TONI MORRISON

D1570809

TONI MORRISON

An Ethical Poetics

Yvette Christiansë

Fordham University Press

New York   2013

Library of Congress Cataloging-in-Publication Data

Christiansë, Yvette.
    Toni Morrison : an ethical poetics / Yvette Christiansë. — 1st ed.
        p. cm.
    Includes bibliographical references and index.
    ISBN 978-0-8232-3915-3 (cloth : alk. paper) —
    ISBN 978-0-8232-3916-0 (pbk. : alk. paper)
    1. Morrison, Toni—Technique.   I. Title.
    PS3563.O8749Z612 2013
    813'.54—dc23
                                                    2012029527

Printed in the United States of America
15 14 13   5 4 3 2 1
First edition

Contents

Abbreviations for Works by Toni Morrison

B	*Beloved*. New York: Alfred A. Knopf, 1987.
BE	*The Bluest Eye*. London: Picador, 1990.
"FP"	"Introduction: Friday on the Potomac." In *Race-ing Justice, En-gendering Power: Essays on Anita Hill, Clarence Thomas, and the Construction of Social Reality*, ed. Toni Morrison, vii–xxx. New York: Pantheon Books, 1992.
"H"	"Home." In *The House That Race Built: Original Essays by Toni Morrison, Angela Y. Davis, Cornel West, and Others on Black Americans and Politics in America Today*, ed. Wahneema Lubiano, 3–12. New York: Vintage Books, 1998.
H	*Home*. New York: Alfred A. Knopf, 2012.
HR	*Honey and Rue*. Deutsche Grammophon, 1995. Recorded by Kathleen Battle with the Orchestra of St. Luke's, conducted by André Previn.
J	*Jazz*. London: Chatto and Windus Ltd, 1992.
L	*Love*. New York: Alfred A. Knopf, 2003.
M	*A Mercy*. New York: Alfred A. Knopf, 2008.
P	*Paradise*. New York: Random House, 1998.
PD	*Playing in the Dark: Whiteness and the Literary Imagination*. Cambridge: Harvard University Press, 1992.
S	*Sula*. London: Picador, 1991.
SS	*Song of Solomon*. London: Chatto and Windus 1978.
TB	*Tar Baby*. London: Picador, 1991.
"UTU"	"Unspeakable Things Unspoken: The Afro-American Presence in American Literature." In *Within the Circle: An Anthology of African American Literary Criticism from the Harlem Renaissance to the Present*, ed. Angelyn Mitchell, 368–98. Durham, N.C.: Duke University Press, 1994.

TONI MORRISON

Introduction

> These were choice documents to me. I read them over and over
> again with unabated interest. They gave tongue to interesting
> thoughts of my own soul, which had frequently flashed through my
> mind, and died away for want of utterance.
>
> —Frederick Douglass, *Narrative of the Life of Frederick Douglass*

> It is a widely held belief that modern literature is characterized by a
> doubling-back that enables it to designate itself; this self-reference
> supposedly allows it both to interiorize to the extreme (to state
> nothing but itself) and to manifest itself in the shimmering sign of
> its distant existence. In fact, the event that gave rise to what we call
> "literature" in the strict sense is only superficially an interioriza-
> tion; it is far more a question of a passage to the "outside."
>
> —Michel Foucault, "The Thought of the Outside"

> In *Jazz* the dynamite fuse to be lit was under narrative voice—the
> voice that could begin with claims of knowledge, inside knowl-
> edge, and indisputable authority . . . and end with the blissful
> epiphany of its vulnerable humanity and its own needs. . . . I want
> to imagine . . . the concrete thrill of borderlessness.
>
> —"H"

In her reflections on the writing of *Beloved*, Toni Morrison laments the decision to end her novel with the word *kiss*, remarking that her substitution
of that word for a still-unnamed "wrong word" transformed an "assertion
of agency" into "genuflection" ("H," 7–8) The original word, though

wrong, may also have been the only word, she remarks (*P* 8), thereby staging for herself the question of how any writer, especially any African American writer, might resist the gravitational pull of everyday speech toward racialized images, symbols, or metaphors, each of which would drag language back into what she terms the house of race. Such images cluster and provide sequential connections of assumption and conclusion that produce real practices, real actions in the social, embodied world. The predicament she describes in her essay "Home" is one burdened by history—the essay preceding her later novel of the same title by some seventeen years. She narrates her responses to that predicament in terms of an evolution away from the concerns with "community and individuality," which defined *Song of Solomon* and *Tar Baby*, toward the "revelatory possibilities of historical narration when the mind-body, subject-object, past-present oppositions, viewed through the lens of race, collapse." A writing that can "enunciate and then eclipse" the racial gaze is the horizon toward which *Beloved*, *Jazz*, and the later novels, including *Paradise*, *Love*, and *A Mercy*, all move. The later novel *Home* recovers Morrison's earlier interest in the relation between individuals and community. It also reviews the persistence of a racial gaze after the attempt to imagine that horizon, returning to the early moments of the Civil Rights Movement in an effort to grasp the particular form of race that made insurrection necessary and necessarily compromised.

Nevertheless, the movement away from a literature that aims to redeem the individual and the community toward one that explores the "concrete thrill of borderlessness" might well be read as a recapitulation of a history of African American literature that is poised between the reflective, self-present moments of Frederick Douglass's autobiographical writings and the deliriously self-conscious but more decentered writing of novels like Jean Toomer's *Cane* and Ralph Ellison's *Juneteenth*, with *Jazz* moving emphatically toward the latter.[1] The space of African American literature is, in this sense, the space of modern literature, and it is not coincidental that Morrison's fiction emerges from and depends upon her own scholarship about and reading of modernism, particularly that of Woolf and Faulkner.[2] The epigraphs opening the present chapter are an attempt to stage the two extremes of this space, the two ends of a trajectory. At one end are the reader and writer, whose assumption of full, which is to say recognized, personhood requires the writer to perform the interior life of a mind that must assert itself via other people's utterances, appropriating the existing normative idioms for expressing (white) subjectivity in order to assert the possibility of black subjectivity.[3] This is Frederick Douglass as the reader of newspapers and other documents that give "tongue to [his] soul."

At the other end of the space that African American literatures call into view is the radically dispersed and fragmented narratorial space of modernist fiction, as found in *Beloved*, where the narrative emanates less from a character than from a place, a house saturated with spite.

The relationship between reader and writer is made the object of reflective play as early as *The Bluest Eye*, where the narrating writer, Claudia McTeer, addresses the reader in a direct first person that interrupts her third person storytelling. The narrator of *Jazz* similarly addresses the reader, especially at the novel's end. This form of address is also strangely present in *Love* in the moments of rupture in which L seems more oriented toward the reader than toward the dead Bill Cosey, with whom she converses. Morrison redirects the relation in *Home*, where a character, Frank Money, directly challenges the third person accounts of his life by interrupting and correcting the narrator. The move alerts the reader that third person narration is not an unimpeachable mode. In a way, Frank Money performs a doubled fiction: a character speaks as if independent of the narration, from a place to which narration must turn but to which it does not have full access or which it cannot account for with full reliability. The move is also reminiscent of nineteenth- and early-twentieth-century debates about character and autonomy in theater and theater's metacommentary on political and social contexts—these debates centered on the relation between characters and actors and not characters and authors. Is a character the automaton that Strindberg decried in middle-class aesthetic values, or the autonomous creation that comes alive in, say, Pirandello's *Six Characters in Search of an Author*?[4] My point here is not to draw comparisons between Morrison's work and Pirandello's or Strindberg's, but to draw out those elements of her fiction that make excess a basis for politics. Given *Home*'s temporal setting—just after the Korean conflict and as the Civil Rights Movement commences—Frank Money's challenge to an invisible, defining presence that has the power of language suggests a parallel with the political landscape at his moment, in which radicalism often understood itself to be "speaking truth to power," although this is not, yet, Frank's understanding. Frank's questioning also places him in the position of a reader. He is the reader of the narrative about himself without denying the presence of other readers. It is for them, as much as for him, that he seeks to correct the invisible narrator.

Nonetheless, Frank's address is contained by the fiction he disputes. A corrective narrative undertaking is thus limited. When he says that he lied about something or when he says that something is more complicated than the narration suggests, he makes or remakes the fictive figuring of history's resistance to narration. In excess, like history, he is the characterological form of resistance to dominant narratives but also the sign of a limit to the corrective simplifications of oppositional narratives.

Jazz opens with a mere sound, the announcement of a speaking voice that discloses itself to be a knowing voice, but one whose face we do not see, and one that turns out to be far more unstable, far less reliable than the fantasy of omniscience so central to the realist novel. This voice is, indeed, less a speaking voice than the announcement of voicing before it takes the form of language, and it calls both the reader and the characters to a problematizing consciousness of language that is itself the legacy of modernist aesthetics.

A reader of the tradition that Douglass helped to found, Morrison seems to reiterate the movement of his text and his epiphany, in which freedom is discovered in reading but experienced in speech—a speech that insists on full presence and the possibility of disclosing interiority without distortion or encumbrance. Douglass ends his autobiography by remarking that "the idea of speaking to white people weighed me down." Yet, he "spoke but a few moments, when [he] felt a degree of freedom."[5] Speech and freedom are correlates for Douglass, the former both enabling and expressing the latter. Undoubtedly, Douglass's experience of such freedom in speech is something other than the borderlessness about which Morrison writes, and Morrison's aspiration to the outside of racist language is not imagined in Foucauldean terms, as an outward movement into the pure language that Foucault describes as the "neutral space," the locus of a speech opposed to thought. Foucault's reading of the "entire tradition wider than philosophy" as that which teaches us "that thought leads us to the deepest interiority" posits speech about speech as the path to dispersal and effacement.[6] Speech about speech is the condition of modern literature, in his analysis, but it is also where the author dies, the subject disappears.

Morrison is herself concerned with the predicament of such death, and with its haunting. And she will play endlessly at the boundary between text and context, between fiction and criticism. The essay "Home," for example, comments upon and cites *Paradise* while it is still being written, which novel later appears as the citation of "Home," itself cited by the novel *Home*. At the same time, Morrison's deployment of the inside/outside trope and her exploration of the history in which African Americans were simultaneously asked to prove an interiority (it was never assumed) and to suffer the fragmenting effects of a discourse that worked through violent exclusion seeks something other than the generalities offered by Foucault.[7] Her work is an attempt to negotiate the twin seductions of interiorization and exteriorization. And she undertakes this labor through the figuration of characters who are simultaneously compelled by the possibility of interiority and undone by the fact of a language that is, emphatically, not neutral or capable of neutrality—even in the sense given that term by Roland Barthes.[8] For Barthes, to retreat from declamatory language and to embrace silence is the avenue of escape from ideology, but he cannot address what Morrison asks us to consider, namely, the predicament of those whose silence cannot signify or even be recognized as an agentive gesture, precisely because it is thought to be evidence of an incapacity for self-expression. For Morrison, as for Douglass so many years ago, the goal is not to retreat from language. It is to analyze and redeem language, though without ever imagining that language could constitute the basis for an escape into purity. Her writing performs this exploration of language with a poetics of uncommon precision.

The present book offers a reading of Morrison's writing as the staging of these questions, a reading that takes its energy from Morrison's own labor to find a language that resists history and its clichés, while making that history visible as the history of *a* language. My own reading is devoted first and foremost to recognizing Morrison as a writer who writes about writing as much as she writes about the condition of African American historical consciousness and the kinds of traumatic experiences that are its foundation.[9] Being an author grounded in modernism, Morrison produces writing that listens to itself and that becomes citational, not only of the African American, American, modernist and classical Greek canons with which she associates herself but also of itself. Here, one has a chance to read a body of work that begins to understand itself as a corpus, a body of literature.

In this book, I am especially concerned to understand how Morrison transforms her thematics into an ethical poetics that increasingly tries to understand the relation of her writing to the production or reproduction of a canon, and what being drawn into a canon also demands of her writing. It is her awareness of the latter, revealed by the circling back of *A Mercy* to a time before America was America, that enables her to treat the "before" of tropes whose torquelike narrative energy continues to drive cultural production, politics, and even her own fiction. Such tropes include the conflation of slavery and blackness, to the exclusion of the labor politics that indentured poor white Europeans and American Indians.

To understand how Morrison's thematics is transformed into an ethical poetics, one must read her fiction on at least three distinct but related levels. The first is that of figure and narrative. The second is that of metanarrative, which is also the level on which figures are intertextually linked to others in the vast body of modern (American and African American) literature, as well as the biblical literatures that inform African American religious culture. The third level is that of poetic practice. In stitching these levels together Morrison produces a distinctively self-conscious writing. Before moving to consider the fiction, and before undertaking the kind of reading that will define the rest of this book, however, I want to pause to consider some of the philosophical and historical questions and trajectories to which Morrison's work addresses itself.

The Prisonhouse of Race and the Outside of Language

Morrison follows a long tradition of critical and postcolonial writers concerned to understand how colonial and slaving discourse works to violate a subjectivity constituted in and by its language. In effect, her fiction poses the question of how language can be experienced as an exteriority, which is also an aftermath, when it is also fundamentally the origin of speaking being. From *The Bluest Eye* forward, this can be seen in the struggle of individuals and groups against a language that is felt to emanate from elsewhere, only to be interiorized, where it establishes its rule with psychically shattering effect. The process is not one of simple absorption or introjection, however, and the experience of interiorization is itself a point at which characters can become conscious of racial logics. Morrison's famous use of the house as a metaphor for this relation between individuals and language invokes and troubles a dialectical relationship between interiority and exteriority. The writing or speaking self who resides in the house of race but who intuits an exterior becomes aware of the dominance of the language that appears as second nature.

This dramaturgy of discovery is written as a threshold narrative in which race presses in on and marks (writes on) the speaker. It allows Morrison and her readers to comprehend the distinction between a language and what we can call idiomaticity. For native speakers, of course, a given language assumes the appearance of language in general, and one speaks colloquially of "languages" internal to such a historically particular language as "idioms" or "discourses." Thus the opposition between *a* language and an idiom appears from within as the mere opposition between language and discourse, if by discourse we mean a historically sedimented set of statements and practices that govern what can be said and thought within its terrain. Indeed, native language, to the extent that it is naturalized (to the extent that it *is* native), loses its sense of specificity and appears universal. All speakers are in some sense the recipients and speakers of languages that exceed and precede them, and hence that come from elsewhere. Nevertheless, the predicament of the slave redoubles this fact, for he or she was first stripped of a native language before being subjected to a foreign language that laid claim to universality. The slave thus had to take up the self-generalizing language of the slaving society *and* the idiomaticity, the specific racialized discourses of its historical moment—all shrouded by ideology in the aura of the natural, the given, the originary. The additional burden afflicting postslaving societies is that these racialized idioms and discourses disavowed their own historicity, and their status as idiom. In the moment that idiomaticity is recognized, or that the specificities of discourse are felt, it is as an enclosure, that which limits the "spreading forth of language in its raw state."[10]

The question for Morrison, at least as she states the matter in "Home," is how to "blow up [the] all-encompassing shelter" of this enclosure (*P* 9). Other writers have also faced this dilemma and they are distinguished by the way in which they grapple with the question of difference in and between languages. It might therefore repay us to consider some of their positions. For René Girard, the only outside to language is that of the world itself, and any attempt to speak out will only fold back into what he calls "the system in which [writers] were first imprisoned with their contemporaries."[11] For Blanchot, writers take in the meanings and values, or even the simple effects, of the world of which they are a part, and then they reproduce, from within themselves, work that "emerges into the monumental reality of the outside as something which is necessarily true."[12] Moreover, Girard contends, great writers "apprehend" the world, or the world as system, "intuitively and concretely, through the medium of their art." His position owes something to Jacques Lacan's sense of the radical disjuncture between the Real and the Symbolic, though he implies a greater porosity between the two. By contrast, Foucault pays heed to a multiplicity and possible discontinuity of discourses and the universal force of language, even as he attempts to historicize such an understanding of language and its relationship to the orders of things and words. Accordingly, he asks how a writer might resist stitching "the old fabric of interiority back together in the form of an imagined outside."[13] Morrison shares this ambition to avoid the mere repetition or reinstatement of a logic, in this case, the logic that structures the "architecture of race" (*P* 8). However, the legacy of wounding to which she turns her attention is not simply the hemorrhage of meaning, but history as a *particular* structure of racialized violence: "Whatever the forays of my imagination, the keeper, whose keys tinkled always within earshot, was race" (*P* 3). She does not say as much, but it is clear that the structure is one that resists even as it is constituted by oppositionality. It is a structure for which the wound and the tear are themselves figures. Hence her fictions often stage a violation of the interior/exterior opposition in theatrical gestures of cutting and opening, splaying and imploding. Nonetheless, the architectural metaphors retain their power. How then, is one to escape? For Morrison, this question amounts to asking, how is one to write?

Morrison couches her dilemma about writing in yet another series of architecturally grounded metaphors, ones that suggest the linkage between spatial logic and law itself. She refers to the "racial house" of thought, which lives only according to the "house rules" of language. And she writes of "rebuilding" the space that she occupies in this house so that it will not be a "windowless prison" into which she has been forced. The claustrophobia of this condition is evoked in imagery whose literalism is suggestive of the "thick-walled, impenetrable container" around her (*P* 4). Within this metaphor of the house of race, then, we find another—that of the prison of the mind, a prison in which "the keeper" is invisible but audible through warning indicators, those metaphorically shaken keys. The literality and the absoluteness of this image are, perhaps, surprising, despite the possible citation of Kafka. The surprise stems from at least two points. The first is that the speaker is Morrison, whose presence in the American literary canon can be called simply formidable. This is a novelist who has received literature's highest awards and whose work has been central in the rethinking of the status of America's slave past in the larger American imaginary. One does not expect an admission of limitation to fall into an expression of its physicality. Nonetheless, the second and more important dimension of this surprise arises from the fact that Morrison has opened her essay "Home" with an admission: "From the beginning I was looking for a sovereignty—an authority—which I believed was available to me only in fiction writing. In that activity alone did I feel coherent, unfettered. There, in the process of writing, was the willed illusion, the control, and the pleasure of nestling up ever closer to meaning" (*P* 3). This admission of a "willed illusion" appears as an always already prior gesture underlying her work.

For Morrison, this willed illusion is at the heart of the "process" of writing. One does not suspend disbelief so much as willingly embrace the illusion that is the work of fiction. Unless such illusion is reduced to escapist nihilism, however, Morrison's realization that she is imprisoned in the house of race calls fiction itself radically into question. She openly exposes the possibility that the illusion of will contained in the notion of "willed illusion" is, in fact, the delusion of (absolute) freedom. There has always been a prior will, that of the invisible keeper. The impulse would be to read this will as exterior and free to move. As *A Mercy* will show us, this is not so. Only a master discourse deeply embedded in the language of the everyday can maintain the house of race, and those trapped in it are necessary to its futurity. The "keeper's" relation to language seems to be one of overdetermination. We are left to ask what happened to sovereignty. That extraordinarily seductive word has suddenly been hollowed out and mocked. Or at least it is now revealed to have been always already hollow: a small, necessary consolation whose effect has been to support the illusion of autonomy in the context of its radical absence.

The boundaries of freedom are the boundaries of law. When Morrison describes the work of writing as "legislating" what she calls its mystery, she invokes an elaborate set of presumptions not only about the force of law but also about the ways in which fiction participates in a structuration of more radical "borderlessness." The status of knowledge now seems shaky, bereft of its performative and transformative possibilities. Morrison has made it clear that she is, and has for some time been, fully aware of "the master's voice and its assumptions of the all-knowing law" (*P* 5). But this declaration is tantamount to an acknowledgment of impotence, despite the presumption, which she shares, that knowing is empowering. Has that not been the ideal articulated in the motto "knowledge is power?"[14] What could possibly "give" her forays away or, to put it another way, give her back into the jealous domain of this invisible keeper? And what would constitute an adequate resistance to this temptation, this betrayal lurking inside language? The answer, suggests Morrison, is not knowledge but rather fiction, where fiction is understood as something other than the unreal and something always compromised.[15] As late as 1998, Morrison writes that, although her project is oriented by a "permanently unrealizable dream," the work of her novels continues to be an exploration of "whether or not race-specific, race-free language is both possible and meaningful in narration" (*P* 9).

Histories of Enclosure

Unease about the endless adaptability of systems, and especially colonial capitalist systems, undergirded by a definitional sense of their impermeability to opposition has been at the heart of theoretical debates for decades. It is most famously associated with the works of Foucault, whose description of modern disciplinarity assumes the logic of the panopticon and imagines language itself as a totality, albeit one whose horizons are historically contingent. In the 1980s and 1990s it was fueled by discussions about postcolonial authorship and arguments for and against postmodernist claims. Indeed postmodernism assumed the iconic status of both post- and ur-system when architectural theorists and literary critics, especially Fredric Jameson, identified it with the cannibalizing, all-consuming logic of consumer culture. At stake was the capacity of this cultural movement to sustain a politics of opposition. Foucault, who attempted to escape the scientistic claims and aspirations to purity of some Marxian ideology critique, insisted that oppositional discourse is not radically other than what it opposes. And it is important to recognize that, in his writings on literature, he only approached a fantasy of neutrality, holding out for the art of writing (and writing as art) a possibility that he specifically repudiated in the more formal realm of the political. The "passage to the outside" quoted at the opening of this chapter is, of course, not a vision of a pure exteriority; rather, it names a certain movement from within the self-reflexive condition of modernist writing—the improbable achievement from within what Gilles Deleuze, writing of Leibniz after Foucault, called the fold. On this basis, but in a much-simplified form, Linda Hutcheon, for example, has dubbed postmodernism a movement "which works within the very system it attempts to subvert."[16] For Terry Eagleton, this was a politics doomed to complicity with the very economy of the system that it attempted to pry open.[17]

Much earlier, members of the Frankfurt School had staged a comparable theoretical debate. In "The Culture Industry: Enlightenment as Mass Deception," Horkheimer and Adorno expressed anxiety about the diminishing political possibilities of Western art.[18] They were writing out of a particular historical moment in which German fascism had made deadly use of mass culture, and their anxiety was grounded in a sense that Western art had become irredeemably complicit with the commodity culture that was spawned by mass production. Their attention was directed at mass *cultural* production, which they saw reflected in the aesthetics of the film, radio and magazine publishing industries.[19]

In Horkheimer and Adorno's generalized analyses, uniformity is the only possible hallmark of an art that has bound itself to the violence of monopolies.[20] What is rendered uniform or predictable is the experience not only of art but of creating works of art. The "culture industry" can only "serve up the data of experience," partly in response to social demands that are taken up by commercial agencies. The consumer has nothing to do but be passively receptive. As a result, the mass production of "dreamless art for the people fulfils the dreamy idealism which went too far for idealism in its critical form."[21] Narratives become predictable, especially in cinema. Details are "interchangeable," as if there were only a set number of "ready-made clichés." To invoke Eliot's modernist claim, in the beginning of formulaic art is its end. Calculated effect is the predominant aim. Where art once expressed an idea, the idea of making art available to the masses made it vulnerable to such things as market forces, and the idea was "liquidated." The alternatives, for Adorno in particular, were twofold. On the one hand was the pursuit of an aesthetic aimed at freeing the listening/reading/viewing subject from the habits of perception cultivated by capital and reproduced in mass culture. On the other hand was silence. Silence is what Pat Best chooses in *Paradise* when she elects to destroy the stories she has been collecting, stories that the inhabitants of Ruby do not include in the town's "official" history. Hers is not yet a book, not yet a chronicle.

Criticized for their elitism, Horkheimer and Adorno nevertheless articulate a familiar concern about a certain readiness of "gesture, image, and word" in consumer culture to reproduce that which already exists (which is to say, the distortions of a violently hierarchical and unjust society), one that stunts subjects and fails to provide the means for either knowledge or expression. In its industrialized form, art, which had been so closely associated with free expression by the Romantics and Expressionists, was therefore doomed, in their analysis, to extend and recapitulate the system it hoped to undermine or change, to recycle its language, its metaphors, its images, its adaptability. One can legitimately discern in their writing an anticipation of the fatigue and ennui that so many critics associate with postmodernism and its repetitions, or what Jameson terms the transformation of modernist styles into "postmodernist codes."[22] This process, Jameson points out, is one of the ironies of commodity production in general, which produces newness and obsolescence at the same time, and even as the condition of one another. Although Linda Hutcheon rebukes Jameson for neglecting postmodernism's engagement with history, Jameson himself pursues the trajectories of cultural production in "late Capitalism," and the term *late* signals his own effort at historicization. He argues, for example, that the "frenetic economic urgency of producing fresh waves of ever more novel-seeming goods" has resulted in an "increasingly essential structural function and position to aesthetic innovation and experimentation."[23] Moreover, he attends precisely to the kind of historicism that postmodernism generates—namely, a nostalgic orientation to pastness in general. Departing somewhat from Walter Benjamin's more ambivalent recognition of the new beauty that comes to qualify the past in the age of industrial capital, Jameson describes nostalgia as the affect that subtends the emergence of pastiche and that permits the circulation of old ideas, old images, old words. Yet he is in tune with Benjamin when he asserts that pastiche is also the vanishing of an individual subject and personal style, the aesthetic of a commodity-saturated world.[24] It brings with it a loss of political project, as well. Where parody had a "vocation," pastiche now finds itself to be without one.

While Marxian analysis frames Jameson's theoretical project, the terms of his explanation of pastiche are evocative of Freud's discussion of the uncanny in that he reads pastiche as the uncanny doppelgänger of parody, and does so in a manner that suggests something akin to horror on his own part.[25] Both parody and pastiche are initially described in the same way. Jameson says that pastiche, like parody, is "that strange new thing." But the familiar thing that is so strange and new—entirely modernist, then—does something else that is "unlike" and "un" or "nonliking." Pastiche "slowly comes to take" parody's place. The possessive formulation evokes a process of displacement and occupation. Pastiche is assigned a strange agency, whose source is invisible, coming from an elsewhere from which it is compelled or which compels it. Jameson further refers to pastiche as "peculiar" and "blank," and uses a phrase that is truly evocative of Freud's discussion of the uncanny: "a statue with blind eyeballs."[26] Parody, one should recall, is a reproduction born of a critical vision, and derives from the Greek αρα (para) *prefix* + ῷδή (ode) and thus refers to a particular enframement or refocalization, to use Mieke Bal's language, of the text or song to come.[27] Though it can extend all the way to travesty, parody is nonetheless a term of critical judgment, and it is in the usurpation of judgment that Jameson sees the relatively undifferentiating work of pastiche as a threat. One might nonetheless recall here that parody is also a term haunted by its obsolete meaning, itself borne of a mistranslation, namely, "A period of time; the termination or completion of such a period; *esp.* the end of life; death" (*OED*). In contrast to pastiche, parody in this sense is doubly a term of historicist criticism: a criticism of enframement, of seeing through error, made possible by the recognition of temporality, more specifically, periodicity (which is to say, historicization).

One is reminded that, for Freud, Hoffman's Olympia does not have eyes of her own. She has only eyes stolen from living children.[28] Analogously, pastiche represents the effect of those "Faceless masters" who continue to inflect the economic strategies which constrain our existences" but who "no longer need to impose their speech."[29] Facelessness and blankness combine in this moment in which speech is no longer imposed because all has become the surface of pastiche. To facelessness and blankness is now added the sense of the depthless. To depthlessness is added the sense of the automatic, the predictable, the shallow articulation that nevertheless is co-opted and made to serve ideological and social purposes.

It is not difficult to find in these discussions about the historical situation of late-capitalist subjects some resonance with Toni Morrison's diagnosis of the particularly racially marked subject in the latter half of the twentieth century. What makes her interesting from our point of view is her anxiety about repetition, about a language that will turn out to be not only haunted by past usages but also capable only of recirculating the past. This anxiety does not prompt a naïve effort at the conservation or restitution of a free and reflective subject, however. In a way, Morrison points out that any such effort would itself by contaminated by commodity logics and/or the generalizing nostalgia that Jameson sees at the heart of this moment. Accordingly, she does not seek to reclaim a lost subjectivity or individuality, nor does her concern about the residual nature of contemporary iconography limit itself to a lamentation for lost originality. Her fear of repetition is a fear of racism's repetition and therefore its continuity. The opposite to simple nostalgia, Morrison's fiction questions whether return can ever escape repetition or where it can be a way of disrupting repetitions that foreclose through domination. A number of characters pose these questions by returning to places whence they came: Milkman and Pilate in *Song of Solomon*, Sula and Shadrack in the novel named after her, Son in *Tar Baby*, and, most directly, Frank and Cee Money in *Home*. Their returns are forms of repetition that challenge the "data of experience" whose iterations monopolize meaning.

In her concern with the iterability of racial discourse Morrison shares much with more formally postcolonial and often explicitly Marxian writers. This is not surprising, given that postcolonial studies has staged many of the same debates as has the cultural criticism of postmodernism. The location from which such debates have been pitched, however, is often entirely different. In postcolonial studies, the argument about language and the status of art has been shaped less by a generic vision of late capitalism as deterritorializing than by an insistent recognition of its spatialization (its division of the world into North and South, for example) and by a tension between the local and the global, the colonial and metropolitan centers and their languages. The crucial object of criticism, here, is the metropolitan curriculum.

One of the most publicized and ongoing debates concerns the relationship that anticolonial and postcolonial writers have had and can have with colonial languages. Those who would embrace the colonizer's language have argued that, through exceptional mastery, they would be able to disprove stereotypes and in fact effect paradigmatic shifts in the way that language is conceived, especially in the way it is ideologically rendered exterior to, rather than constitutive of, colonial subjects who must always feel that they are more belated vis-à-vis language than are colonizers. As

I have already suggested, colonial discourse, of which slaving discourse is a particular variant, always imagines a double exteriority for its subjects. Those who oppose such strategies declare the colonizer's language to be impossibly deaf to local inflection; there can be no authentic expression of a colonial interiority in and through colonial language.

In these debates, language as language and language as discourse occupy the same status, being conflated in the representations by which English, for example, lays claim to being the proper medium of power in British imperial space. It is disseminated via the colonial curriculum, and the curriculum itself is what remains as the trace of the violence by which local languages were initially displaced. Gauri Viswanathan has argued that the colonial curriculum in India, specifically its literary branch, was a medium for imperialism.[30] Her focus is primarily upon the role of the literary canon in the production of the perfect colonized subject, one who understood the primacy of English Literature as the "*source* of intellectual values, morals, and religion."[31] The study of language itself was governed by the logic of utility, suggests Viswanathan. In this context, the study of other languages, or of language per se, was considered inappropriate in India in the early 1820s precisely because Sanskrit, Arabic, and Persian, for example, were deemed less useful as "means to an end (for instance, conducting legal business)." Rather, they were perceived by English educators as being related to "systems of 'pagan theology'" which were related to "the cause of the intellectual degradation of the Indian people."[32]

A variety of positions have been staked on the terrain on which decolonization and postcoloniality are being pursued. They are perhaps most famously exemplified in the persons of Salman Rushdie, Derek Walcott, and Ngugi wa Thiong'o. Rushdie and Walcott are among the most visible proponents of a redeemed and redemptive English, and their writings are nothing if not testimony to the idea that the master can be mastered by being subverted. But others have opted for more overtly oppositional language practices. For his part, Ngugi attempted literally to bid farewell to English in order to write only in Gikuyu,[33] not simply on the assumption that there is a "purer" language than English but precisely because English is so heavily burdened with the historical-political agendas of English coloniality in Kenya. This does not mean that Ngugi's decision to write in Gikuyu is a utopian move, in that it will overlook the particularities of that language's own discursive limitations. But it does suggest that Ngugi initially embraced the idea of a nonuniversalized and nonuniversalizable language: "Language carries culture, and culture carries, particularly through orature and literature, the entire body of values by which we perceive ourselves and our place in the world."[34] That he has since returned to English suggests how complex and economically overdetermined is the possibility of writing and publishing outside of English or the other globally dominant languages, but the insistent and insurgent claims about the hegemonic status of English he made three decades ago are perhaps only proven further by the fact that he has been forced to work in it.

The counterpoint to such local absolutism comes in the form of the idea of internal subversion, often in the idiom of dialect or inflection. Rushdie and Walcott, for example, have argued that the provincialized English that they speak and write has inflected and in fact changed what was standard English in the process. Their language partakes of and resembles its original form. But it is not the same, and the difference is the mark of historical violence in their analyses—both what compels them to speak, read, and write in English in the first place and what has allowed them to appropriate and instrumentalize it toward different ends. Mark and terrain. Cite and site. For Rushdie, English is the linguistic site in which he must struggle against colonial language and its cultural as well as historical baggage, and in which he must do so through a hyperbolically masterful citation of other literatures, other canonical texts from the colonial curriculum.[35]

Like Rushdie, and unlike Ngugi, Walcott's relationship to English is that of the ironically native speaker. English is Walcott's first language despite the fact that colonized and once-colonized people are always, in some ways, belated to the language that comes through colonialism's patriarchy, rather than the mother tongue, though the latter is invariably also the tongue of patriarchy.[36] Walcott has insisted that he possesses two kinds of E/english. Both localized English and standard English are his, and he once termed himself their "monstrous prodigy," the one who is "of the wrong age and colour" but whose mastery of the master's language is so consummate that he can call into question the very idea that language and its speakers can be entirely contained within a possessive economy.[37]

As editors of the influential *The Empire Writes Back*, Bill Ashcroft, Helen Tiffin, and Gareth Griffiths critique the relation between colonial oppression and the colonial education system, which gave normative status to the language of the metropol, with a corollary displacement of indigenous tongues.[38] The sedimented, creolized, and/or localized forms of these languages, rendered mere "variants" of the master tongue, were "impurities."[39] In such a system, language "becomes the medium through which a hierarchical structure of power is perpetuated, and the medium through which conceptions of 'truth,' and 'order,' and 'reality' become established." Anticolonialism—Ashcroft et al. call this "post-colonial"—therefore becomes a "process" of the recovery of the language of the dominant culture. The terms of this process are violent and are described as a seizure: "The crucial function of language as a medium of power demands that post-colonial writing define itself by seizing the language of the centre and re-placing it in a discourse fully adapted to the colonized place."[40] In this, one finds the residue of colonialism's own legacy of violent seizure. What seems to be the myth of a pure language is revealed as more complicated when, for example, the power of the *Oxford English Dictionary* is taken seriously: rather than mask the contributions of the many other languages that make up English, the dictionary performs the power of English to absorb and occupy these languages.

This ostensibly subversive appropriation of colonialism's own idiomaticity—which grounds the claim to sovereignty in seizure—is specified and disaggregated by Ashcroft, Griffiths, and Tiffin as two stages of linguistic recovery, namely "abrogation" and "accommodation." Abrogation is defined in terms of refusal, a "refusal of the categories of the imperial culture, its aesthetic, its illusory standard of normative or 'correct' usage, and its assumption of a traditional and fixed meaning 'inscribed' in the words."[41] Appropriation is, according to Ashcroft, Griffiths, and Tiffin, the acknowledgment that abrogation must avoid the simplistic "reversal of the assumptions of privilege" and normative inscription. It is their term for the way that language is "taken and made to 'bear the burden' of one's own cultural experience."[42] Simon Gikandi has tracked Caribbean writers' long struggle with these issues as they seek to negotiate their relationship with history through an uneasy relationship with modernism and modernity.[43] For Gikandi, Caribbean writers from radically different ideological positions "realize that the time inaugurated by the European colonization of the Americas sets up a modern tradition of representation which still haunts the Caribbean."[44] These writers have been presented with a dilemma. They can neither adopt nor escape "the history and culture of European modernism, especially as defined by the colonizing structures."

The overarching legacy of that history is its pervasive structure, and to ignore it and one's invagination in and by it is folly. Gikandi finds in Derek Walcott this kind of folly. In rejecting the pervasive model of Eurocentric history, Walcott only "seems to become enmeshed in history the more he tries to escape from it."[45] On the other hand, for Gikandi, Wilson Harris is a model writer, whose Caribbean modernism is "highly revisionary." Like Glissant's, Harris's work attempts to respond to "ancestral sources and the colonizing structures."[46] Glissant himself describes his existence as hyphenated in that his writing comprises a poetics of colonialism and does not so much expand Eurocentrism as learn half to remember, half to forget. Hyphenation and partiality thus name a condition of historical location that is not English, but not not English, or, as Homi Bhabha says, not quite, not (English) white.[47] Like Glissant, Derek Walcott has long acknowledged the complex interrelations between the various cultural force fields that he traverses. In the end, his memory is also a vengeance. To this end, he has repeatedly refused to disown the influence of the colonial curriculum in his work, despite the fact that he was fully aware that the curriculum once *intended* to exclude him and his worldview.[48]

Having rehearsed a few of the arguments in the fields of discussion about language and coloniality, I should note that is nonetheless not my aim to extend the debates about postcolonial and anticolonial conversations with and against colonial curricula. Nor do I intend to extend the debates for and against postmodernism. I have raised these two major fields of discussion in the briefest way for one reason only. This is to suggest that, in this present moment, the ironically termed posthistorical moment, art, especially literary art, is burdened with a residual self-conception in which the writer's task is to originate newness, which must appear as the introduction of something from without, *into* a totality which nonetheless works through exclusion. The fantasy of absolute exteriority (and hence absolute newness) has been largely relinquished by writers working in the long shadow of modernism (which is not yet to say entirely within postmodernism) and complicates this task enormously. For the aesthetics of heroic invention have given way to a more complex conception of intervention, the valorization of historical truth has given way to the ambivalences that inhere in discourses of memory. Yet many African American writers refuse to relinquish the question of history and the aspiration to renarrate it more adequately. It is for this reason that Morrison has so systematically made her fiction a scene for the interrogation of representation itself.

Eschatology and Apocalypse: Beginning with the Word

Let me return, then, to Morrison's question: How does one escape a system when that system is language itself and when one is a writer? Morrison's own stated position does not seem to abandon the language into which she was born. Rather, she seeks to trouble and dislodge the racialized discourse that has "housed" itself so comfortably. Her description of this vocation names a process of attempts and is written in the past tense. She writes of a fundamental knowledge of the ready positions that her work could occupy, positions that she has rejected. Thus, she would not "reproduce the Master's voice and its assumptions of the all-knowing law of the white father" (*P* 4). Nor would she "substitute his voice with that of his fawning mistress or his worthy opponent," since both positions remain defined by the house rules and their structures of legibility. The most extreme option, which would make her entirely subject to the house's rules, would be transgression, to counter the rules with their mirror image in the form of counterracism. This, Morrison states, "was never an option." Rather, transformation and not transgression became an option. The "impenetrable container" would be "renovated" into an architecture of accommodation by being opened with a "generous . . . supply of windows and doors."

The implication of unimpeded sight and mobility is clearly stated. A linguistic substitution does in fact take place. The language of renovation substitutes for what is in effect a revolutionist language, one that has nowhere else to go but into a language of transcendence. An impenetrable fortress of racialized discourse is opened by the "imperative" that Morrison says drove her desire to "transform" the house of race "completely." The imperative is revealed to have been a temptation, however, and here she reaches for another discourse, a familiar one usually associated with things mystical. Morrison writes of temptation and conversion in the same breath: "I was tempted to convert" the prison-house of race. An apocalyptic tone shimmers just at the edges of this statement, to reveal the *locus amoenus* of apocalypticism, the transcendent place that is the goal of an apocalypticist vision. It is a place that transcends corrupted time-space and appears both as that which is to come and as that which will have been, which has always already been in the mode of a "to come." It does so in the form of an idealized architecture, a palace where corruption no longer exists. Thus, Morrison's palace would have been a place "where racism didn't hurt so much" (*P* 4). The conditional future anterior tense is important, for it generates both doubt (or a multiplicity of futures) and pastness, albeit a pastness that will only be perceivable from the future. The palace *would have been* such a place, and such a place *was* the temptation. The temptation was nothing less than "the delusion of agency." Now, Morrison literally dismantles the apocalyptic vision. The palace becomes a house again, the house becomes scaffolding, the scaffolding becomes the structure of a traveling fair or circus: "At some point I tried to use the race house as a scaffolding from which to launch a moveable feast that could operate, be celebrated on any number of chosen sites" (*P* 4). This too would be abandoned as yet another dangerous illusion of freedom. The danger was "eternal homelessness" in another's discourse, subject to the melancholia of nostalgia for a "race-free home"—a state reminiscent of the consciousness of exile so familiar to us from the writings of Edward Said. It is at this point that Morrison restates her question: "how to convert a racist house into a race-specific yet nonracist home" (*P* 5). She must do so in writing, and for this reason she must also theorize language as something other than the lexicon of racial epithets, as something more than words.

Benjamin has stated the question of escape in a way that retains the problematized messianicity of Morrison's rejected palace. Clearly, for him there is "no event or thing in either animate or inanimate nature that does not in some way partake of language, for it is in the nature of all to communicate their mental meanings."[49] In another instance, he asserts that language "shows clearly that memory is not an instrument for exploring the past, but its theatre."[50] Here, what appears as the essence of language's clarity lies in its ability to show, to be transparent, to, in fact, disappear in order for something other than itself to be seen. Benjamin writes further that language is "the medium of past experience, as the ground is the medium in which dead cities lie interred."[51] To approach one's own "buried past," one must "conduct" oneself through simile: one must conduct oneself "like a man digging." One digs into the ground of experience, in which the medium itself is the domain of the dead. Clarity is deceiving here, as Benjamin himself concludes. Language ultimately communicates only itself, or rather, the communicability of itself. The question is deferred. The answer can only be the act itself.

Morrison's response is an oeuvre in which language constantly comes into view only to place itself under erasure in order that story and history appear as the outside that is also inside, yet always vanishing. In answer to her own staging of the question of how to "convert" one discourse in order to accommodate another—surely a question of the most profound ethical challenge in a Levinasian sense—she withdraws from one kind of language, that of critical engagement with fellow conference attendees on the occasion in which she presented her essay "Home." She withdraws from this language, charging the conference of scholars of literature, race, and society to continue their form of dialogue with "literary and extraliterary analyses [on] . . . matters of race." It is in this moment that she can return to the specific form of her own "writerly excursions" in order to continue, in the language of *fiction*, her own engagements with "what seems to lie about in discourses on race," namely, "legitimacy, authenticity, community, belonging," or a thought that carries from the dependent title of an essay "Home" to the promise of a *Home*.

Writing on/of Toni Morrison: The Problem of Memory

One of the difficulties in writing about Morrison's work stems from its relationship to history and her interrogation of a tendency to posit history as the oddly agentless cause of future events. The enormity of America's slave past and the legacies of this are everywhere in her fiction and nonfiction— that is, until *A Mercy*, in which she attempts to narrate a moment prior to that in which slavery had become codified and solidified by law, and naturalized through custom. With the exception of her intervention in *A Mercy*, in her fiction the history of slavery has assumed the status of a collective and verily spectral entity, one that shadows the other entity that must always be negotiated in her work: "the community" or, rather, the idea of "community." Even as the notion of community transforms itself across the body of her literature, history remains, settling as more than remains into the deep foundational structure of its future in the form of an injunction: the injunction to remember. Indeed, memory or "rememory" is the gift that the living give, constantly, daily, to the dead. Memory is the gift of a survivor *and*, as a gift, it is the medium of obligation in a logic that loops back to where the living have "presence" *because of* those who have gone before and those who come after. The gift of the dead is the gift of the future, which is the present of the living. Remembrance is the gift that they return, with an aura that now exceeds itself with the power to compel.[52]

It is important to mark the fact of excess, of what escapes the economy of conservation and compensation, though I shall later argue that this excess is not reducible to a material exceeding but is also identified, in Morrison's writing, with the persistent effect and force of vanishing—a vanishing that is not merely a subtraction but also a positive and palpable phenomenon (a positivity in Foucault's idiom). *Toni Morrison: An Ethical Poetics* is premised upon the fundamental distinction between the art of memory and the art of mourning. The former is directed at the recovery, recuperation, and restoration of some presumed totality, whose very idea generates a ukase that it be narrated in familiar and familiarizing terms and forms. In Morrison's writing, however, mourning dominates, in an art of incompletion that seeks to register, if not accommodate, the realities of trauma. As Sharon Holland argues, historically "black subjects share the space the dead inhabit," a subject position that is "almost unspeakable" but still linked to nation formation.[53] Nonetheless, a melancholy fascination with death cannot be mistaken for a galvanizing epiphany. Nor can a nationalist reaction formation to suffice as the answer to fragmentation. It is for this reason that Morrison's fiction is so full of interrupted funerals. These must be read not as a call for a more idealized funereal project and an aesthetics of resolution but as the legacy of the trope of "living death" that runs directly from the holds of slave ships, into which living people were squeezed only to encounter themselves as not-there, not-here. It is the ghost of a *place* into which they have been inserted that is uncanny, rendered so by their presence, as much as slavery rendered them uncanny, strangers to themselves. At the same time, Morrison's fiction creates a series of heterotopic locations wherein ideas of and longings for "home" seek a commensurate language, one that will in fact attempt to escape or resolve the stasis of this liminality. Significantly, this is frequently a language of interruption, of stuttering, of lacunae, and of sound without meaning. At the end of *Home*, it is still a destination to be reached, the unobtained goal of a journey that the Civil Rights Movement makes newly possible.

The uncanny instability of home is, as Saidiya Hartman notes,[54] to be found in the very name African American, whether hyphenated or spaced. The name is not merely uncanny but performative of an aporetic relationship between the general and the particular, one that is grafted onto the minority figure, who is simultaneously deindividuated by stereotypy and refused the capacity to signify the universal. For the characters in Morrison's fictions, the strategies for managing that aporia have entailed something like "double consciousness,"[55] even as the effect of that double consciousness has manifested itself in the relentless experience of the un-canny and the sensation of belatedness.[56] But she has also staged the risks of a turn to communitarianism—a necessary but ultimately inadequate answer to this predicament, and one to which she as an author has also been uncomfortably subject.

Partly because of its testimonial relationship to history, and partly be-cause of her place in the histories of which her books are a part, Mor-rison's work has had a particularly transformative effect on the forms and ideas of canon and canonicity in American literature. Morrison might have received the highest recognition for her work through the Nobel Prize (1993), but the admission of black writers, and black women writers, into the American canon is a recent and still incomplete affair and until the closing decades of the twentieth century African American literature was largely relegated to a parallel canon or the status of a subdivision of a larger, dominant canon within which their work existed in a merely para-textual relationship. Such parallelism has in itself effected great changes in the logocentrism of canon. African American literature, Asian American literatures, Latina/o American literatures, Chicano/a American literatures all insist upon a multivocality that has been at the theoretical heart of the *idea* of American democracy but that has, at the same time, been repeat-edly repudiated, banished, exiled.

Morrison's *Playing in the Dark: Whiteness and the Literary Imagination* takes up this issue directly, offering itself as an argument against literary criticism's deafness and blindness to the role of slavery in the building of America's canon. Her fictional work has also accepted the mantle of responsibility that was first sewn by the authors of slave narratives, the responsibility of creating fiction that is also work for the larger group. This work not only allegorizes losses and survivals, endurances and resistances. It allegorizes the deep and abiding grief that lies in that slave history and its legacies. In short, one cannot read African American writings without being aware of their place in the history of being black in America. Morrison's most famous novel, *Beloved*, suggests that this grief is a matter to be addressed by the nation itself. Implicit in this is an accusation that the violence that pro-duced such grief was structured into the nation, and that such centrality should in itself elicit grief. One of contemporary literature's most famous specters appears to warn that the refusal to acknowledge the necessity of coming face-to-face with the deep and abiding grief that the descendants of slaves have had to bear will not ensure a psychic stability.[57]

Compelling as these arguments are, they also constitute a daunting field of cultural imperatives. These must be addressed when taking up the oeuvre of a writer who has made them the ground out of which her work emerges and upon which it stands. There are a series of potent entities that have assumed the status of givens in Morrison's novels, so much so that some have become veritably invisible. Or rather, their status as "natural" has come to be invisible. One of the entities that has received considerable attention is, indeed, the omnipresent idea of community. But community functions in extraordinary ways in Morrison's fiction, enforcing ethical injunctions even as it provides the mise-en-scène for the thought of their failure and the project of reimagining relation. Community has been charged with the work of ensuring and performing "belonging." It has also been charged with the work of remembering, and it is therefore charged with archival practices. These bear within themselves imperatives whose primary, underpinning telos is the injunction "to remember." More than that, the imperative is to remember correctly.

Conjured up by the very reading that her novels solicit, the community is an entity whose formation must always be negotiated. Morrison has addressed the potency of this entity diegetically in every one of her novels, as characters seek to understand their relationship with and obligations to their communities and vice versa.[58] Thus, Sula's presence in The Bottom exposes that community's tenuous purchase upon autonomy in the degree to which that community reacts to her behavior, which it perceives to threaten its values. While mother-daughter, mother-son, wife-husband, friend-friend relations are all tested in extremis—as in Eva Peace's decision to take her son Plum's life in order to save him from drug addiction—it is, for Philip Page, the community that offers an ideal alternative to normative permutations of coupling.[59] This is, of course, the ideal form of communality. However, the ideal is haunted by literalist limitations and, as often as not, it demands submission.

The question of "inheritance" or, more specifically, the inheritance of a duty to remember, will be literalized in *Paradise* by the Morgan twins, who respond to history with brutally literalist and conservationist reading practices, which transform themselves into conservative social practices. They interpret their duty to the past in terms of communal solidarity: a service to the community that takes the form of conserving the community. Inevitably, suggests Morrison, conservationism is the ground of a death-dealing identitarian politics. *Paradise* is a novel in which the only

communal thing reproduced is death. Yet she is too canny to let this notion of literalism stand. She does not let it appear merely as the failed and
resentful response of emancipated blacks, who can only inhabit language
reduced to commandment.[60] She understands that a kind of literalism had
been inscribed by slavery in the act of naming by which people were in-
ducted into the economy that made them things. Slaves were both named
and "overnamed" in Benjamin's sense, robbed of their singularity in the
practice that rendered them property rather than the bearers of proper
names. Readers are reminded of this history when they encounter Stamp
Paid or Macon Dead, Florens or Frank Money.

The limit to this occurs in the fiction itself, when the stories about such
figures restore to them the singular quality of a life lived. The names, as
translatable words, disappear and become the names of characters, people,
to such an extent that characters must explain the origins of their names
in order to remind their listener of the violent moment in which the black
slave was made the fetish of a not yet and always imperfectly free labor.

Not incidentally, such storytelling is often the ground of community
formation. Always passed orally, the knowledges of name can themselves
be transmitted, and at this level story secures the link between people
who become enmeshed in new social formations defined by the demand
to remember. Sometimes, however, the price of memory is a blindness to
the present. But this blindness is merely the reciprocal relation of a blind
embrace of pastness. Consider, for example, the case of *Tar Baby*. In this
novel, community is dispersed from the central terrain of the novel. Any
communal presence is marginal, yet from the margins the demands that
black subjects remember extends even to the demand that they be the
very thing that must be remembered. Thus, on Isle de Chevaliers, Thérèsa
Foucault is the direct connection with the island's slaving history. She provides the narrative of a group of slaves who, viewing from the deck of slave
ship the world into which they were about to be landed, were struck blind
(*TB* 153). The ship on which they were to be delivered to Dominique
foundered and sank. Only the blind slaves survived and swam ashore. The
unbroken "connection" is literally kept alive by Thérèsa. Page refers to
her "spirituality" and "harmony with nature" *and* her storytelling power,
which, in the mode of her possible extra-diegetic namesake, Michel Foucault, offers a "countermyth about Western culture."[61] One might add that
this "countermyth" is precisely the repository, even bulwark, against the
legacy of Western culture—which is to say, the legacy that landed slaves

in the so-called "New World" generated a history whose fragmenting effect has produced the imperative to remember, and to desire to belong together, as community. So potent, then, is the notion of community that literary criticism itself has to resist its further reification. My own concern is to be attentive to Morrison's respectful ambivalence toward this value and to avoid sliding into socially instrumental reading practices. The latter fail to challenge the very imperatives that might make of the abstract idea of community another edifice of yet more embargoes against openness, against the mobility of critical thought. Morrison warns against this, I believe, and it therefore becomes imperative to push beyond the kind of statements that would argue how or why, for example, a failed funeral is bad for a community.

As a trope in Morrison's fiction, the failed funeral indicates an un-propitiated or improper separation between the living and the dead. It can express a disregard for the dead and for the living, and a community may be rent apart as a result, or possessed by the force of those who should otherwise move on. Morrison's work often seems to invite such structural-functionalist anthropological readings. And yet her work also refutes them. It is indeed the refutation, and the way that she stages this refutation, that opens the possibility for a different kind of reading practice, one that can hold open the aporia of the relationship between the has-been and the testimonial stand-in. Here we begin to see what is at stake in the figure of the funeral and the function of failure, when these occur against the backdrop of fiction's memorial project. It is one thing to ask what work a funeral does, and what constitutes failure when that funeral is fictionalized in and through language. It is another thing to ask what this means about the failure of African American community, *outside* the text.

How, then, are we to read Morrison's fiction and its relation to the long history that began with Africans being violently abducted from the mul-tiplicity of African languages and inserted into the functionalized nonlan-guage of command, made the subject of collectivities but only rarely com-munities, and then invited to hypostatize community as a compensation for the loss of both freedom and a more sustaining form of sociality? How are we to read her fictions about African Americans who are not only de-scendants of those Africans, but who are Americans? The answer requires that we traverse the boundary between text and context, between fiction and history. As Paul Ricoeur writes, neither the pastness of an event nor that of its witness can be known after the fact, but the latter at least "is memorable." And this fact, for Ricoeur, propels a writer to produce "fictions" that stand in for or take the place of events, not merely as referential texts and certainly not as indexes, but as obligated forms of testimony:

> the constructions of history are intended to be reconstructions answering to the need for a *Gegenüber*. What is more, I discerned between the standing-for and the *Gegenüber* that is its correlate a relation of indebtedness which assigns to people of the present the task of repaying their due to people of the past—to the dead.[62]

The question remains, nonetheless. To whom or what is the story owed? And to whom is it given?

The complex and provisional answer to these last questions will emerge in the course of this book, which proceeds by reading Morrison's fictions in terms of their "internal" operations and moves to a consideration of their intertextual relations. Here I have merely attempted to map the ground on which such a movement can take place, pointing to the questions of interiority/exteriority, racialization, language, testimonial practice, and the debt of historical consciousness, the politics of subversion and the problem of absence that stand at the core of Morrison's work and African American literature more generally. This book is divided into several differently conceived chapters, some of which focus on relatively few texts, some of which attempt to sketch the broader contours of a movement within the body of Morrison's writing and between it and the tradition of diasporic writing.

1. From Witnessing to Death Dealing: On Speaking of and for the Dead

> wasn't I (wouldn't I always be) tethered to a death-dealing ideology even (and especially) when I honed all my intelligence toward subverting it?
>
> —"H"

In his consideration of the philosophy of witnessing, Giorgio Agamben attempts to map out some of the relationships between injury, survival, witnessing, and testimony. He argues that a twofold impossibility confronts the one who would testify: to bear witness to what one doesn't know, and to bear witness to what cannot be known. He is struck by the lacunae in witnessing, which he understands to be a speech act, an active, outspoken remembering.[1] He argues that those who survive cataclysms and who are called upon to speak of their experiences are trapped in the strict logic or structure that demands they speak in the place of those who cannot. Called upon to account, survivors cannot and do not have the intimate knowledge possessed by those who do not survive a cataclysm, which is to say any event in which survival is at stake.[2] Yet it is through their speech that the lost voice is invariably sought or represented.

Moving from Eli Wiesel's and Primo Levi's reflections upon survival and witnessing, and the possible impossibility of the latter, Agamben turns to Lyotard's observation of the near incredulity with which one confronts situations in which human beings, "endowed with language," are unable to recount their experiences or can only do so partially.[3] If they do speak, for Lyotard theirs is a partial discourse. For Agamben, the possibility of silence is not the same as absence. We may find ourselves in the presence of a person who cannot speak. This mute person is not simply the locus of absent speech. She is proof that human beings can become disconnected from language. In such cases, Agamben would argue that we are left with ourselves, as incredulous, shaken witnesses, not to the cataclysmic event we know to have happened but to the fact of the limit and the seeming impossibility of witnessing.

Agamben's focus is upon Jewish literatures of witnessing that emerged from Nazi death camps. There are innumerable cautions in drawing parallels between the Shoah and slavery, Jews and African Americans. It is not my intention to present here a sustained argument about the parallels and differences between African American and Jewish experiences. Nevertheless, strong and effective arguments have been made for parallels between antiblack and anti-Jewish racism. Writers and scholars who attend to the histories and the poetics of race—which often means a poetics of racism—have been forced to confront this parallel at the level of racism's operations and formal structures, beyond its particular objects and the histories in which they are differently mobilized.[4]

Agamben's commentary upon testimony intervenes in the literatures of witnessing by returning us to etymology, particularly of the word *witness* itself.[5] His intent is not to bind us to these etymologies. Rather, he shows us how meanings have shifted across time in order to argue for an acknowledgment that any term's signification is specific to context. He is also concerned to analyze the imperatives of particular etymologies when these have accrued the authority that history has given them, even when this history is merely the traversal of time by a word. Agamben reminds us that the word *witness* is closely aligned with *martyr*, which originally referred to one who bore witness by speaking out or testifying. Agamben's own critical etymology returns to the Latin, which designates two types of witness. One, derived from *terstis*—hence testimony—refers to the act of speaking on behalf of another, as a third party in a legal sense. The other is the *superstes*, the one who has firsthand experience of an event.[6]

Broadly speaking, then, a witness observes and is called upon to speak up on behalf of what she or he saw. That speaking can be called the animation of what comes from observation, namely, knowledge of what was seen, even if that knowledge is simply an account of who, what, where, and when. But seeing and observing are not limited to what is produced through presence at an event (having been there), as the above statements suggest. Observation can also be historical, in the sense of reading backward into time via both the *terstis* and *superstes*. One can be an observer of the recorded, in all archival formations. That is to say, a reader can witness;

the boundary between these two categories is not only porous but is the product of a political decision that privileges an impossible presence to the event. Against the exclusive claims of the *superstes*, the *terstis* (still privileged but not exclusive) bears witness first by observing and thus reading the event and its signs. A reader of the archive can be aligned with the *terstis* insofar as she animates that which comes from observation, even if what is observed appears in textual or redacted form. This reader must also learn to animate the signs themselves, to see, in an inadvertent remark or a large set of materials ostensibly depicting or designating one or another body of information, a pattern or an event that is not otherwise foregrounded or thematized. Seeing and understanding what one has seen, along with the capacity to convey this knowledge with some insight, are attributes of witnessing as the term has come to us. And sometimes a reader lays claim to having seen what other readers have not, just as the witness to a catastrophe claims to bear a vision that others have not or could not have had. Although the former attempts to open the place of viewing to other readers and the latter asserts an absolutely unique relation to that place, both mediate, for an auditor or receiver of their message, an insight or a truth that they claim to have discerned in the phenomenal event, whether that be the world or the text in which it is inscribed.

In her commentary on the writing of *The Bluest Eye* and in her fictional author's concern with "how" it was that Pecola came to bear her father's child, Morrison takes up the question of how one becomes capable of reading the world that must be spoken on behalf of. What happened to Pecola? The question drives Claudia to tell a story and her eventual reflections on how readers are produced as the recipients of narrative in general and racially normative narrative in particular. In *The Bluest Eye*, one might say, Claudia assumes the role of the *terstis*, and this first of Morrison's books opens onto a recurrent engagement with the possibility of testimony on behalf of those who are not merely absent but whose experiences only rarely and indirectly entered into the archive of hegemonic knowledge.

Beloved is often cited as the author's most testimonial work, and it is frequently thought of as *the* most powerful novel of its generation to "bear witness" to slavery. But how does this witnessing occur? At what level of the fiction can one say that it bears witness to the event of slavery and the events endured by slaves? Avery Gordon remarks that *Beloved* is not only a narrative about a woman who escapes from slavery and acts in a desperate way to save her children, a narrative derived from a journalistic account. For Gordon, it is a novel whose very language makes visible that which still lingers and attaches to the living. This poetic practice converges with the narrative content. To the extent that it achieves the status of witnessing, it does so by drawing on the authority and the rhetorical forms of earlier genres associated with the work of witnessing. This association prompts some critics to read *Beloved* as a neo-slave narrative, for the novel partakes of an earlier testimonial and evidentiary genre (that of the slave narrative) in order to appear as a kind of witnessing to an event that is otherwise distant from and inaccessible to both the writer and the reader—who nonetheless inhabit a world marked by its effects. The levels on which *Beloved* can then be said to bear witness, in the sense of showing through speaking, are manifold. The same argument can be made for *A Mercy*, in which Florens is a placeholder for someone who might have spoken, just as the stories that attempt to push through the spectral woman named Beloved are speculations about what might have been in ships' holds.

To return to Lyotard's pressing question: "How can you know that the situation itself existed?"[7] How can the witness to witnessing know that something is not being fabricated? Agamben's response to Lyotard is to expose a revisionist logic that can resolve itself only in doubt and denial: "Either the situation did not exist as such. Or else it did exist, in which case your informant's testimony is false, either because he or she should have disappeared, or else because he or she should remain silent."[8] The stakes for both are, of course, the denial of the Shoah and, of equal importance, the experiences of those who survived it.

This crisis of disbelief enunciated by Lyotard and Agamben is, in part, about the witness, or potential witness, who is disbelieved precisely because he or she testifies. The auditor often enough doubts the claim about what has happened or quarantines it in an aura of nonreality. This doubt is exemplified in the following forms: I can hardly believe it; or, it is so extreme that one can only believe in it, rather than feel assured in knowledge of it; but in any case, what is the nature of the catastrophe that there could be survivors to recount it? In effect, the discourse about witnessing is afflicted by anxiety about the impossibility of witnessing. *Paradise* stages this anxiety and attempts to resolve it while thematizing the doubt and the labor to assuage it that Lyotard and Agamben theorize. The elders of Ruby, Oklahoma, attempt to resolve the crisis of belief by demanding that the new generations "remember" and bear witness to events that occurred before they were born, and to do so as if the experiences were their own. These experiences stem from the trials of rejection endured by the town's founding families after their departure from Louisiana when Emancipation failed to deliver its promises. Seeking acceptance and a home in town after town, these first families had been turned away not only by white communities but also by black ones. The greatest of these refusals has come to be known by the residents of Ruby as the "Great Disavowing." Their bitterness emanates from the disappointment of being excluded by communities of the similarly dispossessed. "Turned away by rich Choctaw and poor whites, chased by yard dogs, jeered at by camp prostitutes and their children," the freedmen had expected hospitality in all-black towns. Thus spurned, the first families nonetheless become "stiffer, prouder with each misfortune" and vow to fortify themselves against future hurt (*P* 13). They also vow to found a town "away from prairie-dog towns fifty miles wide and Satan's malefactions: abandoned women with no belongings, rumors of riverbed gold" (*P* 14).

Ruby is established on land they promised themselves, the "paradise" of the novel's title. Remembrance is an annual public act of fidelity to the town's history in reenactments of the Great Disavowing. The annual Christmas pageant sees the town's children act out the "nativity" as a double narrative, in which both the Christian myth and the story of their forebears, driven from towns by whites and blacks, converge. In their miniature and mimetic drama, the children stage the original expulsion and thereby encounter it as their own physical experience, even though they are already three generations away from it. They give this recalled event a sacred aura. Mimesis inducts them into the process of personalizing history at an age when young adult self-consciousness is still mute and thus does not pose the threat of rupture in which a refusal to identify with or question the purpose of the drama might result. Their "remembering" holds forgetting at bay. As we shall see when the young adults of Ruby do question the town's history, doubt and forgetting are hinged.

Almost all adults who observe the performance are also one or two generations away from those who actually moved out of slavery's aftermath into Oklahoma. By witnessing the children, they also reencounter and reproduce their own childhood witnessing, as if to see, again, the terrible journey that took their elders from rejection into the seeming stability of their own all-black town. Simultaneously, while securing the descendents of the first families in their own present, as witnesses, their doubled and tripled witnessing also calls forth the past. The children's pageant is thus more than witnessing. Or rather, it explodes the opposition by which the event and its recounting, through the witness, are held apart. It becomes an annual restoration of the past in the present, and hence an immediate incitement to further observation and yet another act of witnessing—in the form of testimonial, which is to say, narrative recounting of the observation.

Remembering as Witnessing: Ghosts in the (Historical) Text

Clearly, *Paradise* troubles such narrativizing of the overt effort to shore up the dialectical relation between forgetting and doubt. Querying a reactionary opposition to forgetting is also part of Morrison's exploration of an injunction to remember. And this injunction may be understood as the secret ground of witnessing, the call for its work and the anxious anticipation of its possible failure. Thus, it is the injunction to remember that orients Morrison's much quoted essay "Unspeakable Things Unspoken."[9] Critics like Lucille P. Fultz cite this essay as the impetus that undergirds Morrison's fiction, as a "search for metaphorical forms that assist African Americans in recovering their lost or diminished selves."[10] In this context, the spectral figures of her work appear to be the literal incarnations of a problematic, namely, the obstructed access to original and traumatic events, and the desire to have a form in which they can, if not be known, then at least be addressed. More than this, the ghostly images that appear in her novels, frequently unbidden and troubling for the characters, permit Morrison to stage a certain compulsiveness in the memory projects to which African American readers are bound. Thematic readings of Morrison's fiction thus identify her deep concern with haunting as a concern with the force of history and the violent, uncanny nature of its incessant returns. Indeed, in a 1989 interview with Bonnie Angelo, Morrison used precisely this language of "compulsions and forces" to describe what lingers in American history.[11] As Gordon remarks, Morrison's fiction treats the "lingering inheritance" of slavery as tantamount to "life" that "continues to live on," and in coining this seemingly redundant phrase she implies a life not only beyond death but beyond life, a life in excess. This is the "something" that remains unresolved, and unattended, says Gordon, and it is this "something" for which the specter and the idea of haunting provide the metaphor in Morrison's *Beloved*.[12]

How does one live with others and other forces whose strange living takes this excessive form? Gordon calls the site of such living a social geography "where peoples reside" in and with strangeness, and not merely with strangers. In her own early discussions about *Beloved*, Morrison spoke of her reluctance to "dwell" in the era of slavery. However, once she realized that she knew very little about it, she was overwhelmed, one might say compelled, by the enormity or force of that past.[13] Moreover, through engagement and research, observation and the attempt to find a language to write and speak, the idea of the past of slavery became for her as much an obstacle to the individuals whose lives are occluded behind that emblematic name, as an opening. Thus, Morrison refers to the "anonymous people called slaves."[14] For Gordon, *Beloved*'s significance is grounded in this understanding and in Morrison's conscious effort to escape the idea of "slavery" as a closed institution whose effects and definitions reach into the twentieth century and still define lives.[15] It is also grounded in her recognition of the enormous chasm separating the nomination of slavery from the accessing of the experience of slaves. It is in her departure from the historical narrative conflating these two that the work of her fiction is undertaken. In this regard, Gordon argues, *Beloved*'s storytelling power does not derive from or model itself upon the sequentialized, ordered example of the historical record. It does not merely fill in or supplant the previously vacant spaces of historical knowledge. It retains asymmetries and opacities, which produce a haunted text and a haunted reader.[16] Haunting, then, is a partial answer to the problem that would afflict the witness whose survival and testimony is doubted because it has survived. It is less a property of the testimony than an effect of the witnessing.

Nonetheless, when Morrison writes of "anonymous people" or what has been rendered "unspeakable" and unacknowledged, as she does in "Unspeakable Things Unspoken" and *Playing in the Dark: Whiteness and the Literary Imagination*, it would seem that she is calling for the recuperation of those silenced by history and that the form of this recuperation would have to be testimonial. Prior to *A Mercy*, it seemed that this recuperation was specifically and exclusively of African American subjects. However, this novel acknowledges differently disenfranchised groups present in America's foundational colonies. While not all of her fiction is overtly drawn from or dependent upon the historical record, as *Beloved* and *A Mercy* are, they all seem to point us to the fact that African Americans have been construed as historical subjects in a particular way that the name *African American* eventually renders audible and visible. The name signifies the history of origins elsewhere and of rupture, rendering subjects who inhabit the American present American, while marking their irreducible history in otherness in a generalized "African" past. The name is the repetition of haunting and works by attaching to the African American subject a historicity that exceeds that of normative (white, unmarked, European-originating) subjects. It is always visible, always named. Like a stubborn ghost. But the generality of the African (that lumpen category) so named should also be recognized. For in its vagueness and overly generalized status, the entire history of European colonization and slavery's violent destruction of particular histories (of language groups, kingdoms, geographical areas) is effaced. What survives as the ghost in the term *African American* is the ghost of lost origins, of subjection to abstraction.

As stated earlier, this relation to history burdened by loss and flattened by generalization, and Morrison's own invocation of those who have been made "anonymous" by time's passing, might encourage an expectation that storytelling in her fiction would do the work of recovery. And many readers treat the fiction as being precisely that: a consoling filling in of blank spaces, a giving voice to the long-muted subjects of history. Yet the narrators of Morrison's fictions often refuse such easy consolations and do not offer themselves in the mode of the witness whose storytelling will stand in where official history failed. The narrators of *The Bluest Eye*, *Jazz*, and *Home*, and the narrative impulses of Pat Best in *Paradise* and Florens in *A Mercy*, intercept any such easy reading of witnessing and testimonial as compensation or substitution. We encounter this interception in instances wherein narrators become acutely self-aware and question their own writing and motives. Or, as I pointed out in my Introduction, a narrator may be forced into this reflexivity by a character's interruption, as when Frank Money challenges the third person narration in a way that never occurs in *The Bluest Eye* or in *Jazz*. In these earlier novels, the narrator retains a form of oversight and control even in her moments of self-questioning, whereas in *Home* Frank's objections or corrections stand as cautionary notices to the reader as well as for the invisible narrator.

In the context of the problematic of remembrance and testimony, these strategies enable fiction to do something other than bear witness to slavery, for example (as in *Beloved* and *A Mercy*), or to the politics of respectability within black communities (as with Geraldine and Hélène in *The Bluest Eye* and *Sula*, and Sydney and Ondine Childs in *Tar Baby*), or gender politics within them (as in *Paradise*).

Home adds a twist to remembrance and witnessing in that, while Frank Money corrects the narrator on matters relating to his own life, there are things he cannot correct because he has no knowledge of them, even though he knows of them. This is true of Cee's experiences of reproductive experimentation at the hands of Dr. Beauregard Scott in Buckhead, a town whose real-world counterpart was once the Atlanta headquarters of the Ku Klux Klan, as well as a printing plant and "sheet factory" that produced Klan regalia.[17] Frank knows nothing of what happened to her there, except its end result. Cee cannot fully articulate what happened to her. Neither could she understand what she was seeing when she first began cleaning the doctor's office. The homonymic irony of her name is that she does not know what she is seeing. She reads the titles of books, but has no idea what they mean or will mean for her. She sees without seeing the titles of her predatory employer's library: *Out of the Night*, *The Passing of the Great Race*, and *Heredity, Race and Society* (*H* 65).[18]

Those familiar with the history of Francis Galton's eugenics movement would recognize these titles. The first and second have subtitles that Cee does not see or know to see. The full title of the first volume is *Out of the Night: A Biologist's View of the Future*—Morrison's fiction flirts here with historiography; universalizable, it nonetheless invokes the verifiable. The volume's author, Hermann J. Muller, had received the Nobel Prize in Physiology or Medicine in 1946 and, along with his former professor, Julian Huxley, was an opponent of the racialization of eugenics and condemned Nazi eugenics. He is also credited with being one of the foremost geneticists, a science whose shift in name allows, or asks for, a forgetting of its troubling prehistory. Muller was aware of how his and others' arguments that humanity could be advanced through biology, primarily through control of reproduction, would be co-opted by race theorists. In his preface to *Out of the Night*, Muller laments the perversion of the movement. He claims that biological intervention could produce "such men as Lenin, Newton, Leonardo, Pasteur, Beethoven, Omar Khayyam, Sun Yat Sen," and Marx.[19] But he underscored his opposition to racial prejudice by pointing out that he had men from different races in his vision of an ideal (masculine) human. Yet the presence of his book on Dr. Scott's shelves suggests that his opposition went unheard and that his work would be used to support race and class prejudice. Muller differed from his contemporaries about the place of communism in American eugenics. Those with whom he differed politically included Leslie Clarence Dunn and T. Dobzhansky, the authors of *Heredity, Race, and Society*. Dunn and Dobzhansky were also critical of Muller's plan to create a sperm bank sourced from ideal donors. Nonetheless, his work shared their conviction that heredity or biology determined intellectual faculties and physical prowess. Not all were endowed with the same faculties, and eugenics had a vital role to play in mankind's future. Despite their political and scientific differences, their appearance on Beauregard Scott's shelves draws them into the doctor's list of ideal theorists and thus the doctor's worldview.

The fate of Muller's high-minded claims and Dunn and Dobzhansky's more moderate views on race can be found in the second book that Cee names. Its full title is *The Passing of the Great Race; or, the Racial Basis of European History*, and its author was Madison Grant—anthropologist, conservationist, and proponent of race hygiene. Grant called for the "elimination of defective infants and the sterilization of such adults as are themselves of no value to the community," citing the "laws of nature" as his authority. He claimed that they "require the obliteration of the unfit" and that "human life is valuable only when it is of use to the community or race."[20] The larger, "responsible" society could not be burdened "with an ever increasing number of moral perverts, mental defectives and hereditary cripples." He deemed his work and that of "far seeing men" to be a practical preservation of the oxymoronically named "native Americans of Colonial descent."[21] Grant's readers were not only biologists.[22] Moreover, Grant's theories gave the Klan a respectable, Ivy League authority. (Grant had attended Yale and received a law degree from Columbia.)[23] Not coincidentally, Hitler's former Reich Minister for Occupied Territories, Alfred Rosenberg, cited the book during his trial at Nuremberg. He claimed that it was in Grant's book (and in French anthropologist Georges Vacher de Lapouge's work) that he came across the notion of a "master race."[24]

Before these titles Cee experiences awe. They prompt her to think how "small, how useless was her schooling" (*H* 64). She has already lamented the fact that she could not attend a better school than the one run by Lotus churchwomen, who taught basic reading and arithmetic, and she surmises that this minimal education contributed to a lack of discernment on her part when it came to "the first thing she saw wearing belted trousers instead of overalls" (*H* 46–47). While she will learn that a lack of one type of schooling does not mean she does not possess other forms of knowledge, this minimal education does fail her. Being able to read the word *eugenics* does not mean understanding it or knowing where to turn to learn about it. Rather, in the future anteriority of what her education means for her in the larger, racialized society, she has been chosen to experience the meaning of the word. When she wakes in the doctor's surgery after he has injected her, something will have happened, but of which she was not conscious. Until then, the books, the doctor's ordered office, and the new word inspire a desire to know and a sense of safety. She thinks of the doctor's home and surgery as "a good place" (*H* 65). When she is in the care of some women in Lotus, she can only give an account of "the little she knew" of what happened to her. Unable to speak about this, she is left with a new knowledge that she is now unable to bear children as a result of the doctor's experiments (*H* 128).

Cee's inability to say more than "the doctor" as explanation for this and for Frank's knowing and not knowing what happened in the doctor's surgery parallels the larger context of what most Americans know and do not know about eugenic experimentation on black bodies, which continued in America even after eugenicist theories and practices had been discredited in the wake of Nazism's excesses. The Tuskegee syphilis experiment is the best-known exception, and, as such, it has displaced a wider, publicly shared recognition of more widespread practices. As Harriet Washington has pointed out, knowledge of what was being done rested with the perpetrators and their victims, the perpetrators often including medical schools.[25] It is not my intention to take up the issue of eugenics in this chapter, but rather to draw attention to the aporia in Cee's ability to speak, even to herself, of what happened to her. That inability stalls any easy depiction of witnessing and remembrance. Yet she, her brother, and those who heal her know the truth of what has happened to her body.

While compromising any simplistic notion of witnessing, *Home* poses a question about the kind of reflection that witnessing might or should provoke. When Frank and Cee discuss the end result of the doctor's experiments, he asks, "Who would do that to a young girl? And a doctor? What the hell for?" (*H* 132). The second question might well be posed of the larger America as well as the doctor, but Frank will have to answer the first himself. He can answer it only once he understands that he is haunted by a self he does not want to be. Facing that self, he will have to give up any simple notion of innocence. Frank initially appears to be like another

Morrison character. Shadrack too is a young man "of hardly twenty, his head full of nothing and his mouth recalling the taste of lipstick" when he witnesses the horrors of battle in the First World War (*S* 7). Frank similarly witnesses such horrors on the battlefields of the Korean War. There the comparison ends, however. When Shadrack witnesses a soldier's head blown off, he retreats from the battle psychically and wakes in a psychiatric ward (*S* 8). When Frank witnesses his friends' deaths, the "copper smell of blood no longer sickened him; it gave him appetite" (*H* 98). An appetite for blood is not all he discovers.

Cee's ability to accept the truth of her body's experience prompts him to admit a truth of his own, and he delivers this truth to the narrator. His first person interruption of the third person narrative corrects his initial account of what happened when he saw a girl scavenging for food while he was on garbage duty in Korea. In the first version, also told in the first person, he describes her approaching another soldier and touching the soldier's crotch, saying "Yum-yum" (*H* 95). The soldier shoots her. Frank says: "Thinking back on it now, I think the guard felt more than disgust. I think he felt tempted and that is what he had to kill" (*H* 96). Having asked the broad question "Who would do that to a young girl?," he must answer. He answers for himself and for the soldier he was when he reveals that it was he who shot and killed the girl when she touched him (*H* 133). Now he asks of himself: "What type of man is that?" and "what type of man thinks he can ever in life pay the price" of the orange that the dead girl was holding (*H* 134).

Frank reveals the detailed truth as if he were an observer. His observation becomes a statement of conscience and a kind of witnessing. Yet Frank's turn to self-questioning after asking questions of Dr. Scott metamorphoses into a form of sponsorship of the most ironic kind, of answering on behalf of someone who cannot or, in the case of Dr. Scott, who would not. His confession is a formal promise to himself to face the truth, and it is a demand. He closes his confession with a challenge to the narrator: "You can keep on writing, but I think you ought to know what's true" (*H* 134).

With the complication of Frank Money's relation to remembrance and testimony, Morrison's narratorial strategies enable something more than a recounting of emerging generational conflicts in the post-Emancipation era or the shifting priorities of younger black men and women who wish to distance themselves from the racially charged and overdetermined history of their parents, as was the case with Milkman Dead in *Song of Solomon*, Jadine in *Tar Baby*, the young people led by Royal and Destry in *Paradise*, and Christine, then Junior and Romen, in *Love*. Because, in a mode characteristic of modernism, her fiction attends to its own fictional status and makes visible the artifice of writing, introjecting the formal dimension of these issues into the narratives themselves, her works stage and underline the question of for whom a testimony is offered, and in relation to whom any narration (fictional, or historical) claims its status of witness. This does not mean that she collapses the distance between historical actuality and fiction. Rather, her fiction holds open the aporetic relation between history—the historical real—and the fiction within which it is and must be treated, drawing attention to the way we come into language, the way that we read and tell stories, and the tropes we receive and reproduce.

Not Only Ghosts

As is widely recognized, Morrison's staging of history's "compulsions and forces" often depends on narrative disruptions by the *Unheimlich*'s many forms. In any one Morrison novel, the *Unheimlich* circles through figurative and literal forms of dying or vanishing, of unbecoming and undoing. Characters may have to contend with a returned and even vindictive spirit or may discover that the direction of their lives has been dictated by an inadequately mourned death or unspoken loss. Morrison grasps that the *Unheimlich* is not ever singular. When *Beloved* closes, the dead are not laid to any easy rest: "Down by the stream in the back of 124 her footprints come and go, come and go. They are so familiar" (*B* 275). In *Tar Baby*, on a Caribbean island, "Just before a storm you can hear" slaves who drowned with Frenchmen and horses, or who "floated and trod water and ended up on that island along with the horses that had swum ashore" (*TB* 153). On the same island, a man is visited by his dead first wife. She comes "flitting around his chair and gliding over his seed flats" (*TB* 143). It does not matter where he is in the world, she will find him. And yet he cannot remember her eyes. Likewise, a man named Son will be haunted by the idea of a living woman, Jadine, and plunge into the waters of that island to find her, but end up, like Ralph Ellison's Invisible Man, in a semi-emergent world at the threshold of the real and the surreal, running like or with those drowned slaves. *Paradise* is similarly haunted. In an abandoned convent, occupied only by women, the laughter of two children moves from room to room (*P* 171). In the novel *Love*, at the once-famous Cosey's Hotel and Resort, a young runaway has an erotic flirtation with her Good Man, who sits at the foot of her bed or gazes from his portrait, painted when he was still alive and wanting "a playground for folks who felt the way he did" (*L* 116, 103). In *A Mercy*, a young woman is learning how to see herself vanish into the deadening gaze that consigns her to the name *slave* and can speak only from what seems a disembodied state, no longer the self she thought she was, yet not wholly acquiescent in her master's house. She is, herself, out of time and out of joint, and she is perhaps the variation of a revenant in the body of Morrison's work. She is mistaken for a ghost, or the ghost of a ghost. This mistake occurs when the two indentured English workers, Scully and Willard, see her light and imagine that it is her master's ghost moving about his house at night. Her night work, writing her account of herself on Vaark's walls, vanishes in their misreading as her master takes her place in their imaginations.

A variation on haunting occurs in *Home*, in which the figure of a strange man appears before Frank. This figure is similar to the man who walks through Dovey Morgan's garden (*P* 88). Frank sees his man while on the train back to Atlanta to rescue Cee. There are many empty seats, and there is a small man dressed in a pale blue zoot suit, wearing white shoes "with unnaturally pointed toes" (*H* 27). The man does not look at Frank, and when he gets up he leaves no indentation. Frank does not dwell on this. Later, given a bed by someone, he wakes to see "the outline of the small man" from the train. When he approaches, the man disappears (*H* 33). He puts this down to one of many living dreams caused by the war. The meaning of this strange man is revealed much later. The image goes back to a childhood experience, when he and Cee saw a body pulled from a wheelbarrow. They knew nothing about the identity of the man or the cause of his death, but they knew enough of the world in which they lived to be afraid of the sight of the "black foot" quivering as it was covered with dirt (*H* 4). That the foot was black and that the body was being carried in a wheelbarrow is redolent with implications about the race of the farm owner and those who wheel the body. Indeed, the owner's race and ideology are implied by Frank's description of the farm as being like "most" farms in the area, which "had plenty of scary warning signs" and "threats" that "hung from wire mesh fences" supported by "wooden stakes" (*H* 3). This reference to wooden stakes invokes a weapon used by Klansmen, as well as the stake to which lynch victims were tied for immolation. Later, when he is an adult returning to Lotus, the possible content of those "scary warning signs" is conjured up but left unspoken. He wants to go into a bathroom, but "the sign on the door stopped him" (*H* 23). The hooded figure need not be in full sight for its threat to be palpable.

When they have both returned to Lotus and confronted the violence in which they were involved—he as a soldier in the Korean action, she at the hands of Dr. Scott in a war at home—the guilt of shooting the Korean girl opens Frank to other "worthwhile things that needed doing" (*H* 135). The first of these is to find out what happened on the horse farm all those years before and to determine whether the body is still buried there. He learns from the other men that they knew what went on at the farm, where the white farmer held "men-treated-like-dog fights" (*H* 138). He also learns that the dead man was the father of a boy named Jerome. And he learns that he was present when the bleeding boy came off the horse farm, although he has forgotten this. The older men of Lotus tell him that the father and boy were brought from Alabama and made to fight each other to the death on the horse farm. Since one death was necessary to avoid two, the father had insisted that the son kill him in order to live. The discovery of this truth now haunts Frank. He takes the first quilt that Cee has made to sell as part of her new plan to earn a living; the two then find the body and bury it in the quilt at the foot of a sweet bay tree. As Frank completes the burial, Cee spots a man across the river. She is the one who sees, now, and Frank does not. It is the ghost man, or someone like the man Frank had seen on the train on his way to save her, a man in a "funny suit swinging a watch chain. And grinning" (*H* 145). Frank does not know that he has been carrying this man's trace for years, and neither does Cee. As they stand at the new grave with the sign that Frank has made, "Here stands a man," theirs becomes an act of partial witnessing of and for a stranger whose name they cannot say.

Almost every novel in Morrison's oeuvre attends to the revenants of the unpropitiated, the violently discarded, of whom there are traces everywhere, as Elle asserts in *Beloved* when she remarks that there is not a house that does not have some haunting presence in it. This statement echoes Baby Suggs's blunt remark, "Not a house in the country ain't packed to its rafters with some dead Negro's grief" (*B* 12). The same might be said of Morrison's novels, particularly the two whose narrators are like specters who know everything and answer to every name: the unnamed narrator in *Jazz* and the observing L, whom we meet and assume to be living but whom we discover has been dead all along, a discovery that comes late, in the closing moments of *Love* (*L* 189).

Not all the vanishings and disappearances are the same, of course. Nor is the uncanny reducible to the failure to maintain a boundary between the living and the dead, as anthropologists would have it—although some are indeed the result of these failures. There is, for example, the spectral man who looks just like the recently murdered father of the then sixteen-year-old Macon Dead, Jr., and his fourteen-year-old sister Pilate in *Song of Solomon* (*SS* 166, 165). Macon Dead, Sr., was shot when he refused to sell his beautiful farm to a neighboring white farmer, and Macon had buried him. But the grave was too shallow, and his body was swept away by a flood, never to be found. Initially taken in by a midwife, Circe, who hides them in the home of her vacationing employers, the brother and sister set off to find family who can take them in. On the third morning of their journey, they wake to see a man sitting on a stump "with such a distance in his eyes" that they run away, scared. When next they see him, they name him "their father." He beckons them to a cave, where they shelter. In the morning, Macon finds an old white man in front of the cave, and his fear and memory of his father's death drive him to attack the man (*SS* 168–69, 170). He does so just as Pilate emerges from the cave and screams, her screams distracting the white man and thus allowing Macon to stab him in the throat. The man calls "What for?" just before he dies. Neither brother nor sister pauses to respond to the question, whose answer lies in the larger histories of displacement and whose logic is out of their now-orphaned reach. None of this is in their minds. They are distracted from the violence in which they are now embroiled by the discovery that they have literally been sleeping next to a gold mine, and that the unnamed white man is its miner, proof of this being found in his bag of gold nuggets. Macon looks away from what he has just done, to envisage a future guaranteed by the gold. As he does, he and his sister see a pair of boots beside the mineshaft that leads into the ground. She calls out, "It *is* Papa" (*SS* 170). Named, affirmed, and given a place in their lives, the specter rolls his eyes backward and whispers, "Sing. Sing," before vanishing (*SS* 170).

Only after she names him as father can Pilate accord the specter's utterance any meaning. It is the first of many misreadings, many misunderstandings, all born of the constitutive violence that leads to and from a history of enslavement. Pilate interprets "Sing. Sing" as a message to her, even as a commandment to sing a song she learnt from him. In the echo, a prison is named, and the commitment to remember becomes nearly incarcerating. She will learn only much later that the word she heard as a verb was the name of Solomon's wife. That the misreading and misunderstanding are a child's has not yet made clear Morrison's concern with the conflation of childhood innocence and untainted wisdom. The implication is there, however. Learning how to read and understand requires tutelage.

Pilate also interprets her father's vanishing as a sign that they should not take the gold. And so she fights Macon and escapes with the sack of gold, which she believes they have acquired improperly and should not use. Macon's interpretation of her motive as selfish incites a lifelong hatred. Misunderstanding of the past and its signs will be the model for their relationship from then on. When Macon learns from Milkman that Pilate has a green canvas bag that no one is allowed to see, he imagines it to contain the unspent gold. When she returns to the place of their birth, he believes she is taking the gold to bury it, in response to which Milkman offers to go in search. He has inherited a distorted memory. Pilate, of course, does not have any gold, but carries instead what she mistakenly believes are the bones of the murdered white man—they are in fact her father's bones. This is what she had gone back to collect and what she now carries as her burden. Having learned the truth about the bones, she is returning in order to bury them properly.

Heir to what he believes is family history, Milkman had heard the story of his grandfather's death and of the final utterance by his grandfather's ghost. What he does not know is the relation between his aunt's singing of a particular song and his family's history. The traces of his family inhabit the song that Pilate Dead sings in her belief that she is honoring her father's wish: "O Sugarman done fly / O Sugarman done gone" (*SS* 9). Not until Milkman has undertaken what he believes is a treasure hunt does he learn that the song is not about Sugarman but about Solomon, his great-grandfather and the Dead family's lost patriarch. Known also as Jake and "the flying African," he is supposedly the subject of the song. Yet the song is not only about him, indeed, it is hardly at all about him. Over the years, it has come to encompass a myriad stories, and insofar as it is still the trace of Solomon, it is only a fugitive one.

This is where naming, or the ability to remember a name, is not enough. The name of the individual cannot be detached from his or her world. To remember a name alone is to forget, not the world, but others who made that world. The full song is a chronicle of Solomon and the family of his wife, Ryna. And it is a chronicle of their vanishing. In return, each name that is sung by the children of the town of Shalimar, a name Milkman only belatedly hears as the original form of Solomon, is invoked as a trace. Ryna's cry is the first audible response to Solomon's vanishing, but it is a cry that, for all of its communicativity, is not yet the kind of language that names or testifies in comprehensible ways her experience as *superstis* or *terstis*. Whether Solomon really flew back to Africa from a "big double-headed rock" above a valley or whether he leapt to his death is unknown. What remains is his wife's cry: "They say she screamed and screamed, lost her mind completely" (*SS* 323). The fact that others, a generalized "they," have and still "say" or tell the story is in itself testimony to the power of her cry and of Solomon's disappearance. What Solomon left behind is, however, not only a heartbroken wife but sixteen children, including his favorite, last son who bore his Anglicized name, possibly his slave name, Jake. This son was Milkman's grandfather, the one who owned his own land only to be murdered for it by white landowners when he refused to sell. Like his father, he leaves no body behind. His father enters the domain of legend; he enters the domain of the lost in this world because his body is not properly buried. Yet his influence moves about in the way that his son Macon and his grandson Milkman conduct themselves. And his haunting whisper, "Sing. Sing" lives on in Pilate's singing.

As suggested above with reference to Dovey's 'friend' in *Paradise* and Frank Money's zoot-suited man in *Home*, there are numerous other hauntings, other "presences." Some harry the living, others do not. The child that Cee sees "smile all through the house, in the air, the clouds" may be the one she can never have, or it may be the dead Korean girl, now fully acknowledged by Frank (*H* 133). Others harry the living in the accumulated memories of those who are absent but not necessarily dead, all of whom would answer to the name *Beloved*. These vanished beings, clamoring in response to the word, the call, and the name *Beloved*, are not the same as those in *Paradise*, where a more absolute disappearance has been effected. In *Paradise*, the town endures in and through a total silence about the mother of the town's leading elders, Deacon and Morgan Steward. Nothing is said or noted about the vanishing of their older brother or about other people who simply drift out of Ruby despite the fact that the town is supposed to be entirely contained and self-sufficient. This fantasy of enclosure is maintained despite the fact that the town draws its electricity from the state power grid and despite the fact that women travel to nearby towns to purchase household appliances. These silences are noted by some of the characters in *Paradise*, but not spoken about. And in *Love*, only L, who bears an uncanny resemblance to the narrator of *Jazz* but who is far more corporeal and participant in the world, remembers the dead wife of Bill Cosey, the powerful, antinomian owner of the fancy hotel for upper-middle-class black people, or the lover that Cosey took even while his wife was still alive and who simply vanishes out of his story. In *Paradise* and *Love* the vanishings are not part of general conversation, but their effect is generated from within a grammar of memory, given within particular social relations and their assumed historical developments.

More often than not, the disappearance in the worlds that Morrison describes, which can be felt but goes without saying, is that of the mother. In other words, the effect of the disappearance may not appear only in the forms of remembrance directed toward it or the labors at recovery that it summons but in the freedoms or violences that it enables. One sees this complex structure inflected in *Paradise* in the story of a son growing up without his mother, or a pair of twins who seem to have no need to recall beyond a passing reference the woman who gave birth to them. There is a question as to whether this absence of feeling frees them to take aim at women they consider outsiders and a threat to their town.

Despite traces and inflections, for the absences that Morrison creates, there is either no would-be witness or no witness who knows anything that could give a name to a trace. They are the discarded for whom there is no room because they have, in some way, broken some rule or brought some embarrassment; in their being or in their deeds, a crime that cannot be answered with the mercy of remembrance is attributed to them. Morrison's attribution of this kind of criminality, that which makes remembrance too generous, is emphatically gendered, as will be seen in Chapter 3, in a discussion of law. Here, we can simply note that Morrison's work, in making visible the active forgetting of some by others, complicates and resists our desire to read her fiction as a simple kind of memory work defined by the positive recovery of that which has been left out of the historical record.

Other hauntings of poignant significance in matters of witnessing are those generated by lives lived and known, lives that may actually continue but that now escape the purview of their former friends and family. In Morrison's fiction, the living experience these vanishings as a kind of death, but what haunts is not a living on after death but the impossibility of knowing whether such living is excessive or ordinary. The spectral is made to stand in for these lost and often mourned figures, who are not yet not of this world. They are, like Sethe's husband Halle, potentially still "of" this world and likely to appear at any instant—perhaps alive, or as a sighting that someone else has had, as when Paul D recounts the last image he had of Halle, broken mentally and physically and crouching with butter smeared all over his face. In *Song of Solomon*, Macon Dead, Jr.'s mother has vanished, and very little is known of her beyond the fact that she was called Bird and, when Milkman travels back to his father's beginnings, that she was American Indian. Bird's presence, like Halle's, is nevertheless pivotal in family history.

In some cases, that spectral presence is a transcendentalized force, emanating less from a person than from a deed and its effect upon the social world. Thus, an "invisible" hand propels Son to shore in *Tar Baby*. This is the name he gives to the strong turning tide, whose naming may be shaped by his own history. For he is responsible for the death of his first wife, into whose dying eyes he could not look, but whom he cannot now forget. On the island, the invisible, feminized hand comes from a story told by the servants, descendents of slaves, who believe that the mangrove trees are female spirits. On a hill, in a mansion, the controlling force is simply the wish and command of a petulant, pampered millionaire, who tries to have everyone serve his worldview.

In *Sula*, the influential "presence" that determines relations between the all-black town known as The Bottom and the rest of the world stems from the way that its inhabitants remember their own foundational narrative, in which two patriarchs—a white farmer and a former slave—compete over their definition of what is good land and poor. The former slave, like the Old Fathers in *Paradise*, leads a group of slaves into labor for a white farmer in return for a piece of "best" land, bottomland, into which the rich loam of a hill slides. After an agreed-upon time, the former slave approaches the farmer, who gives him land on top of a hill. This land, the farmer says duplicitously, is not poor, but at the bottom of heaven. It is significant, in this context, that the former slave goes missing in the narrative, in part because he is unanchored by a name. And we are reminded of a long history in which the absence of a name has severe consequences. Notable in this tradition is Thomas Hobbes's philosophy of memory. For Hobbes, a name not only anchors a person's character and reputation but also grounds that person in a community's memory. A name is, metaphorically, an address through which we locate an individual. For Hobbes, "the right ordering of names" is related to our ability to name everything.[26] And if, for him, this means that power and knowledge require taxonomy, in a manner that might arouse skepticism today, his observation that individual names are continuous with our entry into the symbolic order holds. To lose a name is to become indistinguishable from one's environment. To lose the capacity for naming has the same effect. Indeed, the two are related. I will return to the question of naming below. Here I want to focus on the particular crisis represented by a disappearance of the living.

This is the other side of Lyotard's and Agamben's anxiety. It is not only that disbelief might threaten to cast the fact of an event into doubt, or that this doubt would contribute to the shelving and/or forgetting of the event. It is that the potential witness intuits that an event has occurred but cannot see this, cannot know whether the event has truly occurred. The potential witness is thus tormented by anything and everything that the one who has vanished might have endured. This is a torment that can only be allayed by the one who has vanished, for only the vanished can know the intimate truth of his or her experience. The knowledge that the vanished bear the truth alone is also a torment, as is the sense that the vanished might have their own anguished memories (including memories of those who contemplate them) that compound loss and make it reverberate in endless ways.

Here, of course, Morrison draws on a long tradition (if anxiety can be a tradition) of such worried discourse. One reads, for example, in Frederick Douglass's autobiography of his anguish about his grandmother.[27] In his 1845 preface to Douglass's narrative, William Lloyd Garrison praises the way that Douglass "gives of his feelings."[28] By the eighth chapter of his narrative, Douglass has conveyed the range of anguish that enables Garrison to praise this "giving" of feeling in the service of the Abolitionist cause. By now, Douglass has written of the shocking beatings and murders he has witnessed. His descriptions of his own emotional response to his personal strife and of his fellow feeling for other slaves have all been shaped by the prose and style that so moved Garrison and Wendell Phillips. Each incident described, each person referred to, provides the reader with information—about the psychic and physical cost of slavery, about the scope of its brutality, and about the extent to which slavers distort their own religiosity and go unpunished for their brutality.

Yet, of all the severances—from his mother, whom he barely knew, from his aunt, sister, and brother—the uncertainty about his grandmother's fate is the one that cannot be "contained" by the elegant enunciation of the facts of his experience and witnessing. It was his grandmother who had raised him and been the most consistent caring figure in his life, his mother, having been hired out by their owner, Captain Lloyd, when he was a baby. Even when writing about his mother, Douglass maintains the ability to provide information that is as much a record of her existence and that of his grandparents, and of their captive place in their captors' world as it is a depiction of the psychic and physical landscape of slavery. He writes that his mother, Harriet Bailey, daughter of Isaac and Betsy Bailey, had initially attempted to walk the twelve miles from her new owner to see Douglass at night. He then provides the only other information he can about her. He knows that she was a field slave and therefore subject to the brutal control of the whip if she was not up and present in the field at sunrise. His only memory of her is of her nighttime visits, when she put him to sleep. He has no memories of her in daylight. The last thing he knows of her is that she died after an illness when he was seven. This information contains the facticity of his birth, her parentage, who her owner was and to whom he hired her, and then her death. It also contains the fact of his attempt to recall his emotional attachment to her. On the one hand, he states that she died before he knew her and that, having never "enjoyed, to any considerable extent, her soothing presence, her tender and watchful care, I received the tidings of her death with much the same emotions I should have probably felt at the death of a stranger."[29]

Douglass cannot and does not attempt to conjure up his mother's anguish, evident in her dedication to him. That would be fiction, and fiction is not yet available in the pressing context in which his evidentiary precision is required for the Abolitionist project. On the other hand, he infers a possible mother-son intimacy and affection in which a mother soothes, is tender and watchful. In turn, he, as her son, can only know belatedly and understand fully as an adult that he was not "allowed to be present during her illness, at her death, or burial."[30] This is the precise, careful enunciation of a loss for which he cannot articulate emotion. While the flatness of marking the three final stages of her existence—illness, death, and burial—do suggest a tallying that bespeaks loss, it is not until he writes of his severance from his grandmother that his writing attempts to go where it has not, that is, into the sickroom, to sit by the deathbed or to stand at the graveside.

Night, here, closes whatever Douglass might have seen of his mother and, by his own admission, whatever he might have known of her. She passes, unknown, out of his life and into the unknown. But for his grandmother the death of her daughter is one of many such severances from the children she has borne, children whose birth increased their owners' wealth. Night is thus a figure, part of Douglass's poesis. Darkness combines with a lack of detailed knowledge about his mother to create an emotional shorthand for his inability to render her visible beyond bare fact. For the work of one who submits to being a witness—as the one who experienced events, and as the one who testifies on behalf of others—this is yet another crisis. It adds to the crisis of belief, feared by Abolitionists. Douglass cannot be either third party or firsthand witness to his mother's life. He can only gesture in her direction.

In a world in which slaves' existences were entirely dependent upon their masters, a lack of foresight on their masters' part could bring about yet another dismantling of an already tenuous stability. The owner of Douglass's entire known family, Colonel Anthony Lloyd, died without a will. His estate was therefore divided between two of his children. When they both died, the entire estate was, in Douglass's words, "in the hands of strangers," who had no interest in maintaining it. It is at this point that he turns to his grandmother, because in the wake of this dismantling came the discovery that not a single provision had been made for any slave, especially his grandmother, who had served Lloyd's family "from youth to old age." [31] He moves from pointing out that not only had she wet-nursed Lloyd, served him all his life and sat at his deathbed, but that she had been the "source of his wealth" by "peopling" his plantation with slaves. The thought of her being "left a slave—a slave for life—a slave in the hands of strangers" pulls Douglass into speculation, for what clearly haunts him here is the inability to know what befell her after she was put out as too old to be of use. He notes that she was put in a hut in the woods then "welcomed" to the "privilege of supporting herself . . . in perfect loneliness; thus virtually turning her out to die!"[32] Douglass refers to this loneliness twice, in quick succession. Moreover, the thought that she remembers and mourns in total isolation the loss of all of her children, grandchildren, and great-grandchildren makes him turn to another's writing, to "the language of the slave poet," John Greenleaf Whittier.[33] Douglass now quotes the entire first verse of Whittier's "The Farewell."[34] Providing the affective supplement for his own muted sentiment, the poem conveys the raw emotion whose stylistic repetitions echo Douglass's brief repetition of loneliness. The poem reads:

> GONE, gone,—sold and gone,
> To the rice-swamp dank and lone.
> Where the slave-whip ceaseless swings,
> Where the noisome insect stings,
> Where the fever demon strews
> Poison with the falling dews,
> Where the sickly sunbeams glare
> Through the hot and misty air;
> Gone, gone,—sold and gone,
> To the rice-swamp dank and lone
> From Virginia's hills and waters;
> Woe is me, my stolen daughters!

With its emphasis on "gone" and anaphorical attention to the ambiguity of "where," the poem echoes Douglass's own inability to locate his grandmother in anything but a vague image of a "little hut" in "the woods." He is conjuring an image here. For all its vagueness, it does indeed address a time and event that he could not imagine when contemplating his mother's death. But Douglass stops short of turning to the fuller exploration of his imagination. That would be fiction, and fiction is not what he is writing. It is not the work that his writing is called to do. He is called upon and calls upon himself to be the witness in the case against slavery

For Agamben, the *superstes*, the witness who speaks *of* her own experience and on her own behalf testifies not as one who has gathered facts for the purposes of a trial or even judgment. In this formulation, Douglass might seem to submit his self-representation to the slave narrative's dominant mode of testimony and witnessing in order to assume the position of the third party who enters a lawsuit. Such a witness gathers information for the purposes of testifying on behalf of another or others. Yet the authority of Douglass's third-party testimony rests upon his ability to make his case as an eyewitness. Anything he is told by others, on behalf of others, is granted veracity through this.[35] And, in part his veracity resides in the language and style in which he visibly/textually strives for balance—

acknowledging even the smallest gesture of humanity in a brutal slaver, or resisting blanket contrastive comparisons between Lloyd's plantation and the relative freedom of Baltimore. The added twist is that it is through this submission to the demands of the genre and its place in the Abolitionist project that Douglass's loss of his grandmother and mother is recovered, not as his own knowledge but as further evidence that a reader may take in order to judge slavery to be inhumane. And thus the slave narrative is not only about those called slaves, but, as Morrison fully understands, about the entire system, which includes the slave master and mistress, who could not be looked upon lest looking be deemed speaking back. Douglass's knowledge of the broad facts about his mother's place as a field hand in slavery's division of labor does not empower him. It empowers the Abolitionist cause, but, in the constant reversal that blurs Agamben's distinctions, what empowers the American canon is the art of Douglass's faculty for observing and transforming observation into "an active, outspoken act of remembering," but most especially the outspoken remembering of the demand for forgetting.

Where Douglass's first person narration appears to deflect his submission to the demands of the slave narrative, Harriet Jacobs's pseudonymic self, Linda Brent, does not. In light of this, Jean Fagan Yellin's argument that Jacobs achieved literary subjecthood now takes on added significance, laying bare the self-objectification that the slave narrative required even as it enabled the writer to perform subjectivity.[36] We see something of this vacillation and mutual dependency in the narrative of Claudia's emergence as a writer in *The Bluest Eye*, where Claudia's capacity to write is both enabled and called into question by her growing self-consciousness. But, of course, the central character of the novel in which slavery is most directly thematized, *Beloved*, does not write and cannot write. Sethe's storytelling is shaped by forces and exigencies that are relatively untainted by the demands of Abolitionism, even though Abolitionism provides the background against which the fated dramaturgy of the novel takes place. A note of caution should therefore be applied here, in the slip between fiction and autobiography. In her reading of Harriet Jacobs's *Incidents in the Life of a Slave Girl: Written by Herself* (1861) and the fictions *Beloved* (1987) by Morrison and *Dessa Rose* (1986) by Sherley Anne Williams, Joycelyn K. Moody delineates the differences between slave and neo-slave narrative.[37] The first difference Moody points out is that Jacobs narrates her own story, while the two fictional women do not, because they are illiterate. It is not only that Sethe (or Margaret Garner, on whom she was based) is not the author of her text (obviously an impossibility for a fictional character). Rather, at stake in Moody's reading is the choice to render her as illiterate. Both Morrison and Williams do so, Moody suggests, because literacy is not the prime concern of writers with the "uniquely modern preoccupation" of invoking the vanished of history and the processes of their forgetting.[38] Morrison knows this. She has self-consciously concerned herself with what she has called "discredited knowledges," discredited because, in part, they were not considered those of page-based literate people.

Morrison's recent response (though not, perhaps, directly motivated by Moody's critique) has been to project the question of slavery and literacy back, beyond its enclosure in and by the Abolitionist framework within which writers such as Douglass and Jacobs, as well as Equiano and Wells Brown, had to operate and before the slave narrative provided the only generic conventions for the representation of subjectivity. *A Mercy* takes up the story of a slave who can write even before the emergence of slave narrative. This is Florens, who has been taught, along with her mother, to read and write—her brother is too young to learn. Their teacher is a Catholic priest who defies the codes against such instruction for slaves, which determine that the acquisition of literacy will be, as for so many slaves to come, shrouded in secrecy. Florens learns quickly. The first text she can memorize and write is the Nicene Creed, "including all of the commas" (*M* 6). Although the priest has two books and a slate, she and her mother use whatever they can: sticks on sand, pebbles on rock," extending the page into the environment where they live, which is daily inscribed by the colonists. But Florens also understands the difference between the spoken and written word. Confessions, she notes, are to be spoken, not written. She is not confessing to us. But she is writing, and what she is writing we read. She writes, the fiction leads us to believe, because she has to, and she writes before she understands herself to be a witness—either to herself or for others.

Mercy: Thought Brought to Bear upon the World

A Mercy shares with all of Morrison's a fiction a concern with the necessary condition of being subject to that which exceeds witnessing even as it calls for witnessing. Here, however, the temporality of inheritance and the structures producing it are profoundly different from those that have come to be known in and through the slave-narrative tradition, however overdetermined that genre may have been. *A Mercy* is set in the town of Milton, possibly in upstate New York or Nieuw-Nederland, between 1682 and 1690.[39] Only seventy-three years separate the novel's earliest time from the Dutch arrival in Nieuw-Nederland in 1609, the settlement of Jamestown and the opening of Virginia having taken place a year before, in 1608. The setting of *A Mercy* is thus one in which the full development of the slave-based plantation economy remains a matter of the future.

Drawing on Orlando Patterson's determination that "death" is the social experience of enslaved subjects, Sharon Holland argues that this state is fully realized or completed by the fact of the accumulated dead lost in the Middle Passage and through slavery's other portals to corporeal death.[40] She also argues that it is not only black American subjects who carry this death into their social relations but all of America, by virtue of unacknowledged fatherhoods by slave masters. However, in *A Mercy*'s temporal setting, such accumulation is only just beginning. True, as Lina and Sorrow know in *A Mercy*, those fatherhoods have already begun. It is also true that, as an American Indian, Lina has already witnessed the accumulating depth of the dead, beginning with the mass death of her own people during an outbreak of smallpox (*M* 46–47). Yet the landscape is not the strange home to a kind of peripatetic dead that we encounter in Morrison's other novels. Two men think they see their dead master moving about the rooms of a grand house he did not live to occupy, but we learn later that it is not the dead who have come to live in that home but a living person, a slave, who is only just understanding the distance that is closing between a self she thought she was and a self that is named "slave." This name summons her with the force of a law that has the power to consign her to a living death.

The enormity of the exposure to death is marked only by Lina's memory of people so stricken by disease, without any way of saving themselves, that they simply lay where they fall, to be the prey of wolves and crows. Taking refuge in a tree with two boys whose names she either did not know or cannot remember, Lina spends the night listening to the sounds of the wolves "gnawing, baying, growling, fighting," and when dawn comes, neither she nor the boys "dared to apply a name to the pieces hauled away from a body or left to insect life" (*M* 46). While Lina does not see any of her dead relatives, she carries the memory of their deaths; this and her induction into the Protestant worldview that perceives her to be a worthless heathen shape her psychic world and relations with others (*M* 47). Nonetheless, the dead do not pursue her. Something lingers, to be sure, in the painful memories, but through Lina we learn that not all terrible memories are hauntings. It is what detaches from memory that makes it a haunting, and that is Morrison's concern. In *A Mercy*, it is as much the vanished living as the terribly perished who haunt. More than this, it is the prospect of being forgotten that haunts.

Every character in the novel has experienced the vanishing of someone, often through death, but just as often through travel—whether forced or undertaken voluntarily. In the unstable time of seventeenth-century colonies and provinces, the reality of distance and the delay in correspondence between those who migrated voluntarily or under pressure from economic circumstances, or who were stolen across the Atlantic and dragged in chains to the "New World," meant that, sooner or later, relations faced the possibility of becoming obsolete or forgotten, often irrevocably. These "losses" were of different orders according to how one entered the New World, for, although Florens's owner, Jacob Vaark, was discarded by his family and grew up an orphan, he has inherited land from a repentant, unknown, and unnamed uncle and has thus been able to "afford" a wife from England, two indentured white servants, an American Indian woman orphaned by smallpox, Sorrow—who is a possibly white girl washed ashore from a shipwreck—and Florens, the slave traded to him as a girl. His indentured white servants Scully and Willard are the only "family" each has, and they imagine themselves and all in Vaark's household as family. Their own orphaned and indentured status does not permit even the acknowledgement of loss, except through an inversion, transferring the status of the lost one to the survivor (orphan). Rebekka Vaark's journey to join Jacob in the New World permits a relieved severance from parents she recalls as having only a sour outlook on all who are different. The novel is thus populated by people captivated not by what they have left but by what they might encounter; their fear is thus of their own disappearance from the horizon of these initially open-seeming horizons.

Six of the novel's twelve chapters appear as Florens's first person addresses to her lover. These alternate with six third-person narratives that deal with the key people in her life: Jacob Vaark, who acquires her as part of the settlement of a debt; Lina the American Indian woman who loves her; Vaark's widow Rebecca, who is indifferent to her but in whose hands her fate lies; the enigmatic Sorrow, about whom she thinks little; the indentured white men, Scully and Willard, about whom she also knows and thinks little; and, finally, her lost mother, about whom she recalls little beyond a sense of rejection.

Morrison's shaping of the novel as a shift between first person and third person can be read as the performance of two types of witnessing—that of the first person who speaks about her own experience and that of the "third person," in the form of a narration that causes its "speaker" or writer to vanish. It is in the third person that the full challenge of this form of witnessing is realized: the gift that slave narrators are prepared to give is of themselves in that they will be read as slaves, despite the fact that they are no longer slaves. For all of their claim to subjectivity, the very name *slave narrative* has come to overtake their writing. *A Mercy* defamiliarizes our relation to that genre, just as *Beloved* did. In so doing, it poses not only the question of what it is that a slave might testify to but also the question of the conditions of possibility within which a slave might speak to others and be heard.

The first thing to note about *A Mercy* is the degree to which the women forget—and to which we see their forgetting. Each carries a vanished life within her, and none of them speaks of this. There is no remembrance and no testimonial. Sorrow's past has literally run aground with the sinking of a ship on which she had spent her entire life, and the man she calls Captain and Father has no other name, no face to remember. Lina cannot recall any names and never refers to her own original name, which was replaced when the Presbyterians named her Messalina as a sign of the apocalypse whose arrival they believed immanent (*M* 55). Rebekka deliberately leaves her English family behind to embrace the freshness of the New World. By the novel's end, she is forgetting even this desire for the new and turning toward a secure Christian religiosity when she joins a Baptist congregation. With this, she gives up a capacity for joy and spontaneity in favor of a belief that goodness is under constant threat from evil. Florens sees in her eyes the same vacancy of recognition she had seen in the eyes of the villagers who examined her: "Each time she returns from the meetinghouse her eyes are nowhere and have no inside. Like the eyes of the women who examine me behind the closet door" (*M* 159). In that rigid doctrine, applied uniformly to the world, Rebekka appears exempt from private memory altogether. However, her entry into the congregation is a return. She has, after all, not grown that far away from her parents, and she has slipped back into to a more familiar mode of being in the world, one that she had decried in her parents. In it, a distrust of all things different reinforces a sense of beleaguered community and shared values. However, this is a privilege that Rebekka has. It is not available to the people whom she and others are displacing—including the indentured servants Willard and Scully, whose class status is sedimenting. Yet she can perform an ongoing fiction of newness. Such is the cast of amnesiac characters. Nonetheless, the novel revolves around the labor of self-enunciation, of literate subjectivity, and of the kind of gesture that could reach forward through the time travel of writing in order to be recalled.

Anticipating Remembering

In its historical setting, *A Mercy* circumvents yet invokes the history in which the prerogative of self-articulation was denied Africans in America and the vast majority of the first generations of their descendants. And it addresses that history at its start. It does this by depicting an encounter for which Florens is ill-equipped and which, therefore, has the potential of undoing her attenuated claim to self-possession—attenuated because she is, in 1690, when slavery is still young, nonetheless a slave.

During her journey to fetch the blacksmith whose healing power her mistress seeks in order to survive the plague, and with whom she is in love, Florens enters a village and is taken in by a mother and daughter who live, like Hester Prynne and her daughter Pearl, on the periphery. They are in a precarious position, about to be visited by an inquisitorial group who believe that the daughter, Jane, is a devil because she has a squint. To prove her daughter no devil, the mother, Widow Eeling, has been whipping her to the point of drawing blood because, she reasons from within the superstitious discourse of her own religiosity, devils do not bleed. Mother and daughter take Florens in, but the inquisitors arrive, and Florens finds herself in the hands of others, who see in her skin the sign of evil's first confirmable intrusion into their midst. It is the first lesson of her young adult life that her blackness can cost her dearly.

The cost is initially psychic. In one way, she is innocent when she first speaks to the group. Yet her innocence is also compromised by a naïveté that has been fostered by Lina's pampering and her life on Vaark's farm, where she has not been treated in the way that either Lina or Sorrow were before they arrived there. Warned to be wary of men, she is not warned to be wary of religious white people. Thus, she discovers in a terrible way how much more than clothing is stripped away from her when she is made to undress and submit every part of her body to scrutiny. She does not offer any objection, nor does her account of her experience offer any explanation or excuse. She simply states the fact that she was undressed. Men and women look at her "across distances without recognition" and seem not to hear her explanation that she is not evil, or the harbinger of evil, but on a mission for her mistress. Not even the letter from her mistress allays the group's fears.

The lesson for Florens is that she is seen but not recognized—a development that approaches, but does not succumb to, the full annihilating realization that Pecola Breedlove has when she understands that she is not visible to the shopkeeper Mr. Yacobowski. Or rather, she is not recognized in herself, but appears only in the form of a projection, as a fantasized other. She is as exploded at the surface of the skin as is Fanon, who finds himself the object of a look that does not seek reciprocity but only fixity and subjugation. Protected and favored only by Lina, and fixated on her journey to her lover, Florens's enforced exposure lays bare the truth of a powerful, collective fear that has to find its fugitive face in hers. While enabling her escape, the daughter Jane (the only one not yet fully interpellated into this order, who can find an affinity with the black woman) confirms this, explaining that the inquisitorial group that had come to "test" her had now found a new object worthier in appearance of the accusation of evil. Jane thanks Florens by saying "They look at you and forget about me" (*M* 114). Resuming her journey, Florens realizes that she is no longer alone. With her are those eyes "that do not recognize me, eyes that examine me for a tail, an extra teat, a man's whip between my legs" (*M* 114–15). Her recollection of the examination animates the signs that are now attached to her body through her own understanding. The effect is profound, as she feels herself shrinking inside (*M* 115). Now, after her body has been scoured by the suspicious gaze of the devil hunters, she has a new self, one that has inserted itself between her own prior sense of self and any possibility of communication with the likes of her examiners. This new self is structured by a narrative that has preceded her and that even preceded a child who cried out at the sight of her; both have been overtaken by that narrative, both are riven with fear by the image that she is made to bear. One will be protected, while the other will live forever at risk.

In *A Mercy*, Florens lives at the cusp of the era in which the predicament of black slaves will be the social death described by Orlando Patterson, and her sense of splitting and self-alienation could be seen to constitute a kind of dying or of approaching death. In her response to Patterson, Sharon Holland argues for a form of *ars moriendi*, a way of living that is shaped by knowledge of death's inevitability.[41] What could this mean for a young woman, like Florens, not yet in the full death throe of the world of accumulating corpses that Holland has in mind? What Holland implies is that the artful commemoration of death must be an anticipatory dance. In 1690, when America is still a set of colonies and slavery's laws have not been entirely consolidated, Florens is not yet, in Holland's terms, a subject who has always been denied and who has therefore "*never*" achieved the status of "the 'living.'" Florens does, however, see this fate in her inquisitors' eyes, and she understands the withering forces of "eyes that state and decide" whether she is who she says or a "something" else, a "thing apart" (*M* 115). Her mistress's letter now takes on an added significance. Whereas it had been a passport addressed to anyone who would stop her, it is now the only concrete anchor that "makes" her legitimate and locates her in the strange and unpredictable terrain into which she has been sent: "With the letter I belong and am lawful" (*M* 115).

Florens is exceptional to her interrogators. For them the only explanation of her appearance can be that she is the minion of evil (*M* 111). While it is not clear whether these people are Puritans or not, the date of Florens's journey and encounter with them is significant in American history. It is two years before the Salem witch trials in Massachusetts in 1692, a time of tensions epitomized by contests between religious practices and calls for unity against ungodliness. Spectacular as they were in early American history, the Salem witch trials were merely symptomatic of widespread doctrines about feminine hysteria in the new colonies, as well as in Europe. In England, for example, Joseph Glanvill's *A Philosophical Endeavour towards the Defence of the Being of Witches and Apparitions* became one of the most influential treatises on witchcraft. Completed in 1666, it was published posthumously in 1667 under a slightly different title and with amendments.[42] Ostensibly a counter to claims that witches did not exist, its argument concerned belief itself and tried to present a challenge to a growing atheism. Hobbes was among those who opposed the claim that witches exist. He argued that they could not exist because it is impossible to fathom the spiritual world. Nevertheless, he did believe that those who claimed to be witches should be punished for the mischief that they created.[43] Within this larger contest against atheism, New England Puritanism also faced its own challenges. Historians have argued that the Salem trials were a displacement of a number of crises.[44] These included the continued fallout of the First Indian War, or King Phillip's War, in New England between 1675 and 1678 and the Second Indian War. In 1679, Increase Mather had convened a synod to consider the evils that provoked God to punish the colonies for their sinful ways. He claimed that the war led by the Wampanoag Grand Sachem, Metacomet, also known as King Philip, was one of those punishments.[45] His son, Cotton Mather, had been writing about evil and Satan in New England for decades.

It is across this terrain that Florens moves and into this context of suspicion and fear that she enters and is examined. The appearance of Rebekka's letter gives her interrogators pause, however. It names her as "owned" by "Mistress Rebekka Vaark of Milton," who "vouches for" her (*M* 112). Formally, in tone and address the letter obeys all the rules. The proper names are of this world, as is the date, and it names Florens as a "female person" who is, nevertheless, property. Moreover, it appeals to and expects civil response, the indices of this expectation being its vouching and its request that the reader allow Florens "the courtesie [sic] of safe passage," all language of nicety culminating in the register of the plea that the letter writer's life "on this earthe" depends on the reader's recognition and acceptance.

Without the letter, Florens is vulnerable. She perceives this as her being in a weakened state, which she associates with animals: "a weak calf abandoned," "a turtle without shell, a minion." She feels, already, how her skin is "a darkness" she is born with, without her knowing, which has been moved from the outside of her skin to her "inside." Her narration is thus already tainted by a proximity to the need to remember an articulating, communicating self. If she cannot account for herself, who will? In a recuperative, even triumphalist politics, her writing could be called an overwriting of Rebekka's letter. But Morrison is never simply recuperative and never triumphalist, thus avoiding the conservatism of such gestures. Instead, the novel has two endings, one in which Florens's narration ends with the possibility that she will be sold by her mistress, confirming the letter's power over her. The other is that she might even burn down the house and, with it, the story that she has been writing.

To Be Read at Last

Except for occasions when self-explanation is framed by her relationship to others and what she has learned through their accounts of their experiences, Florens undertakes to speak for herself. She does so in a context in which she cannot and may never be heard, and in a speech that is always already writing. Her writing is a form of utterance through which she seeks to extend herself to where she can be comprehensible to her ideal reader. Her "reader" is her lover, the unnamed blacksmith. Yet he cannot read. Moreover, the literal surface on which she writes is a space of risk, since her writing is actually a scratching on the walls of a massive mansion built by her dead master and rejected by her surviving mistress. In this, Florens's is a very different first person narrative in the body of Morrison's work, in which narrators like Claudia McTeer ask the question: How? Like Celie's first forays into writing/storytelling in Alice Walker's *The Color Purple*, Florens's narrative slips between subject positions, so that when she writes about Lina, the "I" of herself and the "I" of Lina's incorporated story of sexual abuse are no longer distinguished. (Lina's story is not set out as separate dialogue on the page, and the visual structure of the text does nothing to mark the point of separation between narrators.) All is in the present tense, so that the temporally distinct spaces of narrative and experience—Lina's account of being sexually abused, her telling Florens about the experience, and Florens's later remembrance of being told it—are all rendered in the same present tense. Without the temporal sequencing made possible by declension and the subjective differentiation that strict pronominal usage would permit in English, the reader loses the capacity to establish priority or causality, and the story itself becomes at once conflated and fragmented. In the end, Florens tells a story that includes Lina's narrative to her imagined ideal listener, the blacksmith. *A Mercy*, though written as an assemblage of narratives written from different perspectives, never encompasses them all in a single third-person narrative.

Florens bears testimony to her immediate life of having to leave her smallpox-infected mistress for help, which she will get from the free black man with whom she has fallen in love, with a dangerous self-surrender. Not until the novel's end, after she has completed her journey, debased herself before the man and possibly killed him out of a jealous rage when he favors an orphan in his charge over her, does she turn to someone she has lost, her mother. There is no way she can ever close the gap between herself and that beloved lost object. Yet, unlike Morrison's prior novels, *A Mercy* permits the confrontation with the lost mother that eluded Douglass. It takes us to the *minha mãe* who gave her daughter up to a man whom she believed would never violate her, as she herself had been by slavery. Yet, rather than consolation, the encounter with the *minha mãe* only underscores the impossibility of all returns, all recuperations. For the daughter believes that the mother has forgotten her. If, ultimately, the mother's voice calls out, as it does in the final chapter, it is to someone who cannot hear her, because she believes herself forgotten. Such are the stories that will not be passed on, though their traces will continue to linger. Remembering and possibly bearing witness would also be to remember the fear of being forgotten, which is what Florens carries forth and enacts in her relationship to the blacksmith.

In this searing twist, the space into which fiction can go, the space into which Douglass's remembering of scant details about his grandmother's fate and even scanter details about his mother's *cannot* go, ends up as the scene of an analogous violence. At the end of *A Mercy*, Florens disappears from the story, her disappearance being the mirror image of her mother's vanishing, as well as her mother's giving her away, all bound together in the knot of a feared nonremembrance. Like Douglass, her knowledge of her mother is cast into darkness, one that has overtaken her and already inserted itself deep within, between her and her mother.

This darkness, which now seems to encroach from within, drives Florens to write as much as does her need to explain herself to her abused lover, the blacksmith. She writes in order to anchor her disappearing self. However, "witnessing" is not yet her clearly formulated objective. Rather, she writes against the destitution of isolation and loneliness that continues to settle in her, after her encounter with those eyes that do not see her and that she fears no longer even look upon her. This double destitution, of being unseen because she is excessively visible (her blackness obtruding between her visibility and her recognizability) and of being unseen because she is "unlooked," defines the slave's predicament. This is especially so in the separation from a natal tradition. That *A Mercy* gives that destitution as the future and not only the past not only deepens the history of those who will become African Americans but renders their predicament as the long anticipation of a demand for witnessing that is, from the beginning, endlessly haunted by its already painful failure.

Death Dealing: The Seduction of Language That Speaks for the Unspeakable

There is one crucial indicator of a shift in Morrison's refocusing from full concentration upon spectral hauntings to other, more worldly and proximate anxieties. This shift is not diegetic and is not contained by the narrative, but emerges as an intra-diegetic phenomenon, namely, in the shift between two books, *Beloved* and *Jazz*. In Jazz, the haunting is not only by a specter, and it is not only characters who are haunted when, in Harlem, a voice rife and potent with evocation hisses, "Sth, I know that woman" (*J* 3). It is my contention that the haunting that shapes *Jazz* enables a rereading of *Beloved* in ways that also prepare future readings of Morrison's work for more than the spectral.

Beginning with Claudia McTeer's first disruption of the School Reader and continued in *Beloved*'s monologues and the first, hissing interjection that signals the start of *Jazz*, Morrison's prose becomes a performative enactment of the consciousness of disappearance that informs her historical sensibility. Her writing increasingly asks: What is the nature of the silence that afflicts the historical record, or the dominant cultural imaginary? By writing, and not just storytelling in a Benjaminean sense, she makes silence visible, utilizing all of the resources of typography and layout to realize in the materiality of her text the fact of disappearance. It is significant that Morrison signals the relationship between audibility and visibility through the "graphic" play that makes visible silence but that she does not in any straightforward sense attempt to "give voice" to those absented from, silenced by, or repressed within the historical record. This specularization of silence opens onto a set of interrogations about who speaks and when that speech can be heard. In this, Morrison's writing is the fictional correlate to Gayatri Chakravorty Spivak's theory about subaltern speech as speech that, though technically legible, is disavowed in its meaningfulness by power. The subaltern, as Spivak has shown us, sometimes attempts to use her body to speak, precisely because her language cannot penetrate the realm of power and be heard or listened to. In the case of slavery, the signifying possibility of the body was often limited to a gesture of negation—suicide or self-mutilation as the refusal to work. And equally often, the slave's body was exchanged between (in the United States, mainly white) property holders. In that case, the body's significations were completely separated from the slave's subjectivity. It is, perhaps, in this context that Morrison's naming of the character in *A Mercy*—namely, her use of a currency unit, Floren(s), as a name—must be read, and I shall discuss this issue further in Chapter 4. Long before *A Mercy*, however, Morrison was concerned with the link between absence, haunting, and writing per se.

One proceeds, then, to ask what a reader reads, or what a reader sees when punctuation is withheld, when writing is presented as a block of letters, or when a speaker calls "Sth!"—a sound that comes out of nowhere, that declares a voice whose speaker is obscured.[46] These questions confront the reader in the first "word" of Morrison's *Jazz*. They are, of course, related to the question of understanding how Morrison responds to the problematic she has set—namely, how to write writing, how to liberate the small *r* reader from the upper case *R* Reader, from ideology secreted as a second nature embedded in the seemingly innocent act of learning how to read. To understand this, one must look at the movement between *Beloved* and *Jazz*, at the relationships between the novels, and at the writing that precedes and follows them. This movement is marked most emphatically and dramatically by the "Sth!" that opens *Jazz*. These three consonants make a wordless word that nevertheless galvanizes the trained reader to look for vowels and to play a game of choosing which vowels to place where. An *a*? Sath. An *e*? Seth? Two *e*'s? Conjuring thus with the alphabet permits one to see something emerge from Morrison's corpus, a name that featured powerfully in her previous novel: Sethe, the woman who so willingly called for the dead to return and whose longing for that return was also a willingness to give up her claim to innocence. And so, we might read the opening of *Jazz* as the invocation of a name, *Sethe*. Here, in another novel in another context, the memory and forgetting of Sethe occurs in and through a word that resembles but does not fully reproduce or reiterate it and that arrives in *Jazz* as exclamation and exhortation rather than in the form of the proper name. To trace the disjunctive movement between these two novels is to confront what Morrison offers as a theory in answer to the false claims that recovery makes. Her answer posits the constitutive role of absence and disappearance in the formation of subjects and communities, in literature and in history. It confronts even the discourse that wants to escape the house of race.[47] And it confronts vanishings of difference that occur within and as the conditions of possibility for discursive authority. In effect, Morrison's play with vanishings, disappearances, and the absent presence—which is not to say absence *represented*—offers readings that introduce a moral imperative in the face of a fascination with the dead and lost, while drawing attention to disappearance effected within African American communities

The background to the transformation from a figure in history to a figure in fiction, *Beloved*, is well known. According to the historical record, in 1851, a young slave named Margaret Garner escaped Kentucky into Cincinnati with her three children, only to be tracked down by slave catchers. Faced with recapture, she ran into a woodshed and took up a shovel, with which she managed to kill one child and wound the other two, intending to kill them as well. Tried and convicted, she explained herself by stating, "I will not let those children live how I have lived." Her mother-in-law, who witnessed her actions, reportedly said, "I watched her and I neither encouraged her nor discouraged her."[48] In *Beloved*, Sethe is a former runaway slave who has smuggled her two sons and baby girl off the plantation Sweet Home and into freedom via the Underground Railroad, which delivered them to their paternal grandmother, Baby Suggs, in the Bluestone Community set aside by Abolitionists in Ohio. Baby Suggs's manumission was paid for through the labor of her son, Sethe's "husband"—insofar as slaves could be called husband and wife—but he has vanished, unable to join Sethe during her escape. Pregnant with her fourth child, she escapes, and it is during her journey to join her family that she gives birth to her second daughter, Denver. Having crossed the river into Ohio, she is reunited with her two boys and the baby girl whom she refers to as the "crawlin already baby" (*B* 93). However, when she is cornered by slave catchers and her former owner, she runs into a shed, where she attempts to save all of her children from slavery's reach by killing them. She succeeds only in killing the "crawlin already baby" before another slave, Stamp Paid, prevents her from killing her two sons, Howard and Buglar, and the newborn Denver.

Arrested, tried, and imprisoned, Sethe is finally released but is shunned by the rest of the community of former slaves. For a time, her family at 124 Bluestone Road consists of herself, Baby Suggs, and her surviving three children. They are not alone, however. They share the house with disturbances that are believed to be the vengeful spirit of the "crawlin already baby," who makes her presence visible through signs—overturned canisters, handprints on surfaces, overturned chairs. The boys run away, and Baby Suggs retreats from the world to die, leaving Sethe and Denver to live with the haunting. Denver increasingly longs for the baby ghost to be her friend and calls to her, but Sethe needs to see her fully. When they join hands to call the baby ghost forth, their speech enacts a desire to be in touch with the invisible writer of those strange domestic signs. Sethe, the body that longs to remember, and Denver, the body that longs, call forth and seem to produce an answering presence in the form of a strange woman who walks out of the river and claims the name *Beloved*. The novel's third- person narration then gives way to individuated first person monologues—Sethe has one, Denver one, and Beloved two.

Like *Beloved*, *Jazz* grew out of Morrison's speculation upon an actual event. In Harlem, over a century after Margaret Garner's case became a *cause célèbre* for Abolitionists, James Van de Zee's *The Harlem Book of the Dead* featured the picture of a young girl in her coffin.[49] She had died at age eighteen after collapsing and bleeding, but saying only "I'll tell you tomorrow. I'll tell you tomorrow" when asked what had happened. It was later discovered that she had been shot by a jealous boyfriend, whom she had allowed time to escape by keeping silent. The impetus for a novel, she is not its central character, as Margaret Garner is for *Beloved*. In *Jazz*, we are propelled by an invisible narrator into what she proclaims is her knowledge of Violet Trace and, through Violet, her husband Joe and all the others whom they have encountered in significant ways—including that of the young girl, Dorcas, with whom Joe had an affair and whom he had shot and killed.

Like Claudia McTeer in *The Bluest* Eye, this self-pronouncing narrator of *Jazz* appears, disappears behind the stories she tells, and then reappears. Unlike Claudia, she has no past and is never visibly part of the stories. Her self-reflection, when it comes, is not upon her own life but upon her story- telling and, although she and Claudia catch themselves up and question their motives for telling the stories they have just told, she does not turn back to Joe or Violet as Claudia does to Pecola. She turns outward and addresses the reader in the second person, in a way that inverts Claudia's use of the "we" and its implication of the reader, who then has to ask: Am I included in this reference? Rather than be folded into the indictment of Claudia's "we," the reader is not drawn to join the narrating voice of *Jazz*. The reader is, instead, asked to retain a distance that enables a face-to-face encounter with the narrator who calls.

This narrator's first sound calls attention both to herself and to what is disappearing in the closing of one book and the opening of another in

Morrison's oeuvre: the name of a prior character whose actions have had real historical impact, as well as literary force. To understand this relation between what carries over, or escapes, from one novel to the other, it is necessary to return to the central, first person chapters or monologues in *Beloved*, to the utterances of Sethe, Denver, and the woman who takes the name Beloved. Each speaks of knowing, and it is their knowing that marks these chapters off from the rest of the narrative. The first to speak is Sethe, who lays claim to the newly arrived spectral woman as her dead baby, now returned as a miraculously grown woman. Her monologue begins with the utterance of Beloved's name: "Beloved, she my daughter. She mine. See" (*B* 200). It may be that this citational play extends to the novel *Home*, where the child born in transit who anchors the narrative is named Cee. Here, homonymy allows for a play between imperative or command and name, while calling forth a prior story of death and life in the space between. But in *Beloved*, before such playful extension has occurred, Sethe enunciates recognition in the possessive form. The brevity of her first statement becomes the statement of simple fact shaped by the logic of ownership, of private property: if this woman is named Beloved, she is "my daughter," and if she is "my daughter," she is "mine." Already, in this swift shift, the rhetorical act of a pseudo-performative utterance has routed any potential doubt and settled the matter for Sethe. Her naming has not only called the woman Beloved, but daughter. Both the proper name and the concrete noun ritualize her claim to the woman-child as well as her claim to the ability to designate.

The nouns also reiterate and summon Sethe's earlier history, where the one word on her dead baby's grave is Beloved. The nouns also draw from another, political context and the shifting social terrain on which the terms *mother* and *child* moved and signified. Her rhetorical gesture of inserting herself and the newly arrived (or returned) Beloved into the conventions of a mother-daughter relationship, typically withheld from slaves, extends the dominant codes and conventions, appropriating them for slaves and ex-slaves even while undoing them. (Her murderous deeds, as those of a mother against a child, may also leak back into the dominant realm and threaten the boundaries and entailments of the term.) The gesture inevitably recalls a prior moment when, as slave, Sethe could not have had a "husband" or be considered a mother, like Baby Suggs, who had seen all but one child, her son Halle, sold away from her. It was, after all, a time when slave women were deemed self-producing "goods" rather than mothers in the eyes of their owners. In the transforming social context that followed upon the abolition of slavery, Sethe can and does lay claim to what was previously denied her. And as a new "mother," she assumes the prerogative that she had exercised before in a deadly way when, having borne life, she also gives the gift of death. In effect, Sethe actualizes her status as a subject beyond or without the protection of the law, violating it in order to save another from being similarly without its protections, similarly outlawed.

Sethe then speaks of her own life on Sweet Home and of her life since leaving it. She also speaks of people who preceded her children, and offers to teach Beloved about them (*B* 201). Here, the fantasy of being able to recover that which was lost, a beloved lost object in Freudian terms, is imagined as possible through narrative language, as if the telling alone will heal. In a profound sense, Beloved comes into being through the mother's narrative voice. But in this realization of a wish, the narrative also obliterates what summons the very act of narration—for if Beloved still exists, if she can be said to be, the events of her having been killed, the horrors of slavery that made it appear necessary, the violence of the law that punished those outside of itself, must all be called into question. Again, the doubt that afflicts the witness appears here; if the story is too successful, it negates the trauma that it is intended to overcome, and if this is to be desired in a therapeutic context, the risks of total amnesia, Morrison's fiction appears to suggest, are those of excessive presence. In *Beloved* this takes the form of a ghost who becomes flesh and commands the living.

While the second of the first person monologues in *Beloved* is crucial in an overall reading of the novel, Denver's narration of people who preceded Beloved is based upon the stories *she* has been told by Baby Suggs. Sethe is not Denver's primary source of narrative, though she is the source of Denver's "canny" sight. Nonetheless, of more importance for our purposes here is the voice of Beloved in the third of the first person chapters. Here, the language is broken by gaps on the page and by shifting references to various people, some of whom are partly recognizable. One of these is Sethe herself, seen in this defamiliarized way as mediated by another. The rest are unfamiliar, unnamed people, who nevertheless come forward as strong traces both of this spectral woman's former life and of the lives that preceded her and—in a structural twist—that preceded even Sethe. The narrative voice in this section of *Beloved* announces herself and, in a gesture that reverses that of Sethe in her claim upon Beloved, lays claim to Sethe:

"I am Beloved and she is mine." The reversal is an impossible one, of course, or at least an asymmetrical one, insofar as the daughter and mother lay claim to one another in a singular fashion. Beloved appropriates from Sethe the prerogative of naming and designates herself. Even as she does so, she cedes herself to Sethe, who, as the first object of Beloved's gaze, becomes the focal point of a language that seeks transparency in description. In an aura of detached omnipresence, Beloved describes her thus: "I see her take flowers away from leaves she puts them in a round basket the leaves are not for her she fills the basket she opens the grass" (*B* 210).

The temporal instability created by the reversal of the mother-daughter relation is extended. Beloved speaks of things that preceded her birth: for example, Sethe as a young girl picking flowers to place in the kitchen at the plantation Sweet Home. Thus, very quickly, and like her mother, Beloved has learned how to narrate things that occurred in times that precede her own experience. All of her knowledge comes through watching Sethe, even though the barrier between the living and the dead, metaphorized as clouds, is "in the way." The novel in fact requires the reader to accept that this tension exists between the living and the dead and that it materializes itself in the form of a scopic relation, but also as an anxiety about loss. Beloved says, "there will never be a time when I am not crouching and watching others who are crouching too," and, later, "I cannot lose her again" (*B* 210, 212). Interestingly, although Sethe and Denver speak her name at the opening of their monologues, Beloved never mentions Sethe's name until she has herself been called by Denver. She can name by being named, although the instability between the adjectival and nominal forms of the name Beloved constantly threatens to make her name a question mark. But whereas Beloved's self-naming claims affective attachment, she ends with an accusation, "Sethe's is the face that left me" (*Beloved* 213). Her next monologue follows immediately, and it opens with Sethe's name in this possessive form. What began as an imitation, a kind of subjectless citation, has now become a fully predicating and designating speech. Beloved is present. And though she is initially a very carnal force, she achieves her full presence as a knowing and indeed increasingly omnipotent being, unrestrained by the usual boundaries that confine living, flesh-bound humans. It is as though Beloved is moving from one state of spectrality to another by passing through the world of the living. But that is where the book ends.

It is no small surprise, then, to encounter the first line of *Jazz* and to realize that the voice that utters "Sth! I know that woman" is strangely familiar. Rife with knowing, powerful, and having given up the corporeal body that she so desired but from which she was expelled at the end of *Beloved*, the spectral woman has taken on the body of the text itself, the body of language. She is still speaking the first and last name from which she has derived all knowing, even of how to tell stories, "S[e]th[e]!" In this instant, Morrison's self-citation opens one narrative only through the partial return of another. But the repetition occurs, incompletely, fleetingly (the absent letters complicate the reading of repetition), troubling the reader familiar with her work. In this way, her writing performs a self-haunting while interpolating the reader as a knowing but haunted subject. If Beloved was "the laugh" and Sethe the "laugher," Sethe is now the deceased mother who is the hiss in her daughter's speech. The "Sth!" is an impartial acknowledgement of the M(other). In her recognition and identification with Sethe, Beloved reveals an aggressivity that is also the trace of the M(other)'s traumatizing mark.

Exclaiming the "Back of Words"

What is a hiss written as "Sth!" but an exclamation that is an exhortation, a summons that has yet to enter language in the form of a word? For this hiss, if one is to call it that, is not yet language, although it communicates a presence and attracts attention (*J* 1). It calls the ear and prepares the listener to receive. This exclamation, the sound that lays beyond the word *hiss*, has its precedent in *Beloved*, when a company of thirty women confront the "devil-child" who has taken the form of a pregnant woman calling herself Beloved and who now stands on the porch of 124 Bluestone Road. Most have come with both the "shield and sword" of their Christian faith and whatever talismans they carried in "apron pockets, strung around their necks, lying in the space between their breasts" (*B* 257). Others have come with one or the other. Denver—who, we recall, is the first and only one of Sethe's four children to be born in freedom and the sister of the slain "crawlin already" baby, who has become the "devil-child" haunting 124, assuming the flesh of an adult woman—sees these women and hears only part of their "earnest syllables of agreement that backed" a "lead prayer" (*B* 258). At this point, the words that reach Denver are suddenly broken by a holler. One of the women, Ella, has broken through the prayers to take the company "back to the beginning," when "there were no words" and where there was "the sound, and they all knew what that sounded like" (*B* 259). Inside, Sethe hears this sound as music that recalls for her an earlier, healing time when her husband's mother—there was, as noted above, no law beyond permission to "jump the broom" that would make Baby Suggs Sethe's mother-in-law—had led prayers and gatherings in what the community had called the Clearing. The healing past and the present, a Friday "so hot and wet Cincinnati's stench had traveled to the country" (*B* 257), come together as "the voices of women searched for the right combination, the key, the code, the sound that broke the back of words . . . until they found it" (*B* 261). What they "find" is "a wave of sound wide enough to sound deep water and knock the pods off chestnut trees."

This hiss, the wave of sound that could make water move, comes for the women of the Bluestone community from a time before words. They seem to summon it in order to break "the back of words"—not simply the spine that gives rigor and form, but, one might argue, the limit of words that closes off what is back behind them. But what is the "back" of words? Perhaps silence. Silence that is not simply the absence of speech but a certain speechlessness in the face of horror, and perhaps those secrets that need to be kept. A sound that comes from the "back of words" can be said to send our listening in that direction and, indeed, the sound made by the Bluestone women is enough to send the "devil-child" woman "cutting through the wood" toward the river from which she had emerged, naked and with snakes in her hair (*B* 267). This river is an evocation of that other watery crossing into death, the Middle Passage.

In the central first person chapters in which Sethe, Denver, and Beloved speak, Beloved refers to a time of darkness and the crush of many bodies whose state invokes the hold of a slave ship. In that darkness, which millions experienced, the abyss of which philosophers write was made real. But to call that experience a living hell is to fall back on a metaphor that has lost all of its force. (Hence, it is only through the indirection of an unnamed river that Morrison can lead us along this path of associations.) The violence of the hold is not, however, only a matter of corporeal violence and physical suffering; it also afflicts the relationship to language. Beloved's staggering monologue reveals the physicality of the shock in which language is stripped from a subject and reduced to broken phrases, which come back only sporadically. These fragments, with the silences between them rendered visual on the page as spaces without punctuation, is more the sign of a known language being lost than of an ancient one being recovered. Yet it is in the process of fully entering that terrible place that a new language is learned, precisely where the other language is vanishing.

In the monologue of the woman who has differentiated herself as Beloved, then, the river becomes a metaphorical body of water, taking us back to memories that could not possibly have been those of Sethe's child, but of an unnamed other who hungers for recognition and is possessed by a desperation to emerge from an unbounded loneliness in which the historically real crush of bodies is equated with the crush of an abyss that is symbolic of more than death. The abyss is symbolic of the utter isolation into which we imagine the dead travel. If the hold of the slave ship is a proper figure for the abyss, in the indescribable space beyond the back there is only a vanishing sense of touching and being touched, of seeing and being seen, hearing and being heard. And in the darkness, what vanishes first is the possibility of designation, of naming properly. The proper name separates from its referent, can only be sent precariously into the dark. Here, in the space of the disappearing name, all other social ties are lost, and the place from which speech emanates is therefore also lost, as is the possibility of recognition.

The nonspecific nature of the first person "memory" calls itself Beloved, but only in a generalized way, which seeks to move forward from generalization and to find a body that can be seen and know itself to be seen. The fragmentary nature of this memory reflects the delirium of not having a language for the unprecedented experience of being crowded amongst the terrified and the dying. In that space, the figure that calls itself Beloved keeps referring to faces—those of a woman and a man. She refers to the man's face as not being hers, but as dying on hers (*B* 210, 212). Death comes between her and this man to "lock" his eyes (*B* 212). He cannot look back at her, and she cannot know herself as seen. There is also no reciprocity between her and a woman who becomes distinct from all the bodies pressed against each other, a woman we might read as Sethe, given what we know of her by this point in the novel—this woman has earrings, like those given to Sethe by her former slave mistress. It is here, when Beloved looks at Sethe, that the "clouds [get] . . . in the way" (*B* 210, 211). They "empty" Sethe's eyes, just as death emptied those of the man from the ship's hold. Beloved's metaphor shifts death from herself, to some suspended, unshaped, yet powerfully thwarting manifestation between her and Sethe. She does not embrace death and does not want to. Each encounter with death is so close it sits on her face, but she cannot see that, if this is so, it inhabits her already and that the space she inhabits is that of the dead. This is what she fears. Her desire is to join the living, and this is what she narrates of her emergence from the river of death (*B* 213). The strange and painful truth, however, is that she cannot see the life in the living, only that which anticipates death.

What transforms her from an unnamed, undifferentiated "she" into a discrete subject is the act of naming by Sethe. Until then, Denver has simply referred to her with the third-person pronoun. After she has been named, Denver can say that Beloved "whispers to me." The utterance co-incides with her remark that there are no longer any clouds. Now Beloved can at last enter a reciprocal grammar. The verb *whispers to* requires an indirect object, which is occupied by Beloved's pronominal "me." Feeling herself called, Beloved steps into her new name and in the direction of the whisperer, and as she does so, she moves from listening to saying, "I reach for her" (*B* 213). Again, the object is indirect. She moves toward the other, entering the social world of the living at last. Through the language that precedes her, Beloved becomes eligible for a full identity. She names herself belatedly, once she has emerged from that whispering call and answer. And even that name is borrowed, as I have already noted. The name that Denver whispers is the only one on her sister's headstone, the one word that her mother could "afford" and that survives as a fragment of a sermon that began with "Dearly Beloved." But in this process, as in any process of naming, the generalized word comes to attach itself to a particular being, even if its initial use by Denver has been an act of desperate nomination intended to fix the poltergeist presence that overturns canisters and makes 124 loud and spiteful. In the carnal Beloved, the generalized has become singular, personal. Whispered, it is answered by one who experiences herself as lost, unseen, vanishing. Her answer thus literally embodies the shift from de-individuation to individuation, and with that process comes the possibility of a *self*-consciousness.

It is this claimed self that has a hungry grasp on the living body of Sethe. The hunger is constantly fueled by what one character, Ella, understands, suddenly and instinctively. She understands that hunger is always present in this becoming body, just as it is in herself. It is a fear of the "back there" of the abyss, with which the "devil-child" seems to retain an intimate familiarity. Ella's holler sends her back. As soon as Ella hollers, abandoning the name and all the fixity that language engenders, what has been gap and space in Beloved's memory is reopened. And what has been gap and space—all that testimony seeks to mediate—in the community of Bluestone is also reopened. When the women look at Beloved after this holler, they do not see her. They see only an "it," an undifferentiated "devil-child." Beloved cannot see what Sethe and Denver see when they look at her. And she sees the community for whom she has lost her named personhood also as a mass, no longer as Ella or any of the other named women who have been leaving food on the tree stump outside of 124 and whom Denver has come to know by name.

What had been a disintegrating voice that had no body of its own but that could remember the crush of bodies and that had a memory of an "I" and a "me" is returned to where "there is no one to want me to say my name" (*B* 212). In that expulsion, the "back" of words is returned to its place as the limit we might sense to all testimonial language. It is this limit that is also invoked in exclamation, when language fails, and only a sound from its outside can suffice, or when meaning is so completely shared that speech is not necessary but a gesture of affirmation is called for. There is the "Un huh" that Sethe mutters when her boss is speaking to her and all she can do is think of speeding home to the newly arrived young woman who calls herself Beloved, or the "Uh uh" that comes from Ella when confronted by Stamp Paid about her stubborn refusal to help Sethe, or that Paul D utters every now and then, but especially when he learns that Sethe had murdered her baby (*B* 191, 187, 157). "Uh huh" is also all that Sethe's "husband" Halle says when she tries to make an argument that Garner, their slave master, was not as bad as other white people (*B* 197). What, then, are we to make of these sounds that we have wanted to imagine as coming before language? The impulse is to imagine that precedence as a state of no language. Yet Stamp Paid hears something "undecipherable" when he approaches 124.

Perhaps we should hear his desire for a still-undecipherable language as the flip side of the force that is represented by the hissing "Sth." This is the force of communicability itself, the origins of the social, the horizon toward which the witness always moves and from which the annihilated victim always recedes. It is also the impossible purity in relation to which testimony is always found to be lacking. In the testimony that emanates from a catastrophe such as slavery, the witness, as Agamben shows us, lives the aporia of having to communicate what exceeds communicability, while suffering the burden of one whose very survival calls into question the status of any communication he or she attempts to make. Morrison's characters live and negotiate these burdens, just as her fiction seeks to do—in its thematizations and its formal operations. Again and again, Morrison's answer to the demand for witnessing is to tempt the reader with a sense of immediate access to the fictional world through which we also might gain proximity to the real.

But with each invitation to recovery, there is an interruption. The narrators' claims to omniscience unravel for us, and often for them. The specters who emerge from the past, and who appear to be reclaiming carnal life, consume the living and recede into the netherworld whence they came. Characters who come into being through the act of naming, both by the author and by the other characters in books, traverse the boundaries of the fictions bounded as books but lose their substantiality. And if, across the body of her own literary corpus, Morrison endlessly engages the problematic of testifying to the effects of slavery (rather than the event itself), her turn to slavery's origins upends the presumptive temporality of witnessing by revealing the entanglement of a future catastrophe with the desire for amnesia and severance from the past that so often appears, initially, to be a source of freedom. For Morrison, neither the plenitude of a full re-presence in that impossible ideal of the perfect testimony nor the bliss of forgetfulness is to be sought. And, from *The Bluest Eye* through *Tar Baby, Song of Solomon, Beloved, Jazz, Paradise, A Mercy,* and *Home,* each posing the question of how to witness, of who is eligible to witness and for whom, there is the insistent and visible inscription of gaps and silences, performing and redoubling what the diegetic aspiration of each novel stages, namely, the necessity of remembering forgetting.

2.   Burnt Offerings: Law and Sacrifice

At the center of *Paradise*'s Ruby, deep in Oklahoma, is the Oven. Nails have inscribed into its surface the imperative phrase, "Beware the Furrow of His Brow" (*P* 7). The descendants of fifteen families, who migrated "from Mississippi and two Louisiana parishes" and the failed Restoration, live in obedient, though increasingly tested observance of this command (*P* 13). They, however, call it by different names. It is a command to some, a motto to others.

The Oven is Ruby's social and psychic hearth, perhaps even its most sacred space, more sacred than the two churches that face each other on diagonal corners where two short roads cross. Built by a founding father, Zechariah (also Coffee/Kufi), who originally led the "one hundred and fifty-eight freedmen" comprising Ruby's first generation, the Oven still shows the scarification of his tools. When the elders look at the Oven, they see the homelessness out of which Zechariah led their parents, and they see the mystery of his logic, to which they have no access but which they nonetheless obey. They obey the motto because they ignore the questions that it also poses, namely, what it means, or what is the story behind Zechariah's choice of phrase. Serene in its force and confident in its opacity, the source of the authority behind the motto/command remains unknown and cannot be accessed.[1] Its force has a linguistic form recognizable as a performative. It is a call that comes from somewhere else. And each act by which the inscription is recognized is an enactment of the command "Beware." It is not, therefore, the content of the commandment but the gesture that summons attention, which succeeds or not. The referent—whose brow—and the rationale—why and what happens if one fails to obey—are unsignified, unknown. And thus, although the Oven calls from the past and commands a terrified backward glance from those who pass by it, thereby seeming to summon recollection, it offers no content for memory. Perhaps in this way it partakes of the iconicity of the oven in twentieth-century Euro-American consciousness more generally: an iconicity in which an unspeakable horror and the specter of a violent lawfulness are somehow conjoined without being explained. To this possibility I shall return at the end of this chapter.

The Oven and its motto/command also works like Sethe's scarred back in *Beloved*, or the brand under her mother Ma'am's breast, in that they are all trace structures of historical violence. As traces, they have within them incentives to narrate. If not "why" these signs came to be, then "how" is the question secreted within them—a structure reminiscent of the one orienting *The Bluest Eye*. Here, as there, "why" and "how" have, as their correlate, the "what" of meaning. "How" entails explanation in the form of accounting. As an account, a narrative is also held on behalf of someone else, or on behalf of some characters, in the body of the work. The work of telling vaults over and around the story, containing it and shaping it. The difference between the violence made visible in the description of Sethe and Ma'am and that of the Oven called forth by the Oven derives from the very different structures of signification and power in which they operate. Sethe's and Ma'am's bodies are made to bear the sign of a power that claims them and regulates them. It is inscribed in and on their flesh and is the sign of a rule by force. The Oven's phrase is not written into a body—the scarification applies to the surface of the Oven itself— and it is not the sign of a slaver's claim to power or the mark of his will. It is abstraction; its status as word rather than laceration marks the motto/command of the Oven as located in the space of transition to a new order, the order of law in the instance where it seeks to achieve autonomy and to gather into itself the full force of violence, but in an abstract mode, whereas the law of slavery had been backed by force and applied through force, but was not yet the law as force in the sense it would become later. The motto/command is talismanic, absorbing and warding off a history from which the elders seek to remove themselves—the same history of slavery, which once operated so differently yet remains encrypted as a structuring principle after slavery itself has ended. While the symbolic aura around the notion of an oven is gendered—as a feminine shape associated with the womb—its creation in Ruby was a masculine initiative, that of Big Daddy Zechariah Morgan. As such, it is also the instantiation of black patriarchy's assumption of the prerogatives and the logics of its white counterpart—a theme long familiar to Morrison's readers.

In *Paradise*, the figure of the Oven permits the development of a historicized conception of the rule embedded in the motto. It is a transitional figure, the mark of an emergent order still contaminated by its predecessors, which it can only partially leave behind. If a motto announces a belief and/or code, for which it stands as a reduced signpost, it also makes rules of them. A rule is not yet law in the fullest, codified, and therefore rationalized sense, of course, but it can be an individual and constituent part of a larger assemblage. Accordingly, it too can have something of the force of law when granted that by readers. But there is another dimension of the motto's status, which exceeds the teleology of law's abstraction. If the rule is not yet de jure, if it is not yet part of a fully systematized code, it could be called de facto, but the aura that accrues to it renders it potentially untouchable, even pristine, which is to say, sacred. Relatively enigmatic because of its lack of integration into a visible set of comparable regulative imperatives, oblique in its significations and functioning as a question as much as a commandment, it has the aura of a god's will, or a fated element. In this sense, it is an element of language before a language per se becomes visible. It can be analogized to a word before it has been incorporated into a full sentence, *motto* deriving from the Latin for word. It is a singular component, apparently autonomous, despite its dependence on all of the other elements of the signifying system. The point, however, is that this priority and autonomy are illusory, deriving more from the secreting of the history of the motto's making or of a kind of repression than from its actual anteriority to other laws, such as that which grants patriarchs the right to legislate. The point of the motto is not, then, that it is actually prior to law but that, at least in *Paradise*, it represents the moment of assemblage. Their interrelation and status is one of seriality or contiguity rather than hierarchical integration, and in this manner, it is more like the Mosaic commandments than the stipulations of the U.S. Constitution.

The motto as law in *Paradise* does not yet have the same status as the laws written under the category of Law, codified and legislated at municipal, governmental, or other institutional levels. Neither is Ruby's motto parallel to the officially and constitutionally recognized laws that appear elsewhere in Morrison's fiction, where they are remarkable mainly for the fact that they are disavowed by people in power, or interpreted and twisted by those in dominant positions and manipulated to conceal the interest of racial or gendered power in the mendacious language of universality. Such law has a history, and Morrison's fiction has consistently draw attention to this. It is the law from which women and black people are endlessly exiled, even as they are subject to the prerogatives that others derive from it—the prerogatives of property owners and citizens understood as the bearers of rights. This is the law that is so remote and inaccessible from the Breedloves' lives that no one in their community reports Cholly's rape of his daughter, just as Cholly would not and could not think of reporting the two white hunters who manhandled him and the young girl Darlene on the night of his Aunt Jimmy's funeral (*BE* 146–49). This is also the law that is absent from Joe Trace's murder of young Dorcas in *Jazz*, and which offers neither justice nor retribution on her behalf. The same law is visible in the overzealous sheriff who comes to claim Rose Dear's furniture when her husband abandons her, taking even the chair she is sitting in and leaving her and her children without anything—a "policing" act on behalf of a debtor that drove Rose Dear to commit suicide by jumping into a well shaft (*J* 99). It is the law of the "bad cops" from whom Sandler feels he has to protect his nephew, Romen, in *Love*, and it is the law that Christine and the underground movement to which she belongs resists after the Emmet Till murder (*L* 164), the law represented by the ironically named sheriff, Buddy Silk who is happy to make a profit out of racial prejudice against black business proprietors by providing protection to a paying, successful black hotelier.

Home's reflection upon law covers two periods associated with public disregard for it by segregationists. The first is the early 1930s, possibly 1933, when Frank and Cee slip onto the horse farm and see the callous disposal of a black man's body—the timing is suggested by Frank's reference to being four years old when his family was driven from their home in Texas, some twenty years earlier than his return from the Korean action, which ended in 1953 (*H* 9). The second is just after the Korean War and therefore in either 1953 or 1954. Although shaken by the Depression, the Ku Klux Klan had been revived and was firmly established in Atlanta.[2] By 1923, a decade or so before Frank and Cee would witness the disposal of that body, the Klan claimed that it controlled the state of Georgia, and its membership included some of the country's most powerful and influential lawmakers and politicians.[3] By the early 1930s, when they must have seen that disposal, a very young Frank knew how to read the signs posted on farm fences as indications that the farmers were laws unto themselves. More, he knew that he and his sister were subject to the warnings, de facto. The second period in which the law figures as something to which they have no access occurs when neither of the Money siblings nor any of the women who have been sterilized in Dr. Scott's surgery thinks of calling upon the law to report his experiments. Frank's return links this second period with the first when he learns that, back when he and Cee saw the body, the adult inhabitants of Lotus knew not to approach the law over the murderous sport on the nearby horse farm because a bleeding survivor would have been automatically imprisoned (*H* 139). More importantly for this second period, Atlanta is where Eldon Lee Edwards began regrouping the Ku Klux Klan in 1953. His U.S. Klan, Knights of the Ku Klux Klan, became one of the largest in the country and incorporated itself as a business.[4]

As a returning black soldier, Frank was at risk, as returning black soldiers had been after both world wars. Nancy MacLean points out that the alarm about returning black soldiers was not restricted to the Klan after the First World War: even the federal government was concerned that black soldiers would demand their rights and that this would pose a danger of "impudence or arrogance."[5] For African Americans, whether soldiers or civilian men, women, or children, the periods surrounding the two world wars were fraught with the sense of a danger from which there was no legal protection.

This sense of inaccessibility persisted, despite the fact that the law was in fact used to counter the Klan or to challenge unfair labor practices. Catherine and Richard Lewis point out that between 1937 and 1938 Congress was presented with ten civil rights bills and that by 1950 it had been presented with seventy-two.[6] In Morrison's novel, however, there is no sense of organized resistance to Jim Crow.[7] There is no sense that the May 17, 1954, *Brown v. Board of Education* ruling has or will change education for African Americans in Lotus, Georgia—Cee's reference to her schooling might prompt readers to think of this landmark case, but it is far removed from her awareness. De jure and de facto power existed side by side in often contradictory ways, sometimes used to different ends, as when police and legislators were members of the Klan. The Jim Crow era ended with the Civil Rights Act of 1964. This legislation came as a response to the Civil Rights Movement, whose concerted effort was marked by the Montgomery bus boycotts of 1955–56, the same period in which Frank and

Cee are facing the local forms of de facto power. This brings into focus a difference between de jure and de facto intervention. For Frank and Cee, as for all in Lotus, de jure intervention is distant. De facto rule is as near as the town, or a neighboring farm on which a black father and son are made to fight each other so that one might live, while the National Association for the Advancement of Colored People was mounting legal and other campaigns to break de jure violence.

Despite the NAACP's full awareness of and action to overcome such violence, the novel's silence about it is telling. This silence suggests a gap between the urban and rural lives of African Americans at the time, underscored by a lag between national forms of action and local effectiveness. In an example that has a direct bearing on Frank, a document produced by Fiske University's Social Science Institute in 1946 outlined the gap between federal legislation for black veterans supposedly covered by the G.I. Bill and the realities facing those who tried to access their entitlements.[8] The report claims that some 522,000 veterans, comprising 43.5 percent of enlisted black men, had indicated their desire to return to school, but the 112 black colleges had a combined overenrollment of 50,000 students and anticipated having to admit 22,000 black veterans. This was in contexts in which their coverage by the G.I. Bill was clearly stated. The Fiske report claims that this information was withheld in Jim Crow states.[9] Yet black veterans organized the World War II Veterans Association and the Georgia Veterans League, the latter headquartered in Atlanta, with branches elsewhere in Georgia.[10] Both were active in voter registration and brought successful pressure on state governments to improve employment opportunities for African Americans.

In *Home*, Frank has no awareness of this or of the fact that there was solidarity between black and white veterans in efforts to combat discrimination.[11] As Reverend Locke tells him, he has served in a desegregated army, but the world has yet to catch up: "Listen here, you from Georgia and you been in a desegregated army and maybe you think up North is way different from down South. Don't believe it and don't count on it" (*H* 19).

It is in response to laxity on the part of the police and judiciary in pursuing those who harm or murder black people that a group of black men form their own vigilante group called the Seven Days in *Song of Solomon*. Their secret society mirrors groups like the Ku Klux Klan in a parodic vindictiveness. The law of the Seven Days exacts a narrow, economized retribution without the display of power that white supremacist societies perform, but which nonetheless works by sowing terror through forms of public secrecy, the secret lying at the "very core of power" for Elias Canetti, a notion taken up by Michael Taussig, who argues that public secrecy is the dynamic at the heart of state societies.[12] In their calculus, each black man killed must be paid for by a white man in a direct equation that follows the biblical paradigm of an eye for an eye, but that is politicized when it literalizes the claim that a black life is not worth less than a white one.

In each of these fictional examples of the law's cooptation by a racialized worldview, one might say that a haunting occurs. In *Jazz*, we find an emblematic image for the negative power of a racialized law. This image is the well into which Rose Dear throws herself in despair. Through the direct impact of the law's grasp of property, what should nourish does not, as it does elsewhere in *Paradise*, when the narrator attempts to reconstruct her negative and demanding depiction of the beautifully pampered Golden Grey, son of a black man and white woman, and cared for by Rose Dear. The narrator wants him standing "next to a well dug quite clear from trees and twigs and leaves will not fall into the deep water" (*J* 161). There, all sorrow and hopelessness "from knowing too little and feeling too much (so brittle, so dry he is in danger)" is put in perspective. From the safety of the well's rim, the depth does not haunt him in a melancholy way. For Violet Trace, however, the suicide of her mother is a haunting she cannot escape. The well into which her mother threw herself has a force that pulls at her, and "sucked her sleep" with a "limitless beckoning" (*J* 104, 102, 101).

Ruby's rule has been "forged" on the periphery of the country whose founding Constitution eventually made provision for slavery and whose early obligations to "the better security of peace and friendship" between states in the union had meant that fugitive slaves could be taken back to their slave owners from nonslaving states.[13] The history of the Constitution is what anchors the larger scope of legislative rule from which the Oven's motto/command excludes itself, but which it mimics. This history includes the law that overtook Sethe in *Beloved* and that, in its early formations, as nontotalized fugitive codes, required Florens in *A Mercy* to have a letter of passage to protect her from being arrested as a fugitive slave. In Florens's world, the fugitive codes had not fully racialized labor; they encompassed white indentured and American Indian laborers as well.[14] It would take the fully developed plantation economy associated with cash cropping and the full tidal wave of African slavery, on top of the final decimation of Indian populations, to permit the exclusive conflation of blackness with servitude with labor. But *A Mercy* is inscribed before that conflation has been completed.

Vouchsafe Relations

It may be useful here to reflect upon the context in which Morrison sets her fictions, and upon which those fictions reflect. In 1690, when Florens is traveling to fetch the blacksmith to save her mistress, colonial slave laws were only newly forming. At a time when indentured labor and slave labor were barely distinguishable, slavery was not directly named in early laws, which concerned themselves with fugitive labor per se. The retrieval of runaway slaves was, at the time of *A Mercy's* setting, extrajudicial and largely a matter for their owners.

Various attempts had been made to secure the return of fugitive labor without creating enmity between early colonies. Specifically, Article 8 in New England's 1643 Articles of Confederation provided for an intercolonial agreement for the return of "those that remove from one Plantation to another without due certificate."[15] Article 8 effectively draws any and all fugitive labor and American Indians into criminality. But while "Indians" are named as a specific category subject to the law, labor is not as yet narrowly and exclusively ethnicized or racialized. Yet neither was the colonial apparatus entirely blind to its own implacable tendency to racialization. Ironically, and presciently, the rhetorical structure through which opposition to racialization would express itself was one of self-blinding, a structure that has sightless justice as its model. But this would also entail a disavowal of the actual forms of racial violence, thanks to an extreme valorization of law itself. Moreover, this self-blinding would come much later and be given precedence in *Plessy v. Ferguson* (1896), in the single dissenting argument against the majority opinion that racial segregation was constitutional.[16] In his dissenting opinion, Justice Harlen argued, "Our Constitution is color-blind" (*Plessy v. Ferguson* 559). Of this later legal opinion, Neil Gotanda has remarked that color-blind constitutionalism could not provide for subtle forms of racial subordination, even though it could engage overt forms such as Jim Crow rules.[17] Neither does it engage implicit assumptions that devalue black culture relative to white culture, and it thereby does nothing to undermine the logic of the divisive "separate but equal" rule.[18] However, long before *Plessy v. Ferguson*, Article 8 in New England's 1643 Articles of Confederation was most concerned with healthy relations between neighbors, linking the high-minded notions of peace and justice to the political health of the signatory plantation colonies, Massachusetts, Plymouth, Connecticut, and New Haven. Good neighbors return labor. They "help" in the "safe" return of offenders.

By the time Sethe is tracked by a slave catcher in 1855, the Continental Congress had entered Article IV, Clause Three into the Constitution to ensure the legal extradition of fugitive slaves. Two Fugitive Slave Acts had also been passed in 1793 and 1850. These were ratified by the renamed Congress of the Confederation, and one could argue that the Congress's act of naming and renaming parallels the founding national imaginary, at the heart of which is a self-definition of mastery whose range includes that of mastery over others' labor, enslaved and colonized. Moreover, in the shift from a general concern about fugitive labor to an emphasis on fugitive slaves, these acts encapsulate the consolidation and racialization of labor and property, a consolidation in which the fugitive laborer's face is now black and named "slave." The early indentured Europeans have, by now, been drawn into whiteness and thus separated from the fugitive humanity of black slave labor. They have been saved, as it were, from themselves.

Don E. Fehrenbacher argues that it was in response to the Abolitionist movement that slavers called for legal codification of their rights, specifically in the matter of border crossings between states. The result was the insertion of clauses about fugitive slaves into state laws and interstate agreements.[19] This argument about cause and effect reveals the centrality of ideas about those who are "constituting" subjects and those who are subject to their desires in nation formation. In the moralism that Fehrenbacher observes, slavery is written into the heart of nation building as an axiomatic principle, wrapped in the cloak of virtue and accorded the status of natural law. All else is deviation by default. In other words, the high-minded idealism of the Constitution fused statements of ideal order with those of knowledge, claiming to express not merely the way things should be but the way they are. Within this doubled and deceiving formulation, there emerged a fundamental set of distinctions between citizens and subjects, with the citizen being accorded a fuller subjectivity than those subjects whose interiority and capacity for self-representation was entirely occluded by the same laws.

Foucault argues that juridical practices are one set of critical "social practices whose historical analysis enables one to locate the emergence of new forms of subjectivity" in the nineteenth century.[20] While this date can be pushed back in the American case to the period in which law was emerging from the assemblage of property owners' rules, what remains relevant is Foucault's formulation of the juridical as something other than the strict practice of the law, as the practice of power relations in the act of defining themselves, as power. In a strict sense, the juridical pertains to the law, but it is not reducible to the law. As such, the juridical is a set of procedures, administrations of assumptions and operations, structures of legibility and of sayability. In this light, the fugitive clauses in state and federal constitutions, and in state and federal Acts reveal the jockeying power relations between the early colonies and states, as well as between slave owners and slaves. And they reveal these power relations to be determined by possessive economies, whence they originate but which they also refine.

Freedom, then, is not the easy opposite of enslavement when laws are themselves at once visible manifestation and productive incitements of assumptions that constitute power relations on the basis of property and possessiveness. Such a notion of freedom would rest upon a claim to natural law, in which all people are naturally free and equal, with the (birth) right to freedom and property. It would also rest upon the further assumption that these rights exceed any earthly laws. In other words, the very rationalist tenets expressed in the United States' Declaration of Independence would be summoned to speak for the indentured, the enslaved, and the dispossessed. These tenets reflected the principles of natural law outlined by Locke and, through the influence of his writings on the earliest shape of government in Virginia and Carolina colonies and from thence to Jefferson, they carry into the Declaration and later Constitution the same conflicts that Locke faced in his definition of natural rights and natural liberty.[21]

For Locke, reason would dictate the truth of the claim to freedom. As the creations of God, all humans are to be considered as God's property and therefore no one human can own another. Indeed, the entire purpose of his *Two Treatises of Government* is to map out ways of securing and maintaining freedom through a doctrine that seeks to balance self-government with legislated, societal government. Its opposite or coeval is slavery, the very first word of his *First Treatise*: "Slavery is so vile and miserable an

estate of man, and so directly opposite to the general temper and cour-
age of our nation, that it is hardly to be conceived, that an Englishman,
much less a gentleman, should plead for it." In truth, Locke's concern is
for Englishmen and not African slaves, although he was fully aware of the
trade in Africans, having been a founding shareholder in the Royal African Company, set up in 1672 to control trade with Africa, with special
provisions for the slave trade.[22] The second sentence of the *First Treatise*
makes clear that he is engaging another Englishman, Sir Robert Filmer,
whose *Patriarcha* had argued for absolute monarchy as the divine right of
kings. For Locke, this was tantamount to making slaves of Englishmen
(*First Treatise* §1–2).[23]

Locke's opposition to Filmer's argument echoes Hobbes's ninth law of
nature, that every man "acknowledge another for his equal by nature."[24]
He nevertheless circumvents the question of the tension between natural
law and natural rights in his theory of the public good, in which government is charged with protecting property, more specifically, private property.[25] Chapter 4 of his *Second Treatise* opens with a statement that freedom
from any "superior power on earth" and the "will or legislative authority
of man" constitutes natural liberty (*Second Treatise* §22). In society, however, freedom is not without bounds. Legislative power is by consent, and
consent is tantamount to placing a trust in legislature. There are two exceptions. The first is war, and the second is the absence of government.

In a state of war and "lawful" conquest or just war, natural freedom
from a "superior power on earth" is suspended. Captivity yields to "the
perfect condition of slavery" (*Second Treatise* §23). Furthermore, captivity
is equated with forfeiture. A man forfeits his life "by some act that deserves death." This perfect condition is imagined as a "compact," in which
the captor agrees to limited power and the captive agrees to be obedient
(*Second Treatise* §24). In effect, Locke's argument returns to the captive
the responsibility for his/her state "for . . . no man can, by agreement,
pass over to another that which he hath not in himself, a power over his
own life." Further, captivity is a suspended death or a state of living in
proximity to a death that captivity prevents.[26] This reference is curiously
abstract—as Nancy Morrow points out[27]—given the fact that by 1698,
when Locke published his treatises, the Royal African Company had been
trading slaves for England for twenty-five years. In addition to holding
shares in the African Trading Company, Locke had assured the Gover-

nor of Virginia that enslavement of Africans was justified, for they had forfeited their liberty. Thus, captive Africans, caught in just wars, agree to substitute obedient life for death. It is not, therefore, because they are not human but because they are vanquished that they can be encompassed within a legal structure that grounds itself on natural law.

Locke makes clear that these captives are not on the same footing as those who "sell themselves" into menial work. Such menial workers are not slaves. Here he singles out Jews, among a vaguely drawn group of "other nations," thus contributing to a social and political hierarchy that is not announced as overtly ethnic and/or raced but that nevertheless singles out a group without stated reason, any reasons being, by implication, already known, that is, as circulating "knowledge" (*Second Treatise* §24) or what we might call "common sense."

Forfeiture of liberty is also a condition of living without government. In his *Second Treatise*, Locke remarks that, in the "Woods of America," a Swiss who encounters "an *Indian*" does so in a state of nature, the "Swiss" here standing in for all Europeans transported to a natural fellowship. For all this "naturalism," the European differs from the "native." Locke turns to unsourced proto-ethnographic reports about American Indian family structures and remarks that it is the mother who cares and provides for children, and not a husband (*Second Treatise* §65). Although not overtly stated, Locke's implication is that there is a relation between this family structure and a "lack" of headship, reflected in European reports that, "in many parts of *America* there [is] no Government at all" (*Second Treatise* §108). Of keen interest to Locke is what "several Nations of the *Americans*" do with their property, comparing their hunting and agriculture with English practices, and their leaders with Englishmen. Thus, a "king of a large and fruitful Territory . . . feeds, lodges, and is clad worse than a day Labourer in *England*" (*Second Treatise* §43).

Debates about natural law and natural rights have never been able to determine which has paramount status. For critical race theorists, the Civil Rights Movement's recourse to civil rights floundered on the presumed relation between these and natural rights. Indeed, Derek Bell argues that the U. S. Constitution was framed around property rights that continued to influence the country's legal institutions. Bell's claim exposes what is at the heart of the Lockean influence in the Constitution, namely Locke's argument that law and natural rights are interwoven, the latter deriving from the former, and both having direct political implications in the laws that govern "lives, liberties and estates, which I call by the general name, property" (*Second Treatise* §123).

Fiction is, of course, not critical race theory, even when, as with Morrison's work, it is informed by and articulates positions that resonate with critical race theory and even though it undertakes theoretical labor. In a novel, however, one has what Morrison has recently described as the effort to imagine the subjectivity of those who act in ways that are, for us, now unthinkable, without at the same time being mad.[28] Thus, in *Beloved* and in *A Mercy*, two novels that constitute the temporal bookends of a history that stretches across America's becoming—the history of which I have written here, the history of law's emergence, of the long reach of Lockean theories of natural right, and of the intensifying and consolidating racialization of conceptions of both property and labor—that history is inscribed in the environment and negotiated by characters whose lives are not proof of any actuality so much as evidence of a reading of history, which remains at once external to the diegesis and internal to the imagined world of the fiction. Let me return to the fictive worlds in which these histories appear as the determining structures of narrative and as the environmental condition in which Morrison imagines the otherwise foreclosed subjectivity of slaves, their forebears and descendents.

No Contest

Founded in 1951, Ruby was not the original home of the Oven and its command. The first town established by Ruby's founding families was in fact Haven, 240 miles to the east. It was created in 1890 on land that Zechariah and the other men of the first generation of travelers had bargained from the Creek Nation to settle, "away from prairie-dog towns fifty miles wide and Satan's malefactions: abandoned women with no belongings, rumors of riverbed gold" (*P* 14). It was a town forged in the crucible of exile, born of realism, free of rumors, and a sense of moral propriety anchored in patriarchal fantasies of domesticated women and in the aspiration to purity as isolation. Most importantly, Haven fortified itself against those towns, "from Yazoo to Fort Smith," that had rejected the band of freedmen. It was a town that insisted on its right to be but that bore the scars of having been cast out, a diasporic town, one might say. In this narration, disavowal by others is conflated with the desire to find a safe home. The history of rejection, disavowal, and escape is recalled in the historical recountings and reenactments that bind the town together. Like the motto inscribed on the Oven, the greatest rejection, the Great Disavowing, is also "engraved" upon the memories of two of Zechariah's grandsons, the twins Deacon and Steward Morgan (*P* 13, 14). And just as the Oven fires food and transforms it into cultural material, so Deacon and Steward Morgan fire history in their minds, and transform it into memory.

Born in 1924 to a nameless mother, who "vanishes" from Ruby's foundational narratives, and to Rector Morgan, Zechariah's second son, the twins attribute to themselves "powerful memories" and, "Between them . . . remember the details of everything that ever happened—things they . . . witnessed and things they [had] not" (*P* 13). What they rehearse over and over is "the story that explained why neither the founders of Haven nor their descendants could tolerate anybody but themselves." The story thrills them, bringing, each time, "a jolt of pleasure, erotic as a dream" (*P* 16). It is a story that everyone in Haven shares in the communal space around the Oven.

Haven is not secure, though. The twins decide this when they return from the Second World War. Theirs is a familiar story about African American soldiers who returned to disparity between the high ideals of liberty for which they had just fought and continuing discrimination at home. Such is the case with *Sula*'s Shadrack and, in the same novel, Plum Peace. We know little about Plum's experience or thoughts beyond the bare details of his entry into the war in 1917, his return in 1919, and his wandering the country until his return to the Bottom in 1920. When he arrives, he is a drug addict. The point is that the Bottom is the only place for them, no matter how problematic its history or how strong the "spite that galloped all over" the place (*S* 171). Frank Money also understands as much after deferring his return to Lotus. When he does so, he finds more than an isolated, "unforgiving population, indifferent to the future" (*H* 16). There is still the sense of a place menaced and tortured, even by nature (*H* 117), but he also sees that nothing can silence the town. The novel's sparse descriptive prose gives way to a richness that reflects his new sight. Frank does not see a perfect town, but he does see care and attention: "There were no sidewalks, but every front yard and backyard sported flowers protecting vegetables from disease and predators." The men on Fish Eye Anderson's porch spend their time playing cards or other games and drinking. All veterans save for his uncle, Salem Money, they understand the First and Second World Wars but do not respect what they do not understand about the Korean action. Yet even with this understanding, Frank refuses to see only dissipation in them. He sees liveliness in friendship and signs of activity, even though fishing poles "leaned against the railing" and a "vegetable basket waited to be taken home" (*H* 137). These, the empty soda bottles, and newspapers are "all the gatherings that made men comfortable."

The Morgan twins do not look upon Haven with such understanding when they return from the Second World War. They see "weed-choked" streets and dissipation. They see the neglected Oven. Although they do not say as much, their recollection of what it took to create Haven and the Oven is tantamount to an accusation that this history, too, has been neglected. The details of that history become "out-thrilling and more purposeful than even the war they had fought in." They undertake two main acts of reconsolidation. First, they secure their own family through marriage. They marry two sisters, Soane and Dovey, whose family is never mentioned and with whom the sisters never again have any dealings. The twins also marry their sister Ruby to one of their "army buddies," a man who is unrelated to any of the original families and who also vanishes once he has played a very basic, biological role in fecundating the family line. Their own family now secured, Deacon and Steward move with a band of people from each of the original families, leaving behind "eighteen stubborn people wondering how they could get to the post office where there might be a letter from long gone grandchildren" (*P* 17). The eighteen are not named. If they included the twins' relatives there is no mention of this. The eighteen are consigned to outsider status and do not bear any names through which kinship can be invoked. Remembered only with a glancing contempt, these unnamed people are not necessary to the new town, the one that the Morgan twins insist on "getting right."

The twins' second act is to dismantle the Oven and resurrect it in their newly constituted town, the one they establish "deeper in Oklahoma, as far as they could climb from the grovel contaminating the town their grandfather had made" (*P* 16). They flee from a history of rejection and disavowal whose contaminating reach they blame for Haven's failure. They settle near land once owned by a robber baron, who is long gone but who had willed his bullet-shaped home to a Convent. Although they had considered calling the new town New Haven, the twins leave it unnamed until 1954. That is the year in which their sister dies in childbirth after a white hospital refuses to admit her during labor. The town is named, after "one of their own . . . Ruby. Young Ruby" (*P* 17).

This language of possession, referenced in the phrase "their own," draws a veil between Ruby and the outsider buddy whose military service was exchanged, through fraternity, into serving the Morgan family's need for regeneration. The twins' unnamed friend ensured that the Morgans avoid the fate of the Fleetwood family, whose women give birth to sickly children. These children are a source of embarrassment about which no one in the town wants to speak. The significance of the twins' army buddy is to be an unspoken assurance against such births. In a closed community, there are simple dilemmas of marriage, which always demands alliance with some individual or group outside of the natal family, however that is defined. No single man in the group that left Haven and settled Ruby could be permitted to compete for Ruby. Her brothers saw to that.

The buddy brother-in-law's significance increases when Deacon and his wife lose their sons, also twins, in Vietnam. Thanks to their foresight, the Morgans have an heir, the only one, born of their sister. This nephew's name is K. D. He was named after a horse, itself named after an annual event, the Kentucky Derby. It is a strange name for one on whom so much rests. A race implies chance and the world of pure competition. The deeper family secret might point to the chance that Deacon and Steward took in bringing their army buddy into their family's midst, the chance they gave that buddy, and the gamble that they took, in the end, with their sister's free will and, finally, with her life in the name of lineage.

From their assumed position as the town's leaders, the twins guard over the Oven and the motto. And it is the phrase "Beware the Furrow of His Brow" that stands in the place of a rule of law in Ruby. The disjuncture between the well-rehearsed narratives of the town's becoming and the mystery of the motto's origins is only overcome in the connotation of suspicion—both the suspicion of outsiders and the sense that one is also always suspect in the eyes of He whose brow is furrowed—that clings to the latter and that explains and is explained by the former. This rule is one that, despite the opacity of its possible meaning and source, is associated with a rejection of the "outside" in which the larger, American nation's laws, its Constitution, were so deeply implicated in the imposition and support of slavery.

The contours of most critical readings of the motto are determined by the elders' rigid attempt to impose upon it a single, mysterious meaning. Yet, on one level, the motto's centrality in Ruby's worldview is not as easily dismissed. Although it looks backward, it does so with what we readers, like the younger generation of Ruby, sense is a knowing. The fact that its meaning is the subject of intense debate suggests a content that Zechariah knew or that he learned from elsewhere. The motto eschews the Lockean principles of law that authorized and inspired the ideals of the Declaration of Independence and U.S. Constitution and that, in this aspiration, obscured histories of injustice. In its own most ambitious aspiration, the motto makes visible injustices and their flawed institutions. This is also what the Morgan twins remember, and it is what they attempt to keep Ruby away from. But Misner and Pat Best see what has been happening. The twins' claim to knowledge has become all-consuming, and it has drawn all attention to itself, deflecting attention from other social practices that produce violence within Ruby.

Set in direct and fierce opposition to the outside, Ruby's inside is utterly utopic. So dominant is the idea of the inside that very little real conversation takes place in the novel. We are primarily in the inside of the inside, in the thoughts of Soane and Dovey, their husbands Steward and Deacon, their nephew K. D., Reverend Misner, Pat Best, and others. They all move increasingly inward, eerily isolated from each other by self-imposed injunctions against speaking out about things that disturb them. Through this inward movement, they restage the town's contraction and severance from the wider world.

As will become clear, Ruby's rule requires total submission. In this, *Paradise* is a new and important book for Morrison, because it engages not only what happened to the descendents of those dragged across the Atlantic but what they became—not in the accidental way that The Bottom was settled and clung to in *Sula* or in the way that the Bluestone community was dependent upon the goodwill of Abolitionists in *Beloved*. This novel draws attention to a less than attractive but comprehensible mimesis of race and a conservatism that kept the descendants of Africans in America deep within the house of race, for all their hope of escaping it.

Each of the letters forged by Zechariah testifies to a presence behind the law. Enigmatic, immanent, and receding, this law nonetheless appears to the citizens of Ruby only through the signage inscribed by Zechariah, and only because it can be assumed to be the rule of the group. Playing on the metaphoricity of signage, Morrison's prose seems to want to dramatize the degree to which such rules lay claim to a transcendental signified but are, in fact, merely signs of themselves. In this case, the sign is multiplied. It appears in the motto per se, but also in its referent, the furrow of his brow, and it is in the imperative, or infinitive, verb "Beware." The last is nonetheless a sign of a different order, in that its grammatical form signifies the very fact of commandment and of the power structures whence it issues. Concealed and displayed in the motto, then, is the obligation of the descendants to the original fifteen families. They left the corrupted Haven to retreat deeper into their own closed world. It is their covenant. And it is their commandment and their right to command that is handed down by Zechariah.

Any attempt by the younger generation to "interpret" or change the law is futile, as Steward's wife, Dovey, knows. She keeps this to herself. Pat Best, or Patricia (Pat) Best Cato, also has her private opinion. Pat Best is far more inclusive. For her, the ambiguity in the motto/command can only suggest more than one meaning. For her it is a "conundrum" (*P* 195). Her opinion is at direct odds with Dovey's. The latter secretly understands that the word "Beware" is redundant. The furrowing of the brow is already a signification of power and of its vindictive displeasure. Accordingly, for Dovey, the motto/command would be as powerful if it simply read "Furrow of His Brow," since, alone, it "was enough for any age or generation" (*P* 93). In her version, there is no definite article, no verb. The subject is the object, the object the subject. Therefore, "specifying it, particularizing it, nailing its meaning down, was futile. The only nailing needing to be done had already taken place. On the Cross. Wasn't that so?" (*P* 93). Dovey's question, and the doubt it implies, will never be voiced aloud. But contemplating it reveals the face of rule that she knows precedes her.

Dovey's insistence that the motto could be reduced to "Furrow of His Brow" also performs an inversion: though the commandment to beware is already signified by the furrow, it is the furrow that is redundant to the imperative. "Beware" is the essence of the rule. It is the name of a rule whose presence is also its concealment. "Beware" warns that a force will make its appearance, as punishment. Moreover, Dovey's reference to the cross suggests that something else has been invested in the Oven, something that would elsewhere be a blasphemy. According to the logic of her question, the Oven and its command should not be permitted to displace a sacrifice in which nails played a different part, namely, "the" nailing on "the" Cross. Dovey's question also alerts us to the dangers of historical appropriations. Not only has the nailing of the motto displaced the nailing of flesh, but also, in order to partake of a sacred authority, Zechariah has inadvertently reproduced the gesture of the persecuting Romans and assumed the position of Jesus' executioner. It is tempting to say that Morrison wants us to read the deeds of Ruby's founder as a reversal of Christian logic, a turning back of the word made flesh in the gesture that returns all power to the word, the motto, and rule (not merely a rule) as such.

The verb in its imperative form, "Beware" is the sign that, as Foucault writes, the law in general "haunts" all places and conduct so that "whatever one does, however great the disorder and carelessness, it has already applied its might."[29] This is exemplified in a contest over meaning between two ministers, Reverends Pulliam and Misner. When Reverend Pulliam questions Richard Misner's use of the word "motto" to describe the phrase, he insists that the phrase is a command and he repeats it, "'Beware the Furrow of His Brow.' That's what it says clear as daylight. That's not a suggestion; that's an order!" (*P* 86). In contrast to what Dovey believes, Pulliam's focus is upon the word "Beware." And his reading adheres to the signification of the word as a grammatical form, rather than treating it as a transparent window onto deeper meaning. For the grammatical form signifies power, commands obedience. Whatever the particular rule may be, it is the announcement of rule. Whatever the particular form of order it is assumed to authorize, it is the signifier of order as such.

In its representativeness, and in the namelessness of the author, the motto/command operates without any gesture toward representativeness. It needs no constitution to justify its existence and makes no claims to express the will of a people. Nothing frames or redacts it in order for Ruby's citizens to feel that they are "the" people who govern and are governed. But the concept of the people, which implies equality, is internally stratified. The Morgans are the principle property-owning family, and they are also the bank owners and financiers to whom an unspecified but presumably significant number of people are indebted—they think nothing of foreclosing on houses, one of which has become Dovey's haven in town. The bank is not public and is not subject to any laws of finance other than those imposed by the brothers. Two churches comprise the only other institutions, one Baptist, one Methodist, and the pastors of both defer to the Morgans even as their congregations constantly reenact the Great Disavowing. Neither the Passion nor the Nativity occupies them as much as the Great Disavowing/Little Exodus does. And it is exile more than redemption that centers their theatrical and narrative activities.

Without need for a Constitution, the command is not sustained by any legal institutions, and certainly not by formal political institutions in the basic sense of "the practice of government or administration" (*OED*). Consequently, there are no courtrooms, and there is no elected or appointed judiciary. There are no lawyers. There are no police stations, because there is no police force. There are no offices of town counselors, because there is no elected or appointed town counsel. In Ruby, the rule is universal, on the basis of the Morgan's claim that the town is homogeneous, and its members are supposedly all equally subject to the terror of the motto/command.

Paradise seems to have been written around the following questions: In the absence of a Constitution, and on the basis of a rejection of the document that orients the larger America, where does power reside? How does order constitute itself? Does the disavowal of a corruptible law and the fantasy of an outside to law's rule throw one back onto a kind of order that can be sustained only by the demand for absolute conformity and a totalizing homogeneity? And is this order in the end anything more than the rule of might?

The men of Ruby understand that, insofar as they are led by Steward and Deacon, there are rules and that it is their duty to enforce them. Yet the novel leaves us to ask: Where *does* the Morgan power reside? We note that, when differences do emerge between the Morgans and another dominant family, the Fleetwoods, they turn to Misner, the Baptist minister, for arbitration. Yet Misner does not have the final say and is taken for a fool, an outsider. Neither his office nor his church has any real influence. Even the institution of the church fails to exercise a mitigating force on the battle between aspiring powers.

Misner demonstrates this understanding during K.D.'s wedding to Arnette Fleetwood. The ceremony becomes a battleground between his definition of love and Reverend Pulliam's. Everyone in town knows that the real wedding is not between K. D. and Arnette. Its purpose is to settle a growing feud between their families. In this spirit, the ceremony is held in Misner's Baptist church, with Pulliam invited to give a guest sermon. When Pulliam remonstrates against idle love, Misner feels himself challenged but speechless. He is reduced to physical gesture and reaches for a cross, which he holds high above his head in tense silence. One of the town's wrongly discredited young women, Billie Delia, understands what is at stake. It is something larger than the acrimony between the Morgans and Fleetwoods, but something to which they and the entire town are attached. It is a battle between the Old Testament and the New Testament. Pulliam quotes from Jeremiah 1:5, "Before I formed thee in the belly I knew thee, and before thou camest forth out of the womb I sanctified thee." Misner quotes from I Corinthians, "the greatest of these is love" (*P* 150). Billie Delia understands what Misner also realizes, that Pulliam has the force of scripture and the past on his side. To which one might add that Pulliam's recourse to Jeremiah finds an echo in Locke's reverberating argument that all human beings are the created property of God. Misner, by contrast, strives for free will, encouraging the young people to think, to ask questions. He has been brought to Ruby from outside, where he was part of the Civil Rights Movement, a movement absent and deemed irrelevant to Ruby's lives. Misner has learned that there is a "stubbornness" and "venom against asserting rights, claiming a wider role in the affairs of black people" (*P* 161). All of Ruby, he realizes, is turned toward the past. For Billie Delia, this is the past of an Old Testament law. Misner may have scripture and the future on his side, but Pulliam has scripture and the history memorialized in the Oven on his (*P* 150). After all, Pulliam is the one who insists that the phrase on the Oven is a command and not a motto. The two churches are not united, and, because of the directions in which they gaze, they cannot meet, not even on the subject of love. They are therefore ineffectual in controlling what Misner understands is a dangerous, growing dissatisfaction that will be deaf, even to divine intervention (*P* 161).

For all of Pulliam's alignment with the worldview favored by Ruby's elders, he has no more moral power than Misner. This power lies with the Morgan twins. And the Morgans, like the other men of their generation, know and believe it is their duty to keep the town alive, to prevent it from becoming a place in which eighteen stubborn people watch for mail that will not come. In other words, their duty is as much to themselves, to keep themselves relevant, as it is to the town. Yet the same desire for meaningful life and for a sense of autonomy rather than abandonment or mere exteriority drives the subsequent generation, just as it did Deacon and Steward before them, and Zechariah before them. Generation is the principle of continuity, but also of a possible rupture. It is in the confrontation between each generation and the Oven that the question of the meaning of the motto/command is posed.

The one place in which the twenty-year olds of the town can make their "stand" is at the Oven, specifically, in front of the inscribed "Beware" that marks the limit of their knowledge while offering the thrill of testing that limit. Led by Royal and Destry, two young sons from one of the original families, other young people speculate on the command's possible meaning—in effect, they ask for meaning from something that has always obscured its intentionality and its referents. This speculation coincides with their discussion of their own history and that of their forebears, who are described as "former slaves" (*P* 84). Deacon Morgan interrupts Royal to say, "That's my grandfather you're talking about. Quit calling him an ex-slave like that's all there was." Royal is impatient with a past that has always been dictated to him and that now reduces all his existence to a structural position and that overwhelms the fuller dimension of his life. He rankles at the lesson of stewardship: the younger generation is once again reminded that their elders mediate their knowledge, their history.[30]

But Deacon is concerned about more than the possibility that the next generation does not understand their history. The source of this concern is highlighted by Royal's insistence that, by definition, someone born into slavery must be a slave. He cannot understand Deacon's argument that there is a gap between the name and the state of being, or that there is a comparable gap between the terms *ex-slave* and *freed man*. There is an irony in Deacon's objection to this literalism. Disturbing for Deacon is the fact that Royal and the other younger people want to look further back than their American-born forebears to those born in Africa. The entire continent is summoned here as a lost paradise. That gesture is not without its opponents, however. In a context in which one elder seems to speak publicly for all, Deacon's wife, Soane, might be read as articulating, albeit without speaking aloud, what might be the general resistance of her generation to Royal's argument. His claim that Africans should be considered "neighbors or, worse, family" is a fiction she cannot understand (*P* 104). Moreover, she apprehends this "worsening" of the elder generation's relations with the younger as grounded in Royal's attempt to make "real" his connection with that fictitious paradise, while reducing his "real" forebears to the surface meaning assigned them. For Steward Morgan, the younger generation's pronouncements about the motto/command and their nostalgia for Africa is a dangerous rot. While Royal, Destry, and their peers strain to be relevant, which is to say, of the present, Steward wonders if they "would have to be sacrificed to get to the next one. The grand- and great-grandchildren who could be trained and honed" (*P* 94). The aspiration to relevance as timelessness is, for him, a threat to the indebtedness to the past and therefore a threat to all that underpins his own authority.

Unlike the young adults, who seem constantly to threaten departure form the old ways, the grand- and great-grandchildren are present to him (and to us via Morrison's fiction). They attend Sunday School, and they all come together once a year to perform that pageant of the Great Disavowing. Like the scarification on the Oven, the children's performance keeps visible the reason for the performance, namely the injunction to remember. In addition, the children's proximity to "the dried blood"[31] of history is part of the injunction and makes their innocence remarkable. This juxtaposition enhances the sign of their innocence. This, in turn, intensifies their vulnerable proximity to what Deacon and Steward, as well as the other elder men, increasingly feel is an evil that has to be excised from the purity of Ruby's environs.

In the end, though Steward contemplates sacrificing the young adults, the children are quasi sacrificial in that they are not actually sacrificed or allied with the dispensable middle generation. However, their autonomy is sacrificed for them. For Ruby, as Steward sees it, the children are "naturalized" as "innocent" participants in the drama of protection. As the newest, as opposed to the immediately next generation, and as putatively more promising bearers of future generations, they (and their mothers) could, at any time, be overcome by what lies outside of Ruby's *heim*. The violence is just one story away. Hence they are caught in a constant deferral, their futures being subsumed in and displaced by the history of Ruby and its rule, for which they are the alibi and the means.

A similar but less draconian effacement of a middle generation in order to preserve place is found in Gloria Naylor's *Mamma Day*.[32] In this novel, set in the Gala Islands off the Carolinas, the place is a quasi-mythical black settlement on a small island named Willow Springs. Once the property of a white slave owner, Bascomb Wade, it has been deeded to all of his slaves, thanks to the intervention of Sapphira Wade, the slave woman he had taken as his concubine. Like Ruby, Willow Springs is difficult to pinpoint on a map, even though it is linked to the wider world by an accessible road. Unlike Ruby, it is women who preside in a more encompassing world, watching out for bad tricksters and ensuring that the beneficial, historical, trick of Sapphira's legacy of the land is not undone.

That trick was ensuring that Wade wrote a legal deed registered in Norway, whence he had emigrated. That trick of securing it "outside" of America ensured for Willow Springs a mythic quality of being outside of American legal reach. In an ironic invocation of the Constitution that excluded them, and implicitly invoking *Plessy v. Ferguson*, the Wade descendants claim their land in a collective first-person narration: "We wasn't even Americans when we got it—was slaves. And the laws about slaves not owning nothing in Georgia and South Carolina don't apply, 'cas the land wasn't then—and isn't now—in either of them places."[33]

Willow Springs and Ruby look out at the same history as The Bottom in *Sula*. It is the history in which Macon Dead, Sr., lost his farm and life in *Song of Solomon* and in which the "Residents of fifteen houses" in a "little neighborhood on the edge" of a Texas town were told to leave, "or else. 'Else' meaning 'die'" (*H* 9–10). This is a history of peoples not considered as subjects before the law but as property, and then as subjects acquiring property that becomes desirable.

When property developers approach Mama Day, the elder descendent of Sapphira, about purchasing Willow Springs, she and everyone else knows what their promises about "community uplift" and jobs mean:

> Hadn't we seen it happen back in the '80s on St. Helena, Daufuskie, and St. John's? And before that in the '60s on Hilton Head? Got them folks' land, built fences around it first from mainside—ain't nobody on them islands benefited. And the only dark faces you see now in them "vacation paradises" is the ones cleaning the toilets and cutting the grass. On their own land, mind you, their own land. Weren't gonna happen in Willow Springs."[34]

One reason that Willow Springs cannot be sold is Sapphira's added trick in the deed. While the island belongs to her and Wade's descendants, no living present generation can sell it. Only the seventh generation *from* the living one has that right. In effect, they are caretakers for the future, a view that is entirely opposite to that of Steward and Deacon Morgan, who insist on being caretakers of the past. Steward's willingness to discard the generation immediately following his own is literal, while Sapphira's deeding is a symbolic sacrifice of the right to sell the property she had tricked Wade into handing over. In Willow Springs, the past is a story that is told in a collective first person voice that speaks as a "we" and remembers all the different versions of the same events. The narrators of that story do not have to relive the events, or to choose one version over another. All exist simultaneously, as stories that are told. The present is lived, the future is secured but, in the end, it is left up to the generations to come.

In Ruby, the pageant in which the children perform draws attention to the history, and not to the heirs of the power that emerged from that history—the Morgan twins. In this way, the pageant is of a piece with a literalism of reading. In its penumbra of innocence this literalism reproduces only what is believed to have come from the past and is thereby limited to the endgame of recognition. There is no acknowledged metaphoricity in such readings, merely the reproduction of the surface content of their sign. Hence the irony of Deacon's anger with Royal's pronouncement upon "former slaves," an objection coming from one who is literal minded in all other things.

This theatrics of power as the protector of innocence was laid bare in *The Bluest Eye*, which begins with a citation and the immediate dismantling of the text cited—the (per)formative Dick and Jane School Reader, whose centrality in teaching children how to read is sustained by the "simplicity" of its sentences, a simplicity that is conflated with childhood innocence. Conversely, the innocence of childhood seems to find its "natural" voice in the Reader's simple sentences. From such simple sentences, children would grow, and their language ability would parallel their developing mental acumen and analytical abilities. The innocence of those first readings would always remain, as if at the heart of language, an originary innocence that would also be the originary innocence of the simple sentence. This innocence is also related to being grounded in the phenomenal world in *The Bluest Eye*. We are first introduced to the world in which we will encounter Jane and Dick, Mother and Father, the cat. The green-and-white house with its red door, the prettiness assigned to the house, all give a context to the family but also direct our response to them. This pedagogy of Morrison's text is built upon the redoubling of imperatives, which structure both the school primer and our reading as a kind of overhearing. We are told to "see" Jane, to look upon her and Dick, to see mother and father, to look upon them. We are told to look at their home, their relations. Reading and learning how to read and write are inseparable from learning how to look at the world and—the novel suggests very quickly—how to discern what deserves our looking, what deserves to be seen. An entire normative order conflating the ideal with the visible is hereby produced. Yet Claudia McTeer gradually learns to see through this specular economy.

In the world of *Paradise*, however, the possibility of a Claudia McTeer arising seems foreclosed. Almost nothing intrudes upon Ruby's own pedagogy of looking and learning, for Ruby's dominant curriculum is not that which forms the basis of what the schoolteacher, Pat Best, applies in her small school on the town's main road. Rather, it is the "everything" that matters to the elders, particularly the Morgans, who apply the rule of what must be remembered, of what deserves to be looked at and what deserves to be seen. The Morgan twins think as one that they "remember the details of everything that ever happened" (*P* 13). The inevitable truth is that "everything" is a misleading term, covering the unspoken caveat that their memory is itself selective. What they remember are deaths and affronts. They can memorialize their sister's death, but they never offer more than a glancing remark about their mother or father, and they are silent about Zechariah's death, which would surely have been a significant event for Haven, the town he founded. In this, Zechariah's foundational role is also one that must vanish, like that of the unnamed former slave who bargained for land on behalf of the group in *Sula*. Forgetting here emerges as a constitutive factor in the production of collective identity, particularly the kind of identity premised on absolute discontinuity with others, with the surrounding world.

Pat Best and her father know only too well the implications of the strict direction in which Ruby is commanded to look. Her father has committed the cardinal sin of going outside of Ruby's fold to marry a clearly miscegenated woman. When he brings her home, she is shunned to the point that, during a difficult labor, she dies from neglect when the town's men refuse to drive her to hospital. The women, led by Soane and Dovey Morgan, finally disavow the rule. Their help comes too late. This is Pat Best's private story, which she shares with her father and which the town seems to have set aside. Like the Reverend Misner, she wonders where the other stories are. For Misner, the inhabitants of Ruby are like any black community in all but two things. They enclose themselves in a protective *heim* of god-fearing morality that dictates thrift and reserve in all things, including admitted needs for comfort and ornament (*P* 160–61). Yet they have taken self-protection to the extreme in their isolation. That is the first difference he finds. The other is their beauty: "All of them were hand-some, some exceptionally so" (*P* 160). He names them as an entirety, their beauty unabated even with the exceptions of "three or four" who are not the same "coal black." Those three or four are also "all" because what is beautiful and black in them is enough. It is the all of the all. And it is what is protected in Ruby. These twinned categories of isolation and beauty turn the town inward and focused only on the past, so that the present generation seems to have no stories of itself and threatens to dissolve into a narrative blank spot (*P* 161).

Writing Against History, from the Inside: The Burnt Book

Horkheimer and Adorno offer silence as one alternative to the deathly in formulaic art. If Morrison metaphorizes her art as being trapped in the house of race, that house is structured according to a plan, a predeter-mined grid into which she has been inserted. As in so many of her fictions, the way out of the impasses imposed by the house of race, in this case a house rebuilt by those attempting to flee it, is suggested by a character who is also a writer. Or it is suggested by a character who functions as the critical eye amid the otherwise naturalized principle of reality by which the other characters live. Sula or L in *Love* and Frank Money in *Home* represent this critical function. At once exception and thus evidence of the rule, and capable of reflecting upon the rule itself, such characters orient the critical project that is Morrison's fiction. In *Paradise*, this character and would-be writer is Pat Best.

Unlike her neighbors, Pat Best cannot ignore the silences that beg ques-tions. She finds herself compelled to ask them about family histories. Once she begins, she is further enlivened with the energy of a chronicler trying to record steady losses or disappearances. Thanks to the Morgan twins' claim to be the bearers of memories for all experiences, these losses go unspoken, but they are not invisible. Pat Best's text becomes, and can only become, a counter-history, gleaned from bits of information from her stu-dents, from family trees in family Bibles. Hers is an archive of fragments, scraps, and marginalia—as is so much of history written by and about Af-rican Americans, extracted as it is from the archive, where African Ameri-cans appear mainly when they have directly confronted power.

Pat Best eventually burns her growing book out of a sense of the harm it would do. Her burning, a burnt offering perhaps, is private, a real gift, since no one else is present, and no one can therefore be indebted to her through the awareness of what she has done to relieve them of knowledge's burden. The erasure of names, the disappearances of family branches like that of Elder Morgan, Zechariah's eldest son, all remain secret, and the town's population can go on seeing only what they want to see, a community unchallenged, a community intact.

In any case, Pat Best's putative history of the town's families does not and cannot receive formal recognition because her compilation of stories has no official, public sanction. Were Pat Best's work to surface, it would have the subversive potential that accrues to the unofficial narrative extracted from institutional histories. In part, the subversion constitutes the publicizing of things that families have all agreed to treat as if they had not existed. That Pat is able to find their traces points to the fact that none of these things has been fully excised. They exist in the silence around them, and they exist as silences, or places into which the families never want to drift, yet around which their entire lives are made to circle. Thus, in the place in which peace was to be guaranteed, histories of violence have been accommodated in silence. It is a palpable silence, but one that can only be made to signify as evidence of a repression. Its content is never fully recoverable. And even Pat Best's marginal stories of events long forgotten remain fragmentary and elusive.

Against Pat Best's quiet and selfless sacrifice in the interest of the community's self-image, Steward's notion of sacrifice is shocking. Where she has surrendered all economism and sought no return for her gift, he invokes an idea of sacrifice as the instrument of commensuration and gain. As a result, his discourse raises challenging questions about the notion of narrative as testimony and witnessing when these are read through the etymological history of martyrdom to which Agamben has already drawn our attention. The concept of sacrifice has become twin to that of martyrdom. It is not normally applied in the way that Steward thinks of it, as a way of giving up on others who are less than exemplary witnesses to history. We might call this "triage." Yet there is a sense in which he does evoke the notion of exchange or substitution inherent in the idea of sacrifice. He will give up the present generation of adults in exchange for the upcoming generation in order to secure Ruby's future.

Renè Girard, George Buchanan Gray, and Victor Turner all have argued that the purpose or motive of sacrifice in numerous religions is to propitiate or defer to the will or pleasure of a deity.[35] In Durkheimian social analysis, sacrifice functions to perpetuate or renew relations between groups or individuals. In secular terms, the notion of sacrifice is abstracted, moving from deity to value. Nonetheless, sacrifice persists as an instrument of social reproduction and of the reproduction of social norms. For Girard, the scapegoat comes to substitute for an originary sacrifice, and this constitutes the reduction of sacrifice to murder, which would have saved the community by transferring internecine violence outside of itself. For believers, such murder continues to be read as sacrifice, and in this sense we may say that ritual sacrifice is legitimate murder. For her part, Morrison consistently exposes the groundlessness of the distinction between murder and sacrifice, which is otherwise naturalized through ritual.

Morrison also emphasizes the gendered patterns associated with this derivative development. She points to the fact that the violence of ritual sacrifice takes a particular form in patrilineal traditions. In most cases cited by Girard, the sacrificed subject is male. Of course, the sacrifice of females is frequent in the history of patriliny and, more importantly, patriarchy—the former a principle of descent, the latter a principle of power—but it is rarely made the source of value, and insofar as sacrifice entails the prior valorization of the offering and then its destruction, women's deaths are frequently denied the status of sacrifice, for their inherently devalued state often makes them ineligible for the representative function within sacrifice. The being sacrificed in a ritual intended to sustain a community is representative of that community. Only in places where Woman can signify the universal is female sacrifice set off from female death. But in almost all cases, the communal sacrifice is intended to secure a future reproduction of the existing order; it is a means of achieving life through death.

As Christians, the patriarchs of Ruby have a rich mythopoetic tradition from which to draw for their murderous sacrificial method. Steward's recollection of those families who leave Louisiana and Mississippi in search of a land promised in newspaper advertisements as open and free, ready to be turned into home, echoes Abraham leading his tribe into a new, promised land. After the Great Disavowing, Big Papa Zechariah and those who follow him have been sleeping in pine woods. On the third night, Big Papa Zechariah wakes Rector, the twins' father, and the two move away from the sleeping group to where Big Papa can pray with Rector in attendance. The son observes his father in silence as Big Papa addresses the sky in an imitation of Abraham's prayer: "My Father . . . Zechariah here " (*P* 96). A vigil follows. Big Papa takes up a "humming prayer," which overwhelms Rector. He sinks back, his throat exposed. The sky seems to close in on him, while he feels himself dissolving into it. At a crucial moment, a strange, semi-angelic harbinger figure appears, and Zechariah commands Rector to fetch everyone. The group then follows this figure until he produces a magnificent male guinea fowl, which Zechariah takes to be a gift from God. Haven is founded on the site of that appearance and, by implication, the sacrifice of the fowl. Rector, like Isaac, is spared whatever secret fate had been agreed upon between Zechariah and God.

In this scene, *Paradise* takes further the ideas of sacrifice that are present or at work in Morrison's earlier fiction, wherein sacrifice is "a gift that does not know itself to be a gift" and is therefore not indebting. Halle's sacrifice in *Beloved* and Golden Gray's in *Jazz* are gifts that do not indebt, even though they enable and strengthen familial and social bonds diegetically. [36] Extra-diegetically, their gifts work as placeholders for exemplary acts that have gone unnoticed in history. In *Beloved*, it is, of course, Sethe who gives her "crawling already baby" the gift of death as a gift of freedom. Sethe's sacrifice is of and on behalf of generation—an act for which she, unlike Abraham in Derrida's reading, takes public responsibility. [37]

In *Paradise*, the "gift of death" is a calculated gesture directed toward the long-term recollection of the past. Steward thinks of the newest, youngest generation as the ideal servants and reproducers of the past. As I suggested earlier, he in a sense sacrifices them—or their autonomy—for a communal future defined by its reproduction of the past. But he is also sacrificing them to something older. He is, after all, the steward, one who controls domestic affairs (*OED*) in the service of a master, particularly a master's table. A steward caters to a master and has control over the master's house or, more importantly, the master's land. He even dispenses justice on that master's behalf. In a biblical sense, a steward's master is God. In another sense, a steward fulfills a disciplinary function, meting out justice against "treason and felony" (*OED*). A steward is thus one who ensures the untroubled continuity or regeneration of power, presiding over all performances of power, its every stage and its enthronement.

One irony concerning Steward Morgan's name is that it is also associated with a specific role in a specific religion: in Methodism, a steward is a "layman anointed to manage the financial affairs of a congregation," as a society or chapel steward (*OED*). In Ruby, he and Deacon attend the Baptist church, not the Methodist church, but Steward is concerned about the Baptist Minister Misner's loan society to help out parishioners who cannot service their debts to the Morgan bank. Morgan, one notes, is the name of a "counterfeit" coin and a measure of distance, especially between two linked genes (*OED*). For the Morgan twins, the claim to knowledge and to truth is thus wedded to the conjoining of wealth with power and lineage—but only by the same act of fiat that makes a coin a signifying value. Foucault reminds us that, in the particular episteme associated with capitalist modernity, truth has to be produced in the same way that wealth is produced and truth is produced in order to produce wealth. All is subjected to truth "in the sense that truth lays down the law."[38] As bearers of wealth, Steward and Deacon also lay down the law. They are an incarnation of the principle by which wealth comes to the one who masters truth and the law, and who can make law appear to be the expression of truth, with wealth as its rightful end and its own evidentiary principle. A steward is the one who holds the purse, but not on his own behalf. Rather, he does so on behalf of the presence that he knows resides in the Oven—the receptacle that transmutes the raw into sustenance, but which is also a tomb, a crematorium, and a womb. Frank Money's question about what kind of man could do violence has no place in this space of mastery, yet it is relevant. While the men of Ruby believe they protect their women from the predatory attention of white men and the white world in general, their creation of a self-referential power is a mimesis of foundational violence in which mere murder pretends to be sacrifice and women's value is effaced by men's renown.

Tomb, Womb, and Crypt

The metaphorical conjoining of the spaces of death and birth mirrors the logic of sacrifice as the pursuit of generation through death. By instrumentalizing death in the simulation of a gift, *Paradise* opens onto a sharp critique of the gendering of power in all forms of purism and in all identitarian political projects, especially those which promise freedom in the mode of exile or separation. The movement of that critique can be discerned in the questions that unfold from another primary question, namely: Where is Big Daddy Zechariah buried?

The twins are silent about his death. We know only that, on the night that Steward and Deacon summon all but the eighteen stubborn elders to leave Haven, sometime after the mid 1940s, Steward recalls that Big Papa was "loaded" onto a vehicle. But he is referring to the Oven. While this might suggest that the Oven has come to stand for Big Papa's memory and therefore has become a placeholder for him, there is also a strange slippage. When read against Steward's increasing literal mindedness another set of references is called to mind. These are the horrors of the Shoah and cremation in general. For if the motto/command and the Oven together form a kind of promise to God, as in a covenant, one is reminded that, in biblical usage, the covenant is always amenable to being moved and relocated. If Big Papa has been cremated, he has been fused with the Oven, and his is the burial secreted within Ruby, as that of the absent/present father. There would be a question as to the nature of his cremation, whether it can be read as sacrificial in Steward's sense or whether Big Papa's cremation should be read as a burnt offering that is not strictly the *olah* described in the priestly Torah; the *olah* is a complete sacrifice, which is not eaten by the one who sacrifices. It is a burnt offering, tendered to God as ash. It is not the *zebah*, which is a sacrifice shared, or partially eaten by the one who is sacrificing.

In what has become a signature gesture, Morrison's acknowledgment of the power of old tropes partakes of their force and demonstrates how only the most rigid application would make a trope speak in the same way for all time and on all occasions. In her work, the tropes speak *as if* this is true, while mobilizing the dialectical tension between this impulse and contextual reality, in which context makes the trope speak. In other words, what her play with the possible cremation of Big Papa reveals is the context, and all that is at stake in maintaining it. And her play also reveals why that context, in this case the idea of a pure Ruby, derives from tropes offered by the Old Testament of Reverend Pulliam's Methodism.

Through the cremation and internment of Big Daddy, however, the Morgan twins have parted from Old Testament prophetic attitudes toward sacrifice. With one crucial, Abrahamic exception, *olah* and *zebah* relate specifically to the sacrifice of animals. Temple and other priestly sacrifices are generally criticized by the prophets and are associated with debased worship and moral failure. When the Lord calls upon Isaiah to speak to Sodom, the first utterance is to condemn sacrifice:

To what purpose *is* the multitude of your sacrifices unto me? saith the Lord: I am full of the burnt offerings of rams, and the fat of fed beasts; and I delight not in the blood of bullocks, or of lambs, or of he goats.

When ye come to appear before me, who hath required this at your hand, to tread my courts? (Isaiah 1:11)

Not only is the source of this desire to make burnt offerings questioned and condemned as a human attempt to decipher divine desire, the practice is condemned as vanity (Isaiah 1:12). Furthermore, hands covered in the blood of sacrifice are called unclean (Isaiah 1:15).

In the book of Jeremiah, the prophet is sent by God to stand at the Temple gate to remind the people of the morality of, among other things, hospitality. Employing the same, classic if/then logic of coercion that propels Isaiah's rhetoric, Jeremiah quotes the Lord as saying:

If ye oppress not the stranger, the fatherless, and the widow, and shed not innocent blood in this place, neither walk after other gods to your hurt.
   Then will I cause you to dwell in this place, in the land that I gave to your fathers, for ever and ever. (Jeremiah 7:6–7).

Jeremiah is also told to warn those who enter the Temple of God's wrath against Shiloh, where God's name had first been ensconced (Jeremiah 7:12). Not following God's ways will be tantamount to provocation: "Therefore thus saith the Lord God; Behold, mine anger and my fury shall be poured out upon this place, upon man, and upon beast, and upon the trees of the field, and upon the fruit of the ground; and it shall burn, and shall not be quenched"(Jeremiah 20). Jeremiah is also told to inform all the houses of Israel that burnt offerings, the *olah*, are not enough: "For I spake not unto your fathers nor commanded them in the day I brought them out of the land of Egypt, concerning burnt offerings or sacrifices" (Jeremiah 7:20–21). Sacrifice is also criticized elsewhere.

In Amos, for example, a merchant is criticized for completing his sacrifice by drinking wine he has seized from a debtor who could not repay his loan (Amos 2:8). In Isaiah, Jeremiah, and Amos, the offerings open what Israel Knohl calls a "schism between morality and ritual."[39] Ritual is, here, the empty effrontery of priestliness; morality is the true divine desire. Knohl points out a foundational division in the biblical Israel, for what Amos and Jeremiah say about the crossing of the desert contradicts a central part of Exodus. Both have God saying that sacrifice was not practiced during the exodus. Yet Exodus describes how, three months after leaving Egypt (Exodus 19:1), God commanded Moses to "make a tabernacle" that houses "an altar" that has a pan to receive unspecified ashes (Exodus 26:1,

27:1–2). Aaron and his sons are given the task of maintaining the tabernacle on behalf of Israel (Exodus 26:21).

If Steward and Deacon have conflated *olah* and *zebah*, while also assuming a priestly prerogative of maintaining the Oven—as opposed to the pastoral function performed by Reverends Pulliam and Misner—they have also either literally interned Big Papa's ashes, to (re)create the tabernacle of Isaiah, or interned the idea of Big Papa in the Oven for the same reason. Either way, this reference to "loading" the Oven as "loading" him in the exodus from Haven transforms him from an Abrahamic figure into a form of sacrifice and hence opens the possibility for his becoming spectral. Whether literally or figuratively "loaded" in the Oven, Big Papa becomes the specter that will do more than haunt the future. His haunting will make the future all past, uncoupling one part of time and setting it adrift as yet another sacrifice, in the name of Ruby. If this is so, sacrifice becomes the model of an auto-reproductivity, one that is sealed off from sexual difference and one that indeed permits the violent rejection of women.

Thus, when Steward resists the younger generation's attempt to "interpret" the motto/command, he is acting as a steward, one who controls the domestic, supervising the master's table and therefore controlling consumption (*OED*). As one who inhabits an official status embodied in his name, he is thus in the service of a master or, in Ruby, in the service of the (absent master's) mastering command. At best, he serves that which orients the town. More sinisterly, he serves that which orients the town toward itself, closing or entombing the town's future. For this reason, Steward articulates the "discourse of truth" that makes all decisions, conveying and propelling what Foucault calls all "truth effects."[40] The power to which Steward is bound judges and condemns according to its mystery. This is why, in this fantasy of a self-reproducing generation of men, the women are absent or absented. We might say, figuratively, that the women are sacrificed in and to this fantasy. And Morrison's *Paradise* explores precisely this possibility.

Where the narrative of the Great Disavowing draws attention to Ruby's prehistory and away from the heirs to the power that emerged from that history, Steward's foregrounding of the need to sacrifice two sons, not his, but brothers and possible leaders of the next generation, draws attention away from other sacrifices that have been performed and that will be necessary for Ruby to survive. If Ruby survives, so does the command and its resting place, the Oven. More specifically, Steward's fixation occludes the sacrifices and other contributions of women. Nor is this without biblical precedent.

Mieke Bal's analysis of the Book of Judges draws attention to the pivotal role of women's violable bodies in the formation of a new mode of patriarchy in which a contest between fathers and sons is resolved into a single, transmittable headship. In her introduction to *Death and Dissymmetry: the Politics of Coherence in the Book of Judges*, Bal argues for a shift in focus on the book's perspective.[41] Where Judges memorializes the triumph of monotheism and the power of the judges, she draws attention to those who are largely overlooked. Her interest is, she states, in the tombs not of the judges "but of the judges' daughters, the young girls who are killed."[42] Her work tracks the terrible cost of being female and in close proximity to those who ruled and stewarded the ancient Israelites. With the exception of Deborah (and possibly Ruth, who is assigned her own book), twelve of the thirteen judges were male. Bal points out that, more often than not, women become "caught" between men, as in the case of Jephthah's daughter, who is given as a sacrifice to Yahweh in return for a victory in war. Similar figures include Kallah, bride of Samson, and Beth, the wife of a Levite in Judges 19.[43]

One other female figure who is sacrificed is Abraham's wife Sarai. Hers is not a sacrifice through death, but a sexual or erotic one that enables Abraham to escape a direct threat from Pharaoh. Sarai is subjected to the whims of Pharaoh, but only after Abraham has concocted a subterfuge that sacrifices her on his behalf. Having been given the land of Canaan by God, Abraham continues his journey and arrives in Egypt, where he believes he will be killed once the men look upon Sarai's fairness. Abraham equates her fairness with irresistible attraction, and irresistible attraction with the cause of trouble. Desire is here the origin of death. Hence, he tells her, "thou *art* a fair woman to look upon; Therefore it shall come to pass, when the Egyptians shall see thee, that they shall say, This *is* his wife: and they will kill me, but they will save thee alive" (Genesis 12:11–12). He asks her to pass as his sister. The responsibility for this lie rests with her: "Say, I pray thee, thou *art* my sister" (Genesis 12:12). She is asked to participate in her own sacrifice in order "that it may be well with me for thy sake; and my soul shall live because of thee" (Genesis 12:12). Implicitly, she will be given in either marriage or violation because the brother is defined by his willingness to exchange his sister to produce alliance. A husband cannot do so with his wife (Abraham's deception regarding his wife notwithstanding).

The men who follow Big Papa out of Louisiana and Mississippi are driven by a pride that would be appalled by Abraham's example. They could not "bear to contemplate" the certainty or distinct possibility that any one of their women could be desired or raped by a white man or that their desirability could lead to the men's own death, if only because, as men who have laid claim to property in women, they must be eliminated to permit another such claim. This is the terrible fate that awaits Tom Burwell in Jean Toomer's *Cane*.[44] His competitor for the love of a woman named Louisa is a white man named Bob Stone, who looks back to the past, when his family still owned slaves. In his present, postslaving world, the loss of slaves is equated to the loss of ground. And this loss of ground is also the loss of a masculinity he admires, that of the master who would have been able to go into the hearth where Louisa works, to go in "as a master should and [take] her."[45] He thinks of her as his and of the talk about Tom Burwell being with her when she went home as an affront: "No sir. No nigger had ever been with his girl." When he sets off to meet Louisa in the cane field, he has already imagined a scenario in which he, as a white man, masters Burwell, and he imagines this as tasting his blood.[46] When the two men confront each other in Louisa's presence, Bob Stone pulls a knife to assert his claim, but this is a game at which Tom is master. He cuts Stone's throat. Yet when Stone staggers toward the town for help, Tom and Louisa are unable to run, as the other black people do. Slavery might be over, but they know, as does Stone, that Jim Crow will ensure that his family still "practically" owns the black people in the town. One might say that this is what roots Tom to the spot while Stone's friends converge, silent but for the "taut hum of their moving."[47] Armed, they go in search of Tom, the "moving body of their silence" going ahead "over the crest of the hill into the factory town" where it "flattened the Negroes beneath it."[48] This silence of the mob is also the silence of a power that does not need language but is all action, collective action, since on his own the would-be bearer of power, Bob Stone, has learned that deference is not his automatic due. Only in the collective can Tom be overcome, bound, tied to a stake, doused in kerosene, and burned alive.

An elimination like Tom's is precisely what the men of Ruby wish to forestall. At the same time, they do not give up the kind of competitive claim that drove Tom Burwell to attack Bob Stone. Accordingly, the men of Ruby cannot bear to look upon anyone who is the sign of "racial tampering" (*P* 197), for this would be the sign of precisely that displacement of property rights. It seems at first that they fantasize their own survival as the place from which they will witness a woman's wounding, just as Abraham posited the possibility of a woman's wounding as the condition of possibility for his own survival.

Zachariah and the other men who travel with him are "proud that none of their women had ever worked in a white-man's kitchen or nursed a white child" (*P* 99), because domestic work placed black women in physical jeopardy, where rape was "if not a certainty a distinct possibility."[49] Yet, there is an exchange of a sister, Ruby—the precious name of a dynastic bride in medieval literature. The brothers choose a man for their sister to marry, a man who will be of no real consequence and who will vanish from their narrative, who is indeed spent and discarded by it between the closing of one statement and the start of another. This man, we might say, will be sacrificed to that narrative and its future, just as their sister will be. Despite the fact that there is someone among them who can save lives, the elderly Lone, who has a "gift," the brothers insist on taking Ruby to a white town and a white hospital, where she is rejected and redirected to a veterinarian. In all of their obedient remembering of the Great Disavowing and all of their instruction against turning outside of their community for help, the brothers decide to do this. When she dies, in New Haven, death has entered. By changing the town's name to Ruby, she is immortalized, as is the town and the Oven and its command—a blood sacrifice has occurred, one for which no substitute was offered and which was, in the end, the *real* substitution for the slaying of a son. As Bal notes, women are actually sacrificed in the Bible. God stays the hand when a male—other than Jesus—is to be slain, on that cross. It is this sacrifice—endlessly concealed in and by patriarchal narrative, yet nonetheless the condition of possibility for male fantasies of generational renewal—that Morrison makes visible in *Paradise*.

Biblically, sacrifice is associated with the prerogative of fathers—to which I would add, fathers who are also husbands, patriarchs who make of their sisters wives and objects of exchange between other potential patriarchs. An argument can thus be made that Ruby was in fact the sacrificial subject, whose death in childbirth has made possible the only future that the family would have, through her son, K. D., "the last male in a line that included a lieutenant governor, a state auditor and two mayors" (*P* 55).

The redness of Ruby's "birth," then, is the redness of a secret. The blood price ensures Ruby's success as well as that of Steward and Deacon. And it is this secret sacrifice that is being defiled in the present novel, wherein a new generation of young adults, the direct heirs to Steward and Deacon, question the motto, and thereby negate its status as command, while also desecrating it by drinking alcohol in its vicinity and with outsiders, the women from the Convent. However, the twins' actions are already dictated by the narrative force of exemplary founding fathers, namely, Abraham and Zechariah, the alpha and omega of their symbolic order. Given this, substitutes must be found in order to preserve even that immediate generation, offending as it is. The directional forces of these foundational narratives point outside of Ruby to the contesting female presences in the Convent. There, although not of any religious order, the women of the Convent live in a sister space and might be called sisters who have left and not returned to the system of kinship. It is at them that Deacon, Steward, their nephew K. D., and the other men of Ruby take aim and through whom they seek expiation with "God at their side. . . . For Ruby" (*P* 18).

In the scene that opens the novel and that constitutes the enigma whose unfolding will occupy the rest of the narrative, one sees what will turn out to be the "reconstitution" of Ruby. We now encounter sacrifice in the form Bal has made familiar to us: the sacrifice of women in the service of patriarchal relations, forged through the transmission of property from fathers to sons and the production of solidarity among men of a single generation.

In Ruby's case, it is the women as both maternal figures and sisters who are sacrificed in the production of democracy as a politics of fraternity. The corporeal finitude of this town is strangely transcended—as it must be, in the absence of women, for no one in Ruby dies. Ruby's magical capacity for endurance and self-generation depends on a logic of sacrifice that has traveled within the Abrahamic narrative that sacrifices Sarai to Pharaoh's desires. The covenant of sacrifice into which Zechariah Morgan admits his own people is ultimately enacted in full by his grandsons when they similarly hand their sister over to one of their soldier buddies. By then, Ruby is not simply the home of the descendents of the original fifteen families, it is the resting place of the Oven and all that it reveals *and* obscures—the *corpus mysticum* of a stern, watchful presence and the need to sacrifice women.

It is also necessary for the men of Ruby to ensure that women in the town are intently aware of this "home." As social anthropology has shown us, women, young women in particular, are often moved from one status to another through rites of passage that require them to leave the homes of their fathers and, in many residential systems, to enter their husband's home in and around marriage. While this might be essential to some kinship systems, as Lévi-Strauss and others have told us, it also ruptures the bond that binds a woman to the paternal household in the way that a death might. Thus is the paternal household made vulnerable, opened to the outside and to the possibility of an unexpected arrival.

When the women of the Convent are attacked—some slain, some perhaps having survived the attack—it is with a libidinously charged rage against women's autonomy and their escape from patriarchal oversight, one unrelieved by their passage into the marital contract and hence into the status of objects of exchange. The reader asks, Why? What can explain this murderous fraternity? Frank Money asks a similar question of himself in *Home*. But he takes responsibility by asking what "type" of man can kill a girl for inciting desire. He answers, in effect, "I am." In *Paradise* the question is not asked by any of the patriarchal leaders. Yet the answer to what can explain their murderous fraternity is self-referential. It is that the murderous fraternity, the self-interrupting and self-limiting legacy of patriarchy, is the explanation of the murder. Here is the dark side of a nation that was founded on brotherly love, and on the constitutive exclusion of women from power, but also on the constitutive exclusion of African Americans from citizenship. The parodic reenactment of fraternity in the shootings and murders at the Convent reveals the stakes in seeking remedy for the exclusions of the Constitution through the pursuit of a paradise born of resentment and a desire to have only what has been denied. In Ruby's fraternal system, where democracy regenerates itself through selection rather than election, sorority has no place and acquires its value only in the mode of sacrifice.

The Fire Next Time

One final note is in order here, for it would be a mistake not to notice Morrison's insistent working of the metaphoricity that links firing to fire. The women are fired upon. The Oven is the scene of a different kind of firing. And the ur-form of the sacrifice is, of course, the burnt offering discussed earlier. *Paradise* draws forth a set of figures that have appeared in her other novels and makes it the basis of a complex metacommentary upon the violence of sacrifice in African American history and perhaps too on the burden of Christological rhetorics. How does Morrison make this metaphoricity central to the material world that her narrative draws for us and the analytic vision to which the narrative points us? Let us read this metaphor a little more deeply, in order to grasp not only how this metaphorics of fire works to integrate Morrison's oeuvre but also how it works to link her fiction to other works in the African American canon, in which her writing is situated despite her engagement with the wider range of Modernist writing epitomized by Faulkner and Woolf, as well as her interest in classical Greek literature.

We are bidden to read the Oven, first and foremost because Morrison has given it a proper name and because it is therefore set aside from all other ovens, even as it invokes them. An oven is a chamber in or under which a fire is lit, of course. Together, they transform whatever substance or object is placed within. When one refers to an oven, it is primarily to the chamber and not the furnace that houses the real transmuting power of fire. On one level, then, the Oven in Ruby would seem to be the obvious, concrete chamber in which the practical necessities of feeding the body are taken care of. Bread is baked in it and other foods are cooked in it. It is, however, impossible to limit the structure to this functionality. For in Ruby it is through the Oven that individuals are daily transformed into a community, bound by the act of coming together. Zechariah created the Oven for women to transform meal into bread to feed the community. Baking, specifically of bread, is associated with divine creation. In Luke 13:20–21, the Kingdom of God is likened to "leaven" made, specifically, by a woman who takes and hides the meal until it is ready, a further association that suggests pregnancy and regeneration. If the Oven is female, as seems to be the case, the fire in its furnace brings the necessary ignition to the reproductive process—rendering the Oven a space that waits to be heated by the fire.

But we know from the reference to the 'loading' of Big Papa that the Oven is also a crypt. It is the place of incineration and not merely cooking. And with its sacrificed surface, it is the locus of law's encryption in the form of a motto. It contains secrets that are nevertheless not merely the dead letters of the (father's) law. Each letter of the motto/command is a critical component of the motto in that each is a sign of Zechariah's labor. Miss Esther, one of the oldest members of Ruby's community, attests to this before she dies. Blind and a child when Zechariah had forged the letters, Deacon and Steward nevertheless assign to her the earliest, firmest memory of the forging. They describe her as knowing each letter's shape through her "finger" reading (*P* 86–87). This touching of each letter emphasizes the materiality of the motto's presence and thus of Zechariah's hand and handiwork.

The assemblage of letters that produces the motto occupies the imagination of the young by troubling it. One might see it as condensing the four-part epistemic structure that Gayatri Chakravorty Spivak discerns in Hindu law prior to its rationalization by British colonialism. Spivak observes that late-eighteenth-century Hindu law was organized around the following principles: what is heard (*sruti*), what is remembered (*smriti*), what is learned from another (*sastra*), and what is performed (*vyavahara*). Each part or staging defines a subject's use of memory. However, there is no guaranteed continuity between the origin or what was heard and what was remembered, even though the invocation of what was heard is also a reopening of "the originary 'hearing' or revelation."[50] The epistemic violence of colonialism addresses itself to this complex epistemic structure and transforms it by renaming ritual as crime and by making law a matter of conformity or transgression. In Ruby, however, the motto/command is already the reduction of these elements into a single point, and the violence of the motto lies in its amenability to being read as command, as proto-law.

In this way, the Oven stands for a certain transition on the way to law as totality, but also as the sign of a transition that has occurred long ago and absorbed all that went before it. The Oven thus recalls for the reader, if not the characters, the transformation accompanying the codification and integration of colonial laws integral to nation formation. As I have mentioned earlier, the forging of intercolonial relations was achieved partly through regulation of the movement of slaves and conflict over the status to be attributed to slaves as they were subjected to law.

In this process, the concept of *rus nullius* was gradually altered as the central legislative bodies at both the state and federal levels came to acknowledge that blacks were subjects within the law. This is what slavers discovered with Abolitionists' use of the law to sue for freedom in the John Davis case, in 1791. If a governor of one state could petition the governor of another to return a slave and to sue slave catchers, slaves could claim protection by the law. The refutation of such a claim came in the firm language of the *Dred Scott v. Sandford* ruling, in 1857, in which the Supreme Court declared that Africans and their descendents were not citizens and therefore not protected by the Constitution, though they could be subjected to the lawful activities of those recognized from within the Constitution. The decision also ruled that Congress could not abolish slavery in federal territories. Effectively, this prevented slaves and free blacks from turning to courts. Declared outside of the law, blacks could therefore be subjected to extra-juridical "justice" or to a form of vengeful display of slavery's residual power, epitomized by lynching and immolation.

Now, while these acts are authorized by the early Constitution's relative empowerment of whites, they are also the mark of a persisting logic of "trial by fire" that haunts the law from within and that is encrypted in the desperate and ultimately failed histories to establish towns like The Bottom in *Sula* and Haven in *Paradise*. It is here that Morrison's Oven acquires its full significance, a significance we can perhaps best assess when reading it in relation to a Harlem Renaissance intertext, namely, James Weldon Johnson's *Autobiography of an Ex-Colored Man*. In Johnson's book, the narrator witnesses a black man being burned. Even though he can pass as a white man, the narrator understands that the message of the man's agony is directed at someone "like" him. Whether passing or not, the black subject who is made to observe or hears talk of a lynching or burning knows herself, or himself, to be addressed *as* a black person. The act and the knowledge of the act reconstruct and assert what blackness is meant to be and what black subjects are meant to understand about their being in the world. In other words, the lynching and burning are forms of spectacular justice, in Foucault's sense, which not only announce the inherent guilt of the victim whose elimination is deemed necessary for the good of the society but which operate through terror rather than the solicitation of self-disciplined subjectivity. The point is that this spectacular justice solicits a self-recognition on the part of the black spectator but does not hail him or her as a full subject. In effect, the burnings, a familiar technique of terror among the Ku Klux Klan, work by announcing the black spectator's exteriority to the institutions of law to which whites might have recourse in the face of such trials by fire.

Consider, for example, Walter White's account of his boyhood encounter with a white mob intent on burning his family's house down during the September 1906 Atlanta race riot. Although light-skinned, blond, and blue-eyed, he understood who and what he was *in relation* to the mob:

In the flickering light the mob swayed, paused, and began to flow toward us. In that instant there opened within me a great awareness; I knew then who I was. I was a Negro, a human being with an invisible pigmentation which marked me as a person to be hunted, hanged, abused, discriminated against, kept in poverty and ignorance, in order that those whose skin was white would have readily at hand a proof of their superiority, a proof patent and inclusive, accessible to the moron and the idiot as well as to the wise man and the genius. No matter how low a white man fell, he could always hold fast to the smug conviction that he was superior to two-thirds of the world's population, for those-two-thirds were not white.[51]

When White was writing, such public burnings also asserted with ferocious resentment the mob's rejection of any legislative attempt to correct the Constitution by extending citizenship to blacks. This was Walter White's discovery when he investigated lynchings for the NAACP.[52] Reporting on a 1918 lynching of a pregnant woman and ten men in a small Georgia town, White described his conversation with one of the mob leaders, a general merchant, who assumed him to be white. Among the merchant's first comments were remarks about the federal government and the power of the local law elected by the local knowledge, the "real" knowledge of black/white relations, about which Federal lawmakers knew little. His comments suggest that the federal government is weaker than local opinion and powerless to act. And his comments echo what Anne P. Rice has called a perception by lynchers that authority is ineffectual or misguided, even weak, in black-white relations.[53] This perception made lynching's intent visible. It is more than the performance of extrajudicial prerogative upon the bodies of the subordinate. Indeed, the subordinate are the terrain across which a different contest rages, namely, the contest between the local interpreters of law and justice and the federal legislature. In these theaters of violence, lynching and its attendant immolation of victims and castration of male victims became a commentary upon the law, on its exteriority and inadequacy to the will of the white population. As Robyn Wiegman argues, a "response to the ideological incommensurability between white supremacy and black enfranchisement, lynching marks the excess of discourses of race and rights, serving as a chief mechanism for defining relations of power in postwar years."[54]

Morrison has given us figures of such violation in her fiction, but as often as not she has been concerned to show us that the mesmerizing effect of this system of spectacular violence has been most pernicious in its reproduction within black communities. And here she insists that the concept-metaphor of firing be opened wide to include being fired upon (with guns) and being burned, being sacrificed and being incited. In *Paradise*, it is the fire of armaments that wreaks havoc, displaying masculine prerogative as murderousness. In *Sula*, it is the disabling thrall in the face of Hannah Peace's burning that summons the recollection of lynchings and burnings, only to reveal their simultaneous naturalization and specularization in everyday life as a vulnerability to fire among impoverished blacks. This is what we find in *Jazz*, with the death of Dorcas's mother in a house fire because the fire engine did not come into the black neighborhood but stood "polished and poised in another part of town" (*J* 38). In *Paradise*, however, a realm typically thought of as opposed to the world of hell-fire, these metaphors proliferate to an unusual degree, gathering their force around the Oven and in the rampaging shooting at the Convent.

What shall we make of this complex deployment of a metaphor that otherwise threatens to sink into banality or nonrecognizability? Perhaps here we should remember Horkheimer and Adorno's account of twentieth-century modernity's obsession with law. They believed that the promise of reason had been betrayed in the fetish of rationalism, which had returned the world to a form of mythic violence: "Enlightenment is mythical fear radicalized."[55] In the long development of fantasy's mastery over nature, Horkheimer and Adorno discerned the perversion of law's possibility. Accordingly, the barbarism that rationalism believed it had expunged had become incorporated in its heart. For them, the primary sign of this dialectic was the ovens of the Third Reich. In these ovens, the figure of the law was haunted by the trial by fire. There the liberating violence of equivalence, which makes possible the notion of equal rights, was transformed into the gross commodification of humans. What Horkheimer and Adorno offered as the history of the Enlightenment and the nullification of European claims to civilization appears, in *Paradise*, as something else, namely, a risk internal to the emancipatory project as conceived from within the house of race and internal to the culture of law, which remains, historically and conceptually, dependent upon the always-gendered fantasy of rule.

3.   *Time Out of Joint: The Temporal Logic of Morrison's Modernist Apocalyptics*

Leaving, then, the white world, I have stepped within the Veil, raising it that you may view faintly its deeper recesses—the meaning of its religion, the passion of its human sorrow, and the struggle of its greater souls.

—W. E. B. Du Bois, *The Souls of Black Folk*

The sublime always begins with the chord "And then I saw," following which apocalyptic cumuli curl and divide and the light with its silently widening voice might say: From that whirling rose that broadens its rings in the void here come my horsemen: Famine, Plague, Death and War.

—Derek Walcott, *Bounty*

In a moment of delirious optimism, the invisible, unnamed narrator of *Jazz* virtually sings out, "Here comes the new. Look out. There goes the sad stuff. The bad stuff. The things-nobody-could-help-stuff" (*J* 7). We are invited to bear witness to the end of a time, not its residue. This end occurs in language, as the narrator utters the lyrical phrases that are already redefining and modulating the "sad stuff." What was before is already under erasure, disappearing out of detail, into the generalization of "The way everybody was then and there." We are invited to "Forget that" as the narrator declares history to be over, vanished before a future that lies, immanently, ahead. This is far from *Beloved*'s warning consequences about ignoring the past or trying to forget it.

Although history will be revealed to be far from over, the claim about its passing in *Jazz* announces the narrator's sense of "the times" as subject to both periodization and historicization. Black migration from the South to the North was driven by a desire to render the "want and violence" of the South geographically and temporally past.[1] The South is to be spatialized and its space temporalized, both cast into some domain of exteriority.[2] The urban space of the North, by contrast, stands as a utopic dream image and marvelous counterpoint to rural Southern squalor in *Beloved*.[3] The Northern city is a place that promises the newly arrived "everything you ever dreamed of," as Baby Suggs is told by her ex-slave owner when he delivers her to freedom in Ohio, a freedom purchased through her son's willingness to be doubly enslaved—to their master and to those to whom he is loaned out (*B* 137). Silence surrounds her own expectations of this freedom and whether or not she dreams of the city per se.

Whatever her expectations, however, Garner's description is a lesson in longing—Baby Suggs is to learn how to long for the city, how to succumb to the idea of it. This lesson also warns that this longing is already spatialized, because the fully admiring gaze that it requires can only be shaped by distance, by segregation. Although technically free, Baby Suggs will learn that the dream that produces the place of unlimited access to a material utopia will remain elusive for her because it was illusionary to begin with. The direct experience of the city and what it offers will not only be withheld, but has already been withheld as she arrives in a place in which everyone already has their place and in which she will be told to stay "in her place." In this manner, the characteristic "vagueness" of urban descriptions in slave narrative operates in *Beloved*, even as it is transformed into a symbolic space for such writing. Peripherality dominates the novel, both in the sense of its topological significance and in that it emanates from the center. The distance between the city and the community of Bluestone to which Baby Suggs is moved is, in fact, generated from within the city, from within a house—the kitchen into which Baby Suggs is sent immediately upon her arrival at the home of an Abolitionist family that has agreed to take her in. Even though this family gives her a house in which to live, that house is at a distance, in what is already a segregated community of freed blacks. She never moves from the kitchen to the parlor.

The city of the narrator's dreams in *Jazz* shares that segregated reality with aspiration and home, especially the dream of a home, albeit in a not fully realized dream, as the unnamed narrator in Ellison's *Invisible Man* discovers. The excitement exists within the state of compromise even in Jadine Child's enthusiasm for a post-1960s, early 1970s New York in *Tar*

Baby. In *Song of Solomon*, Macon Dead, Jr., pursues the aspiration not simply to find a home but to own houses he can rent out to others. For him, stability can only come from the "bunchy solidity" of the keys that open all the doors of the houses he owns (*SS* 17). These keys and the city in which he could become the envy of other black people help distance him from the background that his sister represents. As the head of his family's first urban generation, he understands that full citizenship in the world he admires is related to material wealth. And yet, the security that a house should give him is not secured. He dreams of moving to a wealthy white neighborhood, but knows that he has reached the limits of the city's willingness to permit his ambition.[4]

Tar Baby's Jadine does not imagine herself to be escaping the South in her "giggling" happiness at being back in New York after years of study abroad and, most recently, a holiday at her white benefactor's home on a Caribbean island. She understands the city to be all possibility. Like the narrator of *Jazz*, she does not see the city as being only, and always already, mapped and divided into racially and class-marked spaces. Nevertheless, it is a city that has its clear demarcations, as even the narrator of knows. Her time is close to that of Ann Petry's Lutie Johnson in *The Street*. Pressed into an express train that rushes passengers from Eighth Avenue and 59th Street, Lutie observes passengers closing off from each other to create an "illusion" of personal space.[5] The advertisement at which Lutie stares is of a white woman in a "miracle of a kitchen" against which the reality of her own kitchen on 116th Street pales.[6] The distance between Lutie and the advertisement emblematizes that between Harlem and the generalized view of the rest of (white) Manhattan, just as it does the chasm between her world and that of the rich Chandlers, for whom she had worked as a domestic servant. Yet, segregated as the city is, she is relieved to reach the problematic familiarity of Harlem. Walking in Harlem in the 1950s, Lutie is heir to the accumulated gaze that framed the looking endured by the girl named Florens in *A Mercy* (*M* 115). In the middle of the twentieth century, however, Lutie Johnson feels that reaching Harlem is tantamount to an escape from "the hostility in the eyes of the white women who stared at her on the downtown streets and in the subway" and from the "openly appraising looks of the white men whose eyes seemed to go through her clothing to her long brown legs."[7] Where the gaze that Florens encountered had not yet known how to look upon and was just learning how to see her and all like her as a sign of evil, the looks that Lutie encounters claim to be knowing. This later looking has had over two hundred and sixty years of practice and of discoursing about the status of blackness and black femininity. In the 1950s, such looking could still exclude Lutie from the promised wealth and euphoria of the heavenly kitchens of Connecticut unless she entered them, like Baby Suggs, as a servant. In *Home*, Lillian Florence Jones, or Lily, is confronted by "restrictions" imposed by white property owners and residents in an unspecified area in or near Seattle. In search of a home to buy, she is pointed to the fine print in an advertisement: "No part of said property hereby conveyed shall ever be used or occupied by any Hebrew or by any person of the Ethiopian, Malay or Asiatic race excepting only employees in domestic service" (*H* 73).

Insulting as they are, these restrictions cannot help but also be a sign of the presences they seek to exclude. Thus while Lutie Johnson, Lily Jones, and Macon Dead, Jr., have trouble entering the wider suburban America, they put pressure on its boundaries. The victories are small in, say, *Song of Solomon*, where the black population wins its contest to name a street as they wish. But their pressure on the sharp racial divide is nevertheless palpable, as in Lorraine Hansberry's 1959 *Raisin in the Sun*, in which the Younger family moves from the south side to the white neighborhood of Clybourne Park.[8] Restricted, divided, urban space is nonetheless not the totally fixed domain and possession of the city fathers that bounded Chicago into south side and north side in *Song of Solomon*.

Distance and Temporality

Elements of *Jazz* fall into the category of euphoric utopian fiction, figuring emancipation as a project whose ultimate achievement lies in the city, albeit one not yet radicalized as proletarian. But the timing of the novel's writing (as opposed to the timing of the events narrated) casts this vision in a different light. Published in 1992, the novel seems to take its distance from the "libidinal historicism" that Fredric Jameson associates with the postmodern condition: an eclectic and generalized, oddly depthless concern with the past motivated by an absence of faith in the future.[9] Morrison's *Jazz* speaks to the consciousness of a dissonance between dominant (white) forms of (a)historicism—the forms that are fetishistically nostalgic in Jameson's reading—and black American desires to recall a past that is violent ("bad stuff") and therefore to be disavowed, but that also demands fidelity. Indeed, it is this complex historical consciousness that runs throughout Morrison's oeuvre and makes it resistant to a more straightforwardly postmodernist reading, despite the fact that the city of *Jazz* is, after all, nothing if not eclectic.

One needs, therefore, to understand Morrison's engagement with history and with the disjunctive forms of historicism that define her moment through reference to something other than postmodernism—regardless of whether that condition is understood to be a continuation of modernism or a radical departure from it.[10] The reading practice—and indeed the writing practice—that Morrison brings to bear upon these questions is informed by the Christian eschatological imagination of the (often ecstatic) religions so central to African American cultural life. What Jacques Derrida terms an "apocalyptic tone" surfaces in *Beloved*, *Sula*, and *Jazz*, less as a narrative force than as a violent and subvertable logic that is everywhere present in her characters' lives. Whether in the overt citations of Revelation in *The Bluest* Eye, or in the enigmatic figure of the book as headstone in *Beloved*, or in the stern warning of *Paradise*'s enigmatic motto, apocalyptics is grounded for Morrison in the religions tradition of her own experience and her characters' histories. In apocalyptics, she recognizes not merely a messianism run amok but a technology of writerly habit, a technology of the book. Accordingly, in her novels apocalypticism is worked out on several levels: the figural, the structural, and the poetic, none of which can be read independently of each other.

Most obviously, of course, the genre of apocalyptics offers an array of images and devices with which to stage diegetic and extra-diegetic complaint. In Morrison's novels these images and tropes abound as the effects of the corrupting discourses of race, gender, and class upon the social and political landscape. This is the landscape that her writing has been examining since *The Bluest Eye* and that she has spatialized as, broadly speaking, spaces of risk and spaces in which an "out of doors safety" might be possible ("H" 9). This is not to say that her writing has ignored those whose race would presumably privilege them but who are still subjected to class prejudice, like Amy Denver in *Beloved* or Scully and Willard in *A Mercy*. Each Morrison novel shows how those who are discriminated against are subject to discourses of mastery. The Breedloves and McTeers of *The Bluest Eye* and the residents of the *Beloved*'s Bluestone community live in times of trouble. The world in which Cholly Breedlove is "exposed" to two white hunters and then forced at gunpoint to copulate with Darlene for their amusement is corrupt (*BE* 147–49). The white hunters are a sign of the corruption that is abroad in the land. There is no "out of doors safety" for Cholly or Darlene, and there will be no indoors safety for Cholly's daughter, because he internalizes a humiliation and rage that distort his ability to parent. His wife Pauline's experience in the maternity section of the hospital is yet another sign of corruption. She and Cee experience the distortion of medicine's hypocratic foundation by racism. So, too, does Ruby Morgan in *Paradise*.

The Breedloves' and McTeers' neighbor, Soaphead Church, views the world through a corrupting theory of race that claims to be science. Through it, the idea of affiliation, if not family itself, is corrupted for him. His relationship with himself and his family has been corrupted by his distaste for what is black about himself. He has absorbed the spurious science of Arthur de Gobineau, a key contributor to the nineteenth-century development of race theories, especially claims that there was a scientific basis for race studies.[11] De Gobineau's theories would find their echo in Madison Grant's work, but in *The Bluest Eye* Soaphead is no scientist or doctor. He is a man clinging to the idea of a pure, racial ideal of whiteness in order to escape what he has read about the supposed degeneracy of interbreeding with his black forebears. Being a man who has black and white forebears, he refuses to be familiar with the former but blinds himself to the fact that he will always be the unfamiliar descendant of the latter. He rejects being at home with one but is unhomely to the other. The same could be said for Helene, another neighbor in *The Bluest Eye*. And it could be said of Macon Dead, Jr., in *Song of Solomon*.

Such tropes and figures aside, it is at the level of temporal and therefore narrative structure that Morrison's use of apocalyptics is most interesting. Consider, for example, the rewriting of apocalypse in *Beloved*. By the time the four horsemen appear in *Beloved*, all that will flow forward from their arrival has already occurred. In effect, Morrison has drawn back the veil of apocalyptic writing itself. Perhaps the key organizing principle of this genre is its temporal sleight of hand. Traditionally, the apocalypticist looks back at an event so traumatic and so close to the limits of meaning that it can be remarked upon only *after* the fact. However, the apocalypticist presents the past as a vision of times to come. The vision serves a pedagogical function of warning. In its "if/then" logic, the vision literally shows the reader what lies ahead for those who have participated in the corruption of history.

The structure of *Beloved* reveals this process in action. We know that 124 Bluestone is "spiteful," and we know that something catastrophic has occurred. Things have come to pass. Yet we will move forward in the narrative time to the arrival of the four horsemen, as if we were moving to a vision of things to come while sustaining narrative suspense. Other signs and portents prepare us for this, point to the immanence of some convergence of things we have yet to coin. Language itself converges into the image of worst things: the quantifier "four" takes on a descriptive, assigning function. It gives meaning to the horsemen. The phrase sets foot upon the page with the weight of nearly two millennia of representation in the Western canon. It is a phrase that most have learned to recognize as the invocation of plague, pestilence, famine, and death. Derek Walcott, cited in the epigraph to this chapter, names the four horsemen as "Famine, Plague, Death and War," militarizing the end and collapsing plague with pestilence, while linking it to the sublime specular pleasures of revelation: "And then I saw."[12]

And then. I saw. It has already occurred. It occurred as a becoming visible. Morrison also explodes the spatial and visual metaphorics of eventfulness with her extraordinary poetics of place, emphasizing the "taking" and the "taken" dimension that defines postslave consciousness and slave existence. What is revealed is the moment outside, the moment that conditions a future possibility inside slavery's law of appropriation and property. That law, it will be remembered, justified itself through the mythic idea of the gift, if only in the form of sacrifice. What had been given to whites was the prerogative to take to themselves those whom God had rejected (in the story of Ham) or who had been unworthy of Him "in the first place." In *Beloved*, Morrison goes directly in pursuit of the meaning within the statement that an apocalypse has taken place; she radicalizes the apocalyptic traditions by insisting that what Christianity posited as the future is already a matter of historical experience for blacks in America, even as she staves off analogizing the Middle Passage with the Holocaust (the other metaphor through which to conceive of slavery's cataclysm). While that analogy is not entirely absent from Morrison's writing, as it is not absent in African American criticism, the turn to apocalyptics permits a different kind of historicization on Morrison's part, precisely because it points out the violence of effacing by projecting into the future a suffering that has been enacted in the past on others. The result is an immediate challenge to the more conventional univocality of Christian apocalyptics.

Beloved begins with place, and temporalizes it. The evocation of Number 124 suggests a place of beginning. The number "one" itself sets up the first suggestion that this is a beginning of beginnings. And yet, the place of beginning is not the beginning of the story. In the utterance of the first line alone there is a clue to an order that precedes the starting "one" of 124. It is the system of numbers. That is, *number,* with all that it implies about linearity, rationality, and calculability, is the order and the frame within which the house takes its place. The novel's opening statement, then, foregrounds time and place by remarking the time of a named, numbered, and located place, simultaneously conjuring up the necromancy of biblical prophecy and the grotesque numerology of social surveys, such as those about which Du Bois wrote and which he attempted to redeem at the turn of the century.[13]

But what does it mean to say that a house, a place, was spiteful, as if it were a character? What does it mean to utter a statement about a past that is no longer past but leaks into the future in the way that spite leaks into a place? And what does it mean to say that something, an apocalypse, has taken place by the time Number 124 no longer *is* but *was* spiteful? Opening in Ohio—before it had become a state—*Beloved* remarks upon the irony of Sethe's inhabitation of what is ostensibly the space of freedom. This space is also that of an untenable present in which she and her family live. It is a present that is haunted by the past. The house at 124 Bluestone is, in this sense, at a temporal impasse. The lives in this place cannot move forward. Time has been corrupted, is out of joint, as Derrida, invoking Hamlet, a play of plays about haunting, says about all messianic discourse.[14] Behind Sethe and Paul D lies the novel's only (if ironically named) utopic site—the slave plantation from which both have come, the plantation Sweet Home. The deep and bitter truth about this place from which they have sought escape is that it will always retain for them its former role as "home"—one which was not chosen but thrust upon them, and one whose definition of "home" referred to being "at home" as a slave in the "house of race," where belonging did not entail security and stability, but being owned.

Sweet Home was Garner's dream plantation, but like any plantation, it has displaced many thousands of individuals, one of whom is Sethe's mother. But Sweet Home did not just remove such people from their "place," it displaced time. At Sweet Home the past dissolves in the perpetual present of slavery, where time is made the space of function and utility and where everything is rationalized to an absurd degree, but without the enabling abstraction that generates equality. This is the rule of time on the plantation, and it is hierarchical. On one end of the hierarchy, "the bottom," time is marked by the slave bell that signals sunrise and sunset. On the other end is the excess time for the plantation owner, the leisure time in which Garner, for example, can visit neighbors and boast of his idyllic form of slavery. Always in this present, slaves are prohibited from knowing other possible times: the past and futures of a radically different sort. Their lives are consumed by labor, their time absorbed by tasks, their social lives and the possibility of both shared experience and reflection constantly foreclosed by the demands of the plantation.

Apart from a brief contact with her mother on a prior plantation, Sethe has no knowledge of a life other than that lived on Sweet Home. The plantation has taken the place of her mother, of her own memories, of any possibilities for existence other than that of chattel. All she knows about her mother is that she was one of a number of women who worked in a field and who paused to speak with her. Of her mother's past life and her own familial relations, Sethe also knows nothing except that her mother had a "circle and a cross burnt right in the skin" under her breast. This mark of ownership is the literal underside of that other bodily mark in that other idyllic place so sought after by the white settlers of the United States and West Indies—the New Jerusalem, where God's obedient servants, as they are named in Revelation 22:3, bear his name on their foreheads. In a moment of prescience, Ma'am (the only name we have for Sethe's mother) shows the mark to the young Sethe and says it is a way to identify her.[15] The nature, or source, of this mark is intriguing. Like the motto of *Paradise*, it is one of the "secrets" or undisclosed elements of an awful utopia that, in coming into being, has drawn veils around itself, foreclosing all other competing visions. It fills the horizon. Ma'am's mark comes to have many possible meanings, all of which may be true, but all of which create a longing for what is beyond the veil of unknowing. Ma'am herself disappears behind this veil. Like Sethe, Florens in *A Mercy* never knows her mother's name—an ironic fact in the history of slavery, which always recorded mothers as the sole parents of offspring and often erased the names of the fathers. Both women only know their mothers through general nouns: Ma'am for Sethe, and *Minha Mãe*, or the Portuguese for "my mother," for Florens.

As Sally Keenan suggests: "If, in psychoanalytical terms, the mother as source, or origin, is problematic and irrecoverable, so too African Americans, perhaps above all peoples, have learned through their particularly fractured past that history is problematic and often irrecoverable."[16] The mystery of the human body and history figure this predicament, without making the mother the sole or privileged locus of unnarratable loss. Saidiya Hartman has restored this privileged identification of the maternal by identifying it with the irrecoverable. *Beloved* extends this problematic to the disappearance of nonmaternal others. Baby Suggs makes a small attempt to know what has happened to all of her children, but she learns that the veil is not easily lifted. It is powerfully controlled by the same system that makes it impossible to know more than the trace of catastrophe in Ma'am's life. This veil is in fact history, the representation of a past that Keenan suggests may be irrecoverable. History here is the language of the master, not the events and experiences of the servants. In this sense, its mediations are as occluding as they are revealing.[17]

Perhaps the mark on Sethe's mother was a secret sign with meaning for those of whom she says she is the only survivor. Perhaps it was put there when she was a child, before she had developed breasts. If the circle belongs to another time, beyond or behind the Middle Passage, the cross—with the text's emphasis on its being "burnt right in the skin" like a brand—shares the fate of her history and that of the others brought into the country of sweet homes. Like place names on maps, they have been overstamped by the unisonic discourse of possession. The truth of Ma'am's mark is on the other side of the silence surrounding it and her name. This silence parallels that of Revelation, where it constitutes the space of a transformation as the many, competing, and simultaneous languages of the Whore of Babylon give way to the universal language of the New Jerusalem. In Ma'am's case, personal history is absorbed into and by the silence of a new language. Yet in the trace the sign of that catastrophe is made visible. Thus, the trace, the mark itself, is the site of an apocalypse that is withheld—something that the characters Joe and Violet Trace, in the later novel *Jazz*, will enact in their celebratory and then insistent and finally ambivalent residence in the city of their own paradisiacal dreams. Their very name suggests the receding possibility of recovering the history of those who preceded them. In *Beloved*, which already anticipates the transforming of sign into trace, nothing is definitively revealed, although all is sign, begging reading and mocking the imagination of reading as mere disclosure.

What Is in a Name?

In its closure of one time, save that which opens ambiguously in the mark on Sethe's mother, Sweet Home occupies the place of beginning for Sethe and Paul D and stands as an origin to which they look from their vantage point on the edge of Ohio. Sixo is the only register of an attempt to recall an alternative temporality, being the only Sweet Home slave who has remnants of a pre-Atlantic memory. Yet he too succumbs, because at Sweet Home "Time never worked the way [he] thought, so of course he never got it right" (*B* 21). This is perhaps because the sweetness of this "home" is not meant for him or any of the others who have been enslaved. Its ironic name anticipates the question that will be asked in the second song of Morrison's 1995 song cycle *Honey and Rue*: "Whose house is this?" (*HR*). The persona of this song asks, "Whose house is this? / Whose night keeps out the light / In here? / Say, who owns this house?" The answer will come immediately: "It's not mine."

A plantation like Sweet Home is not a bounded temporal order, however. It extends outward, extends the rule of its time in an effort to encompass the surrounding world. Thus Sweet Home is located near a "deserted stone structure that Redmen used way back when they thought the land was theirs" (*B* 24). In this manner, the plantation intercepts even Native history in the claim to priority that Garner makes on its behalf. As the idyllic source of an emergent capitalism, it roots itself "way back" in a time past, one whose passing has been a literal overtaking of slaves and American Indians. Yet there is a deeper implication behind Morrison's suggestion of the eternal present time of the slave's life. It is in this stalled time that a legible, narratable, and even writable history must be found—because it is in this time that history is written.[18] Morrison's reading of the plantation thus offers a powerful and ironic counterpoint to the "now-time" of Walter Benjamin's messianic dialectics.[19] Her mode of seeing, explosive and urgent, written with an eye to the "emergency" of her own present, as well as that of slavery's past present, enacts something of Benjamin's demands for the historical materialist. Nor is it incidental that Morrison's vision of slavery's violence hinges on its perversion of the prerogative of naming. Benjamin similarly identified naming as the site of a possible redemption, one that had first to escape the awful legacy of "over-naming."[20] Like Benjamin, Morrison stages a contest over naming, a contest between the regimes of naming, and finds history to have been the history of language's betrayal. But hers is not a general discovery. It is the discovery of a racialized betrayal, a failure to include slaves in the category of humanity rather than a failure of humanity to realize itself.

In the domain of his own paternalistic oversight, *Beloved*'s Garner takes for himself the Adamic prerogative of naming. He defines his plantation as exemplary, distinguishing it from other plantations and other slaveries and giving it a name that claims mere domesticity. Yet his gestures of naming are also part of slavery's amnesiac practices. The violence of the latter are made clear and played out in a discussion about Baby Suggs's names, as Garner drives her to the freedom for which he makes her son, Halle, pay. In reply to her question about his insistence on calling her Jenny, he takes as correct and irrefutable the name written on her sale ticket by another slaver, whose surname has been recorded as hers. She is, according to the sales ticket, Jenny Whitlow (*B* 142). Although she has been at Sweet Home for ten years, Garner is surprised to learn that she has another name for herself and that she takes it from a man whom she regards as her husband. Garner rejects both the notion of her marriage to this man and the fact that he called himself "Suggs." To Garner, the man's name was also Whitlow, since that is the name given to him on the slave ticket by his previous owner. Insistent on the ascendancy of written documentation and white social and religious laws governing the legal status of men and women living together, despite the interruptions of such relations by slavery itself, Garner shares the general views of slavery.

He even defines what manhood is, by encouraging his male slaves to challenge him and "invent ways of doing things; to see what was needed and attack it without permission. To buy a mother, choose a horse or a wife, handle guns, even learn reading if they wanted to" (*B* 125). This is merely a mask, however, and Garner hides behind it to claim an originary masculinity that then constitutes the paradigm for the slaves, who can only imitate him. Master of slaves of whom he is unafraid, despite the guns he has placed in their hands for hunting purposes, he boasts his fetishized

manhood loudly. Indeed, in his eyes his "manly" slaves imitate his masculinity and are therefore the very proof of his own manliness. He occupies
all positions, like a demiurge.

Only Morrison can alienate him from his presumed prerogative by
making him suffer what he wanted to effect, namely, to be his own name.
Garner is, after all, one who garners. Throughout her fictions, names function as ciphers and signs, but they are also the means by which Morrison
herself enters into and subverts the violence or logic of naming that was
written into the heart of slavery. It also permits her to reveal the force of
literalism, for the reading of the name as a sign and not merely as a deictic
mark transparent to the object of its identificatory gesture is at once the
poison of apocalypticism and the remedying demand for critical reading.

Sweet Home is depicted by Morrison as a fragile illusion, imprisoned
by its own literalism (an inclination that she will show elsewhere to be
the awful and dangerous legacy that can also be one of the hauntings of
African American historical consciousness). The name itself is incomplete,
and the plantation is unsecured except in Garner's imagination, ending—
inevitably—with his death. Its inherent partiality is implied in the name
he gives it, alluding as it does to the song "Home Sweet Home," which
is fully encompassed in the circling return of the word "Home." Sweet
Home, the plantation, is therefore without its own beginnings in this reference, the first "Home" having been removed or expunged in the manner that home is expunged in its slaves. Morrison, one notes, makes silence
and absence signify as well; she realizes the other dimension of language—
not just the "muteness of things," as Benjamin would say,[21] but the muting
of people treated as things.

In Baby Suggs's eyes, Garner is a man who treats the world as "a toy
he was supposed to have fun with" (*B* 139). His wife fits into this "game,"
humming in the kitchen as she and Baby Suggs move in constant production of "home" goods: preserves, candles, clothes, soap, cider, butter, fires
(*B* 139–40). Although his plantation is clearly better than the places Baby
Suggs has experienced before arriving at Sweet Home, she is aware that
Garner is "courting" danger of some kind by "creating" "men-bred slaves"
(*B* 141). It is as though his bravado is an incitement to reencompassment by
the dominant regime. When his male slaves leave Sweet Home, they are
drawn back into the larger order against which Garner's experiment defines itself. They become "trespassers among the human race. Watchdogs
without teeth; steer bulls without horns; gelded workhorses whose neigh

and whinny could not be translated into a language responsible humans spoke" (*B* 125). Here their newly imitative masculinity is emphasized in a language that substitutes emasculation for virility and wild illiteracy for the lettered man. And although they had not been prevented from learning to read, none accepted the opportunity, because "nothing important to them could be put down on paper" (*B* 125). [22]

The letter, the alphabet, has not, of course, been given to women. It remains the prerogative of men. For women, the plantation has only gesture. It is in such extra-linguistic space that Sweet Home "plants" a tree on Sethe's back, its roots setting deep into her. In a sense, it literally and figuratively takes/makes its place in her—though critically it does not create a "family" tree, since there is no vaginal rape of Sethe and no child is born to a white slave owner as a result. Instead, Sethe is made to bear the tree of a knowledge that is both physically and symbolically "behind" in the form of Sweet Home. Schoolteacher has "taught" her what it means to be in the plantation's language. He has "taught" her that this language speaks to her in actions only, writing and reading her as its animalistic, prelinguistic other. The lesson is epitomized in Schoolteacher's physiognomy lesson to his nephews, wherein he instructs them to place her animal "characteristics" in one column and her human in the other—this is the affiliate discourse of eugenics that awaits Cee in *Home* (*B* 193). Overhearing this lesson, Sethe becomes an interloper in the language of Sweet Home's apocalyptic space. She stops to listen because she hears her name, but her seeming recognition is quickly displaced as she confronts the disparity between herself and the descriptions in the two columns. Indeed, she is rent by the dichotomy and by the trauma of overhearing it, split psychically in the way that Fanon has described as the very structure of psychic colonization.[23] Her meaning is not Schoolteacher's and it is not Sweet Home's. Her name is "slave," and it has meaning only in the taxonomy of commodities and other objects.

Schoolteacher presides over the order of Sweet Home as one of Foucault's teacher-judges.[24] He instructs his nephews, the heirs to his power, and the plantation's slaves, those who will be subject to this power. The force of his power will extend through generations, shaping their social and racial relations and together heirs, subjects, and power will ascend into normativity.

When Sethe hears the lesson and begins to understand its content, she steps back (*B* 193). Her reaction is important, acting out the fact that she has been drawn back by Schoolteacher's pedagogy into the language of slavery, a language she had been forgetting in the slippages that make her want to personalize the Sweet Home kitchen with sprigs of flowers or clear a piece of ground in which her sons, Howard and Buglar, could play (*B* 193). The overheard lesson not only foreshadows the brutality of the bodily lesson she will be taught for speaking against Schoolteacher's nephews to Mrs. Garner but foreshadows the step back, the temporal disjuncture that will pursue her across the Ohio River when the four horsemen appear.

When she escapes after she has been beaten, Sethe is cornered by discipline's knowledge as it literally comes up from behind her in the form of four horsemen. [25] In this moment, what was behind in every sense appears as the future to which her children will be consigned. Sweet Home, now fully revealed in all its brutal gluttony, takes up all temporal place, even the future. Indeed, Sethe is haunted by this displacement of her own future to such an extent that, years after the beating, her escape, the arrival of the four horsemen, the killing of her child, her imprisonment, and her release and ostracization by the community, Sethe indulges in a flawed nostalgia for Sweet Home. When Paul D arrives, the tree on Sethe's back takes on new meaning, and the nostalgia turns out to be the trace of the discursive planting and implanting by which she was made subject to slavery. It has written itself upon her in the language of violence—in the scar, which parodies the covenant that, Derrida reminds us, is repeatedly marked on the male body in the form of circumcision. The scar—this inscription or writing on the body, as anthropologists describe it—is also the gesture by which Sethe is excluded from possession of language. She is its surface only. Lacan might say that this is how she becomes the phallus, which the patriarchal subject can own (the masculine being for Lacan that which has the phallus, the feminine that which is the phallus). But Morrison's narrative focuses on the fact that the event is traumatic, and, as Freud would tell us of all such events, it compels repetition. The novel/story is one form of that repetition. The narrative itself is structured by repetition. Each time Sethe thinks of the event, Sweet Home overtakes the present. When Paul D traces the scar with his fingertips in a form of blind reading, he can only liken it to a chokecherry tree. The failure of correspondence between the image and the scar explodes the space of signification, so that it must fall back onto the language that has planted itself into her body as mere index, what Charles Sanders Peirce thought through the image of the bullet hole. It is interesting that the most powerful metaphors for the index, even within the heart of linguistics, so often entail this invocation of violence, just as the metaphors for writing so often entail cutting and marking, as Derrida has shown.

Sacrificing Purity

The "writer" of Sethe's scar has made meaning in the most powerful and visceral way. Such is the sovereign performative power of the slave master. Sixo learns this when he attempts to assert and explain his economy of labor and exchange after Schoolteacher accuses him of stealing and eating a shoat. He explains that, "Sixo plant rye to give the high piece a better chance. Sixo take and feed the soil, give you more crop. Sixo take and feed Sixo give you more work" (*B* 190). The beating that Sixo receives from Schoolteacher is "to show him that definitions belonged to the definers—not the defined." In effect, the beating is the only "payment" he can receive for ill-gotten gains. They are the wages of his "sin." At the same time, these wages remain in the order of the material; there is no abstraction, no translation of command into representation, no transmuting of the index into the symbol. Here explanation is supplement. It does not obviate the need for the beating.

The laws of Sweet Home produce criminality by generating an appetite that it then outlaws, and in relation to which it claims its own fullness, its proportional completeness. Sixo's meanings are not those of Sweet Home. Moreover, they insist on a prior set of meanings, an entire signifying universe beyond the enclosures of the plantation. And this is his crime. Where he sees a shoat as a legitimate and logical reward for labor, or as an object of future use to be taken for consumption rather than exchange, the logos of Sweet Home shows no sign of recognition— for either his rationale or his claim of prerogative. He is its outlaw, always and already criminal. When his body is finally burned, it becomes the brutal inversion of the biblical tradition of sacrifice upon which Sweet Home stakes its foundations, and it enters into the litany of figures so central to Morrison's work (as discussed in the previous chapter), by which the racialization of sacrifice is made visible. In the case of Sixo and the unnamed child of whom all that remains is a charred fragment of scalp still wearing its red ribbon (*B* 193), such burnings are not the *olah*, or burnt offering, which "expiates a broad range of sins."[26] According to J. Milgrom, such offering atones for the neglect of "performative commands" in the Old Testament, and therefore it "answers to all the emotional needs of the worshipper."[27] In *Beloved*, the command that is neglected is that of slave owners, and the burning that takes place is the price exacted from slaves for claiming freedom. As Stamp Paid discerns, this is a world of violence and chaos masked as one of order (*B* 180). These burnings are not read as sacrifices from within the episteme of slavery; they become such by being reread by Morrison, a gesture that confers upon the victim the value that the concept of sacrifice would otherwise have demanded and that the rituals of sacrifice, as anthropologically understood, would have conferred.

The foundational and informing biblical narratives in which fire is a purifying element are rendered impotent when the desired purity is racial. Sweet Home writes these racialized meanings upon the charred body of Sixo, as it does on Sethe's back. The scars themselves are also the indices of commandments. As writing or inscription, they express more than the commanding power of Sweet Home, however. They testify to the slave owner's right over the body of the slave. If their effect is to announce, "Thou shalt obey or be wounded," their actual signification is more simply that of his having exercised power. In the first instance, the scarring is the result of a direct address; in the second, it is the trace of a signifying process that wants to be read by others, overhead by slaves and masters alike. The first claims immediacy; the second seeks futurity. But in either case, the scar is the sign; it communicates. It acquires its wordlike status precisely because it is not only violence but violence that communicates itself as transcendent of the moment. Insofar as apocalypticism requires this signification but promises a moment when the sign will revert to flesh, when what will be will be and ambiguity will vanish, the opening of violence to reading is both a gesture on the way to the prophecy of apocalypticism's fulfillment and a deferral of its realization.

Thus, even within this equivalence between the word/scar and its claim to be Sweet Home's power, other meanings abound. They do so because those who have already been pushed beyond meaning are reading them. Sethe runs as much from the *discursive violence* that authorizes Sweet Home as she does from bodily violence. Like Sixo, Halle, and other slaves who attempt to escape, Sethe refuses to be relegated to the status of the merely "defined" (*B* 190). Their refusal reveals their persistent insistence on the simultaneity of their views within the apocalyptic space that constitutes Sweet Home. To the extent that this simultaneity of meanings exists, however, apocalyptic discourse will have violence as its modus operandi.

Paul D's reading of the scar on Sethe's back is also a sign that Sweet Home is doomed to return to the realm of the sign and therefore that its apocalyptic discourse is doomed to failure. His reading and her account of the beating begin to make history of the sign. Critical distance begins here, and it takes the form of interruption. The possibility of freedom is seeded within the gesture. Paul D begins to read Sethe's scar when she begins to long for "a little space . . . a little time, some way to hold off eventfulness, to push busyness into the corners of the room and just stand there a minute or two naked from shoulder blade to waist" (*B* 18). Time and space coalesce, though not in an apocalyptic way that would narrate this coalescence as a final closure, or end. The time and space that coalesce around Sethe and Paul produce privacy. Again, the interplay between inside and outside is blurred as Sethe's "little time" and "little space" is inserted into Sweet Home's legacy. Until this moment, Sweet Home has obstructed their access to the past as something that does belong to them, no matter how problematically. Obstructed and unable to admit the compromised truth that the place was the only home, albeit awful, that she had, Sethe could only move numbly through the world (*B* 18), and Paul D has kept his emotions in a rusty tin. Their rereading of Sweet Home's writing upon her therefore marks the beginning of a personal history, a view from under the floor of heaven, so to speak, even as the panoptic view from its more exalted heights attempts to reassert itself. The privacy and quietude of Sethe's changing are almost the exact opposite of apocalypticism's theatrics. Traditionally, the genre calls for language that signals and performs. Sethe's language stalls this, even though structurally her "minute or two" adheres to the classic Judeo-Christian pattern of pause before the loud, shouting arrival of a new time. While Paul D's loud excising of the baby ghost announces that its time is over, that entire confrontation remains a deeply private one, far removed from the panoramic scope of traditional apocalypticism.

Denver facilitates this change for Sethe and Paul D when she asks why they talk so much about Sweet Home when it was the site of their slavery and personal abuse and grief. They reply in different and revealing ways. Paul D admits that it was neither sweet nor home (*B* 13–14). Yet he still remembers the attractive prospects of Sweet Home as having "more pretty trees than any farm around" (*B* 21). Sethe, by contrast, replies, "But it's where we were. . . . All together. Comes back whether we want it to or not" (*B* 14). There is no new place in which the past has been radically erased. The same logic—that home is where one finds oneself—underpins Sethe's refusal to leave Number 124, even when Paul D asks why she does not. She rejects his suggestion and its implication that "a house was a little thing—a shirtwaist or a sewing basket you could walk off from or give away any old time" (*B* 23). For Sethe, remembering when she even tried to feel that something of the kitchen at Sweet Home was hers, the critical gesture is the desire for the stability of place. She has to find a way to "take place" existentially, *to be*, to *dwell*. Her psychic and physical displacement demands this.

It is perhaps for this reason that Morrison opens *Beloved* by staging place as a problem. Writing "124 was spiteful," she assigns a past tense to the condition in which the novel opens. The condition is of the precisely numbered and named 124 Bluestone Road, in which Sethe and her daughter Denver live after all other family have died or left. The number and name suggest the existence of a rational grid. The house bearing this numbered name has a place that, through the sense of assignment via the name and number, implies fixity and locality within a legitimized and recognized system of ordering place—a notion of local municipality structured around the daily lives of citizens who, as Althusser suggests, can be "addressed" and whose very addressability signifies their being solicited by power.[28] It is unclear whether the subaltern who emerges from slavery is ever fully addressed in Althusser's sense, being deprived of many of the attributes of subjectivity that are constituted in and through processes of recognition. Nonetheless, Morrison's fiction opens up questions that Althusser and Foucault's understanding of population management and the order of biopolitics barely recognize: namely, that a deep metaphoricity binds the logic of the grid, the rationality of urban space, and the ideological operations of a state that remains, as we have seen, haunted by its violent and racialized origins. This metaphoricity and the history of rationalism's failures are exquisitely concretized in that simple address, which takes the form of an interrupted numerical sequence: 1, 2, . . . 4. However, the spite that becomes the condition of this place precedes and exceeds all order. It is already "in situ" long before the house is numbered "because Cincinnati didn't stretch that far. In fact, Ohio had been calling itself a state only seventy years" (*B* 3). Only the name seems to have existed, and it exists in the private speech or thought of the residents. Baby Suggs, lying on her sickbed and listening to her grandsons escape the spite, refers to the house merely as being on Bluestone Road (*B* 3).

When read as a compound, the *number* 124 is presented as a closed unit. In the history of Sethe's life prior to her arrival at this place, she has been disconnected from the possibility of belonging in a personal way except through the "belonging" of slavery, in which she had been a possession and an abstraction (which is to say, a commodity). There, as a young girl, she "had to bring a fistful of salsify into Mrs. Garner's kitchen every day just to be able to work in it, feel like some part of it was hers, because she wanted to love the work she did, to take the ugly out of it, and the only way she could feel at home on Sweet Home was if she picked some pretty growing thing and took it with her" (B 22). She places whatever "pretty growing thing" she likes into the handle of a pressing iron, garlanding the instruments of her labor. Once Garner is dead and Schoolteacher arrives, she learns that even this simple exercising of an aesthetic preference is not open to her. The sense of choice has been but an illusion, and the illusion can no longer be sustained. A "handful of myrtle stuck in the handle of a pressing iron propped against the door in a white woman's kitchen" cannot make the iron, the kitchen, or the experience hers.

At 124 Bluestone Road, by contrast, she arrives at a place that seems to offer her placement and definition, even redefinition and belonging. Immediately after her arrival, she experiences "Days of healing, ease and real-talk. Days of company: knowing the names of forty, fifty other Negroes, their views, habits; where they had been and what done; of feeling their fun and sorrow along with her own" (B 95). When taught the alphabet by one person and a new stitch by another, she begins to enter the literacy of this new world as well as a self-sufficiency of skills. And for her, as for Claudia McTeer in *The Bluest Eye* and Florens in *A Mercy*, this acquisition of literacy is correlate with the emergence of a new critical faculty. In this sense, *Beloved* continues a thematics of pedagogy through lettering—the stitch being a supplementary metaphor for the weave of the text—as central to Morrison's fiction as is the problematic of race, figured as an architecture. For a time, then, the place is removed from the past vagueness of the Sweet Home that was not home, whose brutal reality is subject to obfuscation by the *idea* of sweetness. The promise is in its name, a promise that disables even Sethe's critical memory from full condemnation of Garner. For a brief time, Sethe can also begin to redefine herself, to give herself definition as the daughter-in-law of Baby Suggs, and as the mother of her children, as a freed woman, as a woman capable of bounty. In this place, Sethe permits herself the same fleeting desire for happiness that Baby Suggs dared upon her arrival in the land of promise, when she dreams briefly of being united with Halle as well as her children.

However, the offer of this place is not guaranteed, and her presence is not secure. For all of her attempts at redefinition, she remains subject to the omnipresent fact of slavery, especially in the legal shadow that it casts during the period of her escape. The failure of geographical distance as a guarantee of freedom is nowhere more poignantly depicted than in the many stories of recapture of runaway slaves, a practice sanctioned by the Fugitive Slave Act. Few writers have more compellingly imagined the consequences of this legal document or rendered its "fictitious force," its performative effectivity, more real.

In the language of the Fugitive Slave Act, Sethe remains a slave. The Fugitive Slave Law of 1793 and the Fugitive Slave Act of 1850 lumped slaves together with criminal fugitives in order to extend the rights of slave owners into nonslaving states. In the eyes of both laws, slaves were not considered subjects who could testify to their own freedom in court hearings.[29] Sethe's experience of this law is that it has provided the bridge across which the past of slavery can travel and attempt to overtake the future as alpha and omega. Here is the crux of Morrison's subversive apocalyptics then: a reading of the conflation of law and, specifically, the law of the State, with Godhead, in a Christian nation that fantasizes itself as secular and modern. Long before she arrives across the river, the long reach of slavery waits for her. It is therefore behind her and in front of her. It is in all places. It takes all place, just as it has taken place before she was born and before her children were. When Schoolteacher, his nephew, the slave catcher, and the local sheriff arrive, the geographic and psychic "pastness" of the slavery Sethe believes she has left behind breaks its boundaries. This sense of the past overtaking the future is marked by Baby Suggs when, the morning after the feast at 124, she detects "way way back behind" the community's belated, postpleasure "scent of . . . disapproval," something that is "Dark and coming. Something she couldn't get at because the other odor hid it" (*B* 138, 137). But Baby Suggs lacks the vision. Her view is thwarted by the present disapproval in which the community questions her ability as its healer. All she can sense is something approaching, and all she can see are "high-topped shoes she didn't like the look of" (*B* 138).

Past, present, and future collide with the arrival of the "something" in the form of the horsemen. "There" and "here" merge, as space and time collapse. In a truly catastrophic way, *Beloved* is born of and in a repetition of the past, in a moment in which a nubile young woman flees white men. The moment is symbolic and fraught with undercurrents of sexuality and bodily threat, since Sethe is, in the eyes of Schoolteacher, a good that can reproduce itself, as all slaves are goods that reproduce themselves—a slave woman being more "valuable" as the "bearing reproducer"—though male slaves are also goods that reproduce the possibility of more goods through labor. His disappointment at the scene he witnesses in the barn into which Sethe has run with her children is marked by his concern for the plantation and reveals the necessary role that young female slaves were forced to play in the continuation of the plantation, the basis of the country's emergent capitalism. Viewing two children "lying open-eyed in sawdust" and a third pumping blood down Sethe's dress as she tries to swing the head of a baby "toward the wall planks," he sees "nothing there to claim," as he had hoped, given that there is "work Sweet Home desperately needed" (*B* 149). He had tracked her children down as much as he had sought her for having, as he believed, "at least ten breeding years left." Yet the woman he sees in the barn is useless, having clearly "gone wild, due to the mishandling of the nephew who'd overbeat her and made her cut and run." Schoolteacher sees "loss," and indeed this appears to be the case. Sethe appears to have lost the future to the past, and she appears to have lost her place in the present of the freedom she had attempted to secure. But the negative, Schoolteacher's destructive impact, is reiterated and projected into the murderous Sethe in that he has destroyed the "value" he placed in her as property. He can no longer "appropriate" her value, even symbolically. She is a "nothing" now, not even a slave. Her capture will not convert itself into any currency. She is rendered aneconomic. Excess is here mirrored in waste, and a Bataillean reader would perhaps not be surprised, for Morrison has suggested elsewhere that slavery's economy is not ultimately amenable to or explicable through the, terms of use, exchange, and rational choice. The nonreproductive assault is the sign of this. It is a violence generated by the pursuit of pleasure, one that produces only blood, death, and horror—and more death.

This emphasis on appearance is crucial. The scene is unclear, despite being visible. This is because, in her use of simultaneous narrative and in the promise of a scene, Morrison both parallels and undoes apocalypticism. The representation that claims to be the final and only representation of a single and only story, one whose meaning unfolds as the negation of interpretation, in a total presence and a complete immediacy, is here transgressed. Under the law that has permitted Schoolteacher to extend his deeds of contract across borders, there can only be one story about Sethe's actions in the barn. This is a story of unprecedented disaster and crime. In the logics of the religious doctrines upon which the law is founded, this latter is a moral crime of enormous proportions. Yet there is another narrative that insists in *Beloved*, and it is Sethe's. Having resisted revisiting the moment in which she killed her child, she succumbs to the decision to give Paul D an account of her actions when he confronts her with what he has learned from Stamp Paid. She will also tell this story again when she succumbs to the need to explain herself to the spectral woman who emerges from the river and claims the name Beloved. In telling her story to Paul D, Sethe challenges the single narrative domination of the postapocalyptic frame in which her life has been cast since the arrival of the four horsemen. Yet she knows that she is in narrative competition, for there is no language for her experience of her actions. She "knew that the circle she was making around the room, him, the subject, would remain one. That she could never close in, pin it down for anybody who had to ask. If they didn't get it right off—she could never explain. Because the truth was simple, not a long-drawn-out record of flowered shifts, tree cages, selfishness, ankle ropes and wells" (*B* 163). The truth is the event, what happened, not its explanation or contextualization. The event, of course, remains beyond language. But it is the referent, and the effort to explain it is perhaps the index of its externality to her own narrative. That externality summons disbelief or revulsion. Equally important, it is because she narrates, because she fails to transform the event into a secret, that she is expelled from the narrative of normativity. In essence, her story transgresses the laws of legibility.

Between her story, her ability to tell it, and Paul D's hearing of it lie the community's disgust, Stamp Paid's disbelief, and the newspaper clipping in which she is completely redefined and unrecognizable. Paul D looks at the clipping, and his first reaction is, "That ain't her mouth" (*B* 154). When she speaks to him, the reaction continues, because what she says is always held at bay by Paul D's disbelief and by hope of reprieve from what he dreads hearing, which shatters his idealization of her—this idealization being the binary opposite of Schoolteacher's degradation of her. In this space of conceptual illegibility, the text itself decomposes, as it does in *The Bluest Eye*, into the materiality of its medium. The writing is simply "those black scratches" to him. They speak, and he refuses to accept what they say. Yet the clipping is what "moves" him to confront her, and its narrative, which he cannot read but which is handed to him as corroboration for Stamp Paid's version of the story, hangs between them. She tells the story to herself as much as she does to Paul D:

> Simple: she was squatting in the garden and when she saw them coming and recognized schoolteacher's hat, she heard wings. Little hummingbirds struck their needle beaks right through her headcloth into her hair and beat their wings. And if she thought anything, it was No. No Nono. Nonono. Simple. She just flew. Collected every bit of life she had made, all parts of her that were precious and fine and beautiful, and carried, pushed, dragged them. Over there. Outside this place, where they could be safe. And the hummingbird wings beat on. (*B* 163)

In this refusal to answer yes to the demand for her return, implicit in the appearance of Schoolteacher's hat alone, Sethe is beyond all help and left to her own resources. Given that she has been rendered part human, part animal by Schoolteacher's lesson, her running into the barn might seem to be an overdetermined dead end of acceptance. Yet it is the only immediate shelter. Like the law, it is already mapped into a landscape dominated by slavery's reach and slavery's seeming ability to make meaning of all things for those called slaves. A barn is not a barn. It is a dead end. And in slaving's discourse, a being seen as having "animal attributes" will behave like an animal. This is why Paul D's accusation that she behaved like an animal when she killed her child is both salutary and troubling. He might seek to disrupt the automatic reach of slavery's bestializing discourse, but that is because he is still fearful of it himself—he is, after all, employed in a slaughterhouse, where he presumably asserts on a daily basis the difference between animals and people. What he does not understand is that her flight into the shed underscores the boundaries of the spaces that are permitted her and her acceptance of the burden of responsibility for "every bit of life she had made." This responsibility forces her into the "selfish pleasure" of refusal: "I couldn't let all that go back to where it was, and I couldn't let her nor any of em alive under Schoolteacher. That was out" (*B* 163). As Marcel Mauss suggests, refusal is the only moment of empowerment for one who is indebted in a gift economy. But Morrison is here also concerned to make clear that, in a world where sovereignty is the prerogative of the propertied, every gesture of sovereignty is inevitably both self-assertion and the assertion of selfishness. Within a commodified world, individual personhood is constantly severed from its historical imbrications with others. Sethe refuses to be indebted to the past that seeks to violate her, and that refusal calls African American historical consciousness radically into question. It asks: What is owed to the past? Is memory repayment? Is one responsible for that repayment in the form of memory or, as Morrison terms it, "re-memory"? Or is one responsible for surviving the past?

Sethe's acceptance of her responsibility for her own past takes the form of a knowing that she moves into by degrees, beginning with her actions in the barn and then her remembrance and speaking with Paul D. For the killing of the baby in the barn and the attempt to kill her other children, she submits to being a murderer in the eyes of the law and her community. She does this in order to give the gift of freedom. That is, she ultimately obeys the law of the gift as it has been transformed by economy, which is to say, as debt in exchange; acknowledging debt, she agrees to repay it. The freedom that she gives, however, is enabled precisely by her prior refusal. This freedom is an escape from the corrupted time in which their future would be stolen from them by consignment to the eternal present of slavery's hellish excess. In this excess they can be only body. And so, Sethe literally sends the baby "Outside this place."

Challenged by Paul D, who voices the community's disapproval, her rejoinder remains simple: "I should have gone back there? Taken my babies back there?" Yet for Paul D and the community her violence remains both excessive and illegible. It crosses the threshold of acceptability. The law as norm is also, as Foucault has taught us, the law of intelligibility. While Sethe's narrative of the event reiterates her refusal to have the past overtake her and swallow up the future for her children, Paul D's resistance to her account expresses a wish for a reversal of time. His resistance is a desire for a scenario in which Sethe stepped out to confront the slave catchers, stalling them with her appearance, while, perhaps magically, perhaps through the help of others, her children were spirited away. Paul D is reminded and does not want to know how voracious Sweet Home's appetite was. The Fugitive Slave Act would have permitted the slavers to continue their pursuit of that which they considered their property, and the children's escape and survival would have depended upon community assistance that was withheld at the time.

Growing in the period just prior to and during Reconstruction, the Bluestone community too is caught in a time out of joint. The chaos of the violent past is still freshly with them, and the present is too close to this past for it to be anything but unstable. The future is unclear. Denise Heinze describes the existential terror behind the elation of Emancipation.[30] Faced with the task of reconstructing an ability to form social units outside the imposed relationships of slavery and having to negotiate a relationship with a world not shaped by the time and order of slavery, freed slaves were faced with the unregimented, unregulated material and emotional reality of freedom, of co-presence without community, and freedom without imaginations prepared for the task—a slightly problematic presumption on Heinze's part if generalized, and if one overlooks the reality that slaves clearly imagined freedom, pursued it, and made their own worlds out of stolen freedom, whether as politically effective as a Douglass or Truth, or as politically ordinary as those who simply slipped over into a mundane, workday freedom. In addition, they were faced with the backlash of slavers who perceived themselves robbed of "property." Paul D remembers the freed slaves as "stunned." His description partakes of a post-apocalyptic vision in the most common usage of the term.[31] Freed slaves are so "tired and bereft" that they suffer amnesia, live in caves, compete with animals for food or, in extreme cases, like the woman jailed and hanged for stealing ducks, mistake these animals for their children (*B* 66). Heinze cites this scene to support her argument that Emancipation meant a "total loss of the civilized society of which [black people] were adjunct."[32] It can be argued that the community of Bluestone perceives itself at risk of sliding backward toward the control of the "civilized" people of the dominant white society. In a manner that will be more fully developed and thematized in *Paradise*, they therefore impose their own strict rules against all excesses, all hungers caused by deprivation and the sight of plenitude just a way down the road in the city that has everything. In their attempt to secure time in the present and to make sense of their freedom, Sethe's actions are excessive. But it was not always thus.

When she was a young, untutored woman, her arrival in the community was marked by increasing joy and a potentially excessive emotion for which a space had been set aside—the Clearing, to which the community went for the sermons of Baby Suggs. Beyond this space, excess would reveal what came to be feared at this point in the community's time—namely, the orgiastic, and its perception as not only further chaos but potential excuse for white intervention and the reinstatement of overt white control over the community's lives. It is therefore the community's narrative of excess and criminality that has dominated the surrounds of Bluestone. Sethe's story may be present to herself when she is able to tell it to Paul D, yet she has been removed from her place in her own community, the Bluestone community, by the intervention of slavery and thus drawn back into participation in a pattern of disruptions designed to break families, friendships, and other relationships between slaves. Having given the gift of freedom through death, a gift in which the recipient is the victim, she inhabits a paradoxical atemporality. The baby ghost and all around her are drawn into this state. The baby ghost dictates it and makes it a constant sign of the past, whose simultaneity with the present is out of balance. The novel itself is revealed as a space of temporal fluidity. All stories or moments inhabit the same plane. Paul D's arrival is juxtaposed with Sethe's reminiscences of Sweet Home and the dead Baby Suggs's living memories of arriving at Bluestone. Baby Suggs is always arriving, as is Sethe; Denver is always being born; Stamp Paid is always bringing mother and child across the river.

The inherent instability of the world into which Baby Suggs is delivered by her son's sacrifice and into which Sethe delivers herself and her children is visible in signs all around them, but it is drawn most clearly in Stamp Paid's list of contemporary troubles. He intones these after discovering a scrap of scalp, tied with a ribbon, in the river across which he ferries escaping slaves:

> Eighteen seventy-four and whitefolks were still on the loose. Whole towns wiped clean of Negroes; eighty-seven lynchings in one year alone in Kentucky; four colored schools burned to the ground; grown men whipped like children; children whipped like adults; black women raped by the crew; property taken, necks broken. He smelled skin, skin and hot blood. The skin was one thing, but human blood cooked in a lynch fire was a whole other thing. The stench stank. Stank up off the pages of the *North Star*, out of the mouths of witnesses, etched in crooked handwriting in letters delivered by hand. Detailed in documents and petitions full of *whereas* and presented to any legal body who'd read it, it stand. But none of that had worn out his marrow. None of that. It was the ribbon. (*B* 180)

Disorder and distress surround the death of Baby Suggs. The community's spiritual leader until Sethe's actions, Baby Suggs withdraws from the world to "fix on something harmless in this world" until her death

(*B* 179). The consequences of Baby Suggs's absence are considerable. As a spiritual leader she has audited and guided the psychological and spiritual clearing of her community's psychic distress. Once she is removed, the community's spiritual needs are unministered, and excessive "pride, fear, condemnation and spite" dance where she had "devoted her freed life to harmony" (*B* 171). Her demise signals the entry of the untimely and chaotic into her unprotected community, since it is shortly after this that a series of events occur in which a number of temporalities converge.

Paul D's arrival coincides with the season's change and a carnival in whose charmed space prescribed order and rules are inverted, while taboos are relaxed. It is a device of inversion and, in Bakhtinian terms, the triumph of the grotesque.[33] The change of season, heralded by dying old roses, marks a threshold period. In the trope of passage from birth to death to birth, it is a time of great vulnerability and change. The unexpected abundance of the old roses signals unusual times within the normal seasonal shift. The roses, planted as a propitiatory gesture by the sawyer "to take the sin out of slicing trees for a living," seem to crawl, like the murdered baby, "all over the stake-and-post fence that separated the lumberyard from the open field" in which disorder reigns in the form of the homeless, unchecked children and the annual carnival (*B* 47). Boundaries between order and chaos, life and death, are being transgressed. Death and a resistance to the ordered cycle from life into death are signaled by further references to the roses: "The closer the roses got to death, the louder their scent" (*B* 47). Everyone who attends the carnival associates it with the stench of rotten roses.

Uncannily evoking the rose of Isaiah's promised land, the rotting bizarreness of the flowers foreshadows the strange disorder of the carnival, where social order will be reversed, but only in the manner of a death that is not a death (for the order will be returned). The rot is inextricable from the carnival, where the imposed order governing the lives of Sethe's community is overturned as white people serve black people: "Denver bought horehound, licorice, peppermint and lemonade at a table manned by a little whitegirl in ladies' high-topped shoes" (*B* 48). This is the land of the "Big Rock Candy Mountain" in which excess abounds. Bodily time is confused as children play at being adults, and social time is equally disrupted as white people, normally the leisured class, play at being slaves. "Freakish" racist epithets for black people are cast at whites, as they fall under a counter-gaze that fixes them, making, therefore, a spectacle out of that which had previously organized the spectacle with its gaze:

> Breathless with the excitement of seeing white people loose . . . without heads or with two heads, twenty feet tall or two feet tall, weighing a ton, completely tattooed, eating glass, swallowing fire, spitting ribbons, twisted into knots, forming pyramids, playing with snakes and beating each other up. (B 48)

The strangeness of carnival is earthly, however, and not nearly as uncanny as the life that Sethe inhabits or the house at 124 Bluestone. In any case, here, as everywhere, the carnivalesque is a momentary respite in the continuing narrative of inequality. Its false catharsis functions more like an escape hatch or pressure release for the guilty accumulations of slaving's excesses than the opening of a radical possibility in which the equality of all, rather than inversion of hierarchy, is contemplated. Indeed, the carnival displaces and banalizes through its theatricalization the absurdity of the lived order.

Two main strands of thought have engaged inversion and reversal of the sort depicted in *Beloved*. One is the structural functionalist analysis of anthropologist Victor Turner, who understands liminality to be antistructural.[34] The other is the materialist analysis of linguist Mikhail Bakhtin, who conceives of it in terms of the carnivalesque and in the idiom of play and transgression.[35] Both recognize occasions where social norms are suspended and the usual principles of boundary maintenance are put aside. In these states, hierarchies are reversed and power is humbled. Both Turner and Bakhtin consider what happens within these spaces of excess, especially when they cannot be contained. Turner calls them "liminal" and argues that they make possible the imaginative recombination of signifying elements within the social field. Bakhtin's concern with ribald excess concentrates on the corporeal transgressions within the carnivalesque, particularly in the work of artists like Rabelais. At the time of Morrison's writing of *Beloved*, these two theoretical traditions were being reinflected and brought together in the widely read work of Peter Stallybrass and Allon White, but Bakhtin's concern with transgression dominated and was read as opening the possibilities for resistance.[36]

In *Beloved*, the carnival opens on those moments of inversion in which social norms are suspended. More than a moment of resistance, it makes a space for understanding the absurdity of the lived order. The most potent evidence of this, and of the instability inherent in it, is the hiccup in the number 124 itself. When broken from its compound structure as one-hundred-and-twenty-four into a sequence, it embodies disruption. Just outside the city in which the Bodwins live and which has "Everything you ever dreamed of," the place to which Sethe comes embodies sequential disruption through the missing "3" in 1-2-?-4. This is a space of liminality, of "betwixt and betweenness," as Victor Turner calls it.[37] But where Turner's notion of liminality is transitional, a momentary disturbance on the path to structural resolution and hierarchical reintegration, the emblematic interrupted sequence of Sethe's address has no such relation to a future fullness. It merely signifies rupture, openness, leakage, and the impossibility of maintaining boundaries. One of those boundaries is that between the living and the dead—which is the boundary most essential to any cultural order.

Into 124's liminality comes a figure who exposes the nightmare in which the living and the dead "live" in a collapsed time, where the past of the dead takes its place in the present of the living and makes the future one of only the living (and the) dead. This is the figure for whom the book is named, "Beloved," the uncanny trace of an encounter so traumatic that it was not fully apprehended in the moment of its occurrence and remains mysterious even afterward, in the repetitions of a narrative marked by partiality.[38] The "baby ghost" that comes to haunt 124 takes the place of Sethe's "crawling already" baby, and its existence is marked by the temporal and spatial miscegenation of the moment of its birth. The "baby ghost" is the past and present, the "here" and "there." All time merges in the stalled present, which is signified by the present tense participle, "crawling." Born in the moment of temporal disruption where the past comes in through the medium of the law that dictates her future, the baby ghost embodies this disruption, repeats it, just as the disruption itself embodies an earlier disruption in the constant repetition of the eschatalogical catastrophe of slavery. This coming into being of "the" Beloved is, then, the coming back of the past. As Derrida writes in *Specters of Marx*, "what seems to be out front, the future, comes back in advance from the past, from the back."[39] This is the sleight of hand of an apocalyptic utterance, which writes of something to come or makes something *appear* to be coming, to *be* the future, when it has already been. It is apocalypticism's gluttony, as the woman who claims the name Beloved will demonstrate.

Impossible Futures?

The movement of the past as the future is the kind of rhetorical gesture that makes space for notions of repetition, such as "The Second Coming." For Derrida, repetition is inseparable from notions of a "first," but it is also bound up with last things "since the singularity of any *first time* makes of it also a *last time*" in the discourse of apocalypse.[40] In *Beloved*, the reappearance of the past catastrophe as a spectral young woman is also a reconfiguration of the future, coming from behind. In a Benjaminian sense, she is the angel of history, albeit an unexpected, black female angel, caught in the storm of progress that drew so heavily upon slavery and that, in turn, was caught up in and generated further progress. In this storm, she is eternally displaced from the past in what Benjamin has described as "one single catastrophe that keeps piling wreckage upon wreckage."[41] Where this wreckage is piled up at the feet of Benjamin's "angel of history," however, Morrison has the wreckage pile up at the feet of Sethe, Denver, Paul D, and other members of the Bluestone community as their own lives. They are, in effect, the wreckage of slavery as they arrive and are literally "piled" up on the fringe of the city—a thematic more fully developed in *Jazz*. Moreover, as the embodiment of that history of catastrophic repetition, Beloved is the conglomerate arrival of their many histories. She also arrives from the dead (and Benjamin's angel could be mistaken for death, with "His eyes . . . staring, his mouth . . . open, his wings . . . spread").[42] Where Benjamin's angel stares back toward the past, Morrison's Beloved walks out of the river, wearing a white dress in place of wings— she is dressed for the present, her eyes fixed on what is ahead. Overtaken by catastrophe, she is now the catastrophe that can only overtake. Displaced forever from the past, she can find and make her home only in the present and its future. Her presence *is* the apocalyptic embedded within the narrative that *is* the narrative of the headstone, if not the headstone itself. It is the marker or signifier of an ending, yet the beginning of the story of that ending, a beginning and story compressed into an epitaph and requiring explosion or opening, as her body will by the novel's end. And so the book *Beloved* itself performs the entire preordained past of the figure Beloved, who is, in turn, required to fulfill its prediction. She is the presence invoked but covered by the headstone as book.

The figure of Beloved—or the specter believed to be Beloved–is a potent embodiment of Morrison's argument that an apocalypse, in its most cataclysmic mode, has taken place. For Sethe and her family, what is supposed to come to pass–the future, in whatever form–is not coming anymore, except as a haunting, because it has *come* to pass, it has taken *place*. Emphatically, the phantasm of the once-dead, once-murdered child seeks a place. If, as Marilyn Ivy points out, "the phantasm is understood as an epistemological object whose presence or absence cannot be definitively located,"[43] Beloved is a phantasm and not merely a ghost. Dis-located, the past attempts to relocate to the present and thus enter the future.

The future will not be entered in *Beloved*, however. That dreamy possibility must wait for Morrison's later novel, *Jazz*, in which two characters named as the residue of both the previous fiction and the fact of the past arrive in New York. When Joe and Violet Trace leave the South, they ride high, traveling in the "colored section of the Southern Sky," on a journey in the above-ground railroad that parallels the historical northward flight out of slavery via the Underground Railroad. En route, they cross the water of symbolic proverb, and as they do, time and space converge in a rupture of more positively sublime proportions. They and the sky become one: "the train trembled approaching the water surrounding the City . . . like them: nervous at having gotten there at last, but terrified of what was on the other side" (*J* 30). Through the Traces, the South enters the North, as does their dream of a future. The city appears to be the space in which the dream comes true, yet they learn that it is not. It is a place in which their dream will be stalled by the waiting segregation between uptown and downtown.

Perhaps this is why the Southern sky prevails in this novel. Although the "people down there in the shadow are happy" that history is over, the sky is "unbelievable" (*J* 7, 35), the surface upon which the dream of a future can still display itself or be projected. It does so above the earthly city, whose carnality is slowly revealed in mundane events and quotidian experience despite the excitement that makes so many "feel more like themselves" (*J* 35). The sky's spectacular performance is linked to the earthly city's time. The earthly city attracts and distracts so that dreaming is deferred. It is the city's time that the Traces read as filled with multitudinous possibilities and that makes the narrator delirious. "I'm crazy about this City," she says. Although "Below is shadow where any blasé thing takes place," (*J* 7) New York is the architectural realization of a fantasy of modernity whose mantra is: "Here comes the new. Look out. There goes the sad stuff. The bad stuff. The things nobody-could-help stuff" (*J* 37).

The Traces' crossover into the new space and order of the city nonetheless requires a psychic transformation. The Traces are "read" as signs of a past and, as such, are subjected to a violent makeover. Someone dies. Joe Trace shoots his young lover, and something in him and in Violet dies as well. Murder displaces the fact of a crisis of memory for Joe and Violet. On one hand, successful integration into the new order asks for amnesia. The narrator states the rule of entry that is perhaps the motto of apocalyptics: "Forget that" (*J* 7). It is only in forgetting that Joe and Violet can "take place" in the present of the modern. Initially, they see in this forgetfulness a liberatory possibility, although later they will be haunted by that very embrace of forgetting. "History is over," says the narrator, and with this statement comes, not the promise of the negative finality of an eschaton, but the possibility that "everything's ahead at last." And all revel in this apocalyptic transcendence of an episteme. Yet Joe and Violet struggle to cling to the traces of who they were.

As with all of Morrison's novels, nothing is as simple as it first seems, and everything is haunted by ambiguity. Even the seeming gravitas of *Home*'s title is unsettled by that novel's close when Cee says to Frank, "Let's go home" (*H* 147). The invitation suggests that there is a "there" to go to, yet it is in the future, still a dream, despite the sense of arrival (as in *Jazz*) or return (as in *Home*). In *Paradise*, that ambiguity afflicts historical consciousness and the narratives of origins as much or more than anything else. In *Jazz*, the phrase "everything's ahead at last" keeps the trace of the past in the utterance "at last." Something has come before, and this something is always necessary, even as a trace, in order for the present-future to know itself as such, distinguishable from what has been left behind. The implication is even more ambiguous still. If everything is ahead, there is nothing behind. If nothing is behind, there can be nothing ahead, since nothing comes from nothing. In this head-spinning series of implications, the narrator herself goes crazy, is "crazy about this City." The real and the phantasmatic become indistinguishable and in a moment reminiscent of Eliot's *The Waste Land*, "Daylight slants like a razor cutting the buildings in half," as the narrator sees faces impossible to tell apart from the stonework.

The people who inhabit this city have been carved into it on the architect's blueprints, or in the imaginations of artisans. Or they are ghosts that haunt the architects and artisans and drive them to plan and execute cities. In this space where reality and imagination coincide, dreams are "tall," but vision penetrates even the shadow, taking its strength from the sheer extravagance of the buildings that rise above the ground-level past. The city makes craziness and other dreams enter here as well—under the grandly performative sky, sheered off from reality like the image-riven movie screen in which the city has become the space of dream. Its dreams are not all freeing, however. Some are nightmarish, none more so than the promise of elevation that first seduces Joe and Violet and then abandons them. Joe and Violet have entered the amnesia of the future willingly, but they have not recognized that utopia is bought at a price, one that has been determined above them, in the "halls and offices" where "people are sitting around thinking future thoughts about projects and bridges and fast-clicking trains underneath" (*J* 7).

It is in the halls and offices, perhaps, that dreams have always taken place, and it is for this reason that their authors have imagined such magnificent alternatives. Columbus's Enterprise of the Indies belongs as much in the market or the merchant's office as it does in the sacred space of the sacred text from which he claims his authority. Writing to Prince John in 1500, Columbus claims to have been guided to his discovery of the New World by two of Christianity's most powerful prophetic voices, the writer of Revelation and the prophet Isaiah: "God made me the messenger of the New Heaven and the New Earth of which he spoke through St. John in the Apocalypse, after having spoken of it through Isaiah; and He showed me to that location."[44] That "location" is the land at which he eventually arrives from across the Atlantic Ocean.

In his self-representation as a messenger trumpeting the vision of a "New World," Columbus claims to be merely the vehicle of a divine plan. In practice he is deploying an apocalypticist's hermeneutic skill, which masks as much as it claims to reveal. The full quotation to which Columbus alludes is: "For, behold, I create new heavens and a new earth: and the former shall not be remembered, nor come into mind" (Isaiah 65:17). Columbus's silence about God's full promise evades its implications for the Europe from which he sails. But silence is not the only tool in this evasion. He reasserts Europe's relevance by claiming that its textual traditions guide and authorize his journey. This both enables him to assume the role of interpreter and authorizes his role as agent. He achieves this through a display of virtuoso reading, which in itself is a performance of knowledge—the apocalypticist knows, and therefore knows how to access, the correct and unchallengeable authority of textual tradition.[45] In a later letter to the Spanish monarchs, Columbus assuages any fears they may have of impending marginality by confirming the centrality of biblical literary tradition for his voyages. He asserts in the grammar of future anteriority that "for the execution of the enterprise of the Indies neither reason nor mathematics nor map serve me, plainly Isaiah's prophecy was fulfilled."[46]

Columbus read other literary traditions through the lens of prophecy. Earlier, in 1481, he wrote four postilles in the margin of Piccolomini's *Historia rerum ubique gestarum*.[47] The first postille is titled "Auctoritates in brevia"— "Summary of Authorities"—and quotes Isaiah, II Chronicles (9:21), and Psalm 73 ([74]:12), followed by Columbus's own brief comments. The combined themes of the postilles comprise a narrative of sea voyages, King Solomon's ideal shipping fleets, remote locations or "islands of the sea," and a promised land that waits for the word of God, and where gold is the reward for the intrepid, God-delivering voyager. The second postille refers to Augustine's *City of God*. Columbus lists the canonical Hebrew prophets of post-Babylonian Judaism; these are said to have predicted Christ and the formation of the Christian Church. They also refer to the acquisition of gold by Solomon's fleet. The third postille quotes the first-century Roman-Jewish historian Titus Flavius Josephus on the shipbuilding technology of King Solomon's rule. In the fourth postille, Columbus attempts to calculate the arrival of the Golden Age by charting the generations of Adam.

His utopian dreams reflected the spirit of his time. Marjorie Reeves has documented the psychological state of fifteenth-century southern Europeans, particularly in Florence, Rome, Milan, Siena, and Genoa, in which Columbus moved as a boy and young man.[48] Christian Europe faced a crisis after the fall Constantinople to Sultan Muhammed II in 1453. For European Christians, this was the loss of a holy land. The crisis coincided with a radical shift from traditional apocalyptic belief, represented by Augustine, to the ideas of the late-twelfth-century Calabrian abbot Joachim de Fiore. Augustine had calculated that the Golden Age would come after the time of trouble spoken of in Daniel 12:1. De Fiore preached a different message. Just as apocalyptic as his forebears and contemporaries, his calculations differed in a key way: he predicted that the advent of the Golden Age would occur *before* the eschaton. Thus, crucially, it would occur within history. For soon-to-be-subjugated peoples, the most devastating aspect of Joachim's vision was that it inspired beliefs in worldly global kingdoms.[49] By the end of the fifteenth century, messianism had reached peak levels in Spain. At a time when rulers were vying with each other to be the Messiah-Emperor of the world, Columbus frequently signed himself *Xpo ferens*, or "Christ-bearer," and he is referred to as such by Bartolomeo de las Casas, who documented the atrocities inflicted by the Spanish conquerors and settlers.[50]

Columbus's readings blur and conflate cause and effect. Without him there would be no messenger to whom the divine word could make sense and reveal the route to the new heaven and new earth, and without the texts there could be no new heaven and new earth. This logic affirms the durability of biblical topoi and tropes. The ideal, this-worldly place becomes epistemologically available through the texts, and because of these texts European imperialists could commit themselves to building the place. The texts were both incitement to and evidence of an existence not yet encountered. The new heavens and new earth that Columbus envisioned were places of a wealth that could be shipped back to the "old" earth. In the infinite regression of Columbus's circular logics, he found authority for his actions in the literary tradition that he inhabited. Therefore, reaching what he believed was his destination, he found the "fresh lands" and "delightful groves" he so desired. Las Casas records this in his account.[51]

This tradition of textual validation of action was shared by the early settlers of Virginia Plantation. It also informed Puritan efforts to establish a New Jerusalem, free and far away from the corrupted time of the old world—as Rebekka Vaark so hoped, although she was not a Puritan. Biblically inspired pastoral and paradisiacal tropes can be glimpsed, for example, behind Captain John Smith's persuasive accounts of the Virginia colony. He depicts a voluptuous, almost sentient natural world awaiting English settlers and describes the coast's bays as harbors with the capacity to anchor between five hundred and five thousand ships. He writes of "divers sorts of woods" and the possibilities of planting vines, fruits, herbs, fields, gardens, and orchards, and of building houses, ships, "and other works."[52] Sovereignty and gain are not merely subtexts. Settlers will be able to "recreate themselves before their owne doors, in their owne boats upon the Sea; where man, woman and childe, with a small hooke and line, by angling, may take diverse sorts of excellent fish, at their pleasure." Natural abundance will produce pleasure, and both are bound up in a nexus of social and economic opportunity. Such is the extraordinary plenitude of this place that servants, masters, and merchants will all have the same opportunities for wealth:

> He is a very bad fisher [that] cannot kill in one day with his hooke and line, one, two, or three hundred Cods: which dressed and dried, if they be sould there for ten shillings the hundred, though in England they will give more than twentie, may not both the servant, the master and marchant, bet well content with this gaine? If a man worke but three dayes in seaven, he may get more then hee can spend, unlesse he will be excessive. Now that Carpenter, Mason, Gardiner, Taylor, Smith, Sailer, Forgers, or what other, may they not take more than they ate in a weeke? or if they will not eate it, because there is so much better choice; yet sell it, or change it, with the fisher men, or marchants, for any thing they want.[53]

A Mercy rehearses this brute economic truth in both Vaark and D'Ortega's profiteering, and *Jazz* exposes the actuality of a deep interpenetration of spaces that were imagined to be different only as the condition of possibility for the one negating the other. And, as I suggested in Chapter 1, the narrative of *Jazz* ends up being one of compromise as much as of plenitude and liberation. That compromise was spatialized in a segregation that meant "any blasé thing could happen" only within the limits of Harlem. It is an ironic fact that Georg Simmel defines "the blasé attitude" as the quintessence of modernity, linking it as a survival device to the manic pace and sensory overload of an urbanity that can be survived only through the practice of indifference.[54] Marx suggests that capitalism mistakes indifference for individualism,[55] but Simmel means something else. He means to invoke something not unlike what Benjamin, reading Baudelaire's "flaneur," describes as the relation to the *passante*, the one who passes.[56] In Harlem, "passing" is a complex trope, and it is not coincidental that this scene of *Jazz*, where anything can "come to pass," takes place there. The more immediate referent, of course, is the possibility stripped of surprise that characterizes the commodified landscape and its desiring consumers. *Jazz* is ultimately a story of all that comes to pass in Harlem.

Indeed, in *Jazz*, sacred text and sacred space are shown to have been built on the mercantilism of the New World, New York, the new Harlem. This is the madness of the vision revealed: that heaven does not descend but rests upon the earth, and that the view from below is not of gold. It was, after all, the same lunacy that named the plantation Sweet Home, and the same delirium that planted a tree on the back of a woman whom it had made over as the slate for power's script—"made over," because of the violent injunction in this refashioning. It was, suggests Morrison, this very fantasy of a dream "taking place" that made slavery possible and brutality its unnecessary angel.

4. Beginnings and Endings, Part One: Old Languages / New Bodies

In the early pages of *Jazz*, Joe Trace utters these words: "you could say, 'I was scared to death,' but you could not retrieve the fear" (*J* 29). Any scene, no matter how intense, can be replayed, but insofar as it is replayed in narrative, his earlier experiences make him afraid that all memories will remain, for him, "drained of everything but the language to say it in." He tells himself that this fear, of feeling's dissipation or absence and the desire to recover or perpetuate it, is why he shot his young lover, Dorcas. It was "just to keep the feeling going" (*J* 3). It is a remarkable passage, distilling within itself the belatedness and the affectively reduced status of narrative vis-à-vis the event that it recounts, but also the longing toward emotional plenitude that compels such narrative. In a gesture typical of her maturing prose, Morrison stages for us the problem of the relation between event and discourse, and through it the question of how narrative and language, more generally, function in the always compromised and nonetheless necessary project of representation—whether historical or personal. Although the question of race remains central to that interrogation, it does not exhaust the problematic as Morrison conceives it.

In the play of simile, metaphor, and nomination, a play that becomes visible across several different texts, Morrison undertakes a more general exploration of how language compels action despite an ineradicable gap between actuality and its representation. In this gap, the demand for representation grows, and is filled by competing traditions, many of which aspire to cover over that gap and to claim totality. Indeed, this very process of claiming totality is what Laclau calls ideology, and Morrison's most recent fiction, most notably *A Mercy*, is concerned with the establishment of ideological dominance or hegemony in a space that I shall call, following Mary Louise Pratt, the "contact zone." I mean by this both a temporal and spatial location prior to the entrenchment of the plantation economy and the acceleration of the Atlantic slave trade, when competing imperialisms, economic migrants, slaves, indentured European laborers, indigenous people, and religious exiles were vying to make the landscape of the new world legible in terms that claimed continuity with their prior *Weltanschauung.*

Morrison's fiction has always been concerned with the force of tradition, including both white and black patriarchal traditions, in the lives of her characters. This is staged, at least partly through the re-iteration of different similes, metaphors, and names within but also across different novels. References to the Pauline legacy in colonial Christianity, for example, recur in the names of characters such as Pauline Breedlove and Paul D, and through the overt citations of Romans and I and II Corinthians. There are many other recurrent terms, of course. The figure of the house as a metaphor for racial discourse is present in *The Bluest Eye* and again in *Beloved* and in *Love*, where Bill Cosey's wife and daughter, once friends and now old women, are in a bitter struggle to own what has never been a real house but a hotel that once housed all of their aspirations. The metonymy that permits the Oven to signify both sacrifice and covenant is at the heart of both *Paradise* and *Love*. The examples are legion. But what work is performed by the recurrence of such figures?

In any tradition, a question arises as to what ensures the continuing relevance of older knowledge, idioms, similes, and metaphoricities to a changing present. What authorizes them and enforces their persisting use? For Morrison, this question has a doubled aspect. In response, her fiction examines the forms of resemblance, or what we might term the discursive conditions of intelligibility, that enable the comparison of one moment with another, such that the language of an earlier period can continue to function in a later one, and with it the presumptions about how social life ought to be ordered. For the assumptions of any tradition to retain their force, resemblance must be perceived across time and between environments. This is powerfully staged in the genre of apocalypticism, taken up in Chapter 3, which is premised upon the idea of an absolute identity between past and future, to be effected when the gap between word and thing is completely overcome. As discussed in Chapter 3, the Christological tradition that informed Columbus's American fantasy was saturated with apocalypticism and other forms of prophecy. In this chapter, I pursue the matter further by considering the relationship between apocalyptic discourse and the ordinary, even banal forms of similitude that lie at the heart of everyday life and burden the lives of all who would seek change—as Morrison urges us to do.

Increasingly, in her later fiction Morrison has become concerned with the disjuncture between past and present, and the violence that is necessary to claim continuity on the basis of resemblances that are not all recognized or granted by different characters. In novels like *Song of Solomon* and *Paradise*, gender is a condition that sharply inflects the perception of relations between moments, and leads to a certain estrangement from the taken-for-granted similitudes by which tradition operates. And, of course, patriarchal figures often respond in her novels by clinging vehemently to the former sources of their power by effacing what time and history have transformed. By insisting on perfect similitude, which is to say, identity of past and present, they make claims for the continued legitimacy of the traditional discourse within which their power is legitimated. As will be seen in Chapter 5, *A Mercy* extends Morrison's exploration of these issues by turning to an apparently originary time in order to imagine how difficult it must have been to inhabit a time before the language of one world (the colonizer's world) had been inscribed onto the New World, when the resemblances between the colonizers' new heaven and the new earth were only shakily conjured, and when the labor to discern continuities between prophecy and history required the violent expulsion of difference, the silencing of women's voices, and the destruction of indigenous life worlds from which alternative idioms, similes, metaphors, and worldviews might have been learned by the abducted and forcibly landed migrants who would soon staff the plantations and underwrite the birth of America.

In the pages that follow, I consider the politics and the poetics of similitude in Morrison's fiction. To do so, I commence with a treatment of the idea of simile itself, move on to a discussion of naming in *Paradise* and *Tar Baby*, and conclude with a treatment of the conflict of signs in *A Mercy*. In *Paradise*, the politics of naming as insult both derives its power from and confirms the iterability of sacred texts when these are read as the literal model for the readers' own circumstances. The names chosen by eight men of Ruby for the women in the Convent announce and justify the action they will take, revealing the force of naming not only for the one named (the usual limits of theories of the performative) but for the ones who name. In this case, the names will determine the action of the men, calling them to murderousness . . . or so it will seem until the novel's end.

In *Tar Baby*, the island paradise of Isle des Chevaliers would appear to be far from the lives and worlds that the protagonists have left behind and might suggest that they see each other differently from how they once did. Instead, to the material possessions that they have brought to ease their way into the new world are added the old "comforts of home" that maintain class and racial boundaries, namely, the fixed and frozen lexicons of their prior lives. The thought experiment that was the Isle des Chevaliers is taken further in *A Mercy* and relocated at the ur-moment of America itself—when Europeans were first settling on the eastern shores of New England, displaced of their own accord or forced into indenture, and displacing American Indian nations with people they had brought from Africa. In the cacophony of competing traditions, the demand for a new language and a new episteme was answered by the drive to make of money a lingua franca and of nature a "standing reserve."[1] In this process, of course, people of color would be required to learn the language of new masters (themselves competing for supremacy), but it would function for them only as a structure of command, ensuring that the task of decolonization, like the task of literature, would be to resignify the world that race built. The discussion of *A Mercy* must wait until Chapter 5. Here I focus on the texts that precede it.

The Likeness of Things

I begin this discussion of similitude with its most overt literary form, namely, the simile. At a very basic level, of course, a simile performs a comparison of at least one thing with another. In poetry, it often appears to be an embellishment or an ornament. At worst it is superficially decorative but unsubstantial. If on occasion its excessiveness seems to call the reader to reflect upon the materality of poetic language, it is also frequently felt to be that which is dispensable, inessential. However, I want to argue that it performs a more complex translational role, at the boundary between the unknown and the comprehensible, often using the kind of displacement mechanism that Freud identifies as the secondary part or process of the dream interpretation. One might say that the dream and the simile share the same source material, drawing upon an individual's experience, but only if one recognizes that such experience (save in the event of trauma) is itself already translated, already subject to frames of interpretation. In neither case are we speaking of translating immediacy. Rather, the translations performed by simile, as by dreams, should be understood as rendering anew a representation that has become utterly habitual because the interpretive frames have been naturalized.

The dream's material draws upon and re-presents this mediated experience, but the connection between its content and waking reality is obscure and, for Freud, proves most elusive when a subject attempts to put the images and sensations of the dream into language or to explain the sequence of such images as part of a coherent, temporally linear narrative. This is because these images have themselves been produced through processes of concretization—what Freud describes as condensation and displacement— and their status as dream image marks the point of their extrusion from narrativity. The difference between a dream and simile is that, whereas a dream deploys metaphor and metonymy, it arises in the domain of the inexplicable, where the phenomena to be grasped through similitude of one sort or another appear materially present but resistant to representation, or exceeding it. The dream has to be explained because it "hides" its meaning, according to Freud. Whether in more formally poetic discourse or in the naturalized forms of language that occur in everyday conversation, a simile strives for lucidity and comprehension of one thing via another. The substitution marks the point of the original representation's apparent failure to convey the truth or significance of that object. It is, one might argue, an attempt at wakeful connection, and as such, it is the "sign" of the wakeful, thinking, interpreting mind, seeking a language through which to make sense—not through processes of reduction but rather through the proliferation of interpretive possibilities and the valorization of interpretation itself.[2] Where a metaphor presents the process of association as completed and anchored in a (magically produced) identity of attributes (one thing is stated in the assertive form to partake of the being of another), a simile keeps that process visible and holds open the instant in which that association is being made. The copular function, in other words, is staged, and the magical power of language to conjoin what is otherwise distinct is contained and restrained in the realm of visibility. The metaphor could be said to partake of the occult; the simile of the profane. Figuratively and typographically, the nearly invariably present tense in which a simile is expressed makes visible how one thing is being brought into the vicinity of another. The gap is not yet closed. Two things shimmer in relation to each other, one expanding the meaning of the other, but only by virtue of the reader's gaze. The power is not transferred to the words of the comparison.

It resides in the very gesture of "likening." And if two objects or qualities are made to approach each other, it is not in the realm of things but in the realm of language. Simile shares this linguistic nature with metaphor, but it knows itself to be speculative, imaginative, even an illusory substitute for the inadequacy of language in the face of the real, whereas metaphor asserts the truth of its identity and effaces the magic or the violence of the copula in the simple gesture of saying "it is," rather than the speculative "as if," which is what the simile enacts.[3]

A simile also functions in the realm of sensuous perception. It works by laying claim to the material. The gesture of comparison points to inadequacies in the primary designating or nominating term, and the proliferation of figures of resemblance, while being no more material in themselves, on the one hand accumulates specificity, while on the other asserting the impossibility of a one-to-one relationship between word and thing. In this way, simile is the other of the proper name, though both work, as Derrida has shown us, through forms of iterability.[4] Both play a salient role in Morrison's fiction, where, as Avery Gordon has shown, they are part of an insistent hauntology. In Morrison's project, the simile is the mark of a desire to capture in language what escapes it, to make present what is absent. It is an attempt to give the ghost the form of a name and thus put it to rest, as it were, but only by restoring the past. This is what Joe Trace, with whom I began this chapter, attempts. He is a man whose name announces his status as haunted and who seeks, so violently, to restore what is always receding from his affective horizon: "You could say, 'I was scared to death,' but you could not retrieve the fear" (*J* 29). The narration of an event is "drained of everything but the language to say it in." Joe's is an extreme case, a deadly one for young Dorcas. And perhaps all such refusals of language's limits must be deadly. His is a cautionary tale, told by one who has defined race as a house of language. If *A Mercy* tries to take readers back to a time before race mattered, before race became a determinant of slavery and slavery explicable in terms of race, as Morrison says, it is in order to see at what point the limitations of language per se become the limitations of one language and one discourse in particular.

The Politics of Insult: Jezebels and Eves, or Their Ends in Their Beginnings

A simile never works in one direction only. Nor is the relationship merely dyadic. The primary subject of a simile's comparison is not only linked to the second term, and thus made to partake through abstraction of the attributes that they share, but it also receives something from the context of the thing or state to which it is being compared. The logic appears to be one of contamination as much as enlargement or specification. Perhaps for that reason, Morrison takes pains to make the trope of contamination the vehicle for a more generalized staging of the problem of simile as contamination. She does this in order to show us something about language in general, but also to show us how that logic is frequently coded in gendered terms and in ways that rely upon Christian apocalypticism. This has special clarity in *Paradise*, in which the doomed women of the Convent are called Jezebels and bodacious Eves by the men of Ruby, prior to their massacre. These nominations exist in the same sphere as descriptions of the hot peppers that the women make under Connie's guidance, peppers hot as hell. They also call into play myriad other associations with the names *Jezebel* and *Eve*. To call a woman a Jezebel is, after all, to will her into a contest that she cannot survive. Morrison mines this history of naming to great effect.

It is not necessary to know the history of the name *Jezebel* to understand why it functions as it does, but some excavation of how it has come to function as it does will make visible the wishful telos of its semiological chain and its interplay with the name *Eve*. Given the deep intertextuality that links Morrison's fiction to biblical narrative, the specific associations of these names, which initially appear in *Paradise* as banal insults, is worth considering.

Jezebel appears in both books of Kings in the Old Testament and in Revelation in the New Testament. The rhetorical achievement of Revelation in naming another woman Jezebel reveals how a semiological chain enables more than naming, and how the iterability of a name enables forms both of recognition and of insertion into the waiting narratives of patriarchal ideology.

The Jezebel of Revelation is singled out and condemned for naming herself a prophetess, teaching and eating food sacrificed to idols (Revelation 2:20).[5] Her fate is clearly meant to serve as an example, particularly for other contesting prophetic voices at a time when church leaders were healing their own schisms, including the deep differences between Peter and Paul—the latter provides recurrent intertextual referents for Morrison.[6] Calling out the name *Jezebel* summons events in the Old Testament's books of Kings. This name, אִיזֶבֶל / אִיזָבֶל, is initially given to the Phoenician princess whom King Ahab marries (I Kings 16:31). She is blamed for converting him to the worship of Ba'al and, worse still, other gods, including the Canaanite fertility goddess Asherah. Yahweh's prophet Elijah takes her advent and Ahab's conversion as a direct affront. At stake is the primacy of his political position and the religion in which he grounds this primacy. Insults, accusations, contests, and murders ensue. Ahab's susceptibility to Jezebel is seen as a weakness. Her power over him is seen by Elijah and his successor, Elisha, as the contagious corruption of syncretism. For them, proof comes in two epitomizing events. The first is her exercise of power over Yahweh's prophets when she orders their expulsion and murder. The second comes in the form of a letter, written by her in Ahab's name to secure Naboth's vineyard through slander that results in the latter's death by stoning (I Kings 21: 8–16). For the murder of the prophets of Yahweh and the death of Naboth, Yahweh tells Elijah to predict that she, Ahab, and all their offspring will be destroyed (I Kings 21:21–24). Elijah sets this prediction in motion by calling into competition fifty priests of Ba'al and four hundred priests of Asherah, daring their gods to perform miracles. In the absence of miracles, Elijah orders the slaughter of these false prophets (I Kings 18:18–19). When Ahab dies and his son Ahaziah becomes king, Elijah's successor Elisha condemns him for his idolatry and appoints another: Jehu, son of the Judean king Jehoshaphat. At the prophet's instigation and relying on his assurance that Yahweh calls for this, Jehu kills Ahaziah. Elisha then calls for the murder of Jezebel, and Jehu promises that this will be done and that her body will be left to be eaten by dogs (I Kings 9:10). When Jehu arrives to kill her, she prepares herself by painting her eyes and arranging her hair (II Kings 9:30–33). At his instigation, her eunuchs throw her out of a window.

The eunuchs thereby join Jehu in their willingness to unify against the foreigner and her idolatrous ways. In so doing, they elevate the figure of this woman to the status of a necessary player in a drama of unification and the strengthening of faith. Through her, they all perform their allegiance to Yahweh and to the dominant prophets' teachings. One final factor will clinch the merit of their decision: Jehu recants his earlier call for her body to be left for dogs. She is a queen, after all, and as a king he is invested in the proper regard for a royal body, even that of Jezebel. All that remains for burial, however, are her skull, hands, and feet (II Kings 19:34). Jehu reads this retrospectively as the word of the Lord coming true, having been uttered through him earlier as utterance and action but having come to him through the words of Elijah. This confirms the veracity and hence iterability of Yahweh's prophets Elijah and Elisha. As if to drive this home, Jehu also predicts that her body will be "like refuse on the ground in the pot at Jezreel, so that no one will be able to say, 'This is Jezebel'" (II Kings 19:36–37).

Until, that is, her name is invoked again in Revelation, as a term synonymous with refuse and corruption. One could say that, in Revelation, Jezebel has been transformed from a proper name into a generic category for Woman, or at least a kind of woman, "a Jezebel." As a book that announces itself to be "The Revelation of Jesus Christ, which God gave him to show his servants," Revelation is filled with citations and allusions to prior scriptures with which the writer's audience of believers would have been familiar. Indeed, the writer of Revelation, the pseudonymic John of Patmos, associates himself with Old Testament apocalypticists Isaiah, Daniel, and Elijah (Revelation 22:9), thereby inserting himself into the fraternity of classical prophets.[7] The audience of Revelation would have known of the famous political and religious struggle between Elijah and Jezebel and would understand the scenario that is to come. It has, after all, been made to pass before. Elijah's predictions came true once, and the author of Revelation is marshalling every element of that earlier drama to hurry them into place again. Iterable, the predictions become their own conditions of possibility. They also carry forward the paradoxical announcement of their sameness and their distinction.[8] By the time of the early Christian Church's formation, to call a woman "Jezebel" is to use this name as a form of insult.

Like Jezebel in Kings, the Jezebel of Revelation is accused of worshipping other gods. Where Kings' Jezebel shares her table with idolaters, the Jezebel of Revelation is accused of eating food sacrificed to idols. This Jezebel is also associated with the Whore of Babylon in Revelation 12. The Jezebel of Kings paints her eyes, and the Whore of Babylon is dressed in purple and scarlet (Revelation 17:4). Both contrast with the woman clothed only in the natural radiance of the sun (Revelation 12:1) and the divine bride who emerges out of heaven (Revelation 21:2). The Whore's fate is predicted. She will be cast "desolate and naked," and the ten beasts that grow out of her will consume her flesh (Revelation 17:16), just as dogs are predicted to eat Jezebel's flesh.

These two female figures are also spatialized through the Whore, who is simply referred to as Babylon, "that great city, which reigneth over the kings of the earth" (Revelation 17:18). It is within this feminized space that the great battle must be staged before the ideal place can appear, the new heaven, on the new earth. Nothing less than their total destruction is called for. It has in fact already been predicted by Elijah, and that prediction has been fulfilled in II Kings. That the redactors of the Bible chose Revelation to seal all that has gone before is chilling for all women, given the central role that women play in the combat between a corrupt, syncretistic world and an ideal, monolingual one.

As I have already stated, the Bible constitutes a primary intertext for Morrison, as it does in so much African American fiction. It should also be clear from the foregoing that the Bible is itself a palimpsest, an assemblage of interlaced texts organized to appear as a chain of citations that stretches back to a supposedly originary and authentic utterance. *Paradise* calls forth this intertext in its very title, but here the specific reference is to the recursive, gendered stories that ascribe to women the function of both being and signifying contamination. It was, of course, the woman, in the person of Eve, at whose feet was laid blame for the loss of Paradise. What animates the narrative of *Paradise*, however, and perhaps that of the biblical intertext, is not the deeds of women but accusations against them. Morrison would thereby invert the biblical narrative logic, which renders the object of insult and accusation the cause of her own fate, of her own death. *Paradise* opens at the endpoint of the story, with slaughter (described in the previous chapter in terms of the metaphorics of sacrifice, via the rhetoric of the "firing"), so as to pose the question of what caused the deaths of these women and to hold it open—precisely where the name *Jezebel* would have closed it.

The narrative about the Convent women in *Paradise* resembles that of Jezebel's story in Kings and Revelation, even to the point of the women's bodies disappearing after the men raid the Convent—just as they have been reduced to unknowable fragments in the biblical tales. Moreover, the juxtaposition of Jezebel with Eve, and thus the conjoining of seduction and contamination when the men of Ruby refer to "Jezebels" and "bodacious Eves," works in two directions, both revealing the fictional work to be structured by biblical myth and illuminating the operations of the biblical text. From Jezebel, a series of associations extends, in one direction toward the Whore of Babylon in Revelation, and in the other direction toward the Eve of Genesis. As the "MOTHER OF HARLOTS AND ABOMINATIONS OF THE EARTH," who tempts men, and as the woman who heeds other gods and offers forbidden food to men, the Whore and Jezebel are figures in whom is iterated that earlier crime by the first mother, the first temptress, namely, the consumption of forbidden food—the refusal of the taboo and hence of the principle of sacrality.

These associative chains are borne in the proper name when it is used as insult, as it is in *Paradise*. As Judith Butler has shown us, the act of naming can be violently constitutive.[9] Where Butler is concerned with the forms of subjectification accomplished by the kind of categorical naming that is called hate speech (and the possibility of escaping it), Morrison's fiction points to something else: the ways in which the insult of the proper name *Jezebel* impels a narrative that encompasses not only the women who are so named but those who hurl the insult. The name as insult is unmoored from its claim to singularity; it knows itself to be iterative. The one who shouts "Jezebel!" asserts the resemblance of the one insulted to an originary figure or to a set of qualities (in this case filth and feminine sexuality, corruption and desire in excess). In this sense, Jezebel is as violent and as categorical a term as is *nigger* or any other racial epithet, though it masquerades as a proper name. All of the destructive, explosive force that Fanon discerns in the horrified, finger-pointing accusation of the white child confronting the black man in *Black Skin, White Masks* appears here as a feature of the racial purism that underwrites Ruby's utopian separatism, thanks to the sexualized idiom of the Christian mythos in which it has been cast. The act of naming as insulting impels violence, Morrison demonstrates, because it carries the secret burden of those names' first narration and the many repetitions to which they have been subject over time.

In the end, *Paradise* shows us a situation in which names cannot be dislodged from the signifying chains in which they first appeared. This burden, this weight dragging behind the names/words, is not confined to a matter of historical precedent, however. In Ruby, the men seem possessed by those early stories to the extent that they must reenact them. Their naming of the women thus appears to be, or is initially claimed to be, based on their perception of a quality inherent in both Jezebel and the women of the Convent. But, as the novel makes clear, the similitude generated in the act of naming shifts into the boundedness of metaphor. The women are no longer like Jezebel or bodacious Eves. They are Jezebel. They are Eve. The cul-de-sac of such metaphoricity binds them to that of which they are accused. But it also binds the actions of the murderers, the suspicious and accusatory men, to those who have gone before them. Frank Money understands this in *Home*. Words remember, Morrison seems to tell us, and their memory is vengeful. But this is because the names have been granted the power of prophecy. And it is thus that Morrison is able to show us the banality of apocalypticism as a prophetic tradition written in the form of patriarchal insult.

For a New Language of the Body

As the accepted leader of the Convent, Consulata, or Connie, attempts to deliver the women who live there from this burdensome predicament. The Convent is a refuge for strangers and a sign of the foreign that occupies the perimeter of Ruby's carefully bordered world, but it is not, properly speaking, a community. The women have gathered in the Convent for a variety of reasons, but their convergence is accidental until Connie retreats into a deliberative isolation and reemerges to become their strange, "reverend" leader.

The enigmatic character Consolata Sosa has been doubly orphaned. She was discovered parentless in a South American slum as small child and transported to the Convent. When Mother Superior Mary Magna dies, Connie perceives herself to be orphaned yet again—specifically, to be without a mother. This doubling of loss is perhaps what makes itself cognizable to her as loss, giving her name an ironic resonance. Equally important is the fact that her status as doubly orphaned makes her an awkward figure of authority, or at least one in which authority cannot anchor itself in inheritance or any claim to continuity with the past. In the space of her new solitude, following the Mother Superior's death, Connie has only the support of friendship from Soane and Lone, of Ruby, before she is joined by the other women who arrive at the Convent. Despite these friendships and companionships, however, Connie has nothing to tether her to the world (*P* 247).

Having been raised in the idiosyncratic environment of the nuns and Mary Magna, Connie comes from a feminine environment that is far removed from the acquisitiveness and puritanical pursuit of sameness so favored by Ruby's leading men. She listens to others, but rarely speaks. And she almost never compares anyone or anything. It is one of Morrison's great achievements to have created a character that we overhear listening more than speaking. In any case, this absence of the easy simile and the premature judgment (the prejudicial judgment) is also what keeps the

Convent open to and for others. At the same time, however, it ensures the fractiousness of the Convent, where confrontation with difference is the price paid for relinquishing formulaic simile.

The Convent is a place to which individual women are driven and where they are haunted by their immediate pasts. But in this cloistered refuge, the mandatory co-existence of people who would previously never have given each other the time of day means that they are confronted with differences from which they cannot retreat and against which—in the case of Gigi and Mavis, for example—they initially fight. They are neither neighbors nor enemies, but rather strangers thrown together in a new and often uncomfortable intimacy. Connie's withdrawal and descent into the cellar leads them to seek her out by temporarily taking leave of each other. What happens to her will nonetheless take them beyond their old associative chains and the behaviors that haunt them and each other.

Her withdrawal from the world begins much earlier than her physical descent into the Convent's cellar. It commences, paradoxically, when she meets Deacon Morgan in 1954, just after Ruby has been founded and when she is thirty-nine. Steward Morgan ends their brief and ardent affair. Bereft, Connie is comforted by Mother Mary Magna, and it is during this period of grief that she experiences an initial "sunshot" of pain searing her right eye (*P* 241). This is the beginning of what she calls her "bat vision," the fantastic transposition of hallucinatory dreams that enable the prophet to discern the future. In this case, as in the biblical texts that it echoes and ironizes, the "sunshot" is an announcement that "Consolata had been spoken to" (*P* 241). But from whom this communication comes remains unclear, and Connie does not name its source. She does not make the link with her inability to distinguish one twin from the other at a glance. She cannot understand that this was a failed sight to begin with. Neither does she associate Steward's stern warning with having been "spoken to." Having fallen silent about her carnal love in the affair with Deacon, Connie commences a self-transformation in which she emphatically rejects the corporeal existence of her earlier life—in a gesture of repentance that initially appears to be entirely within the tradition of feminine self-effacement so central to Christian penitent movements. She does not totally reject bodily existence, however. Rather, Connie seeks a different way of occupying her body whose hungers have been taught to her even before she could speak and whose satisfactions have also been dictated to her and the other women.

The first gesture in this labor to reclaim her body from the structures of desire and attachment to which she has been subject entails the pursuit of oblivion. Connie attempts to shun all things that remind her of her body's needs through the dislocation that alcohol makes possible, as she drinks her way through the long-deceased benefactor's abandoned liquor store. She tries to get away from the sunlight that hurts her eyes and blinds her but also to hold fast to a self dedicated to her increasingly idiosyncratic faith in a savior/God who communicates through sunlight. She nonetheless remains "wary" of this savior, whom she never addresses but whom she longs to love without the carnality of her love for Deacon Morgan during the brief months of their affair. Her ambivalence extends also to the gifts or marks of grace that mark her off as exceptional among women. Thus Connie also wishes to retreat from the strange "gift" of saving life that Lone DuPres sees in her, the gift of assuming spiritual form and bringing the dead back to life. Lone had pressed her to use that gift by "entering" Soane and Deacon's son Scout when he was fatally hurt in a car accident while on furlough (*P* 245). But Connie's more severe religiosity had been offended by this burdensome gift, which others desired but which she could only comprehend as "devilment" and an "evil craft." Ashamed, she had tried to keep it as secret as the affair with Deacon. When she had used it in an effort to save Mary Magna from dying without the Convent mother's permission, it had been a violation, "anathema," as she put it, doubling the evil of the occult talent that she had otherwise abandoned with that of personal assault (*P* 247).

Freud might term Connie's gift—the capacity to liberate others from death—the dream image of melancholia. But for Connie, it is a moral problem, being one more species of overattachment to the worldly. It is thus of a piece with her physical desire for Deacon, but also barely distinguishable from a relationship to a God that takes the form of a painful, sensuously potent communication.

Despite her aspiration to retreat, Connie steps belatedly into Mary Magna's place as the one to whom the women defer, and she accepts the burden of answering their needs. By 1975, her gift begins to assume another form, as she starts to sense the thoughts of those around her. This is a "gift" she would also like to abandon but which she finally accepts, as she "listens" to each woman's narration of grievance, grief, fear, and longing. She takes charge "like a new and revised Reverend Mother, feeding them bloodless food and water alone to quench their thirst" (*P* 265). Under her maternal and indeed matriarchal care, a form of sorority begins in the space where patriarchal materiality and spirituality have left their powerful traces: the home was, after all, that of a rich embezzler who favored erotic decoration everywhere, though it had also been intended to function as a haven for "Native Girls" under the name Christ the King School. It is this sororal community, unshepherded by masculine authority and increasingly liberated from the idioms, the violent similes, and the persecutory names of mythology, that offends the men of Ruby.

What the men of Ruby and the distant tax collector fear may arise at the Convent does in fact emerge. What they fear is the women's autonomy. But the form that such autonomy may take remains unimaginable to them. What is more, its strange shape—the odd obsessions, demands, and rigors imposed by Connie, the delirium of words and things in which the remnants of Jezebel's story recur in unrecognizable narrative—is unimaginable to the women who inhabit the Convent. And Morrison will lead us to understand that the flight from Ruby, as it unfolds in the Convent, risks reinstalling the power of the mysterium and with it a severe authority. What saves the women of the Convent, for Morrison, is love. It is not incidental that *Paradise* will be followed, in Morrison's oeuvre, with the novel entitled *Love*.

Mysteriousness remains at the Convent, with the dreamlike reappearance of the women at the novels' end. But it is not contained by or reduced to patriarchal self-mystification—as it is in the motto inscribed in the heart of Ruby. Nor will it be grasped through a liberal fantasy of freedom.

Although not the witches' coven (the play between coven and Convent saturates the text) that some in Ruby think it is (P 276), the Convent is beginning to fulfill the promise that Connie had made when Grace first arrived, when she states that: "Lies not allowed in this place. In this place every true thing is okay" (P 38). From this promise of plenitude, of self-presence and unmediated truth, emerges an ambivalent kind of new authority and induction into an as yet unknown world, one that constantly threatens to mimic the patriarchal order but that nonetheless always escapes, always remains somewhat ungraspable. In 1975, Connie gathers all of the women at a table, where they will be served their last, lush meal. She says: "Eat how I say. Sleep when I say." In return, she will teach them to understand their hungers (P 262).

At first the women are confused. They do not understand what she is saying or what she has become, and they try to find a known set of names for the person inhabiting the body of someone each of them has come to know as the "sweet, unthreatening old lady who seemed to love each one of them best; who never criticized, who shared everything but needed little or no care; required no emotional investment; who listened; who locked no doors and accepted each as she was" (*P* 262). As Connie becomes strange, assuming the prerogative of power, the women tend toward unison. In this passage, the women are already thinking as one, or, at least, Connie is the one about whom they all agree. But even here Morrison resists the creation of a perfect feminine space into which a stricter binarity might force her narrative. Connie is not a benign, "unthreatening old lady" at all. She has been irritated by the women who "insist on joining her" in the cellar: "Talking, talking, always talking" (*P* 221).

Sarah Appleton Aguiar reads Consolata as one of Morrison's "symbolic midwives," and while this conveys the sense of one who facilitates and is instrumental in bringing what is hidden to light, the analogy keeps Consolata within a frame that the rest of the novel does not entirely embrace.[10] This is not a story of natality so much as the reproduction of death. Aguiar is nevertheless astute in her identification of the similarities between Consolata and Baby Suggs, who takes upon herself the psychic healing of an entire community of freed or runaway slaves in *Beloved*. Aguiar also sees a similarity between Alice Manfred, who befriends Violet Trace, who finds herself having to teach her the small, everyday things of survival (like how to hold an iron properly), and who listens to her and thus begins to have a sense of her life in *Jazz*. Others could be added to this list of figures who respond to others' needs and enable some form of transition. These figures, invariably women, do so from some unfathomable sense of obligation to strangers, rather than on the basis of a received social or gendered role within a community of mutually recognizing subjects. There is no reason to imagine the midwife as a figure of charity, of course. But Morrison seems to go to great lengths to make the helpmeets of transition be ambivalent characters, as vulnerable to temptation, petty jealousy, covetousness, and rage as is any other character. The list of figures who perform in this way are not all ideal. There is Thérèsa of *Tar Baby*. She is wily, manipulative, and disapproving of Jadine Childs. There is one-legged Eva Peace, who takes in abandoned boys and a floundering white man in *Sula*, but who murders her son Plum rather than see him succumb to addiction or, as she puts it, try to crawl back into her womb. There is the young white woman Amy Denver in *Beloved*, who is running from an abusive family and stops to help Sethe—not only a stranger but a runaway slave. Amy Denver draws on a home remedy to save Sethe and deliver her baby. She is, in Aguiar's sense, a midwife, but she is far more complex. She may be helping Sethe, and she may be saved only by whiteness from being one step above the social status of a black slave. But her language draws upon the racialized realities of the day. She refers to "an old nigger girl" and says at one point that she does not want to see Sethe's "ugly black face hankering" over her (*B* 80, 82). Yet she does help, and when the narration pulls back to observe them, we have a sense why. They are "two women" struggling together as "two throw-away people, two lawless outlaws" (*B* 84).

Amy Denver may not be the most ideal symbol of midwifery, but Morrison does draw figures whose knowledge of physical and psychic healing would imbue them with a symbolic status as curers and the bearers of a supernatural force. One such figure is M'Dear, who arrives to diagnose the illness of Cholly Breedlove's Aunt Jimmy in *The Bluest Eye*. She does not walk, and she looms "taller than the preacher" who comes with her but who cannot administer as she does (*BE* 136). While she possesses medicinal knowledge, she is not the only caring female figure in Cholly's world. The women rally around Aunt Jimmy in much the same way that the women of Lotus rally around Cee when Frank delivers her to Ethel Fordham's care in *Home*. The women in Cholly's world are older and had grown so "Edging into life from the backdoor" (*BE* 138). They were ordered about by white people and their husbands, but did not take orders from black children or each other. In addition:

> They ran the houses of white people, and knew it. When white men beat their men, they cleaned up the blood and went home to receive abuse from the victim. They beat their children with one hand and stole for them with the other. The hands that felled trees also cut umbilical cords; the hands that wrung the necks of chickens and butchered hogs also nudged African violets into bloom; the arms that loaded sheaves, bales, and sacks rocked babies into sleep. They patted biscuits into flaky ovals of innocence—and shrouded the dead. They plowed all day and came home to nestle like plums under the limbs of their men. (*BE* 138)

These are not sentimentalized mothering women, though they will nurse and care as the occasion rises. This is the case in Lotus, when Cee learns how to pay attention to the women who participate in bringing her back to health (*H* 122–23). She sees at last, perhaps, that they are each different in appearance and style but similar in key ways: "There was no excess in their gardens because they shared everything. There was no trash or garbage in their homes because they had a use for everything. They took responsibility for their lives and for whatever, whoever else needed them" (*H* 123). They prize common sense and industry and devote themselves to living useful lives. The point is that solidarity and gender allow the women to care for others without making of them the facile images of the idealized nanny required by and replayed in white fantasies and fictions about black maternity. This is why the Convent is such a useful device for Morrison; it allows another exploration of "the mother" as figure and trope in the house of race.

Thus, while still called Connie, Consolata welcomes each woman to the Convent and cares for her, but she does not mother her. Her caring for the women takes the form of providing that space, but she has regarded the women who arrive at the Convent as broken and afraid, weak and untruthful. Only when she is drunk on the embezzler's vast supply of alcohol can she bear them. Even then, in early 1975, she wants to break their necks to stop their bickering, their badly cooked food, the greed of their need, and, worse than everything, their "drift" (*P* 222). Without any real plans, all they have are empty wishes—that is, until she has a visitation by a strange cowboy with long, tea-colored hair like hers and eyes the color of the green that had filled Deacon with wonder (*P* 251–52).

Not knowing how much they have irritated her, the women know her only as the "ideal parent, friend, company" and the one with whom they feel safest (*P* 262). She is their "granny goose" and "play mother"—until she interrupts this idyllic image by making that feast and turning her blind gaze at them, commanding them to leave or stay according to her rules. In the classic structure of all rituals of transition, the women descend into an atemporal oblivion. Staying, they lose track of habitual time, as they submit to the "template" of the day that she makes out. They clean the cellar and ring it with candles, creating a space within a space of sanctuary. In a ritual wherein the women lie naked in the outlines she has made of their bodies, Consolata begins to speak in an English that is broken, as mysterious in its references as the motto discussed in the previous chapter (*P* 263). The things she tells them are ambiguous, open to innumerable interpretations. Is the "him" for whom her flesh had been so hungry Deacon or Christ? A reader can know this, but the women in the cellar cannot. How, too, can they know that the "her" for whom Connie cares as "her body sickens" is Mother Mary Magna? And what does she mean when she talks about bones and says that what mattered when "she" died is not spirit but bones, and the truth is "like bones" and goodness "like bones"? They can only guess at the gist of what she says:

> After she is dead I can not get past that. My bones on hers the only good thing. Not spirit. Bones. No different from the man. My bones on his the only true thing. So I wondering where is the spirit lost in this? It is true, like bones. It is good, like bones. One sweet, one bitter. Where is it lost? Hear me, listen. Never break them in two. Never put one over the other. Eve is Mary's mother. Mary is the daughter of Eve. (*P* 263)

Here Eve is salvaged from the insult of continuity with Jezebel. Eve, ejected from the chain of iterable associations that links her with corruption, is reinserted into a series that puts her in a position of contiguity with both purity and maternal devotion. But at what cost? And via what irony? For it is the bones, those fragmentable, unknowable traces—vulnerable to being strewn hither and thither—to which Jezebel had been reduced in the hope that she would be forgotten. But Connie insists on the irreducible facticity of bones. Here they are the improbable images of a restored truth value, albeit haunted by the specter of magic. For bones are at the intersection of two traditions—the reliquary and divination. The reliquary tradition is not without its magic, but divination allows predictions of the future. In divination, the throwing or pointing of bones is associated with truth, but at the cost of effacing meaning. Not coincidentally, it is in this zone of semantic instability that Connie claims her authority and demands the women's obedience.

In the Convent, there is no Oven to serve as a social and psychic hearth or a town's possibly most sacred space. But there is a cellar in a misnamed Convent, a place in which the only masculine presence is an uncanny cowboy or a newly defined Christ, divorced from any Church. In this space, the women obey the mystery of Connie's logic and come closest to (though they do not become) the people of Ruby, by ignoring the question of the source of her newly acquired Reverend Mother status. She is as serene and confident as the motto but not contiguous with it. The only contiguity that she seems to observe is that between Mary, who would be the ideal, heavenly bride of the New Testament, and Eve, the source of original sin. As such, of course, Eve is also the origin of redemption. And thus, in Connie's oneiric discourse, Eve is no longer the figure of mere corruption. Once Eve is disinterred from the semiological chains that bound her to Jezebel and kept her from association with Mary, there is nothing between her and Mary but the bare bones of Connie's statement that they are not like but related: kin who must never be broken in two. The result of separation can only mean death for the one who is the other's distaff. Thus is the violence of a patriarchal similitude broken.

We do not have access to the rest of Consolata's speech. All we can know is that her words are "clearer than her introductory speech." We do not have access to the other women's language, either, because it is new, perhaps too new to be understood. This is a sororal rite of passage, into which no one is permitted to blunder. We are reminded here of *Sula*, where young Nel and Sula are drawn into an energy for which they have no name and which, therefore, renders them silent and without control. The boy Chicken Little blunders into their ritual of digging a hole in the ground and dies—as perhaps any unprepared person who enters the liminal zone of ritual must do. Disrupted, it becomes a space of death for him when, displacing an energy that can only be wild, Sula reaches out to him rather than Nel. She grabs his hands, spinning him while he laughs, delighted, until the sweat from both of their hands and the force of their spinning loosens her grip. He sails out and falls into the river, his trousers quickly absorbing water and dragging him down so that all that is left is the place where he sank (*S* 61).

Reading between this and Derrida's remarks on space in representation, Patricia McKee suggests that the place where Chicken Little sinks is exactly the designation of the "nothing" of where a boy once was.[11] To which can be added the argument that this "nothing" is also terrible because the "closed place in the [river's] middle" is where language too has been drowned. This personal event condenses in diminutive form what the narratives of the Middle Passage seek to grasp, namely, the failure of language in the face of death, and the death of language in the face of massive historical violence. But it also reveals the degree to which a secret, especially the secret of violence, binds subjects together in mutual indebtedness and protectiveness. And sometimes, as Morrison's narrator in *Jazz* says of herself, it reveals the tendency of a storyteller to subject her characters to any manner of torment for the sake of dramatic effect. In *Sula*, the girls cannot and never do speak of Chicken Little's death, even though Eva Peace, Sula's grandmother, somehow knows about it. No such demand for sacrifice afflicts the women of the Convent in *Paradise*, whose new community does not depend upon a secret, despite its risking of the mysterium. Under Consolata's guidance, dangerous energy is directed into action that prepares the women for what is to come (and what will be set in motion when they go into the town, to dance at K. D. and Arnette's wedding, where they offend Steward). But there is no violent error of the sort that claims Chicken Little. The women, not needing a sacrificial subject to bind them, go about their own business, oblivious to how they may appear from without. They empty themselves in order to fill the outline that Consolata has drawn for them, abandoning their formal self-images and the structure of identification that they enabled. A sacrificial death would introduce a new triadic structure, which would interrupt the one organized by Consolata. And so the women of the Convent neither seek nor require such an exterior event. Their world remains self-sufficient— hence a challenge to Ruby's fierce autonomy.

Beastly Language: The Monstrous Performative

We receive what Connie says in the deflected form of the third person, the shift performing the emergence of a new "order" or bond between the women, from which we are of necessity excluded but of which we learn through a third-person narrative that condenses and selects only the most persuasive, magical images; not quite a gospel, this section of the text nevertheless transforms Connie into Consolata Sosa, who leads the women away from the carnality of their bodies to face the deep sorrow of their lives and the seduction of the bodies they now inhabit, not needing, not thirsting, just as she promised (P 265). As pointed out in the previous chapter, the women's "muted" manner and calm has an effect on the women from Ruby, who are moved to look from this calm to their own lives, comparing them but not finding any likeness, only lack, a lack of the peace of those who are not haunted.

The Convent has always had its attractions for other women. There is Soane, who came to ask, without satisfaction, for help in aborting her baby and who ended up loving the woman her husband had slept with. And the then unmarried Arnette Flood, who came for the same reason and, when not satisfied, punched herself in the stomach until she miscarried. There is also Sweetie, who fled the unnamed sickness of her children and found herself taken in by the Convent women, and Billie Delia, who was helped when her mother hit her with a clothes iron. For each of these women who sought shelter, the Convent is still within the narrative of a place in which women would be prepared to and did do wicked things. In spite of this, Soane and Billie Delia will remain true to the Convent women. Arnette will claim that the women tricked her, beat her up, and aborted her baby (*P* 275). Sweetie will claim that they tried to poison her and that she heard babies crying where no babies should have been (*P* 275). Billie Delia will think them strange but know to take Pallas to them when she finds her in a state of shock at a clinic. Although Billie Delia will walk away from the town, the men at the Oven will say that the women of the Convent drove her to strike her mother (*P* 276). And a white family who got lost decades earlier and whose bodies are found in a car in Sergeant's field will become the victims of the cloistered "Bitches" (*P* 276).

Lone hears the chain-reacting clauses and phrases turn into "fangs" and a "tail" that are "all slithery in a house full of women." Demon, devil, serpent, Eve, the Whore of Babylon, and Jezebel make them more than "women locked safely away from men." These likenesses, which close into the assertion of metaphor, make them "worse, women who choose themselves for company, which is to say not a convent but a coven." Morrison would have us recognize what structural linguists assert, namely, that the signified of any sign is dependent upon its signifier, that the play of signifiers permits the profound conceptual difference between convent and coven to appear quite simply in the presence or absence of the letter *t*.[12] At the same time, she insists that this superficial play of signifiers is determined by their deployment in and by historical narratives. The matter is irreducible to form, though it cannot appear without form. If there had been any doubt at all, these phrases becoming the features of a demonic creature make clear how Morrison conceives of the language in which the women of the Bible have appeared. It is a monstrous force, announcing and effecting violence.

An either/or logic announces itself in what Lone hears within the men's accusation. This logic parallels and extends the inside/outside, neighbor/stranger opposition, which is also racialized and gendered as "intact" black / contaminated or miscegenated black and good woman / bad woman. She hears them speaking and intuits their thoughts, hearing the slippage from their worry about the town's ruin to the accusations against the women. Present and past are drawn into a simultaneous narrative space as the men begin to link personal woes and the town's crisis with figures for which they have waiting narratives, narratives that hear themselves as predictions and that demand fulfillment in order to save the promise that is Ruby. Lone recognizes, and through her the reader learns, that those narratives are realized when the eight men of Ruby meet at the Oven (also different from the coven only through a single letter's alteration) and determine to rid the town of the Convent's women. They proceed to its grounds, where they "shoot the white girl first." Frank Money's question reverberates backward from Morrison's later *Home*: What kind of man kills a girl? When he asks that question of himself later in Morrison's oeuvre, we are brought back to the night at the Oven in *Paradise* where the townsmen experience narrative as affective compulsions, born of private narratives and personal experience, though both are informed by the larger meta-narratives of the biblical intertext. In all cases, the result is a demand and desire to expel the women.

Thus, although the women in the Convent had shown him kindness by taking him in and cleaning him when he was at his inebriated lowest, Menus Jury can feel only shame at the thought of having needed the women (*P* 165, 277–78). Sergeant Person persuades himself that Steward's call to protect Ruby against the women is justified when he really believes he can push the women out of the Convent and take for good the land he has been leasing from them, as well as the rest (*P* 277). Wisdom Pool would find an explanation for why he could not control his brothers, especially Brood and Apollo, and sisters any longer. He could pin the falling out between his brothers over Billie Delia Best on her friendship with the Convent women. Why else would one brother attempt to murder another for the sake of a woman "like" Billie Delia? And Jeff and Arnold Fleetwood could blame the Convent for the sickly children in their home and not confront any embarrassing questions about incest or intermarriage. K. D. could blame the Convent for Gigi/Grace's rejection of him. He is "a Morgan after all, and they haven't forgotten a thing since 1755" (*P* 278). Steward and Deacon can attack the Convent because they cannot abide what they cannot control (*P* 278–79). All take up arms against the women who can fulfill any need and function as the empty signifier, to which all manner of evil is attached. This is one crucial meaning of the devil from within Christianity, this capacity for metamorphosis, which incites desire and interrupts other relationships. This is why the women must be removed.

Steward himself remembers 1954, when a woman from the Convent almost broke up Deacon's marriage and their vision of a perfect town. As one concerned with others' physical and psychic wellbeing, Lone senses his anger as a malady, "a floating blister in his blood-stream" (*P* 279). Deacon's carelessness is "treason against the fathers' law, the law of continuance and multiplication," in Steward's assessment. And it is a threat to Steward's self-image. He and his brother had, after all, shared an image of perfect femininity when, as boys, they had seen nineteen black women bathed in sunlight and the scent of verbena, a vision that multiplies the perfect, naturally radiant, heavenly bride of Revelation (*P* 279). The women at the Convent are the opposite of these dreamy females and therefore a threat to the one memory that really belongs to the brothers themselves, the memory that is more private than the loss of their sister, because all in Ruby share her death, after all. Deacon can attack the Convent because of his pride and shame. These lingering responses to his affair are inseparable for Lone. He has to erase the shame of being attracted to Consolata, and he has to erase her as the shame itself. Shame can never come to live in him. He can only displace it by seeing in her all the desire that produces a lack of control (*P* 279). He has his own private biblical association. Even though he does not have to invoke the name *Salome*, he casts Consolata in that role, as he imagines what would have happened to him if he had continued seeing her. In a nightmarish hallucination, he sees his head being served on a plate (*P* 280). Through Deacon's narrative, we see that even the most intimate memory, the most private experience, is, in this sense, drawn into the public discourse and shaped by biblical intertexts, given biblical analogies, provided with the terms of biblical similes that convert into metaphors in which one type of person overtakes another in a way that entombs.

Idiomatic Similitude: Bringing the Present into the Past

Long before *Paradise*, of course, Morrison had been concerned with the question of whether one can escape the violence of a particular social order if one does not also forget the language in which it was known. *Tar Baby* offers us a thought experiment of a sort that would be repeated and radicalized in *A Mercy*, drawing on the tradition of utopian fiction (the wish fulfillment of colonialism), which casts characters into new territories in order to imagine if or when they would reproduce the errors of their previous existences. Would they impose anew the grids of intelligibility by which the old world had been structured? Would they relinquish the violent similes by which antiquity was reproduced? Could they learn to think differently? The speculative mode in which any fiction approaches such problems should not be forgotten. Nor should the fact that there is no other way.

In *Tar Baby*, the setting is an island filled with displaced people who are running from secrets or knowledge with which they cannot live and who imagine that this running is not away from these sources of distress but toward something better. *Tar Baby* has three primary sites, including New York and Eloe, Florida. The main setting is the fictional Caribbean island Isle des Chevaliers, which has been overtaken by absentee or permanently holidaying landlords from Europe or America. There, ensconced in his house L'Arbe de la Croix, Valerian Street requires his wife and servants to live in a state of suspension around his insistence that he is only visiting and could return at any time to his home city of Philadelphia.

In *Tar Baby*, Morrison uses Isle des Chevaliers as a setting in which the attitudes and values of each inhabitant of L'Arbe de la Croix are challenged by inherent instability. Thus, for Jadine, Margaret, Sydney, and Ondine, the island's fecundity constantly threatens to overrun the principles of order. Ants plague the hothouse in which Valerian grows plants that could easily grow outdoors on the island. Jadine is caught in the mud of a swamp. The island is a palimpsest of colonial legacies, which include contemporary commodification of people whose forebears were themselves commodities. Thus Valerian orders his seeds from the Portuguese Ferrara Brothers (Domestic and International Company) and listens to Bach's Goldberg Variations, Haydn, and Liszt while growing cyclamens, which come, originally, from the Mediterranean, Iran, and, in Africa, Somalia. The interlacing networks of colonial trade are reproduced in his catalogues and in the microcosm of his hothouse. All legacies and their contemporary beneficiaries and subjects occupy the same temporality, all guarded and maintained, or ordered and possessed.

The blind woman Thérèsa, known by Valerian's household as Mary, guards and replenishes stories about different groups that are said to haunt the island. Through her, we learn one view of a story about Napoleonic chevaliers, who landed on the island and who continue to ride across it. We also learn through her and her nephew Gideon, known by Valerian's household as Yardman, of the race of Africans who arrived on a slave ship, took one look at the place to which they had been brought, and jumped overboard. They too haunt the island and sometimes mate with witches who live in the swamp or with living women. The fantasized new world, it turns out, is utterly overrun by the old, the shades and ghosts of deceased occupants or visitors standing in for a generic predicament of dependency on the past and overdetermination by its idioms. Utopia is simply a displacement and projection of a repressed failure, in particular, a repressed paternalistic failure. The characters live their lives on narrow, well-trodden paths, never venturing beyond the destinations of their carefully planned itineraries. It is only when Son, or William Green, intrudes upon L'Arbe de la Croix and seduces Jadine Childs that she can think of departing from the only road she has known, the one she and Margaret take between the house and the dock to spend time on the water.

We enter *Tar Baby* through Son's pivotal viewpoint. As an outsider, he must look and attend to his surroundings, translating for the reader/ stranger, while staging his escape, given that he is about to jump from the ship on which he works and land, undocumented, on a foreign island. His language is briefly inflected with that of the feminizing, idealizing tourist brochure. This is a language that Derek Walcott has associated with "ardent binoculars" that fix "the blue reflection of eyes" onto the distance of that tourist brochure, a distance emblematized by "the steamers which divide horizons."[13] This fixity is projected onto the island as screen, attributing to it a paradisaical state, where "Time creeps over the patient who are too long patient."[14] Walcott stares backs, using the distance produced by the clichés of brochures as the condition of possibility for his own language. However, Son's eyes are not the empty or emptying blue of distance. Rather, as we will see when Jadine looks into them, they are orange, and what he sees moves quickly from the tourist brochure to his self-masculinizing experiences of women. Where he comes from, the all-black town of Eloe in Florida, women serve and pamper, confirm his masculinity by calling "Come on in, you honey you!" or deceive in childish ways, as his teenage wife Cheyenne does, for whose accidental murder he is on the run (*TB* 176, 224).

His view is one of overdetermined engendering. His lexicon is filled with feminine similes and metaphors for nature. These align in an initially problematic way with a paternalistic view granting an agency of attraction that is then displaced onto women. White cruisers are "girlish" to him (*TB* 1). The island to which he hopes to swim, Queen of France, has "eyelashes," which she "lowers" as if to entice him. He is in a context that is masculinized by the name of the ship on which he has been working, the *Stor Konigsgaarten*. But he is leaving this ship, and when he does so, he enters the water, yet another overly determined gendered sphere, for which he has a ready language to explain the sudden tug of the current. First, it is a "bracelet of water" around his ankle, but very quickly this description does not suffice to explain what is happening to him. He can only find the simile that makes the most sense to him. The current is "like the hand of a persistent woman," which now pushes him from his desired course (*TB* 2). Having done its work, the simile converts to the metaphor of a "water lady," in which all the associations of the word *water* follow the pleasing sense of a "lady" and leave behind the reality of a "rip tide" or boundlessness in which one can drown. He is deposited near a small pleasure craft and climbs on board, hiding below deck, where he falls asleep when the "water lady" returns and "brushes" Son's eyelids with her knuckles (*TB* 3).

While the first female presence is forceful and "persistent," the novel's male protagonist appears passive, captive, and in awe. His language is innocent, trusting, as he gives himself to the current. Indeed, he is the most positive male figure in all of Morrison's novels up until *Tar Baby*—we are introduced to all of the men of this novel before we meet the women (surely a nod in the direction of an earlier scriptural paradise in which the Adamic male is the first creation in a creation story). Valerian Street has the power of wealth and his whiteness. His butler, Sidney Childs, has little or no power. Son's images of women are positive; Valerian's are bitter. When we first meet him, his wife is last in his sequence of priorities. He thinks of all that he brought with him to the island: "records, garden shears, a sixty-four bulb chandelier, a light blue tennis shirt and the Principle Beauty of Maine" (*TB* 9). His worldview is jaded and takes on the tone of the time of day, so that his grey eyes are "like a four o'clock shadow on its way to twilight" (*TB* 9). Although Sydney and Ondine have worked for him for forty years, he refers to them through the service they provide. Sydney is Sydney the Butler (*TB* 10), and, as if infected by Valerian's malaise, Sydney refers to him only as his employer. Compared with the coldness of both men, Son is already warmer and open.

The first feminized presence in these introductions is the natural world, and the only references to "real" women are through distortions. We hear only the sound of women's voices when Son eventually wakes on the small pleasure craft (*TB* 4). We hear his language for the sound of their thighs moving against fabric as they walk, and we see only a white hand (*TB* 9, 10). The voices "sprawl" for him, and "sprawl" takes him back to the world he knows, so that he gives them some familiar form, in which the laughter of women in Eloe would be "sprawling like a quilt" (*TB* 4).

These voices and thighs are those of Jadine Childs. Jadine is the young black woman whose aunt and uncle are Valerian Street's cook/housekeeper and butler, and whom Street has had educated at private schools and sent to university. The hands are those of Margaret Street, Valerian Street's wife. He refers to her as the Principle Beauty in a sardonic reference to his first sight of her, dressed as a beauty queen (*TB* 22).

When the as yet unnamed Son appears in Valerian's house, his unkempt appearance is made to signify Margaret Street's racialized notions of truant black working-class masculinity. Her anxiety about the working class is conjoined to her racialized views, and both are rooted in her own immigrant working-class background. She can accept the college graduate and cover model Jadine at her table, but she needs to distance herself from her friendship with Jadine's aunt, Ondine, who, with her husband Sydney, can never be more than servants. Ironically, Margaret and the Childs share opinions about black masculinity. The Childs view working-class black masculinity as truant and a betrayal of "uplift." When Son appears, he signifies their worst fears. For Margaret, an old language of similitude comes quickly and easily to explain her reaction to the news that Son, when discovered by Sydney, has been hiding in her closet for days.

All the way out in the Caribbean, she draws upon a phrase from the Deep South of the America that the Childs—niece, aunt, and uncle—fear and that is home to Son. He is the "nigger in the pile" (*TB* 85).[15] In this particular structure, this word and its associations freeze into a common purpose. The simile opens a store of further associations, whose narrow semiological course overtakes Margaret, like a tide in its own powerful right, and delivers her to the over-sexualized black male body of her fears. Their hermeneutic energy further animates her, conjuring further fears, naming them, and depicting them for her. All she can think is that Son hid in her closet and masturbated at the sight of her. She can only think how "Black sperm was sticking in clots to her French jeans or down in the toe of her Ann Klein shoes" (*TB* 85). The images bring the general racialized exaggerations into tactile association with her personal possessions (whose expense has to be marked for her, as if she still has to insist that she is a wealthy woman and not the poor woman she once was). Although she is the one who calls the images up and locates them in her jeans and shoes, she has never had to question the semiological system in which she uses words that are in effect also speaking her, to her, and for her. She cannot know that it is she who brings the images into her closet, places them there, "clothes" them, and makes them materialize.

At the same time, familiar associations converge in familiar ambivalence. Son is both hypersexual and dehumanized when, as a cipher, "nigger" is uttered again, this time by Jadine. As soon as it is said, Margaret substitutes for it "gorilla" (*TB* 129). For Jadine, the word *nigger* is all the "black" from which she seeks to distance herself, the "black" that has been fetishized by the same semiological system that articulates Margaret's fears.

Tar Baby is Morrison's fourth book, right after *Song of Solomon*. Its thought experiment of testing the possibilities for love in an island "paradise" never overlooks the nightmare histories that it took to "create" such a fantasy place. The novel's lovers, Jadine and Son, cannot escape their personal histories or the shared "back" story of slavery. Jadine's uncle, Sydney, makes clear the distinction between his small family and the likes of Son or island inhabitants like Thérèsa and Gideon when he proclaims, "We Philadelphia Negroes." Son represents everything that reminds Sydney of a history of subjugation that leads straight back to slavery and its geographical home, the South. Madelyn Jablon makes the distinction between their politics, reading Sydney as an assimilationist and Son as a black nationalist.[16] Until Son's presence forces him to, Sydney does not see that Valerian Street is the presence that blurs the distinctions he so wants to maintain. For Street, Sydney, Ondine, Son, Yardman, and Thérèsa are all ultimately the same. They are black, the face of servitude. Jadine is the one who cannot be "only" black, since she has been schooled to look and sound "like" someone he can talk to. Her individuality and her attempt to be someone in her own right are irrelevant to him. He does not really think about her or anyone else except his blood son. Because of her education and modeling career, Jadine has been inserted into an aestheticized order in which the beauty of blackness can be read only according to a prescribed set of likenesses. She is, therefore, a "Copper Venus" in the modeling world—not the real, but a "likeness" of the "original" maintains the distance between simulacrum and original. Her difference reaffirms the original's transcendence in that she might appear to be the same, but her race makes her different and the name "Copper Venus" confirms the paradigmatic whiteness of the "real" Venus, against whom all "copper" women will be measured.

Further, as a "made up" woman, Jadine figures as the tar baby of the title.[17] The epithet does not overtake her entirely. In what is by now an established Morrison fashion, the older tar baby narrative is invoked, but it is never an unchallenged mold that entirely dictates her characters' lives. It does not close up into a sealed metaphor. Rather, it is one of several narratives that are simultaneously in operation, providing their own tropes, as we see in Thérèsa's stories about the drowned slaves, the French chevaliers, and the witches who live in the swamps. What "sticks" to Jadine and Son is history itself. It is history that distracts them, even though they each try to pull "the other away from the maw of hell—its very ridge top," because each has some knowledge or dream of "the world as it was meant or ought to be" (*TB* 269). This struggle might be a further invocation of the tar baby narrative, but both exceed the folkishness that stereotypy would seek to amplify and make the only mode in which black subjects can be recognized.

Linda Krumholz argues that *Tar Baby* employs the overly determined word *tar* only to expose and disrupt its excessive reach, thereby undermining "the opposition between blackness and whiteness in racial and racist formulations."[18] For Krumholz, Son's entry in to Valerian Sweet's home is an entry into the space in which the self-satisfying politics of liberal humanism are performed as presumptive universal values that Valerian believes he upholds.[19] Valerian's house is itself an announcement of "taste" and "worth," a place that is a portrait of and testimony to the discerning mind that has chosen the right artisans, the right builders. More troubling for Krumholz is the association of innocence and culture, which can be sustained only if the violence behind the universalism of Valerian's principles remains hidden.

Valerian's desire to prevent rifts in truth and to close himself away from the world of flux is reimagined in Morrison's seventh book, *Paradise*. There the thought experiment begun in *Tar Baby* pushes to the deeper past of a place that is not that of the tourist brochure's imagined "island paradise," but a place that was the imagined new heaven and new earth dreamed by other texts, scriptures—namely, the shores of New England in their early colonial formations.

5. Beginnings and Endings, Part Two: The Poetics of Similitude and Disavowal at Utopia's Gates

Morrison has described her project in *A Mercy* as wanting "to separate race from slavery to see what it was like, what it might have been like, to be a slave but without being raced; where your status was being enslaved but there was no application of racial inferiority," when what is called America was "still fluid, ad hoc."[1] The novel also imagines emergent subjectivities in such an ad hoc state.

Two journeys take us into *A Mercy*: that of the young slave Florens and that of Jacob Vaark, her master. Although they traverse the same geography for part of their sojourns, they are on entirely different missions. One is narrated in the first person; one is told in the third person. We learn about Florens's journey through her writing. We learn that she had been taught how to read and write by a priest from an early age, when she was still with her mother and baby brother on D'Ortega's estate. By the mid 1600s, such an act was already frowned upon by slave owners, who were already reserving writing and reading as their privilege. Her writing takes place in secret, and it is inscribed on the only surface available to her. This surface is the walls of her dead master's dream mansion, which is locked up and empty, shunned by Rebekka Vaark, who has forbidden any of her indentured servants or slaves to enter it. Florens's writing is therefore an act of disobedience to her mistress's command, which is, in the end, an extension of her master's voice. She enters the house at night to write with whatever implement she can find, even if it is a stick, so that her writing is a form of scoring and engraving. Her act of disobedience is also an act that obeys her own need, an act of substitution in which she can express her desire, explain herself, and see herself reflected. It is an act of self-reflection, even though it is addressed to the blacksmith. It is an act of accounting for herself and for what has brought her to writing.

Florens's journey takes place eighteen years after Jacob Vaark's death due to smallpox, and his journey was what made her his slave. His death will make clear how tenuous the life of a slave, a woman, and a female slave was in a "new world" that retains the old structures of "headship" so admired by Locke as the sign of a well-organized society. Their journeys are, therefore, those of a subject who can move freely and of a subject who cannot; they are journeys into the worlds of masters and slaves, for Vaark will arrive at his debtor's home to collect monies owed him by a man he loathes as much as he has contempt for the man's trade in slaves, but he will leave owning a slave. He will also invest in sugar and other commodities produced elsewhere by slave labor that he need never see or be reminded of. Florens's journey will bring her face to face with the future that awaits her and all others likened to her.

Although their lives intersect, both Florens and Vaark move through the world in very different ways. Florens has to negotiate the geography between the only home she has, the farm of her widowed mistress Rebekka Vaark, and the home in which she has invested all hope and every aspect of her being, the heart of the man known only as "the blacksmith," a free black man who can come and go as he likes. She, by contrast, must be thankful that her journey to the object of her desire has been made possible by the death of her master due to smallpox and her mistress's belief that the blacksmith can save her from the same fate. Florens must cross a terrain for which she is ill prepared. She does not know her way, though she has been given general directions. She carries a letter of permission from Rebekka Vaark, but its acceptance is not guaranteed, and its legibility depends upon the literacy of any interceptor. Florens has a vivid notion of how she will be received by the blacksmith, but no idea how they would ever be permitted to be together.

As discussed earlier, her journey takes place in a contact zone in which signifiers are unstable and power relations asymmetrical.[2] These encounters bring signifying systems into contest, and the asymmetry of these conditions produces a crisis of legibility born of a crisis of similitude. Florens's encounter with mother and daughter Ealing and their neighbors produces just such a set of crises for her. They perceive her likeness to the satanic figures of their own mythopoetic tradition, whereas she sees only her shadow in their fears. She attempts to comprehend these people by drawing on what she knows, but this does not help her. Florens can only see how what she knows will not suffice: "Swine look at me with more connection" (*M* 133). The women look away from her as they examine her body, and the only explanation Florens can find is the lesson that Lina has taught her, to look away from "bears so they will not come close." Ironically, this explanation bestializes her.

When Florens writes her explanation of her actions in what appears to be a second person form of direct address, the reader is tempted to respond egotistically, or even in a deictic reflexivity, by responding with "me" or "I" to her "you," not knowing, until much later, that she is addressing the blacksmith. The reader is merely listening in or reading over the shoulder of this address. Moreover, Florens's early references and are made stranger by her language, which is not the relatively normativized English of the third person narrations of the other characters' stories. Rather, her English retains a foreign and informal quality that is masked in the speech of others, including Lina and Sorrow or the indentured workers Scully and Willard.

Florens is aware that what she speaks about might seem strange and that what she is writing may not be read—she stages this uncertainty with her question "Can you read?" and notes that her writing may be received as:

> full of curiosities familiar only in dreams and during those moments when a dog's profile plays in the dream of a kettle. Or when a corn-husk doll sitting on a shelf is soon splaying in the corner of a room and the wicked of how it got there is plain. (*M* 3)

Indeed, there is no way of fitting the dog's profile or the doll into any ready schema. They are not part of a general, circulating set of learned signs associated with the period of the novel's setting, and their unexplained or decontextualized appearance troubles any anticipated contract between a writer and reader: the contract in which the reader expects the writer to be committed to making sense. We do intuit that she is already in the midst of "telling" her story, but we can understand only belatedly that telling and writing do not occur at the same time. When the novel opens, it is the beginning of her writing and her learning to tell the story that has been moving through her head.

When she begins, everything is familiar to her, but only partially so for a reader. We can understand the basic concept of a doll made of a corn-husk. But the doll and everything that we first read is rendered strange by the image of the dog's profile, which is not seen in an actual kettle but in a dream of a kettle. As such, as dream imagery, the dog's profile takes on the added significance of an omen. That Florens makes no distinction between the strange and the concrete adds to the sense of strangeness.

The doll is linked to this supernatural phenomenon as if it were interchangeable, through the simple conjunction "or." The doll therefore appears to be animate, as if it had sat itself on the shelf or as if some other force had cast it, splayed it in a corner. The seal on the strangeness comes with the reference to "the wicked of how it got there." This last phrase has no subject. It implies a blameworthy force, however, and that Florens takes this to be normal.

We will learn that the doll belongs to an orphaned boy whom the blacksmith has taken in. The point is that to call her language strange casts her into the periphery of what we, as early-twenty-first-century readers, consider the "normal" or comprehensible speaking voice of fiction. What is audibly strange is the quality of her "English," and this might suggest that she herself is strange.

Strangeness also appears literally, as a foreign language in writing that has already naturalized itself as English, albeit as dialect. This is the Portuguese phrase *minha mãe*. Someone who speaks Portuguese would understand the strict lexical meaning of *minha mãe* as "my mother," but not its specific meaning in Florens's explanation, or the particular formulation in which it appears as a category of person or presence when she refers to "a *minha mãe*" or "the *tua mãe*." The phrase renders the mother as a definite noun but not a possessive one, and thus a categorical term rather than a designator of singularity. The same occurs when Florens later substitutes an "a" for the definite article "the." This further, cumulative effect makes the mother figure possibly anonymous. The mother could be anyone's and not exclusively hers. As we will learn, this too has a logic. It is not a sudden eruption of a sign severed from its referent. Only when we have learned more about her do we understand that the possessive naming of her mother is an ironical, conflicted naming of one she believes has given her away—one whose action she does not understand. All she remembers is that she was standing with her "mother" and baby brother on the Portuguese trader D'Ortega's estate when a man came by with their master and suddenly pointed at her mother, saying that he wanted her. Her mother had pushed her forward, saying, "Take her. Take my daughter" (*M* 16). Florens can only interpret the statement as a choice that favors one child over another, her brother over her. Perhaps this is why she cannot say "my mother." The mother is "a" mother to her and "a" mother to her brother.

She is not "our mother." The truth embedded here is that she does not understand what a "brother" means. Not only is the singularity of the mother-child bond ruptured by slavery, but the singularity of all bonds so insufficiently but necessarily marked by the token possessive is ruptured.

Beyond the question of the singularity and the possessive economy that attempts to name it, the foreign phrase emblematizes Florens's mother. The category of persons who mother is inaccessible and foreign to her. It is significant that the phrase *minha mãe* is also the trace of the first language in which Florens would have learned how to refer to her mother. However, it is not her mother tongue. That tongue, spoken in Angola, from which her mother was taken, is completely inaccessible, even more so than that of Sethe's mother in *Beloved*, in which Sethe has a memory of Ma'am speaking another language. All we eventually know about Florens's mother is that she was taken from Angola to Barbados. Barbados becomes a replacement of its own, consigning Angola to a vague, indefinite status, along with any language Florens's mother would have spoken prior to the death-driven Middle Passage. The language of a master has thus been inserted into the place of a "first" language that is nevertheless not a mother tongue. English is the language of another master. It has established its dominance over Florens, making the initially italicized Portuguese doubly foreign, as foreign as the reason behind her mother's decision is incomprehensible and forever inaccessible, left behind at Jublio, where her mother is always kneeling and saying "Take her. Take my daughter" (*M* 26).

When, at the novel's end, the *minha mãe* addresses Florens, she names herself. The phrase *tua mãe* appears again, but without italics, as the mother entreats, "Oh Florens. My love. Hear a tua mãe" (*M* 167). The marked foreignness is subdued, less declarative in this intimacy of address, for even though the mother would be a stranger to her daughter, she has been imagining her for years and has made her familiar, even as the one who, being lost, she can only fantasize. The mother identifies with all mothers in this gesture, even as she claims the only daughter that is hers.

These distinctions between a mother and a daughter might lead one to draw an anthropological conclusion that theirs was not necessarily a biological relation, but one that extended the kinship obligations of adopting orphans. After all, Florens's mother does not say "your mother" but "a mother" in her closing entreaty: "Hear a tua mãe." However, the *minha mãe* does make clear that she bore Florens after D'Ortega decided to "mate" her and two other slave women to increase his "stock" and to "break" them in

(*M* 165–66). This occurs twice, and she says to the daughter she cannot and will not see again, "the results were you and your brother" (*M* 166). But this acknowledgment and the declaration of love do not mean that she can claim to have "mothered" Florens. This is a brutal, insurmountable fact of slavery. Calling herself "a tua mãe" is truthful. These, too, are details that Florens can never know. Florens is clearly her mother's daughter and not D'Ortega's, as Vaark suspected. However, the sad truth is that Florens and her brother are "fathered" by the paternalism of slavery.

Not knowing, Florens is amnesiac. She has blocked out or forgotten that her mother had said more than "Take her. Take my daughter" (*M* 16). When Vaark had demanded her as partial payment for the debt owed him, her mother had first said, "Please, Senhor, Not me" (*M* 16). Her reason is revealed only at the novel's end, when the final pages are given to "the" *minha mãe*. She had pushed Florens forward to save her daughter from D'Ortega, because she had "read" Vaark correctly, seeing in him a man who seemed to have "no animal in his heart" (*M* 163). For what the *minha mãe* knows of this world in which the Vaarks, husband and wife, imagine liberation from the horrors of old Europe is that: "There is no protection. To be female in this place is to be an open wound that cannot heal." This is in some ways an answer to Florens's own question "Can you read?" which is put to herself as much as it is to the blacksmith or to any reader. Florens cannot. If reading is to be understood as comprehension, she could not "read" her mother's act or speech. Even though she heard her mother speak the phrase *tua mãe*, "your mother," and even though she recalls this phrase, the "pledge" or promise of fidelity within the possessive "your" escapes her.

The indefinite status of "a" *minha mãe* is the crypt in which any real connection is buried. Or, more appropriately, it is the headstone that marks the place where such a connection once lived. Between them accumulate narratives that move forward in time and that might be read as striving to bring them together but that never can. There is only a brief opportunity for Florens's mother to speak before she vanishes, unheard, in the wake of her daughter's movement into the future to which she had sacrificed her. This is the tragedy of *A Mercy* and the tragedy of the untold stories that simply never can be passed on.

This is also what makes the "you" of Florens's first utterances fluid for a reader who has yet to understand her, and it is what fuels her need to write. She simultaneously anticipates and dismisses the possibility that what she is writing will be read as full of anomalous, mystifying signs. She points out that to perceive something as strange is tantamount to asking or looking for a cause, for responsibility, and, when one does not find it, to assigning it to someone or something and its author. Not until late in her telling do we learn what the referents for the doll and the steam are. Yet even then we will not be satisfied, because she does not distinguish between the real and the magical. This is why the kettle image is so redolent with Freudian associations, for kettle logic was adduced by Freud to demonstrate that dreams do not obey logic's rule of noncontradiction. (In kettle logic, several contradictory explanations are adduced as explanation for an event.) The same can be said for both magic and language in the moment of its invention, when metaphor simply conjoins previously unrelated entities, as if by magic.[3]

At the beginning of her story, Florens insists that if one cannot read signs, they remain strange. Hence her question "Can you read?" concerns more than page-based literacy. Taught how to read and write, in secret and by a priest (*M* 6), she reads scripted writing and nature in a continuous way; one mode is not privileged above another. Yet her act of writing is an admission that her way of reading the world is changing. To pinpoint when that change began for the likes of Florens, her mother, her brother, and other slaves—as well as for the Scullys, Willards, and Linas—is impossible. Some incidents seem pivotal. One change begins with a contest of wills between two men and the power that money gives one over the other. With a signature, Vaark or D'Ortega can transform a human being into currency. The change that a written contract makes in Florens's life continues with the power that Rebekka Vaark's letter claims over her. This document draws Florens into a discursive position already dominated by Rebekka. Her writing is equally an understanding of the irrevocability of changes revealed by the death of Jacob Vaark.

The first lines of Florens's writing are directly related to the next, most decisive change, and they are filled with the objects and sensations of her arrival at the blacksmith's home. By then, she is not the child whose desire for shoes is humored by her mistress and master and by their servant Lina. She is not the young slave woman adopted, loved, and protected by Lina. And she is not the young woman whose first sexual encounters filled her with such daring that she could set off with nothing but a few directions, wearing her dead master's boots, to find the object of her affections. By the time she reaches the blacksmith's home, inhabitants of a settlement have read her blackness as the sign of the devil, and she has also been reminded that she is a slave permitted to travel only because of a mistress's letter.

Something else arrives with her. It is the memory that precedes all of the experiences of her journey: her memory of her mother as a woman who gave her away and chose to keep her baby brother. When she enters the blacksmith's hut, ready to begin a new life, this deeper memory will become the frame of reference through which she reads what awaits her. And it is in the blacksmith's home that those figures of her first writings belong—the corn doll, the steam in the dreamed kettle—for what she finds confronts her with the task of reading what is real against the specters of her fears of (further) rejection.

As noted earlier, the doll belongs to an orphaned boy that the black-smith has taken in. The triumph of her successful journey and her joy at seeing the blacksmith ends when she sees the boy, Malaik (*M* 135). In effect, he becomes a rebus for the only other little boy she has known, her brother. Her view of him is therefore distorted. Her behavior follows suit, as she attempts to thwart an estrangement from the unity she feels not only with herself but with the blacksmith, this ego ideal whose function in her life is narcissistic and imaginary.[4] She has, however, already shifted, or been shifted, from a dyadic relationship into a triadic one via her reaction to the boy when she sees the attention paid to him by the blacksmith. The shift is physical: in the turn of his head, which she sees and understands even before she addresses the reason for it. Her prehistory speaks for her as her eyes "follow" to where he looks. Her phrasing and the fact that she casts the boy, whose name she does not yet know, as a location, a "where," are an instant attempt to deny his existence (*M* 135). In effect she attempts to deny what she sees and has already translated.

In the always-present tense of her relation to language, past and present are decompartmentalized. Her past enters the present, informing it through a distortion of her inner and outer worlds. She states simply, "This happens twice before." The pronominal weight of "This" draws what is before her and what has happened "before" into the distorted actuality of looking for her mother's hand "that is only for her little boy." She sees herself as "a pointing screaming little girl hiding behind her mother and clinging to her skirts" (*M* 135, 136). Here is no easy emergence of an "I," but that of a girl to whom she cannot lay claim. Her first self-image is of a struggle that already mimics what Hegel calls the "struggle to the death" in the master-slave dialectic.

These memories occur in the present. They "are full of danger," and they are causal. They also retain their own unreleased logic. The formative separation from her mother is the single, only one. We do not know what the second is, unless it is the separation from her brother, making that first separation manifold. The effect of the memories is the always-present experience of being expelled. Despite the years of respite brought by Lina's care and attention, when confronted with this memory, Florens conjoins her mother's utterance with the flat statement "and I am expel." This is existential and ontological, while also locative. It fixes her in a place where she does not want to be, expelled once more. This time it is from the blacksmith's full attention. In the grammatical construction of her utterance, she is in a time that has stalled.

Left alone to care for Malaik while the blacksmith rides to save her mistress, Florens dreams the haunting figure of one who cannot speak to her, who can only gesture. She sees "a minha mãe" in the doorway, holding the boy's hand. The figure has Florens's shoes in her pockets (*M* 137). No longer distanced by italics to delineate the foreign, she appears to be signaling to Florens, who tries to understand what is being communicated. Florens retells this in the only way that a dream can be told, as a secondary process that displaces. When she wakes and finds that her shoes are indeed missing, she can only interpret that earlier sight of her mother as a sign *from* this figure that the boy has taken her shoes. The question "Can you read?" is now also "Is this true?" A reader can say it is not true but cannot know the nature of any truth about her missing shoes. She assigns blame. She sees Malaik as her rival and his doll as an extension of him—but also as the reminder of that earlier boy, her brother, whose power seems to reach so far into her life. Removing the doll from Malaik, she places it on a high shelf but is astonished and immediately afraid when she finds it thrown in a corner of the blacksmith's hut, with a stool overturned and porridge spilled. She reads and misreads what she believes are signs. She cannot believe that the boy wanted the doll, that he used the chair to reach the doll, and that he had perhaps fallen over and knocked the porridge over, too.

Inanimate objects appear animated, as is always a potential with toys or other objects, which can at any moment, as Susan Stewart points out, suggest "the still life's theme of arrested life."[5] In Florens's case, this arrest is psychic. Both the doll and the boy are miniatures. One is a miniature of a female, the other of a man; one is truly inanimate, the other flesh and blood. For Stewart, miniatures have escaped historical time but distort it through their proximity, a distortion that is incorporated as transcendence and therefore outside of flux.[6] Florens sees the doll and boy as directly associated with her earlier loss of her mother. She also reads them as malevolent forces. In her panic, she grabs the boy's arm and breaks it, just as the blacksmith returns. His reaction is not a misreading as much as it is a response to what is directly in front of him. There is no way he can access Florens's fears, and there is no time for him to ask, or even imagine, an explanation. What "reading" he does is within a frame that his own freedom has given him. He is free. She is not. He berates her by accusing her of having turned herself into a slave. It is a frame already on offer to him, and he does not pause to question his certitude. Her reaction is swift and frenzied: she takes up a hammer and attacks the object of her love, who is now also an object of loss and betrayal. Where her mother had attempted to save her from the fate of a slave woman, the blacksmith has accused her of having the mind of one.[7]

He reads the boy's scream, his pain, his broken arm and sees all he needs to see. Belatedly, she believes that he should have read and understood her love as explanation for her actions, even her accidental breaking of the boy's arm. Her early question about reading signs returns: Who is responsible, who is to blame? Her writing is her attempt to have the blacksmith reread the entire situation, in a space in which his gaze is fixed only on her—like the reader's gaze so desired by the narrator of *Jazz*, who says how she has longed to say out loud:

> That I have loved only you, surrendered my whole self reckless to you
> and nobody else. That I want you to love me back and show it to me.
> That I love the way you hold me, how close you let me be to you. I like
> your fingers on and on, lifting, turning. I have watched your face for
> a long time now, and missed your eyes when you went away from me.
> Talking to you and hearing you answer—that's the kick. (*J* 229).

How might Florens be read without consigning her to the history that Morrison attempts to suspend? That suspension allows us to look to the zones of contact, in which flux brought death and disease to American Indians and in which Africans were enslaved and poor Europeans indentured. Yet that time and place of early America contained the potential for the truly strange—if by strange one might mean playing with a sense of the unexpected as that which, even if briefly, escapes from the violent regime of the calculable and the order of slavery in which people were reduced to and traded as countable things. This is the time and zone to which *A Mercy* returns us. However, it does not attempt any consoling, recuperative gesture. Rather than installing fiction as consolation or redemption of a lost chance, *A Mercy* portrays again and again instances in which characters are caught in the impossible glass bell jar of making sense while being perceived as producing nothing but mystery or senselessness. In other words, the crisis of each moment of contact produces illegibility for Florens, and also for the servant girl Sorrow.

By contrast, Jacob and Rebekka Vaark embrace their setting, whether it is New England or upstate New York, with clear eyes and an unshaken conviction that they can see and understand their new world. They view the world they have left behind in England as decrepit and violently bound up in a class system that left them little or no chance for growth—him as an orphan, she as a working-class girl. Until they both contract smallpox, violence is distant from them, although they do not understand that their presence and the settlements to which they belong are forged in violence. Nor do they understand that they have within their own home someone for whom the arrival of Europeans has meant the end of the world. This is Lina, the American Indian girl who is the same age as Rebekka, just a teenager, when she is sold to Jacob Vaark as a housekeeper. For Vaark, Lina is simply one of Rebekka's "two helpers as reliable as sunrise and strong as posts" (*M* 21).

Lina's childhood has taught her about the arrival of Europeans. She mulls over the inequity and confusing piety of those she refers to as "Europe," who "could calmly cut mothers down, blast old men in the face with muskets" but become "enraged if a not-Europe looked a Europe in the eye" (*M* 46). She is one of three young children who survive the smallpox outbreak that killed her entire people. Her memories are of a world in which death stalks and animals gnaw on the bones of people, making it impossible for children to dare name "the pieces hauled away from a body or left to insect life" (*M* 46). Rescued while French soldiers burn the remains of her people and their infected village, she is sent to live with "Europes." A family of Presbyterians takes her in only because, being a girl, she may grow to become the kind of industrious soul they admire—in their embrace, they echo Locke's depiction of American Indian men as lax, American Indian women as industrious and therefore admirable. In so doing, they turn the truisms of his depiction into proven reality, at least for themselves. They also interpret the fate of her people as a sign of God's displeasure with "the idle and profane"(*M* 47). She grows up under their roof, forced to constrict her relationship with the natural world to their beliefs until she matures physically and becomes a burden to them. They advertise to trade her to Jacob Vaark as a "Hardy female, Christianized, and capable in all matters domestic available for exchange of goods or specie" (*M* 52).

From her prior life, Lina can only draw upon fragments of what her mother had taught her. Otherwise, little from that life prepares her for the one into which she has been inserted, so that not even a reach for similitude as sense making comes easily. Rather, she has to confront the example set by "Europes" at the limit. Isolated in and by her difference from them, she makes her own solutions, drawing upon "scraps" of what she had learned from her mother and combining these with what she learns about European medicine. She brings together the fragments of native lore and Christianity and invents "the hidden meaning of things. She has found a way to be in the world" that ended hers (*M* 48). She becomes "more than one thing," inhabiting the kind of plasticity that the Vaarks imagine is open to them but going beyond anything they could comprehend without calling it "animal." She "cawed with birds, chatted with plants, spoke to squirrels, sang to the cow and opened her mouth to rain" (*M* 48–49). And she swears herself to loyalty in order to endure the shame of survival. In fact, survival is possible if shame does not intercept life, rendering one's purchase upon it ambivalent. Lina's instinct is to resist the way that shame would deepen her isolation because the destruction she has witnessed is a private matter now, since the only other survivors of her village, two boys, were immediately sent elsewhere and there is no one she can talk to— although the possibility of talking is what shame forecloses. In part, her turning outward might also be due to the fact that she has only fragments of visual imagery to draw upon. The world is what gives her a conceptual and emotional language and an escape from shame's paralysis.[8]

In a moral order, the shame of the survivor would have to have its corollary in the guilt of the perpetrator or at least in the guilt of those who did nothing to avert a catastrophe or who were somehow the beneficiaries of it. The Vaarks make absolutely no reference to Lina's past. He is the once "ratty orphan," now a landowner, thanks to an inheritance from an unknown relative (*M* 12). She, at sixteen, has been palmed off by a father keen to be rid of her but is glad to be away from the murderous religious competition between Catholics and Protestants. His sense of newness is a belief that the old class hierarchies can be overcome, especially through the possession of things. This is confirmed through his position as a moneylender, underwriting D'Ortega's plantation economy. He is in a position of power over someone who would, in Europe, be his superior. He is a fledgling mercantilist; he is among those who ultimately will fund the full scope of colonialism and whose relationship to capital will be surpassed by a new investment in the transformation of production and not simply the extraction of surplus through trade. Aware of his financial power, he imagines himself outside of the plantation economy that makes D'Ortega vulnerable to failure.

Husband and wife believe in the newness of their lives, and of the world they understand themselves to be part of. Their fantasy is about what might be ushered in through a radical break with the old. Yet the sense of newness can only be a fantasy about forgetting, for neither can move forward without recalling the past, even in a millennialist hope that they are breaking with a corrupted, misdirected "old" world. Even the triumphant new cannot give up its dialectical, definitional relationship with the old. The latter must remain within memory in order to have its mistake amplify the new and render it legitimate. What passes under the name *new* is a practice or way of being that attempts restoration and renewal of the purity that, for millennialists, preceded the corrupt time.

For Rebekka, restoration begins with a return to health, and in a state of gratitude she renews her faith. That her gratitude does not extend to the blacksmith (or to Lena for nursing her) allows her to discredit the role that his intervention and aid played in her regained health. As indicated earlier, she returns to stern religiosity and embraces an ordering of the world she had attempted to avoid and that she had already seen in the close personal quarters of her parents' religious intolerance and their "glazed indifference" to anything and anyone save religion, including their children. She remembers their religiosity as "a flame fueled by a wondrous hate" (*M* 75). Their desire for a "rampaging avenging god" masks their "enraged envy and sullen disapproval of anyone who was not like them" (*M* 75). Their abhorrence of Catholicism made their Fifth Monarchy Protestantism the central core of their identity and their identification with Englishness. Rebekka's earliest memories include public hangings, and her nightmares are filled with images of a drawing and quartering she had attended when too young to really recall, save for her parents' recounting of it as if it were an entertainment (*M* 75).[9] All the way across the Atlantic, she still thinks of drawing and quartering as if it were her own memory that contributes to the "gore of what she had seen since childhood" (*M* 76).This is Morrison engaging what is, essentially, false memory. When others' memories heal into another's psyche, they may be misrecognized as one's own experience. So, although Rebekka imagines herself as being free from her parents' memory, she is entirely possessed by a narrative that she cannot distinguish from her own experience. We see here the structure of identity formation in a preracial time that will come to govern the historical consciousness of African Americans after slavery. A colonialist thinks she is severing from an old world, while others are abducted and lose their mothers' memories. The violence is that the colonizers have the memories, while the colonized do not; they can only fantasize.

With all of this behind her, Rebekka first looks upon the world she has stepped into, having seen it as bathed in a brand-new rain that falls uncontaminated by the soot of London's skies. Violent religiosity had been a torsional political force in her childhood, structuring her memories. The distance from it is measured by the new natural world's ascendency over earthly, religious architecture, which is dwarfed by "trees taller than a cathedral" and drowned out by swarms of insects "louder than chiming steeple bells" (*M* 76). This is an earthly paradise for her, a new earth filled with birds and fresh water. Plenitude fills her days. Yet the shadow of the past is never far away, providing a symbolic architecture that still shapes and arranges her thought, holding her hope in a dialectical relationship with all she abhors. Thinking of beauty that cannot be marred by violent winter storms or summer's insects, she is still repelled by the memory of "reeking streets," being "spat on by lords and prostitutes, curtseying, curtseying, curtseying" (*M* 77).

And, until her recovery from smallpox, she is under no more obligation than to pay a "polite attendance" to the only presence of formal religion in her vicinity, the Anabaptists. Even here, she cannot refer to them without the image of her parents' condemnation of all Separatists. These Anabaptists are, for her, benign and generous refugees from England's religio-political violence. Without knowing it, she is already linking herself to them as one who has also escaped. Yet she is still on the cusp of what Bachelard would call the "phenomenology of the daydream" in which memory and imagination are bound. Her memories are of things that would be unspeakable had they not been spoken of again and again by her parents. She receives them narratively, not as her own firsthand memories of "frisky live entrails" being held up to a victim's eyes before being cast away (*M* 76). The prurience of her parents' language remains energized and impossible to turn away from.

Their encounters with England's religious struggles have rendered the very image of its architecture impossible for Jacob and Rebekka. Influenced by Protestant polemic, he sees temples of corruption in the Catholic churches. For her, the stability promised by the design of churches, the vaulting announcement of devotion embodied in cathedral steeples, has been undone by the crudity of intolerance. Whatever these architectures meant to communicate, they have seen more. The divine light that Abbot Suger, the theorist of gothic architecture, saw streaming through cathedral windows into naves has been replaced, for Jacob, with sunlight that "fires" fog and turns "the world into thick, hot gold" (*M* 9). One might say that he and Rebekka have taken Abbot Suger's vision of divine energy out of the edifices of power and found it in a world that they believe to be the equivalent of that promised in the scriptures on which this power claims to rest.[10]

For Vaark, the "old" is epitomized by Catholic Maryland, in which priests walk openly (*M* 13). Imagining himself to be entirely open, so much so that he embraces the sense of not knowing what might come his way, he has nevertheless carried into his lexicon an older language of accusation, namely, of paganism, which is tantamount to witchcraft—New England was less than a decade away from the Salem Witch trials when he set off to Virginia and Maryland to force D'Ortega to honor his debt. The Catholic churches of Maryland are therefore temples that menace, and the priests are bound to "sinister missions" that "crop up at the edge of native villages" (*M* 13). Roman Catholicism and the Whore of Babylon align when he reads the "lax, flashy cunning of the Papists" against the unspoken presence of Revelation's depiction of arch-feminine corruption (*M* 14). This is what he had learned as a boy in a poorhouse, where his primer was a catechism of Protestant polemic that he has never questioned. The sight of priests unlocks lines he has remembered as if they were his own thoughts: "And all her blasphemies / Drink not of her cursed cup / Obey not her decrees." At the same time, he avoids organized worship.

Vaark might find his literary echo in some of Amaso Delano's thinking in Melville's *Benito Cereno*. Although of different times, one born into the world begun by the likes of the other, both men are blinded by their own sense of goodness and propriety—and in this they are the forebears of Valerian Sweet's liberal humanism. Vaark is more cautious of his surroundings as he travels through Virginia and then Maryland on his way to D'Ortega's plantation, but he has an air of self-satisfaction that parallels Delano's (and Valerian Street's) sense of himself as a fair-minded, good man. Both assume the ascendancy of their way of living, particularly their Anglo-Protestant, Puritan worldview, for while neither espouses any especially religious sentiment, both are quick to refer to the competing imperial interests of the Spanish (in Delano's case) and Portuguese (in Vaark's) as reflecting a "softness" that they associate with Catholicism. Each expresses a sense of his own humanity, particularly toward animals and the disadvantaged—the slippage is revealing. Both appear to be the still point in a world that is in a state of flux.

As Vaark rides through Virginia and then into Maryland, his view of his surroundings and his language for what he knows of them transforms his attraction to "hardship and adventure" into a sense of restraint and, although not expressed as baldly, a democratic impulse. The last is reflected in the way he remembers the one colony as "a mess" and the other as the private province of a king who permitted papery (*M* 11, 13). While in Virginia, he thinks back with a nascent class consciousness to the "people's war," in which people of different, but not all, races fought against the landed gentry, led by one of that class. The war to which he refers with an almost nostalgic sense of a missed opportunity for "social ease between gentry and laborers, forged before and during the rebellion," was in fact a far more complicated affair. Bacon's Rebellion of 1676 (known in England as the Virginia Rebellion) was led by the planter Nathaniel Bacon. Framed as the revolt of small free-holders and "common" people against Governor Berkeley and his associates, who were grandees in their eyes, the rebellion has come to have an almost utopian aura. In reality, the language of commonality employed by Bacon and his followers in rejecting Berkeley's increase in poll taxes masked a fundamental flaw in their declaration of mutuality or commonality. In the Virginian view of the time, the term *commonality* extended to those who did not own land or who, as exservants or former indentured workers, had acquired some land but were not among the elevated classes eligible for office in the House of Burgesses. Although Nathaniel Bacon was from this class and had been a member of the House, the stories of his rebellion portray him as a man willing to step outside of his class to side with commonality. This supports the view of the rebellion as motivated by an impulse for a more equitable access to government and favor. Drawing upon historical records of growing awareness of and dissatisfaction with leadership and its allies—merchants, religious leaders, and legal counselors—Peter Thompson argues that the term *commonality* was taken to refer to those who were "the actual common people of the colony, often but not always figured as a distinct social and political estate oppressed by corrupt or immoral great planters."[11] Thompson reads "commonality" as "a near synonym for commonwealth, referring to localized polities in which householders were bound together in an organic commonweal."[12] As American Indians who refused to side with Bacon and his militia were to discover, the bond was material, for at the heart of the rebels' dissatisfaction with Berkeley and his taxes was the entire colonial project of land acquisition and labor.[13]

For Vaark—who was not born to land ownership, as were the wealthy who made up the House of Burgesses, and who, through the luck of his inheritance, has been elevated above white indentured servants—the rebellion was one of hope and hope lost. The loss was manifold. The rebellion's failure reinstated the gentry's interests against any impulse to commonwealth, but this failure was also rooted in another factor, one that actually aligned the rebellion with the same interests—the desire for land and control of local nations. Indeed, as Vaark notes in an aside, the rebellion led to the death of the tidewater native peoples, who had come into conflict with the Virginian planters and a growing class of land-grant farmers seeking to expand their colony and their agriculture.

On his journey to collect the debt owed him, Vaark appears to be the still point in a world that is in a state of excitability, a world of colonies in the agitated state of defining their boundaries, of settling land, and of defining themselves as new, even as they rely upon their English or Spanish as well as religious differences. All allegiances have yet to be settled, as well. Having landed in a fog on the shores of Virginia, Vaark compares it with the English fogs he had known in childhood and those where he now lives. His description of the fog would appear to make it heavenly, "sun fired, turning the world into thick, hot gold" (*M* 9). But movement through it is difficult, a struggle. It is like a dream, and he misses its beauty once he has passed through it. He has little fear, none of Florens's anxiety about encountering bears or men. Moreover, he is not without information. He knows the laws of each colony, its history. He relishes the challenge of passing through this "messy" geography. Vaark is as alert for snakes as for robbers. The experience exhilarates and tests him. With each test he finds confirmation of the kind of man he believes himself to be, and even better than he had thought. When he stops to free a raccoon from a trap, the caution that undergirds his attention and reading of his surroundings contributes to a "growing confidence" that began with his landing in the fog (*M* 10). The measure of his confidence is in direct proportion to his disdain of Catholicism's marrying of tobacco and slavery. It is in this state, confident and disdainful, that he arrives at his debtor's plantation, called Jublio.

For all of his confidence and pleasure in being alert to danger, Vaark now confronts a place that has so claimed and "tamed" the terrain that it seems to have the power to announce itself. The place is more like a palace than a house. Its brick walls and many windows are grandiose. The wrought-iron gates through which he must pass, the windows, and the mist through which he views it all build upon a basic impulse that he has held at bay. It is the impulse to find shelter, one that Vaark's memory of being a foundling suggests is never far away.

Bachelard reminds us that the impulse to find shelter is "rooted in the unconscious" and can easily be ignited.[14] He also implies another basic impulse—the impulse to speak about the house of one's dreams or daydreams, even if that house is one of the "real houses of [one's] memory."[15] For Bachelard, the oneiric house "lives" in literary rather than analytic language. When Vaark tries to analyze Jublio, he does so in what seems to be a language of the concrete, noting how easy it would be to build (*M* 15). His language moves between a practiced practicality and the poetic, and ends up in an affectively charged delirium. Where the "sopping weather" damages D'Ortega's tobacco crop, the house already seems to exude "comfortable" odors that Vaark can liken to "fireplaces and good women serving ale," places and contexts he knows. His next phrase brings his past into the dreamlike present as he finds that these odors cloak Jublio "like balm." He notes the second-story windows, which hold sunlight above the mist. This light glitters. The verb echoes the gold of the sunlight earlier in his day. Indeed, this house seems to contain the light, almost the light of the world. He observes the materials that were used. The wood is not simply wood, but "Soft southern wood." The stone is not simply stone but "creamy stone." And he begins to imagine the interior even before he has entered. He sees the "Long hall, probably, parlors, chambers . . . easy work, easy living, but, Lord, the heat" (*M* 15). This dream is so powerful that he feels it physically—foreshadowing the feverish energy with which he will build his own version of this house, but also the smallpox that will claim his life.

At the same time, the ellipsis marks a breakdown of his language. It also inserts a pause and space into which language disappears, and from which it cannot draw anything. Vaark is, after all, not familiar with such houses. He grew up in a workhouse and was only one step away from being an indentured worker himself when he received his unexpected inheritance. He shifts from the concrete but vaguely outlined rooms and passages in which he is already moving as if in a dream and which are already entering him, as if the house were his own house of memory. He stands before a real house, but it is so far removed from anything he has ever known that it can only become a dream. Attempts to render it in language move him deeper into the dream, in which he is already confronting a desire that his self-congratulatory Protestant restraint would find unacceptable.

He and his wife have already seen the natural-world cathedrals of new-ness. He will attempt to build one; she will be appalled and turn to grasp the "greater" dream: a heavenly kingdom, of which the massive trees she so admires—and which her husband will cut down to build his mansion—are but symbolic, earthly reminders.

There is another impulse, which Vaark understands but puts aside. Grandeur can attract and demand respect and, indeed, control the way that a body moves in its presence. Bachelard's two themes in developing his "psychology of the house" are organized around aspirations to vertical-ity and a concentration on centrality.[16] This verticality is the dialectic rela-tion between "high-minded" reason and the "unredeemed" unconscious. Although Bachelard's poetics of space focuses on experience and not pur-pose, this could be the very definition of the Enlightenment, the answer to Kant's question *Was ist Aufklärung?* the aspiration to liberate consciousness from being plagued by irrationality and ignorance. The house of Vaark's dreams might suffer from "Lord, the heat," and its full details might defy coinage. But it already exudes a reasoning and rational confidence. None-theless, his house mimics the announced solidity of D'Ortega's Jublio. And it is rooted in contest. Even before he steps into D'Ortega's house, Vaark has recreated it in his own image and emptied it of those he is just about to meet.

His confidence fails when the reality of the house and its occupants displace the dream. He is returned to hierarchical Europe and to con-sciousness of a self he seeks to escape. The house has, after all, "made" him sweat. Immediately after thinking of the heat in those brick walls, he wipes sweat from his hairline, and he does so with his sleeve (*M* 15). He fingers his "soaking collar" and in these two gestures is more like the boy who has just taken his horse than the master of a palatial mansion. The gap between dream and reality is deepened by the servant who opens the door and is more dignified and well dressed than he is. When D'Ortega appears, he approaches with the confidence of the master of such a house. He uses Vaark's first name, while Vaark calls him "sir." And his clothes seem to announce the superiority of their wearer, just as the house announces its superiority.

The dreamlike ease of Vaark's imagination now pulls away from comfort and shelter to his older life of social exclusion, and he finds the teachings of the workhouse now housing his reactions. He compares himself to the Catholic, Portuguese D'Ortega. He is the antipapist; D'Ortega, the tobacco planter and slave owner, who has callously dumped the bodies of "his cargo" off the coast and now complains about the Lord Proprietary's fine and the chore and cost of having to "scoop" up what remains could be found. Vaark perceives D'Ortega's flat accounting of the cost, measured against the horrific images of bodies piled in "drays (six shillings)" and carted to "where saltweed and alligators would finish the work," more as signs of the slovenly, old Catholic Europe than a basic inhumanity (*M* 16). Whereas he sees softness and a cloying opulence in D'Ortega, he sees restraint, focus, and luck in himself. Whereas he sees avarice in D'Ortega, he reminds himself that he came to this new world, not for the promise of wealth, but attracted by "hardship" and "adventure," notions that we now categorize as the "boot-straps" logic that is part of the nation's self-characterization, though at this point in the novel they are part of a self-proclaimed innocence that precedes such characterization (*M* 12). Vaark's Protestant superiority grows, even though he attempts to couch his objections to D'Ortega in more revolutionary terms of the rotting old world and the fresh, egalitarian new one. Nevertheless, he does so because he is acutely aware of his appearance beside his host's coat, stockings, and "fanciful wig" (*M* 16). His "rough clothes" are in "stark contrast to embroidered silk and lace collar" (*M* 17). His prudence is offended by D'Ortega's wasteful burning of candles in the daytime (*M* 19). His fingers, although "normally deft," have become "clumsy with the tableware" at lunchtime, and he sees his hands still stained with the blood of the raccoon he has freed, while the D'Ortega family's hands are spotless, their skin free of

perspiration. Even this he finds insulting, as part of a "show" and performance whose single aim is his humiliation. He is the English speaker made
to listen to prayers in an indecipherable language, the man of plain food
and simple hunger who cannot eat "heavily seasoned dishes." His disdain
makes him superior and able to look down on D'Ortega's family.

He compares D'Ortega's fecundity—six children, including two older
sons of thirteen and fourteen—with his own childless marriage. He and
Rebekka have lost four children, three of whom were stillborn. The
fourth, a girl named Patrician, was killed by a kick from a horse at age five
(*M* 21). In this comparison, Vaark finds Rebekka the better woman. Her
body is not as excessively fecund as Mrs. D'Ortega's. Rebekka is uncom-
plaining and busy, dutiful. As someone who mourns the failure of Bacon's
Rebellion, Vaark nevertheless draws upon a ready hierarchy in which the
supposedly overdressed Mrs. D'Ortega is a "chattering magpie," whereas
Rebekka had been "cheerful as a bluebird" before what he can only call
a "kind of invisible ash" settled over her after the deaths of her children
(*M* 21). Where Mrs. D'Ortega cannot imagine living in the snow of the
north, Rebekka is more like him, able to adjust to even the worst losses.

Vaark's view of himself as just and hardworking is grounded in an an-
thropocentrism that finds expression in his attitude toward animals. Animals become the conduits through which he can distinguish himself as
human, following the logic by which, according to Derrida's later thought,
all creatures designated "non" human are placed in the single, caged category of "animal" in an act of violence.[17] Derrida's concern with the place
of animals in the construction of the human registered much earlier, in
his critique of Rousseau's *Essay on the Origin of Languages*, in which Rousseau's theory about the development of language makes speech the initial
distinction between humans and animals.[18] In Rousseau's natural philosophy, the acquisition of language that moves beyond what one might call
mere "subsistence communication" is accompanied by, and facilitates, the
development of sympathetic responses. Derrida reads against Rousseau's
privileging of human speech as the delineator of imagination and, especially, pity. The Rousseauean category of the "human" is constituted in
an act of containment and exclusion that reserves for animals the place of
receiving our pity, since, for Rousseau, animals lack the ability "to live . . .
suffering as the suffering of another and as the threat of death."[19] Without
an "affinity with the other as such," Rousseau's treatment of speech as
"living," consigns animals to having "no relation to death."[20] It follows, in

this logic, that an emotion such as pity would become a further delineation of the human. Derrida turns to *Emile*, in which Rousseau writes:

> pity is born, the first relative sentiment which touches the human heart according to the order of nature. To become sensitive and pitiful the child must know he has fellow-creatures who suffer as he has suffered, who feel the pains he has felt, and others which he can form some idea of, being capable of feeling them himself. Indeed, how can we let ourselves be stirred by pity unless we go beyond ourselves, and identify ourselves with the suffering animal, by leaving, so to speak, our own nature and taking his. We only suffer so far as we suppose he suffers; the suffering is not ours but his. So no one becomes sensitive till his imagination is aroused and begins to carry him outside himself.[21]

Vaark's act of liberating a raccoon trapped in a tree break affirms his sensitivity or fellow feeling for another creature. This is one of three occasions on which he reaches out of himself, stirred by concern for animals. He thinks of the horse he has hired after landing not just as any horse but is mindful of her name, Regina. He takes care to rest her, despite his eagerness to get out of Maryland as fast as he can, and he takes care to order D'Ortega's slave to care for her and not to feed her while she is sweating. But there is a slippage in his language. The horse Regina is as hardworking as Rebekka. And the horse has a name, whereas he does not recall Lina or Sorrow, who work beside Rebekka on his farm, as more than "two helpers as reliable as sunrise and strong as posts."

The third instance occurs after he has left Jublio and returned to Virginia Town, where he witnesses a man "beating a horse to its knees" (*M* 28). The horse is saved by other men, "rowdy sailors," but Vaark's anger remains. Indeed, "Few things anger him more than the brutal handling of animals." He experiences raw fury against the infliction of pain, in part because he is appalled by what he sees as the "mute unprotesting surrender glazing" an animal's eyes as it is beaten. He is especially distressed by the fact that it has no capacity to protest save through falling to its knees.

Proximity and Contagion: The Slave's Body

In Freudian terms, a dream works by virtue of condensation and displacement. For Freud, this is why a dream has to be explained—it "hides" its meaning. Lacan sees metonymy and metaphor in the mechanism of the dream. The concept of "a dream" or of "dreaming" is often invoked as a simile when someone tries to explain a mystifying or troubling event that occurs in waking life. In other words, an (experience of an) event that has an aura of unreality is often likened to a dream. The simile is language that works, wakefully, consciously, to make meaning. In this, any one of the haunting presences in Morrison's work is "like a dream" in that it does not and cannot stand for one thing: most famously, Beloved is like a dream because she is the condensation of so many people and encounters, and her body also becomes a metaphor for, say, a slave ship. For Vaark, the entire experience at Jublio has changed his dreamlike pleasure of gold-shot mist into a nightmare. The world blessed by clean rain is also the world of heat and the reality that bodies are needed to produce the wealth he seeks just as much as D'Ortega does. Proximities emerge that he would rather not see, despite his negative comparisons between himself and D'Ortega. In the slave quarters, what should be a wake-up call to reality, is the deepest part of his nightmare.

Although he does not express horror or feel raw fury at D'Ortega's description of discarding humans as so much wasted cargo and leaving their bodies to rot or be eaten by wild animals, Vaark emphatically re-fuses D'Ortega's offer of slaves in lieu of monies owed on the grounds that "Flesh was not his commodity" (*M* 22). When he is taken to see the slaves, he distances himself further from the man, refusing any pity or fel-low feeling for the "Catholic in him" and what goes "beyond" this (*M* 23). D'Ortega's "drooping lids" and softness point to something "sordid and overripe" and soiling. The slaver is one of the Catholic "they" who had been excluded "from Parliament back home" (*M* 23). The past that he believes to be behind him comes forward to shape his emotions. And the shape that emerges is that of vermin, for, although Vaark does not believe that papists "should have been hunted down like vermin," he has conjured up this image and invoked creatures that mark the limit of his capacity for pity or compassion. D'Ortega, financially wounded, deserves nothing.

D'Ortega is oblivious of Vaark's disgust, however, and moves among the slaves, pointing out "talents, weaknesses and possibilities" (*M* 22). The slave women's eyes strike Vaark as "shockproof" long before he remarks upon the glazed eyes of an animal in pain. In effect, and reading backward from his later experience in Virginia Town, the horse seems more capable of feeling pain that the slave women. Standing in front of the slaves, Vaark will feel for them and find the language with which to express that feeling:

"shockproof," while the men look at the ground save for quick glances that he does not interpret. But it is their collective silence that overtakes him and makes him reach for some translation, one coming from as far away from this contaminated world as he can imagine. Although not expressed in the precise mode of a simile, the effect is comparative and "likening" without sealing itself into a metaphor. With the absence of sound so over-whelming, he envisions the silence as "an avalanche seen from a great distance," an event whose roar is not heard.

This is the man who, but for the brief ellipsis when language broke down at the front steps of Jublio, has articulated all he sees and has been able to name his responses to the D'Ortegas in an endless, precise litany of contemptuous comparisons. Here, his invocation of the distant avalanche is a reminder that, in its most direct function, a simile compresses one thing into proximity with another, drawing upon resemblance, likeness. Yet simile achieves some purpose in this act of naming the resemblance between one thing and another—be that thing an object, place, state of being, or a person. The simile might be said to do the work of explanation and familiarization, doubling meaning in order to make meaning possible, as when Vaark finds himself in close proximity to D'Ortega's "passel of slaves." He is not unfamiliar with slavery or captivity. He has on his farm indentured workers and a Native American woman who is virtually in a state of enslavement. Yet he is in utterly foreign quarters in all senses. He is in the papist state or Maryland, on an estate run by a Portuguese trader, whose house is nothing like anything he has ever seen except for a palace. He has endured food that is foreign to his palate and endured prayers in a foreign language. And now the reason for his visit, the collection of a debt, is redirected. In fact, he is physically directed by D'Ortega, who "moves" him toward the slave huts, into yet another proximity of excess, here the excess of control that is required to keep grown men and women from revolting and seizing their freedom. This excess of control is visible in the scars and wounds that Vaark notes on the bodies of the enslaved.

Vaark's response is to lose control. His stomach is "seized" by anxiety. All the rich food he has consumed at lunch blends into the odor of to-bacco. Having initially been "welcoming," the odor now nauseates him. He turns away to the sublime distance of silence and avalanche as a way of interpreting the slaves' silence and proximity in an attempt to remove himself from the unpalatable context of "his host's insistence" (*M* 22). The image of the avalanche does not seem to reflect anything from his past as briefly recounted. Rather, the image suggests a turn to fiction, in which he conjures up a pristine landscape of imagination rather than this world. It is an always-already aesthetic citation.

It is also possible that Morrison is giving us a racialized conception of the sublime here. In many ways, the image of the avalanche provides a figure for an unfathomable alterity and thereby works to contain the abyssal sensation that would otherwise confront Vaark in the moment that he stands face-to-face with the slave's otherness. The avalanche is both suggestive of the nature vistas so beloved by Romantic artists and ironically subversive of them, for it is an image of nature's destructive, death-dealing power, uncontainable as beauty. However, the point of Kant's theory of the sublime is that humans have the capacity to represent the limit of representation, to know that the mind has limits. In this recognition, says Kant, it can make reason a virtue and, confronting its finitude, grasp without actually knowing the idea of God. When Jacob Vaark confronts the slaves, he is overwhelmed. Although he does not say as much, he finds them untenable. That their blackness is as much a reason for this as the state in which he finds them will become apparent in the image for which he reaches, an image that will be the filled with opposite of their blackness. Moreover, although he does not say as much, he has encountered an absolute limit to his reason and, more importantly, to his capacity for similitude. He summons the only figure that he has for this limit—drawn from the extremity of a European landscape of which he himself seems to have had no experience. That he has to invoke a figure of destructive whiteness is Morrison's gesture toward a racialization of the sublime, which otherwise appears to us as a universalizable phenomenon. While the psychic and intellectual process may indeed be universal, she urges her readers to recognize that every history of figuration on which it is inscribed will be relative and, in this case, idiomatized in a color schema that is about to become "race." We know from the later novel *Home* that that schema will eventually supplement the rhetoric of color with the language of code, in the discourse of eugenics, and that the new idiom will both naturalize and biologize the fundamental otherness that Vaark found in black slaves.

Likening the slaves' silence to an avalanche draws upon this aesthetic notion. At the same time, Vaark's imagination meets an immediate limitation. He cannot know what the slave men's quick glances suggest or what thoughts might actually lie behind the "shockproof" eyes of the women. He can see that at least one man bears the warning face brand given a slave who attacks a master. This he can read. It is already a language that he knows, for all his imagined distance from slavery. He hears the silence not as such, then, but as that which he cannot hear, the "roar he could not hear." It is overwhelming, but as natural as an avalanche. He senses sound, but as something inaccessible. And he cannot look away from the signs of what might be immanent. Everything about this incident marks the limit of his control. He has imagined slaves to be distant from himself, and now he is drawn into their proximity by a man he despises.

The world of avalanches is outside of the oppressive heat. A snow-white, alpine nature could not seem further away from the unnatural restriction of black bodies smoldering with rage in D'Ortega's slave quarters. Rather than providing him with the outside of something known, which would enable him to translate this encounter, the simile forges a new association that effectively changes the geography of Vaark's imagination. The distant alpine geography is, in fact, disturbed. The distance across which Vaark's imagination perceives an avalanche is the distance between himself and his known world, but it is also the distance he would seek to put between himself and the slaves, whose silence does indeed have the force of disaster, the disaster that is the slave trade, with which all of the early colonies had already established proximity. Yet, rather than putting distance between him and the slaves, or conveying him to that alpine elsewhere, the simile has conveyed the slaves into his imagination. They have entered that space or have, at least, come to occupy a newly opened proximity to it. They are a new presence in the vista of that old snow, and their presence has animated it, brought it down.

Vaark is blind to this. The simile does not save him. Only a physical departure from the shed can alleviate his nausea. But when he does leave, his resolve against accepting any slave as compensation for the debt D'Ortega owes him is undone. This prudent man acts on a whim and decides to take a slave woman he sees at the cookhouse. He observes her dispassionately, notes that she has two children, "one on her hip; one hiding behind her skirts" (*M* 24). Minor as it appears, he is nevertheless performing his own tallying and is already "measuring" her health. He notes that she appears "better fed." That she is "better fed" is a sign that Vaark reads partially until he notes D'Ortega's unease. Vaark suspects that the "clove-laced sweat" on the woman suggests that the woman does more than cook for Mrs. D'Ortega. His earlier prudence is translated into resolve when he insists that he wants her as the payment, and he articulates this resolve as a selfless purpose—of providing more help for his wife—rather than as the pleasure of winning a contest with D'Ortega who clearly does not want to part with the woman.

Vaark's "selflessness" is deflected, however. Even in this he is out of his depths. A series of quick movements and confrontations have change his resolve again. The little girl steps forward. Distracted by the movement, he looks at her feet and sees that she is wearing a pair of women's shoes. He reacts physically again, this time with the pleasure of his chuckle, and then, at the thought of displeasing D'Ortega, he gives way to a "loud, chest-heaving laugh at the comedy, the hopeless irritation" of his entire visit. While the chuckle has some direct cause, it is still restraint. The laugh, however, overtakes his body, moves it, and restraint gives way to loudness. The laugh overtakes and is the sign of being overtaken.

He also directs his full attention away from what he is engaging. He turns from the present acquisition of a slave to an abstraction, pondering the larger scope of his visit with a kind of hindsight or oversight, revealing what he is right then. He is not the superior creditor, but someone who has temporarily abstracted himself. Not D'Ortega but the slave woman seizes upon this opening, stepping forward and addressing him. What had been a collective roaring silence in the slave quarters is now barely a whisper, whose urgency he hears and which has the power to reach him in ways that the distant roar of the avalanche could not. That roar was not language. The slave woman's whisper is.

It draws him forward, and the woman asks him to take her daughter instead of herself. He is not shocked or brought up short by the woman's daring. Neither does his desire to cause D'Ortega discomfort hold. It slips away as his laugh at the sight of a slave child in shoes comes to a "creaking" close: the shoes are humanizing; they are one of the many things that separate humans from animals or, in a predictive way that *Beloved*'s School-teacher teaches, slaves from free people. In the child, he cannot look away from "the most wretched business" into which he is being drawn (*M* 26). Yet here too he does not linger in thought or reflection. He has already turned from the present to his own life, his own needs, not thinking of what it might mean for a woman to give up her child. His own wife has lost four children, yet he makes no comparison between her grief and what the woman on whom he will inflict a similar loss will feel. All he thinks is that the little slave girl would be the same age as his dead daughter and that she might therefore be a good distraction for the grieving Rebekka. Here is another stalling of his imagination. To imagine what the child might feel is beyond him. The man who pauses to free a raccoon, who experiences fury over mistreatment of a horse, and who thinks himself appalled by trade in flesh thinks that, if the girl before him were to be kicked in the head by a horse as his daughter was, "the loss would not rock Rebekka so" (*M* 26). The silent discourse that has made it natural for him to read the woman at the cookhouse as a slave was never as distant from him as he imagined.

What began as the journey of a man who was the still point of his own world has been compromised by the reality that he deals with slavery, whether directly or indirectly, and the admission that he desires wealth so much that he would be willing to perform mental gymnastics to circumvent his capacity for pity. Animals remain the safe, easy recipients of his form of mercy; humans trapped in slavery are not animal enough for this.

In the space between the old and new worlds there is a chasm. America does not look like England. Rebekka and Jacob reach for similitude because it is the only thing that allows them to survive. Ironically, they are trying to escape. The pursuit of one similitude leads to the enactment of another. The effort of making sense leads to a practice of sameness. The corollary of this is that there is a strange, ironic, and irresistible transference of memory from one generation to another, despite an attempt at rupture. This is the negative side of Derrida's argument about inheritance. For all the effort to escape the violet political order of vengeance and corrupt cruelty, people recall narratives told by parents and eventually those narratives heal into their own narrated memories, which, like dreams, are ultimately known through processes of secondary revision. The result is that one cannot always know the difference between one's own experience and that of others because both pass through narratives that are deeply overdetermined by sets of metaphors, similes, idiomaticities, mythic structures, and interpretive frames. On the one hand, this is the basis of transhistorical or transgenerational identity. On the other hand, it is possession by the past.

Epilogue

This book has treated Morrison as a writer who writes about writing as much as she writes about the condition of African American historical consciousness within the larger America. Over the years, Morrison has increasingly produced writing that cites itself, as well as the canons with which she associates her work. Indeed, the canny practice of self-citation has underscored the relation of her writing to the production or reproduction of canon, and to what being drawn into a canon demands of her writing.

In the figure of the prison house of race, discussed in the Introduction to this book, an unseen presence is heard, not speaking but jingling keys. These, we presume, keep the house locked, but they also open other rooms. Equally important, the key that opens a door is shaped to the lock, and thus the metaphor of the key allows for the recognition that freedom is shaped by slavery. To extend this metaphor, *A Mercy* can be said to have revisited not only America's founding moments but also Morrison's own statement about the unseen logos in which her writing is "housed." That revisiting is also a revision. *A Mercy* wonders what other presences might be inscribed and effaced in the canon, even of African American literatures. A "masterful" doorkeeper is not the only occupant in the house of race. It includes others whose presence is foundational despite being invisible and who have always been speaking and writing in ways that, when seen and understood, render the very notion of the "house of race" or the "master's house" questionable. In *A Mercy*, Morrison asks her readers to rethink the possible slippage between a metaphor about a house of race and one about the master's house. After all, Garner's Sweet Home in *Beloved* is only possible because the slaves that he owns sustain it. But a slave could not articulate this point of view in public. The effort to make such a claim could and did elicit violent repudiation. Hence Schoolteacher punishes Sixo for attempting to explain the relation between his alienated labor and his need to kill a shoat to feed himself (*B* 190). The teacher is also the silencer. Silence has to be learned. And the permanent mystery of African American life is how an alternative conception of the world was learned. *A Mercy* shows one possible experience, by one possible young woman in the twilight between learning what she has to learn and trying to write against it, trying to keep a record of her presence. At the beginning of this difficult process, she has no one to cite, nothing by which to measure how she should tell her story. The literary conceit is that her writing is precanonical. And the canon that has not yet emerged will become the material of Morrison's own knowing citation. Beyond everything else, her novels are a staging of this process, for citation is also performative. But this is to get ahead of a necessary speculation on how it is that Morrison might have arrived at this strategy and the poetics necessary to sustain it.

Perhaps the performative operation of citation becomes most visible in the relation between an epigraph and the text to which it points the way. Starting with *The Bluest Eye*, Morrison's employment of epigraphs has been a theatricalization of a citational practice. While epigraphs often work to establish a readerly skill as authoritative and authorized, Morrison's fiction is a complex play with such authorizing, one that partakes of but also destabilizes the self-legitimizing force of canonicity. Indeed, even though she is now firmly part of the canon of African American writing within American literature, her work could be said to be heir to the figure she imagines scribbling away in an empty house that others imagine to be their exclusive heritage. There is no ghost at the beginning, but henceforth there will be a haunting.

If a parallel between Morrison's work and that of Florens is possible—with due acknowledgment of the limitations of such a parallel—we might go further, to suggest that Morrison destabilizes from their centrality the very traditions from which epigraphs emerge as signs of readerly and writerly authority. She does this by making the epigraph the site of spectrality. From this point of view one might argue, for example, that the relation between the epigraphs of *Beloved* and *Jazz* and the first utterance that opens the latter book constitute a performative poetics of possession. As such, they turn away from the question of haunting in its more conventional and limited sense. What happens to writing as citation at a boundary where it is impossible to know the limit of originality? Is this the place to explore

Morrison's dream of borderlessness? The answer to that question must be speculative, but it is one of the possibilities explored in this chapter.

Morrison's epigraphs partake of the mysterious interplay between the body of a novel and the disappearing body of another text from which a passage has been taken and reconstructed as an epigraph, thereby making visible a textuality that exceeds every corpus. That interplay creates its own unsettling gap, between the event of the prior work and that of the one to come, the one that is imminent and already opening. In the space forged by the epigraph, all truth is suspended and in play at once, and both texts are rendered uncanny to each other: out of time and out of place. And in the politics of Morrison's testing of the walls of an ideology as closely wrought as that which houses race, one text is enabled to take its rightful place. Its rightful place is the other's.

Epigraphs: To Cite Citation

An epigraph is the literal, typographical performance of writing as decontextualization and recontextualization. It is writing that has already taken place and that is positioned in an intermediary state between the material, outer layers of the book and its interior, the author's work. Gérard Genette calls these outer layers peritexts and considers them the responsibility of the publisher.[1] Positioned at the head of a text, an epigraph performs two possible functions. It is either a titular appendage or a canonical gesture. In either case, it "consists of commenting on the *text*, whose meaning it indirectly specifies or emphasizes.[2] As a commentary that attaches itself to a text, an epigraph would also be paratextual in Genette's schema.[3] Yet, unlike other forms of paratext, the epigraph does not give clear instructions—as, say, the paratextual "a novel" beneath a book's title does. Rather, Genette reads an epigraph as mute but gesturing and thus as having a far more open relation to the text that it informs. Rather than announcing how to receive the book—for example, as a novel—the epigraph leaves interpretation "up to the reader."[4] This does not mean that the epigraph is mute. Nor is it always neutral. Genette's brief history of the epigraph in European literature of the eighteenth to twentieth centuries implies a practice very different from that of the framing, supplementing, and authorizing paratexts of writers who come from outside of those traditions and seek entry there. This applies to the writings of former slaves in the Americas, where the genre of slave narrative required the enframement of a validating introduction by a white abolitionist. It also applies to colonized and postcolonial literatures, in which paratexts performed a similar function of validation, often being written by a colonial official or person of note. There is an ironic inversion of this poetically structured demand for paratextuality—in which the supplement is evidence of a lack in the author. It is the "textual elitism that devalues considerations of historical and biographical context" in close reading, as Valerie Smith reminds us.[5] What the suspicious white reader of abolitionist literature needed by way of verification, the contemporary reader of black literature might want as explanation. But Smith's desire for historical context cannot fully escape the double bind that minority writers negotiate. Historically, minority and postcolonial writers have always had to negotiate the expectation and demand that their literature will be autobiographical and that it will signify itself as minority literature without a paratext. This history forces a different relation to paratextuality and epigraphic writing.

Morrison's fiction reclaims the epigraph from its function as verification, partly to attest to her mastery of fiction. As will become clear, however, her epigraphic work signals that she is aware of the risks that attend such a move. Her use of epigraph plays with the limitations of paratextuality and the function of authorization, especially authorization granted by a master discourse in the house of race. And yet two books that come late in Morrison's oeuvre—*Love*, followed by *A Mercy*—have no epigraphs. We might wonder at what might seem a new muteness, or a revisiting of a mode that began Morrison's novelistic career, with *The Bluest Eye*.

As discussed earlier, *A Mercy* does not draw on an existing canon. Morrison has to imagine Florens as writing before being written, so to speak, or before the slave narrative became a genre that had to be inserted into a ready, comprehensible, and legible tradition of the sentimental novel. Florens's citations can draw only upon her immediate experience, even though that experience includes being read through prior knowledges and canons of figurative language that insert her into the condition of an enslaved black woman. *Love*, by contrast, might not have an epigraph, but it draws upon a long history that includes the settling of America and a deeper history of empire out of which Columbus eventually emerged.

The citation of America's early settlement is geographical in that *Love* is set on the mid-Atlantic coast. The setting is a former "broke-down 'whites only' club" in the town of Silk, purchased by Bill Cosey in the 1930s, when the "whole country began to live on Relief" (*L* 102). In its heyday, the resort was where African Americans could have "the best good time this side of the law" (*L* 33). The place allowed a sense of pride in those who came to it and those who observed it from afar, the black cannery workers or fishing families, or the domestic workers or teachers in disadvantaged schools, for example (*L* 41–42). The political turmoil of the Civil Rights Movement and the backlash against it, as well as an unfortunate proximity to the cannery, eventually led to the resort's rundown and closure. For a brief time, Bill Cosey had created a "haven" of leisure time for African Americans in the vicinity of the country's founding geography, but the haven was temporary and never "at home" in that charged landscape.

Names of people and streets in the town of Silk make for a palimpsest of historiography and popular culture that calls forth and undermines the idea of empire and legacy. *Love* invokes history in a twofold way. The first is through a set of names that suggest an engagement with Rome, if not the Roman Empire. But this engagement will be seen to be highly mediated by discourses surrounding the founding of America and American popular culture. The other is the history of the Christian church and its founder, Paul; given the Pauline thread in Morrison's work, the misspelled name of one character, Romen, might signal a misdirection of Paul's entreaty to the Romans to give up carnal love.

Historiography comes through in another misspelling: that of a former fishing friend of the patriarchal hotel owner Bill Cosey, named Sandler Gibbons. His last name calls to mind the mammoth six-volume, eighteenth-century historiography of the Roman Empire by Edward Gibbon. The volumes are often referred to as *Gibbon's History of the Decline and Fall of the Roman Empire*, as if *Gibbon's* were part of the title. This makes for a potential slip, in which Gibbon would become Gibbons. Sandler's surname suggests this common mistake. The spelling of his grandson's name, Romen, suggests another mistake and perhaps a swift nod in the direction of Edward Gibbon, who had blamed the downfall of the Roman Empire on, among other things, barbarian illiteracy.[6] Gibbons and Romen are not the only names that conjure up associations with the Roman Empire. Silk has a street named Gladiator (*L* 84).

On the surface, these names place Silk and the mid-Atlantic coast of America in the tradition of *translatio imperii*, or the transfer of empire (sometimes put more bluntly, as the transfer of civilization), which underpinned the idea of the "rise and fall" of civilizations. This notion was certainly related to the Fifth Monarchist belief that the Book of Daniel's four world orders predicted a fifth kingdom that would herald the return of Christ. And it was also a concept behind claims that Columbus had opened a "New World."[7] The discourse of *translatio imperii* may be narrated via Columbus's colonization of the Americas, but it has trickled down to the suburban aspirations of a street name, Gladiator. In Silk, "Gladiator" belongs to the empire of dreams that feeds the popular, suburban American imaginary. The street name is from a different discourse, one of celluloid heroes and dramas, which has given Silk "epic-movie names" (*L* 84). Thus the discourse of *translatio imperii* is ridiculed, just as it is ridiculed by the name Valerian Sweet in *Tar Baby*.

Morrison's decision to relinquish an epigraph for *Love* makes sense, given that the burden of empire and dreams of transported *imperium* have been so sublated in national storytelling. *Love* resists any literary *imperium* that might stake its futurity in the world that the novel conjures up. *A Mercy* has even greater reason to resist the epigraphic convention, given its proximity to Europe's aspirations to create new empires, on the one hand, and, on the other, the start of centuries of human enslavement, which would seek to destroy any continuity beyond the drudgery of their dire conditions for those who were enslaved.

It is Morrison's next novel, *Home*, that returns us to the epigraphic convention. It does so in a way that takes us back to *The Bluest Eye* and the novels that came immediately after it. In that first novel, the distinction between a prior, enframing text and the novel's beginning is blurred. It opens with a quotation from a Dick and Jane school primer, which is quoted three times and from which some chapters take their headings. The second and third repetitions introduce variations in punctuation and spacing, each signaling a hand at work, so that by the time we turn to the first person statement by the novel's narrator, Claudia McTeer, we have some sense of a writerly presence that is already engaging with, but changing the status of, a prior text. Morrison certainly uses this strategy in *Jazz*, where the transition from epigraph to narrative suggests a story that has already begun when we open the book.

The Bluest Eye's stuttering start focuses attention on the primer. The opening quote from it has the same sink (or placement on a page) as the first chapter of the story per se (i.e., as told by Claudia). The difference between the two is that the quotation has larger leading (or space between the lines), as might be found in a children's book. When the quotation is repeated, all punctuation disappears, and the passage has the same leading as the text of the novel that follows. When the quotation is used in full for the third and final time, spaces between words also disappear. The ensuing disruption works on two levels. One is a mimesis of children's acquisition of reading skills, which would include childhood language play that jumbles words to make a game of nonsense sounds. The other is an invocation of a scriptural tradition that reaches back to undo the histories of reading. *Scriptura continua*, or continuous lettering without spaces between words, was used in Western antiquity and still is the written form of such alphabetic languages as Thai. According to Paul Saenger, Greece was the first ancient civilization in the West to adopt *scriptura continua*. Although initially the Romans maintained an earlier Mediterranean tradition of separating words by "interpuncts placed at mid level in the line," in the second century C.E. the Romans too abandoned such medial points, and *scriptura continua* became the dominant form of writing throughout the remainder of what is known as the classical period.[8] Saenger also suggests that children "tend initially to write in *scriptura continua* because they see its continuity as a faithful representation of uninterrupted oral speech."[9] Edward Tenner makes the point that historically learning how to read run-on writing began with students reciting and memorizing words and then identifying their shapes on the page (or scroll).[10] The system changed in the early medieval period with the (re)introduction of spaces to delineate words, enabling a move away from the orality of a text that had to be read aloud to the privacy of "silent reading" as an act. With that change came the history of Western reading, into which the Dick and Jane primer is inserted and which we may now see as being redone, if not undone, by Morrison.

But, if redone, in what way? If the markers that enable silent reading vanish and if Saenger is correct, the text must be voiced (again). The third repetition of the Dick and Jane primer is followed by a "voice," we will understand later to be that of Claudia McTeer: "Quiet as it's kept, there were no marigolds in the fall of 1941." The speaking voice is personalized by a collective "we," and the speaking quality is signaled typographically by italics, which differ from the story that comes after, the "how" or poetics of Pecola Breedlove's predicament and Claudia McTeer's storytelling attempt to understand it. This section of the novel functions as a prologue in that it introduces us to the key characters and the key themes and concerns. It enters into a space made possible by resemblance to the primer.

Each word in the first version of the Dick and Jane quotation is defined by the white space around it. The white space shows where each word begins and ends as a unit of sense. Only when the white spaces are closed up does blackness come into view—or what Jennifer Brody, writing about the typographical devices that Ralph Ellison uses in *Invisible Man*, calls the "blackness of blackness."[11] In other words, the *scriptura continua* foreshadows the narrative conceit of *A Mercy*'s fiction of turning the clock back to a time before American canonicity existed. In *The Bluest Eye*, the employment of *scriptura continua* plays at undoing the readerly traditions that undergird something as seemingly innocent and unencumbered as a child's primer. The tradition or history of Western literacy makes way for the story of a black child, told by a black writer, imagined by a black woman writer.

Into this space of reassembled time, Claudia McTeer introduces her own house, or, more to the point, she brings readers into "her place" or the place from which (her) narrative emerges. And the pristine ideal of the Dick and Jane house is ironized. The reality for the McTeers is the opposite, but this opposite has an interior, where, instead of the instruction for play that we see in the primer, we see loving care—although this is not idealized. To echo Jennifer Brody's reading of Ellison's *Invisible Man*, the whiteness of the ideal home and ideal reader is opaque, but it is a miscegenated whiteness in the sense that it is dependent upon the blackness of the ink. Brody argues that *Invisible Man* "seeks to re-member the blackness of whiteness that the term American would seek to erase."[12]

The dismantling of the school primer will be cited within the novel when Claudia "dismantles" the dolls that she and her sister were given.[13] When read within the context of *scriptura continua*, Claudia's resistance has larger implications. As she explains, in juxtaposition to her own early acts of creation and inscription, which are tentative acts of self-creation and self-inscription, the dolls seemed to obstruct her early encounters with herself as creator.

Her bald statement that she "destroyed white baby dolls" is set aside as a paragraph of its own, singled out from the paragraphs preceding and following (*BE* 15). This singling out must be read in relation to what Claudia has stated just prior to the destruction. She has been complaining about adults who do not listen to what she would really like for Christmas. Instead of listening, they have bought for her and Frieda the objects of their own desires, namely, the white baby dolls. What she had wanted was to "sit on the low stool in Big Mama's kitchen with my lap full of lilacs and listen to Big Pappa play his violin for me" (*BE* 15). Rather than have anything concrete to possess, she had wanted to "feel something on Christmas Day." In this imagined space, which has its own sentimentality, romance, and idyllic longings, Claudia would be listening to music, a wordless creation charged with affect and the ability to impart and elicit affect. The dream is interrupted, however, by the reality of daily routines. The "lowness of the stool made for [her] body" gives way to the materiality of the preparatory bath in a zinc tub that cools water too quickly. There is no warm kitchen. There is cold metal. There are no lilacs. There are "curtains" of chilly, "soapy water." More importantly, all connection with the outside world is washed away as dirt in favor of an "irritable, unimaginative cleanliness." The effect is one of erasure. But what is it that has been erased, and why does Claudia react with such venom to this?

Claudia has been writing on her own body, inscribing "ink marks" on her legs and face. She refers to these marks as "all my creations and accumulations of the day gone." The possessive noun is emphatic. It is also an articulation of putative self-possession. These ink marks are hers, her body is hers, and the "all" are now all gone. Moreover, the accumulations, as signs of her selective interaction with the world, are also gone. They have all been "replaced by goose pimples" on cleanly scrubbed and rubbed skin. Her skin has become a surface upon which her own will cannot act, but upon which something else can be inscribed—an unimaginative cleanliness that cannot, in effect, imagine her. Imagination itself is being washed away. It is at this moment, when her own putative acts of creation have been washed away in favor of cleanliness, that she breaks the graphic, visible integrity of the paragraph to state: "I destroyed white baby dolls."

In her "worthy" state, she is presentable and is presented with creatures that adults tell her are beautiful. Her own living flesh, upon which she made her own marks, was not "worthy." Because of this too—and not only because of their whiteness—the dolls provoke "unsullied hatred" (*BE* 13). In part, this is a hatred of creatures that are simply the material surface mimicry of the real. It is a hatred of the uncanny, of things that are strangely familiar, yet out of time and out of place, seeking to make themselves at home and relevant. The dolls can cry "Mama" like real girls, except that this cry is more "like the bleat of a dying lamb, or, more precisely, our icebox door opening on rusty hinges in July" (*BE* 14). The narrator's similes insert a distance between the thing and the "real" that it invokes. She describes herself as bemused by "the thing itself, and the way it looked" (*BE* 13). The doll is in fact not real, and who believes that the doll is real anyway? However, what is real is the reaction to the "bleat." Whether it sounds like a dying lamb or contracted metal, "all the world had" already agreed that "a blue-eyed, yellow-haired, pink-skinned doll" was desirable. Calling "Mama" and arriving in Claudia's own home, where her own mother recalls her own childhood longing for such perfection, the doll calls out that she is "here," like Hoffman's mechanical Olympia, a figure that embodies, for Freud, the uncanny and that instills "the idea of being robbed of one's eyes."[14]

For a subject schooled by the Dick and Jane primer and the tradition from which it emerges, seeing and looking are privileged early on. It is only through seeing and looking that a reader can be invited into an encounter with the graphics of language. (The same notion applies to sightless readers, for whom the encounter with language is more material still.) Claudia has her own love object, herself. The dolls arrive like automatons, seeking a home in the midst of ritualistic preparations for Christmas. Scrubbing off "all" of Claudia's "creations and accumulations" becomes more than automatic. It becomes dangerously animating. A "new" girl is expected to step out of the zinc tub, worthy of the new dress in which she will be equal to receiving the doll. Moreover, she will see this doll with new eyes, so to speak, eyes that have been taught to appreciate "real" beauty. In a word, Claudia says no to the animation of this impossible doppelgänger, and she repeats this rejection in what she writes of the dolls. In short, she will not be robbed of her self-articulating "I." Dismantling the dolls exposes the sheer emptiness that "the single-stroke eyebrows," the "pearly teeth," the "red bowline lips" covered over (*BE* 14). Once the "cold and stupid eyeball" has been removed, the "sweet plaintive dry 'Mama'" is undone. All that is left is a broken "Ahhhhhh." The talking doll is rendered as nonsensical as the segment of the Dick and Jane primer whose punctuation has been removed.

The grownup response to Claudia's destructive behavior receives the same redaction. Adults are described as frowning and fussing, and their chiding is collapsed as if into one voice, a voice of complaint that includes Claudia's mother's. The multivocal speech is also presented as if it were one phrase, an extravagant, nonsense-accumulating compounded word: "You-don't-know-how-to-take-care-of-nothing. I-never-had-a-baby-doll-in-my-whole-life-and-used-to-cry-my-eyes-out-for-them. Now-you-got-one-a-beautiful-one-and-you-tear-it-up-what's-the-matter-with-you?" (*BE* 14).

The hyphens achieve two things. They produce the effect of a streaming complaint in all of its breathless outrage—they make the complaint palpable and present, and they make visible in a comic way the senselessness of what is being said. We literally see that the adult cannot make sense of Claudia's action, but we also see that the adult does not make sense to Claudia. Further, we see that the adult Claudia, now fully in control of language, is able to render her parents' and others' confusion because, in hindsight, it was wrong minded, even misguided. Where the child Claudia had sought to accumulate the day through self-inscription that would, in effect, make of her day an emblem, as an inscribing adult she makes nonsense of the others' accumulation of dangerous longings. The complaining accusation is seen as driven by an energy derived from some internal mechanism that cannot stop itself. Her citation of the outraged utterance is an act of incorporation that opens language up in the same way that the dolls were opened, a practice that is connected to what happens to the School Reader. She wants to see "of what it was made" (*BE* 14). With the dolls, she also wants "to discover the dearness, to find the beauty, the desirability that had escaped" her. With the adults of her childhood, she also seeks to discover what had "eluded" her.

Thus, early in the novel we see three instances of disassembly: those that have been imposed upon the School Reader, the dolls, and the adult complaint about their destruction. The Reader is aligned directly with the dolls, while the adult outrage is attached to it in a peripheral, bemused way. The absence of such dolls in the adult speaker's childhood radiates through what the adult says. Childhood disappointment spills up into a grief that can only be expressed in this moment of doubled lack—the adult recalls not having the perfection of such a doll and now witnesses the destruction of this perfection. At the same time, the fate that the Reader suffers reveals the endless power of the images that it generates, as well as their associations, which continue even after nonsense has been made of the Reader's language. The fate of the dolls reveals the empty heart of a verisimilitude that has, in the Aristotelean sense, no character that can persuade a viewer/reader of a "real." The destruction of the dolls does, however, follow that of the Reader in that both do, as Page suggests, enable Claudia to escape their power.

Yet another factor is at play in her "unsullied hatred," which is as much a response to the role the dolls were to play in socializing her as a young female as it is to the curious companionship of these scaled-down replicas of fleshy, real white girls. Claudia is confused by a Baby Doll and by what she senses its presence demands of her. She senses that this demand is for a certain role playing: "What was I supposed to do with it? Pretend to be its mother? I had no interest in babies or the concept of motherhood" (*BE* 13). Resisting what she intuits is the socializing function of the "big, blue-eyed Baby Doll," Claudia nevertheless does learn what was "expected" of her. She learns, from picture books filled with images of girls with dolls, that she is to "rock it, fabricate storied situations around it, even sleep with it." Her revulsion is physical, not only from the whiteness of the dolls but from the premature game of reproduction itself. Moreover, what this game "reproduces" is not reality but "round moronic eyes, the pancake face, and orangeworm hair." Other dolls are equally lifeless, with "hard unyielding limbs" that resist her "flesh." The cold, lifeless facsimile is juxtaposed with the real girl. The cliché about "unfeeling" or "unresponsive" white girls and "passionate" or "hyper-responsive" black girls shimmers just beneath the surface of this juxtaposition. Even here, there is no simple equation.

The uncanny dolls *are* animated. Claudia finds in herself something that is the "true horror" of her dismembering of the dolls" (*BE* 15). It is that she transfers "the same impulse to little white girls." Her articulation of her desire to "axe" the girls is familiar. It echoes her reason for dismembering the dolls in that she claims she does not seek to destroy them so much as to understand how it was that they could enchant "people," who would look at them and utter an "Awwwww" that made no sense. Here it is black adults who mimic the "Ahhhhhh" of broken dolls when they look upon living white girls. Something else has broken, and Claudia is the one who makes the association. It is she who has broken the falseness of language that came out of a doll's mouth. It is she who is in control of what comes out of the adults' mouths. Furthermore, she has already taken pains to draw parallels between the damaged "Mama" call of the dolls and the sound of a "dying lamb" or an "icebox" in winter. Damage infuses the "Awwwww." Where the doll's damaged cry was associated with the removal of "the cold and stupid eyeball," the black women's "Awwwww" is associated with a gaze that is diverted from Claudia, as if in the sway of "the secret magic" that the "real" beauties "weave on others."

The breakage here is of the "proper" accord of the "proper" appreciating gaze between black girl and black mother. The white girls are depicted as having an agency that might even be secret from them, uncannily at home in them but out of their own sight, subjecting them as they move about the world. Unspeaking in the text, these girls do not even cry out "Mama." Their presence is cry and summons enough, and all are obedient to it. The white girls' presence alone disrupts and breaks the gaze between black women and black girls as the magic weaves "on others." Now, all self-inscription has vanished. The automatons have made themselves at home, upon others, in the realm of the visual, where the materiality of language itself is also at home for the sighted.

The tradition out of which that writing has grown has been co-opted and made at home in Claudia's writing, though only after she has unwound time figuratively through the typographical invocation of *scriptura continua*. And yet the question of how to read the situatedness of the Dick and Jane primer remains. Is the Dick and Jane quotation an epigraph, or has the novel already begun with Claudia McTeer mimicking a childlike language play? How are we to read this? Does the Dick and Jane story "leak" into the book, only to be cut off in the space between it and the italicized paragraphs in the narrative voice? Do the second and third repetitions, appearing as if epigraphically, isolate the passage even further, putting it in its place and allowing Claudia McTeer already to begin disassembling it? We are caught in an undecidability that is, for Morrison, the very condition of literature.

This ambivalence is settled in *Sula*, where the delineation between epigraph and the novel per se appears relatively clear. The epigraph comes from Tennessee Williams's *The Rose Tattoo*:

> Nobody knew my rose of the world
> but me . . . I had too much glory.
> They don't want glory like that
> in nobody's heart.

That the original is not set out with such line breaks enhances the epigraphical status of the quote. The line breaks follow a common poetic style of correlating units of meaning with line breaks, then using enjambment to suture the breaks and beginnings. The effect is a shifting and reweighting of emphasis, creating emphases Williams might not have intended. Williams's name is, in fact, absent. Only the title of his play is used. This omission of the name runs counter to Genette's suggestion that the significance of an epigraph is "very often" its authority rather than its content. Morrison's dispensing with the author's name signals that he does not circulate as a figure of authority, but rather that the possible signification of his text can proliferate beyond any intentionality that could be assigned to him.[15]

C. Lynn Munro reads Morrison's choice of epigraph as suggesting the novel's theme. It "implicitly [invites] the reader to consider the play as an analog to the novel."[16] Munro argues further that the play and novel have a "common aim": to "force their audiences to recognize the tragic dimension which colors the most mundane of lives and to realize that much of the tragedy is a result of the individual's ability to transcend or even recognize his or her own self-indulgence."[17] Munro's remark applies to Nel more than to Sula, yet at the novel's, end Eva Peace says to Nel, "Just alike. Both of you. Never was no difference between you" (*S* 169). After Sula's death, Nel herself is not sure where she begins or Sula ends. Both could be read as paratexts of each other. Through the device of citation and the principle of narrative focalization, each organizes how a reader might see the other. More importantly, each finds in the other a citation of herself. One makes the other intelligible to herself. As Nel discovers at the end, after Sula has died, this "echo" produces something else, another self still, the self who is given over to friendship (*S* 174).

Munro might be correct about the correlation between Serafina in *The Rose Tattoo* with Nel in *Sula*. This reading also seeks closure by focusing on the epigraph and thus severing it from the title. By contrast, Morrison's use of the play's title and her elision of Williams's name allows us to emphasize the narrative and the meaning of the tattoo, rather than biographical detail. In the play, the rose tattoo is a birthmark on Rosario Della Rose, Serafina's husband. When a similar mark appears on her breast on the night she conceives her second child, she reads the appearance as a divine blessing upon her marriage. Rosario is not faithful, however. The other woman in his life, Estelle Hohengarten, has a rose tattooed on her breast to signal her love for him—her German surname can be translated as "High Garden," perhaps suggesting paradise. His death leaves the two women to face each other in much the same way that Nel and Sula must face each other when Nel's husband, Jude Greene, leaves after she discovers him with Sula.

These parallels aside, the sign of the tattoo is a hinge that opens to other possible readings the relation between Morrison's text and the Williams play. Perhaps the tattoo is a religious stigmata that Serafina gladly wears, yet members of Sula's community read the birthmark according to their mood or fears. Some see it as a rose, others as a serpent, some as a tadpole. Sula herself does not read it at all. She cannot see it, unless she contemplates herself in a mirror. She can, however, read how others perceive her or how they take the birthmark to be a sign for how they are to respond to her. When men in her community pronounce Sula guilty of sleeping with white men, they read backward to the birthmark and make it authenticate their "knowledge" about her (S 112). The epigraph thus opens the text to a reading in which the violence of literalist readings of intertextuality becomes visible.

A similar correlation between epigraph and novelistic theme occurs in *Song of Solomon*. An epigraph without a source reads:

> The fathers may soar
>> And the children may know their names

Without a source, the epigraph may stand as the vanished utterance of an anonymous speaker/writer, or it might stand as Morrison's own fabrication—a placeholder for one who might have spoken. Given the fact that epigraphs function as authorizing gestures, this ambiguously authored epigraph might be called an unauthorized authority, or a self-authorizing authority. However, the book's title is resonant with biblical authority, and because of this and the epigraph's tone and style, the reader might assume that the epigraph is indeed a biblical citation. But without a citation, biblical rhetoricity lifts away from the Bible, with the result that the apparent citation becomes subject to doubt; it might be mimicry or, worse, dissimulation or violent misrepresentation. All of these practices are enacted in Morrison's novels, where characters commit or are subjected to unspeakable crimes in the name of God, of nation, and of race when the latter are imagined as the sites of God-given rights.

Song of Solomon's epigraph partakes of the biblical rhetoric of the patronym even while invoking the fear that the patronym masks, namely, the uncertainty of paternity. The "may" of the epigraph invokes a structure of permission (and hence of possible prohibition by the father), but also of doubt. The choice of "may" rather than "will" is telling in this regard. But it also grants the text its exalted tone, which partakes of prophetic utterance via the aura emanating from the auxiliary verb formation "may soar." The language has already taken off via the invocation of ascent in "soar."

In fact, the quotation could have been drawn from the Nag Hammadi scriptures, to which Morrison turns for *Jazz* and *Paradise*. For those books, she cites "Thunder, Perfect Mind," which is generally read as the utterance of a female voice. The Nag Hammadi text that comes closest to the epigraph for *Song of Solomon* is "The Father Utters the Names of People Who Know," from the Gospel of Truth. This gospel concerns itself with correcting errors that have been generated and then corrected by "the Father," a transcendent being, though these errors are no fault of his.[18] As we have discussed earlier, Macon Dead, II, and Pilate do not blame their father, Macon, Sr., for the misreadings and misinterpretations that dictate their lives after he is murdered. Like the end of Morrison's novel, which concludes with Milkman's awakening from his self-centered existence to imagine others and Pilate's learning the truth about the bag of bones that she carries, the Nag Hammadi Gospel of Truth ends with an "authentic human existence, imagined in traditional Gnostic terms as a state of wakefulness."[19]

Whatever the real source of the phrase "The fathers may soar / And the children may know their names," its epigraphic aura implies an utterance that comes from elsewhere, imparting or bestowing authority upon what follows. At first sight, it seems to be of the same order as the epigraph to *Sula*, which makes clear and direct references to the book's content. Marianne Hirsch points out that the citation opening *Sula* "raises the novel's central themes: family relations, flight, transmission, origin, knowledge, naming, transcendence, contingency."[20] Hirsch reads the epigraph as evidence of the interplay between familial and linguistic structures, and the symbolic order in the production of self-knowledge as the prerogative of heirs to a father's name—naming here being an acknowledgement of legitimacy,[21] but also the prerogative of the fathers.

In the ambiguity in the second part of the epigraph, this self-knowledge converges with the father's name. In patrilineal societies, to know one's father's name is to know one's own name, and therefore to know one's place in familial and social structures that, in turn, can know one by one's name. For Hirsch, males are the heirs to this knowing in *Song of Solomon*, while women do not share this privilege. Hirsch's remark also bears on Pat Best's "letter" to her dead mother in *Paradise*, where she writes, "they looked down on you Mama, I know it, and despised Daddy for marrying a wife with no last name, a wife without people, a wife of sunlight skin, a wife of racial tampering" (*P* 197).

In *Paradise*, Pat's maternal grandfather has "soared" into a cloak of anonymity, relegating her mother to "bastard" status. In *Song of Solomon*, men are remembered by name, despite the distortions of memory or accidents of document. "Milkman ' is really Macon Dead III. His grandfather, Macon Dead I, was originally named Jake but became Macon officially when, registering with the Freedman's Bureau, a soldier wrote his birthplace where his first name should have been recorded. Despite this, the journey that his grandson, Macon "Milkman" Dead III, undertakes will reveal the truth of not only his name but also that of Macon Dead I's father, the "flying African" named Solomon or Shalimar. As discussed elsewhere in this book, *Song of Solomon* plays out the larger history of naming and naming contests in at least two ways. The first is the careless overwriting of proper names by slavers or slavery's legacies. Slaves were assigned names by their masters or were forced to take their masters' names. The act of naming oneself or naming one's own children was an act of self-assertion. In *Song of Solomon*, Macon Dead Sr. insists on the right to name his children Pilate and Macon Jr. His daughter's name is taken from the Bible, as are those of the granddaughters he would never see, the daughters of Macon Dead Jr.

While the men in *Song of Solomon* are remembered by name, the histories and even the names of women are lost. Macon (Jake) Dead I cannot bear to hear his wife's name said after she dies giving birth to Pilate. As a result, her children never learn her name until the journey undertaken by Milkman. There the novel looks back at the epigraph and shows it up as an ironic promise. If the fathers do indeed "soar" or abandon their families, those families bear the consequences. Pilate's mistaken interpretation of her father's spectral call, "Sing, Sing," is a direct consequence of not knowing her own mother's name (*SS* 333).

The further irony of the epigraph, given the emphasis on the father's names in the novel, is that it has no source. It is unnamed. As such, it has its own transcendent potential, but this potential is persistently undermined by the novel's content. Of course, the novel's title, *Song of Solomon*, is from the Old Testament and functions paratextually as a hinge joining the name to the vast web of intertextuality that is the Bible. Sometimes called the Song of Songs, the Old Testament book comprises a series of songs that praise the absent beloved. This too would seem to have clear resonances in the novel's concern with "flying" fathers and fickle lovers. Like the lamenting Old Testament lover who rose to "go about the city, in the streets and in the squares" to "seek him whom my soul loves" (Song of Solomon 3:2), Hagar in the novel goes looking for Milkman when he abandons her. Such comparative readings abound in both overt and subtle ways: for example, in the Old Testament text, the singer refers to the cedars of Lebanon (Song of Solomon 3:9), and Milkman thinks of Hagar while he is crouched against a cedar (*SS* 301). Yet the books do not fold neatly over each other. For Morrison's book, there is more bitterness than consolation, and the love song meets with ridicule.

More importantly, the singer in the biblical Song of Solomon, or Song of Songs, is a woman. She sings of her pleasure, and even when bemoaning the beloved's absence her singing is not all, or only lament, but a full and knowing articulation of her desire, her longing, and her movement in the world. At the end of *Song of Solomon*, Milkman finally says that "it was the children who sang and kept the story of [the father's] leaving alive." Moreover, he learns that it is not only the fathers' names that are remembered, but the women's as well (*SS* 330). Yet the lineage is patrilineal, and even the town in which he learns of his family's history is named after the great-grandfather who bears the powerful Old Testament name Shalimar, or Solomon.

But other books are summoned in the relation between the title, the epigraphs, and the "interior" of Morrison's novel. Given the novel's concern with names and naming, it is a further profound irony that Milkman's younger sister bears a New Testament name, First Corinthians. The name of a woman, it is also the name of the first letter written by the apostle Paul to the early Christian church in Corinth, and its appearance signals another form of paternity, one that is entirely textual. This New Testament name links the vocation that Paul insisted was his (Galatians 1:15–16) and the congregation at Corinth. Paul demands that the faithful turn from all syncretism, to see and accept their "calling" (1 Corinthians 1:26, 30). This "calling," he claims, has been predicted in earlier scriptures (1 Corinthians 2:9). Not incidentally, this first letter to Corinth is an answer to an appeal for intervention in a divided community. The appeal has come from a woman named Chloe. Hers is not the call of a lover for a beloved, but that of a believer and follower calling for guidance and leadership. In answer to her lost letter, the blessings and greetings that open his letter give way to the cause of concern: "Now this I say, that every one of you saith,

I am of Paul; and I of Apollos; and I of Cephas; and I of Christ" (1 Corinthians 1:12).

Whereas Chloe of Corinth could summon a church leader, Morrison's First Corinthians spends most of her subdued life in a household that favors a male heir, her brother Milkman. Her education at Bryn Mawr opened no doors to her. Instead, she, like her sister, is confined to her home until, in desperation, she answers an advertisement to become a maid to the Chicago state poet laureate, Michael-Mary Graham. This is her secret. She tells her family that she is a secretary. Only under the cover of her lie can she enter a public context in which accidental meetings might take place. While on a bus to her job, she meets Henry Porter, who becomes her lover and who, by abbreviating her name to Corrie, alleviates her of the burden of a name that calls upon a community to restore the ideal city, Jerusalem (1 Corinthians 14:25), and to convert all to witness and worship Israel's God. Richard B. Hays argues that this required the Corinthians and those they would convert to have nothing less than a conversion of the imagination.[22] Only when she defies her father and her brother can First Corinthians, Corrie, imagine a self who can love and be loved by a man she meets on a bus. Imagining, she takes the father's prerogative and flies herself, not subject to the epigraph's implicit warning that those who do not know their father's names do not know their own. Rather, her story bypasses the epigraph's influence, leaving it to her brother and father, and even to her mother. Her name and the novel's title conjoin Old and New Testament. Like the unnamed singer or singers of the biblical book Song of Solomon, she eventually embraces herself in a way resonant with the assertion "I am black, but comely, O ye daughters of Jerusalem" and the further exhortation to "Look not upon me, because I am black, but because the sun hath looked upon me" (Song of Solomon 1:5, 6). The singer in the biblical text does not mention her father, but she refers to her "mother's children," with whom she has quarreled (Song of Solomon 1:6). So Morrison makes the epigraph a hinge, opening her own text outward and receiving into its interior the dense burden and potential of the past.

If, however, the fathers soar and the children know their names, some women seem to sing more forcefully in the space vacated by them. *Tar Baby* likewise draws its epigraph from the Pauline epistle from which Milkman Dead's parents choose his sister's improbable name. *Tar Baby*'s epigraph reads:

For it hath been declared
unto to me of you, my brethren, by them
which are of the house of Chloe, that there are
contentions among you. (1 Corinthians 1:11)

One might be tempted to read Paul's reference to the house of Chloe as an autobiographical signal by Morrison, whose birth name was Chloe Anthony Wofford. The epigraph points paradoxically both toward and away from its Pauline context, as well as the Pauline call for unity. If the epigraph for *Tar Baby* has a personal reference, it remains guarded.

That said, this second reference to Paul's first letter to the Corinthians marks a turn in Morrison's self-citational practice. Here, the name given to a character (First Corinthians) in one novel reappears at the threshold of the next, but only indirectly. Moreover, the name that reappears is not hers alone but rather the source from which hers was derived. But how are we to read this tight self-referentiality, which partakes of Paul's body of work while producing another, Morrison's own? A complex citational text, Paul's letter nonetheless aspires to closure, to unity, to the establishment of a church that is internally homogeneous and self-knowing.

The Pauline letters make at least four overt appearances in Morrison's work. As has been discussed above, I Corinthians provides the epigraph for *Tar Baby*, as well as the name of one of Milkman's sisters in *Song of Solomon*. In sequence, Romans provides the epigraph for *Beloved*, and in *Paradise*, II Corinthians is one of Soane Morgan's favorite books of the Bible along with Deuteronomy. Earlier still, Pecola Breedlove's mother is named Pauline. Although this first connection with the New Testament Paul might seem slim, the early naming of Pauline Breedlove acquires a belated significance when read against the epigraphs and citations of Paul's epistles in Morrison's later novels. The ironically named Breedlove family could not be further from Paul's message of love, and yet the name seems to call forth what is missing in that family—namely, love. It is a Pauline message, the secret in Pauline Breedlove's name. In the movement to this point, one feels that Morrison's oeuvre has offered a response to the call by Martin Luther King, Jr.: namely, to supplement the mastery of the English language with love. King's call came in a 1956 sermon in which he read a fictional letter from St. Paul to Americans. In the "letter," King/Paul states: "American Christians, you may master the intricacies of the English language. You may possess all eloquence of articulate speech. But even if you 'speak with the tongues of Man and angels, and have not love, you are become as sounding brass, or a tinkling cymbal.'"[23]

Beloved turns to Paul's Epistle to the Romans for its epigraph. In this epistle, he proclaims the inclusive nature of his faith: "I will call them my people, which were not my people; and her beloved, which was not beloved" (Romans 9:25). All, including Gentiles and Jews, are encompassed in the notion of a community of the faithful. None are excluded. All are the children of "the living God." In her introduction to the Everyman's Library edition of *Beloved*, A. S. Byatt compares the Pauline inclusion with the failed promise of the Declaration of Independence, whose preamble reads: "We hold these truths to be self-evident, that all men are created equal; that they are endowed by their Creator with certain unalienable rights, that among these are life, liberty and the pursuit of happiness."[24] Byatt argues that this was the declaration that African Americans could sound back at a discriminating America in defiance and outrage.

The epigraph finds an echo in the novel, one that is intimate and filled with a mourning born of an almost-failed assertion of the right to freedom, namely, Sethe's bid for freedom, which resulted in her murder of her child. In the priest's sermon at the funeral for her slain child, she hears him begin, "Dearly Beloved," a salutation directly influenced by Paul's notion of the beloved community of believers. When she is released from her prison sentence for the murder of her child, she hopes to use the phrase as an epitaph on the child's gravestone. Lacking the money to pay for this, she accepts a stonemason's proposition that he carve each word in exchange for sex. She endures "ten minutes for seven letters" that make up the word Beloved and forgoes the cost of another ten minutes because "what she got, settled for, was the one word that mattered" (*B* 11). The intended adjectival clause, "Dearly Beloved," succumbs to the (im)proper noun as an enunciation of disruption itself. There has been a disruption of language and in language by an improper exchange at the site of a body's last home, the grave. And here is the epigraph as abstracted language, turned into an epitaph that speaks for and in the place of the one who has gone and who can no longer speak, and with whom all story has gone. There is no immanence. The epitaph says, "Here lies all story, now."

As a sign of disruption, the word *Beloved* is grammatically and temporally ambiguous. Temporally, it occupies a (forever) present tense, yet it is also the past tense in the sense that love has already been attached to a subject. Grammatically, the word is both the singular beloved and the plural beloved; it is the possessive singular "my" beloved and the plural possessive "our" beloved. It is the singular, too, as the beloved or as the beginning of such adjectival phrases as "beloved daughter," "beloved sister," "beloved mother," "beloved granddaughter," or "beloved friend." As such it becomes a space of all possible addresses, and thereby the single word becomes the visible presence of the invisible, corporeally absent child. The word acts as the space into which the lost body of the child can be written and the space into which loss itself is written. In its ambiguous state, this word speaks not only to one grave, but to many. Through a single word, the speech act of naming becomes an instant and spatial zone of contact. Utterance becomes exposition, naming becomes (re)calling.

For the novels *Jazz* and *Paradise*, Morrison picks up on the way in which Paul's first letter to the Corinthians is a response to signs of division. She leaves the Pauline reference behind to move outside of the singular doctrine and leadership that he sought to enforce. *Jazz* commences with an epigraph from "Thunder, Perfect Mind," the unique articulation of a female figure in the Nag Hammadi library. The presence of this text at the start of *Jazz* underscores the gathering force of Morrison's exploration of feminine utterance, begun by Claudia McTeer in *The Bluest Eye* and extended in *Song of Solomon*.[25]

"Thunder, Perfect Mind" has no individual author. It emerges from a library, that great figure for the infinitude of intertextuality. Nevertheless, in its partially disconnected state the quotation becomes an antegraph. It exists at the division between the past, which has been granted a new immediacy through citation, and the immanent arrival of a newer story. It is there that the pure vocalization "Sth!" takes its place.

If read from the "Sth" alone, the opening of *Jazz* arrests through a sharp interruption, in which the visual effect of the grapheme invokes the excitability of the sound and vice versa. Its effect is a form of synaesthesia, and close to phonemic orthography. As we have already seen, if read within Morrison's corpus, as the first sound that follows *Beloved* and its unstable closure, the sound continues that novel's haunting. In this context, its arrest is a return of the uncanny. It is literally the sound of a hiss coming from elsewhere, unseen but familiar in its strangeness, now out of time at the turn of the twentieth century and out of place in the streets of New York City's Harlem. If read in tandem with Morrison's oeuvre and the epigraph from "Thunder, Perfect Mind," the sound arrests in yet another way:

I am the name of the sound
    and the sound of the name.
I am the sign of the letter
    and the designation of the division

Radiating its fierce deific aura, the epigraph "speaks" itself. It is and claims
to be pure language. It is self-contained. It is its own body, its own appearance, its own auditor. Moreover, it radiates beyond the boundary between itself as epigraph and the novel to which it is attached, because the
very first statement of the novel partakes in the same tone and style as
"Thunder, Perfect Mind." "Sth!" is also a sound that is its own name, and
it designates a division between the epigraph and the story that is about to
be told, a division that would otherwise be contained in the proper place
of the book epigraph, in its paratextual space, divided physically by at least
one blank page from the place where the text commences.

How Will Love Suffice?

The gathering force of Pauline references is only temporarily displaced by
the Nag Hammadi text. It returns, most forcefully, in the title *Love*. Here
the author of the Pauline epistles is missing, and what had been epigraph
transforms into title, fully covering and naming the book, which has no
need for an epigraph.

  Summarizing the retrieval of love as an ethico-political counter to late-
twentieth- and early-twenty-first-century materialism, David Nirenberg
returns us to the etiological history of love's role in formal systems of
exchange, a history that emerges from the ancient Mediterranean basin
and enters European-inflected philosophy via Hebrew scripture, Greek
philosophy, and Christianity.[26] Without suggesting that this etiology has
an inevitable telos, Nirenberg reminds us that the transformation of love
into a liberatory force, if not an emotional and ethical bastion against all
forms of corruption, has come about only because its etymology has been
suppressed. Early kinship and political as well as trading systems of the ancient Mediterranean used the same vocabulary of love and friendship in-
terchangeably, even incestuously. In other words, the terms *love* and *friendship* were employed freely to refer equally to relations between creditors
and debtors, in kinship, in marriage, and in other relations. While this history does not mean that our present uses of the terms *love* and *friendship* are

entirely null and void, Nirenberg's logic parallels Jan Patočka's argument that something Dionysian remains stowed away in Christianity through its early borrowings from other belief systems, and it parallels Derrida's critical extension of Patočka, as well as Horkheimer and Adorno's arguments about the barbarism at the heart of rationalism.[27] It is the obscuring power of the projected ideal that is of interest in each case, since, for Nirenberg, Patočka, Derrida, and Horkheimer and Adorno, an analysis of that surface reveals its dialectical relation with what claims to have been expunged. Thus, to advocate today a return to love as an ideal for confronting one's enemy or for countering the greed epitomized by global capitalism—as Martin Luther King, Jr., did in his 1956 "Pauline" sermon—is to overlook those earlier slippages. To argue, as, in Nirenberg's example, Archbishop Rowan Williams has done, that divine love is the counter to late capitalism's devolution into "infinite exchangeability and timeless, atomized desire" is to apply love to the very matters of reciprocity and exchange that Nirenberg notes were among the earliest documented uses of the term in the ancient Mediterranean.[28] Of course, Morrison does not revisit that early Mediterranean moment. Instead, she looks to the period of capitalism's commencement in slave-based economies during the early conquest years of the Americas. *A Mercy* has no epigraph, in keeping with the many statements that Morrison made upon its 2008 release: namely, that she wanted to imagine an America before it was America and before racial boundaries had solidified. Dispensing with an epigraph, the novel resists becoming an echo of writing that has gone before it, even the body of African American literatures that Morrison's own work as a young editor at Random House brought to light, a time before Hawthorne, Lucy Terry, Whitman, and the American literature that she writes about in *Playing in the Dark: Whiteness and the Literary Imagination*. In that book, she argues that blackness has always been a defining presence in canonical American literature, even when it is not acknowledged. *A Mercy* attempts to enter a time when that presence struggled with the challenge of having to find a new language, a new way of looking at the world and of explaining it. Like *A Mercy*, but published before it, *Love* gave up the temporality that an epigraph creates between a prior text and an immanent one. Both novels appear to occupy their own space without looking backward. In this sense, they could be narratorial heterotopias in Morrison's work, if we are to read Foucault's argument about heterotopic space as more spatial than temporal. For Foucault, heterotopias are spaces that grow out of, but are outside of, normative places. They reflect these normative places but are "absolutely different from all the sites that they reflect and speak about."[29]

The decision to relinquish the epigraph is as much a political act as a literary one—the two always being linked for Morrison, whose work, I have attempted to show, undertakes an ethico-political poetics of American raced, gendered, and politicized psyches and the laboring bodies that inhabit class positions. It is thus entirely to be expected that a novel set in later moments would revert to the practice of epigraphic inscription, and this is certainly the case with *Home.* The novel returns to the convention in a complex and multivalent manner, for its epigraph is taken from Morrison's own song cycle, *Honey and Rue,* with music composed by André Previn and sung by Kathleen Battle. The epigraph is taken from the second of six songs, 'Whose House Is This?' The quote reads:

> Whose house is this?
> Whose night keeps out the light
> In here?
> Say, who owns this house?
> It's not mine.
> I had another sweeter, brighter,
> With a view of lakes crossed in painted boats;
> Of fields wide as arms open for me.
> This house is strange.
> Its shadows lie.
> Say, tell me, why does its lock fit my key?
>
> ("Whose House Is This?," 1–11, *HR*)

The questions bring us full circle, to Morrison's essay "Home" and to the tensions surrounding the house of race, first drawn so brightly and distinctly in the Dick and Jane primer and the McTeer household in *The Bluest Eye.* More to the point, though, the question takes us to the role that black women played as domestic servants, tending houses that were not theirs. While the men of Ruby take pride in knowing that "none of their women had ever worked in a whiteman's kitchen" (*P* 99), the issue of domestic service and its ironic relation to the idea of home was raised in Morrison's first novel, with the work that Pauline Breedlove does to keep the Fishers' house spotless and perfect. The issue appears again in *Tar Baby* in the Caribbean island home that Ondine Childs maintains, and it appears in *Home* as the "large two-story house rising above a church-neat lawn," maintained by the live-in maid, Sarah Williams (*H* 58).

When Pecola Breedlove and the McTeer sisters decide to visit her mother at work, they enter a kitchen that is "a large spacious room" (*BE* 107). This is quite unlike the places in which they live—while the McTeers live in a house, the Breedloves live in a storefront. The girls see Pauline Breedlove as they have never seen her before. Her "skin glowed like taffeta in the reflection of white porcelain, white woodwork, polished cabinets, and brilliant copperware." This is a lakefront, not a storefront house. Claudia declares lakefront houses "the loveliest" (*BE* 105). They are not the kind of mansion that so inspired Jacob Vaark, but the suburban dream of a middle- and upper-middle-class America he could not imagine. The windows of each lakefront house are likened to "shiny eyeglasses," but, like Vaark's house, they appear to be empty. There is "no sign of life." The "life" of these houses is inside, cleaning in the visible invisibility of domestic service. Leisure time has a space provided. It is the Lake Shore Park that waits, "sweetly expectant of clean, white, well-behaved children and parents" (*BE* 105). "Black people were not allowed" to enter it. Beside it is the Fishers' house. It is distinctive in Claudia's mind as "the large white house with the wheelbarrow full of flowers."

When the children enter the Fishers' lakefront house and Pecola accidentally knocks a blackberry pie onto the floor, her mother is enraged. In "a voice thin with anger," she can barely speak to the girls, the ellipses indicative of the places where language fails her: "Crazy fool . . . my floor, mess . . . look what you . . . work . . . get on out . . . now that . . . crazy . . . my floor, my floor . . . my floor" (*BE* 109). When she turns to speak to the Fisher daughter, a "little girl in pink," she finds language: "Hush, baby, hush. Come here. Oh, Lord, look at your dress. Don't cry no more. Polly will change it."

The possessive language is, of course, ironic. Pauline has no right to the floor. She merely cleans it. Nevertheless, the pride is hers, relieved as she is to have found "a permanent job in the home of a well-to-do family whose members were affectionate, appreciative, and generous" (*BE* 127). When she looks at the Fisher house, she smells and loves their linen and draperies, the little girl's "pink nightie," the "white pillow slips edged with embroidery, the sheets with top hems picked out with blue cornflowers." She loves the porcelain bathing tub and its "silvery taps running infinite quantities of hot, clear water," which are a universe away from the zinc tub in her storefront home. In the Fisher home she is in control of "things." She is "queen of canned vegetables bought by the case" and other plenitudes that she orders as if she is, indeed, a steward. The slippage between acting on behalf of someone and presuming that something of their power is hers is apparent in her possessive language: "Power, praise, and luxury were hers in this household" (*BE* 128). In return, she receives the gift of intimacy. Her employers "even gave her what she had never had—a nickname, Polly." That this is a diminutive or a name commonly given to a pet parrot does not occur to her. The name and the kitchen in which she can "survey her handiwork" are hers.

In the Fisher house there are "no buckets of stove-heated water, no flaky, stiff, grayish towels washed in a kitchen sink, dried in a dusty backyard," and where there are little blonde curls to comb, there are "no tangled puffs of rough wool to comb" (*BE* 127). The beauty of the Fisher house sours Pauline Breedlove's view of her own residence. So, for her, the question "Whose House Is This?" does not refer to the perfect home that she cleans but to living quarters that she finds dingy.

In the song 'Whose House Is This?' after the persona sings, "Say, who owns this house? / It's not mine," she goes on with:

> I had another sweeter, brighter,
> With a view of lakes crossed in painted boats;
> Of fields wide as arms open for me. This house is strange.
> Its shadows lie.
> Say, tell me, why does its lock fit my key?
>
>   ("Whose House Is This?," 4–5, 6–11, *HR*)

The inverted logic of a key that fits a lock substitutes for a lock that fits a key. It is a chilling understanding of how a Pauline Breedlove has been drawn into a state in which she seems to have fashioned the means by which she enters and incarcerates herself in the house of race. She may have a beautiful view, but she will be returned to where she belongs in the view of those who own the house and can call her Polly. So in a sense she is right when she turns her disappointed eye to the place in which she lives. It is not her "house," nor is it her home. It is an abandoned storefront "on the southeast corner of Broadway and Thirty-fifth Street in Lorain, Ohio," and it is "the debris of a realtor's whim" (BE 33, 34).

Its appearance is "irritating and melancholy," and visitors who drive through the town "wonder why it has not been torn down" (*BE* 33). As is common with petty bourgeoisie commerce, the storefront is attached to living quarters—so different from the middle- and upper-class distance between living space and work space, epitomized by the lakefront, where there is the added leisure space of the park adjacent to the Fishers' house. A family of Italian immigrants, the Villanuccis, live above a café that they own (*BE* 9). They have made a home at the site of their labor. The Breedloves do not. But their immediate neighbors, the three prostitutes who occupy the apartment above them, do. The address has seen many occupancies before this. It was once a pizza parlor, in which "slow footed teen-aged boys . . . huddled about the corner" and performed their novice masculinity by exposing themselves (*BE* 34–35). It was a real estate office, and it once housed a gypsy family, whose daughters placed themselves in the plate glass window between "yards of velvet draperies and Oriental rugs" to smile, wink, or beckon (*BE* 34). Their "elaborate dresses," with long sleeves and long skirts, add to the girls' allure; some passersby imagine them "as hiding the nakedness that stood in their eyes."

The daughters of the gypsy family seem to understand what being in a storefront means. It is a space to display goods or, when turned into living quarters, where poverty is on display. Who lives in a storefront? The answer might be: someone who cannot afford or gain access to a house. The storefront is where the Breedloves' poverty is on display, but it is also a space in which the history of slavery is, embarrassingly, on display as well. Lorraine, Ohio, is a short distance from Oberlin, which was a terminus on the Underground Railroad before the former slaves escaped across the border into Canada. They were fleeing a history in which people were displayed and examined for sale. The storefront, like the legacies of slavery that determine economic and class status for some, "does not recede into" the "background. . . . Rather, it foists itself on the eye of the passerby in a manner that is both irritating and melancholy" (*BE* 33). Visitors who drive by wonder why it has not been torn down; residents of the town "simply look away when they pass it."

Morrison's fiction has never looked away from how the past inflects or ghosts the surface of the present. The song cycle from which *Home*'s epigraph is taken continues the work of reflection that such forms of repetition as citation permit, and of which epigraphs partake. *Honey and Rue* is a complex set of references to Morrison's oeuvre. Each song contains, in abstracted form, themes and concerns that were present in her fiction before she wrote the cycle and anticipates these revisited elements in her later fiction.

The first song, "Love," prioritizes love: "First / I'll try love." Trying and also testing, the persona has never "heard the word / Referred to even / Me" ("Love," 1–5, *HR*). This is someone who labors, and "sundown," when labor is done, is her time of day. For all of the promise to try love, there is a sense that this persona is alone, perhaps like L in *Love*—a woman with a quiet nature, who has given her life in service and who has never declared her love for anyone openly or received a declaration of love. L meditates on love: "Do they still call it infatuation? That magic ax that chops away the world with one blow, leaving only the couple standing there trembling? . . . Some, the riptide ones, claim exclusive right to the real name, even though everybody drowns in its wake. People with no imagination feed it with sex—the clown of love. They don't know the real kinds, the better kinds, where losses are cut and everybody benefits. It takes a certain intelligence to love like that—softly, without props" (*L* 63). It could be L singing "Love," or it could be the narrator of *Jazz* who longs to be looked at and loved by a reader.

The second song, from which the epigraph for *Home* was taken, returns us to the overt question of home and belonging—its implications for Pauline Breedlove have been discussed above. It also returns us to Morrison's image of herself in the house of race and the challenge to write in language and with narratives, characters, forms, and style that could "enunciate and then eclipse" the racial gaze and the possessive language that has the power to designate and consign. The song's last three lines carry something of the strangeness of Morrison's remarks about the house of race in the essay "Home," and they pull a reader up short with the sense of how adaptive a possessive logic can be so that "its lock" will always seek to fit the singer's key.

Having summoned the image of a house, albeit a house of race, the song cycle shifts into the relation between houses, the communal space that becomes a town. The third song, "The Town Is Lit," begins with the image of a suburban dream, but the dream is speculative, a proposition, a desire uttered by unspecified people who have the invisible aura of the powerful and whose power dissipates into the tone and style of an always already omniscient will:

It's been suggested: well kept lawns and
fences white porch swings and toast by the fire.
It's been requested: puppies, a window of
blossoming pear trees and a place for the robins
to nest.

("The Town," 1–5, *HR*)

The plan is disrupted by a volta and a stanza that is indented, the tone
reminiscent of Langston Hughes's "Harlem Night Song":

But I know that somewhere, out there
The town is lit
The players begin
To make music in all the cafés.

(Ibid., 6–9)

Another life is already underway, making art, collaborating. And although
"Clowns on wheels / Linger to steal" in a less than ideal world, love is now
not only the wistful promise that a solo persona makes to herself, albeit
ironically (ibid., 10–11). Lovers appear in the town and, in a way that is both
mundane and free, they expect that the world will orient itself to protect
them: "Lovers expecting / The night to protect them" (ibid. 13–14).

The first five lines interrupt the jazz riff, and the exact repetition creates
a sense of insistence. Now the phrases "It's been suggested" and "It's been
requested" consolidate into a quasi-bureaucratic tone and style, so that the
perfection of the lawns, porch swings, and other elements of idyllic subur-
bia becomes sterile, even soulless. Interruption occurs via a volta again as
the persona also insists:

But I know that somewhere, out there
Geminis split
Sagittarians kick
To the music in all the cafés

(Ibid., 24–27)

In spaces of sociality, and where individuals are customers and servers paid
for their service, the stars are active, personified, and anthropomorphized
as mythic figures for whom there are ideal pairings. So, Geminis and Sagittarians are joined by Aquarians, who "throw / Gold on the floor / To
rival the glitter it makes" and the mythic creatures of "Pisces swim / Over

the rim" (ibid., 28–32). In this thriving world of affinities, destiny is not so much manifest as something danced by players

> Knowing they've got what it takes
> To cut through the dark
> And get to the heart
> Of the music in all the cafés.

> (Ibid., 33–36)

After the jazz-inflected close so reminiscent of Langston Hughes, the song cycle shifts into another solo presence with the fourth song, which was actually composed last and as the result of an additional request by soprano Kathleen Battle, who debuted the cycle at Carnegie Hall.[30] The song opens with a question:

> Do you know him?
> Easy (My God)
> He's so easy to take, to mistake
> So easy.

> ("Do You," 1–4, *HR*)

On the CD it is sung unaccompanied; on the page it is reminiscent of chapter three of the biblical Song of Solomon, when the beloved is separated from her lover and asks the watchmen, "Saw ye him whom my soul loveth?" (Song of Solomon 3:3).

Through this, Morrison's novel of the same title comes back, and this time it is Hagar who, abandoned by Milkman whom she so loved, wanders the South Side of Chicago, looking for her lover, but as his hopeless stalker (*SS* 128). Expelled from his love, she can no longer be at home with herself. She has lost her ability to be in the world for herself, and she dies. But the novel is not the only intertext for this song. The singer might be Sethe waiting for Halle, or for Paul D in *Beloved*. Or it might be Sula waiting for Ajax to return in *Sula*, or it might be her friend Nel waiting for her husband to return. It might be the narrator of *Jazz* waiting for her Thursday man, or L singing about the antinomian Bill Cosey, whom she has loved since she was a child. And it might be Jadine Childs singing about Son in *Tar Baby*. Or the man may be one of the mysterious, heralding men who seem not of this world, never leaving a dent in a seat when they get up, always dressed anachronistically and somehow thundering through the world even when they are quiet. And then, if it is any one of the men that, say, Connie or Dovey has seen in *Paradise*, or that Cee glimpsed in *Home*, he may point us to work that is still to be done, the work of remembering and recovery, and of proper burials.

The Middle Passage is filled with improper burials. This might be what is invoked in the fifth song in *Honey and Rue*, "I Am Not Seaworthy," which opens with a direct statement followed by mythic imagery:

> I am not seaworthy.
> Look how the fish mistake my hair for home.
> I had a life, like you. I shouldn't be riding the sea.
> I am not seaworthy.

In the "middle passages" of *Beloved*, when Sethe, Denver, and the woman named Beloved are locked in 124 Bluestone, Beloved speaks as if she is many or as if many are trying to speak through her. At the novel's end, once Beloved has been expelled from 124 Bluestone by the women of the community, some report seeing "cutting through the woods, a naked woman with fish for hair" (*B* 308).

The concept of home that maps across Morrison's novelistic fiction enters the song cycle overtly in "Whose House Is This?" and closes it with "Take My Mother Home." The promise of that title is far from easily delivered. Whatever a reader's expectation might be, the first stanza is perplexing. Stylistically, it is set as prose: "My lady rides a Tennessee stud with a tiny whip in her hand. The afternoon sky is kind to her and the wind is in love with her veil. Her coat is as red as her heart. The spurs on her heels glint like knives, where the flesh of the stud is soft." The image of a woman with whom the elements are in love is cut by the callousness of her pleasure. The horse is controlled by a whip and her spurs. The designation "lady" insinuates gentility, but the song unsettles that closed circuit of associations. It unveils the violence through which ladylike femininity is performed.

There are two levels to this femininity, presented as located in Tennessee. One is the surface appearance of a "lady" out riding and therefore in public view as a sociality different from the urban café scene. Her veil belongs to an earlier time. Whether or not she rides in any decade of the twentieth century, her veil announces her allegiance to a time that is, for her, not anachronistic. If set in, say, the mid nineteenth century, she might be riding as taught at any of the finishing schools created for young Southern girls. The veil has a broader feminine allusion to virginity, prized in the hermetically sealed logic of racial discourse, in which the purity of the womb must be protected to reproduce the purity of the race.

This is the narrative of *The Birth of A Nation*, in which miscegenated characters, Lynch and Elsie, force or insinuate their desires and in which a black man, Gus, attempts to rape young Elsie Cameron, who, rather than succumb, commits suicide.[31] These characters are offered as representative, and they become the film's justification for the rise of race heroism by white-hooded men who ride to rescue white women and to forestall all future threat by "cleaning" the streets of a "black menace." And they ride to "clean" the houses in which a Lynch, or an Elsie, or a Gus might imagine himself or herself at home. The film goes to great lengths to show how white women and men comport themselves. Ben Cameron, the eldest son of the ideal Southern family and a race hero, raises his hat to women who ride by in a carriage. His sister Margaret is introduced as "a daughter of the South, trained in manners of the old school."[32] In the north, Elsie Stoneman is introduced in a long, puzzling take of her feet playing behind a curtain—but in a film that relies on heavy-handed symbolism, the curtain-veil-virgin association is driven home and will be confirmed when Ben Cameron rides to save her from an attempted rape by Lynch.[33] The education of Southern daughters was, of course, class-based as much as it was racialized. In the 1850s, just prior to the Civil War, finishing schools were popular among wealthier Southern families. Sentimental images of ideal white Southern femininity flourished, especially in autograph books, in which drawings of young women were accompanied by messages and signatures. Christie Anne Farnham quotes from a message in the autograph book of Harriet Cook, who attended Georgia's Madison Female College: "True beauty dwells in deep retreats, where veil is unremoved. Till heart with heart, in concord beats, And the lover is the beloved."[34]

Jazz mocks this notion of "true" beauty by naming a slave woman True Belle—that this name could have been given to a slave to underscore the paradox between her status and a mastering whim does not undermine the fact that Morrison's choice of the name for a relation between slave woman and mistress deepens the mockery. True Belle's mistress is Vera Louise Gray, a Southern woman, daughter of a Confederate Colonel, and bred to make a perfect marriage. She has instead borne the child of a slave man named Henry Lestory or Les Troy, known as Hunter's Hunter (*J* 148). She is disowned by her father and mother; she is literally put out of her home for having defiled the house of race. Her father cannot control his rage and slaps her. Her mother does control her rage, but it is "Only breeding, careful breeding," the kind so prized by D. W. Griffith and eugenicists, fictionalized in *Home*'s Beauregard Scott, that does not "allow her to spit" (*J* 139). Breeding is, of course, what is at stake. It is also the secret that her father, Wordsworth Gray, keeps. His rage is as much about remembering that there are "seven mulatto children on his land" as it is about "the terrible thing that had happened." Grayness is produced by mixing black and white. There have been "other" births of the nation, about which Wordsworth Gray knows and about which Griffith was silent, in order to maintain the beautiful vista of purity, or the Beauregard.

The opening lines of "Take My Mother Home" create an image of violent feminine perfection, beginning with a possessive clause, "My lady." But the possessive has already been questioned in the first song in the *Honey and Rue* cycle. Might it also be troubled in this song? As with the second and third songs in the cycle, "Take My Mother Home" uses interruption and disruption to destabilize the (white) idyll. In this song, "My lady" may ride on, but a persona breaks free of the mesmerizing image. In doing so, she turns to other familial relations that make the possessive "My lady" ring hollow: the "true bell" rings out "my mother," "my father," and names other relations from which she is estranged because she is not free:

Take my mother home; take my mother on home
I ain't free; never mind about me
Take my mother home.
Take my father home; let my father see his home
I ain't free; don't worry about me
Take my father home.
Take my sister home; lead my sister home
I ain't free; forget about me
Lead my sister home.
Take my brother home; show him the way to get home
I ain't free; it don't matter to me
Take my brother home.

("Take My Mother," 6–17)

In *Jazz*, True Belle may speak of her mistress, like any slave or servant, but the truth is closer to the lock that fits the key in "Whose House Is This?" True Belle, like any slave or servant, is the mistress's. After all, the Fishers speak of Pauline Breedlove with a possessive certainty that masquerades as a complement, like a key that fits a lock. They say, "We'll never let her go" and "Really, she is the ideal servant" (*BE* 128). True Belle discovers how ideal she is, and her realization of the cost accompanying such ideality rings through the lament in "Take My Mother Home." When Vera Louise Gray is given enough money to leave her family to save them from shame, the narrator of *Jazz* interrupts her own storytelling to say: "True Belle was the one she wanted and the one she took. I don't know how hard it was for a slave woman to leave a husband that work and distance kept her from seeing much of anyhow, and to leave two daughters behind with an old aunt to take care of them. Rose Dear and May were eight and ten years old then" (*J* 139–40).

This book on Morrison's novelistic fiction opened with reference to her essay "Home" and its anticipation of *Paradise*, which will come to appear as self-citation. That gesture of citation expands across her work, and the epigraph from *Honey and Rue* points to the novel *Home* as a culmination of Morrison's prioritizing of "matters of race and home," first explicitly addressed in "Home" ("H" 4). When Cee enters Beauregard Scott's house, she enters the house in which race is at home. Its old edifice is now buttressed by science. It is a time of beginnings: the country is on the cusp of the Civil Rights Movement, and it has already been riven by Senator Joseph McCarthy's inquisitorial crusade to protect America from a perceived Communist threat—a fact that slips into *Home* via an aside by Lily, Frank's girlfriend. She has lost her job as a makeup artist for a small theater, which was shut down and its director jailed for staging the agit-prop play *The Morrison Case*, by Hollywood screenwriter Albert Maltz, one of ten writers and filmmakers summoned early before the House Un-American Activities Committee and jailed for their supposed Communist sympathies. The play was in fact never staged, filmed, or published.[35] Its appearance in Morrison's novel makes for a remarkable moment, in which we have a new intricacy of citation that links Morrison, the author, briefly with a fictional character accused of being "un-American" a little before Martin Luther King, Jr., delivered his fictional letter from St. Paul and a few years before white supremacists would fight to insist on exclusive right of whites to citizenship.

As one of Morrison's late novels, *Home* partakes of a strange temporal logic (perhaps most readily associated with the photograph): something has happened and something is yet to happen. If Roland Barthes made this the definition of the photograph, it is also an apt description of what fiction can do.[36] Morrison's novels show an understanding of what it might mean to write in a space in which African Americans produce worlds in spaces where belonging has been challenged and in which their name keeps history and the present within view of each other. The thrill of borderlessness that Morrison voiced in "Home" lies somewhere in this relation between a name and a citizen, a name and a subject who refuses to live in the hyphen but who cannot close the door on its possibilities by entering only into the past or living only in the present. While the past is lost with the myth of origins, it is the one window that keeps the present from forgetting and sealing itself up into a triumphant narrative. One has to recognize that at the end of *Home*, a novel occupied by the narrative of a homeward journey, the final line, "Let's go home," is at once an invitation to collectivity and a gesture toward a path yet to be traveled. In other words, both community and home are destinations still to be reached, and some, like the mother in *A Mercy* and the mother summoned in the last line of the last song of *Honey and Rue*, will never make it. That is the bitter-sweetness to be enjoyed in a future of freedom.

Notes

Introduction

1. Richard Yarborough is much more direct about Morrison's relation to such a genealogy. He places her within a lineage that begins with Gustavas Vassa, Frederick Douglass, and Harriet Jacobs and shifts to Booker T. Washington, James Johnson, and then Ralph Ellison. In his estimation, Morrison is aligned with David Bradley and Alice Walker as contemporary heirs of that genealogy. See Yarborough, "The First-Person in Afro-American Fiction," in *Afro-American Literary Study in the 1990s* (Chicago: University of Chicago Press, 1989), 110. By contrast, Trudier Harris's early writings place Morrison's fiction in a tradition of oral storytelling that stretches from slave narratives through the late-nineteenth-century narratives of such writers as Charles Chesnutt and the early-twentieth-century writings of James Weldon Johnson, Jean Toomer, Langston Hughes, and Zora Neale Hurston. Harris identifies Wright and Ellison as continuing the thematics of folklorist writing and argues that it is with Morrison that folkloric materials and form reach their full, modernist "literary" peak. See Trudier Harris, *Fiction and Folklore: The Novels of Toni Morrison* (Knoxville: University of Tennessee Press, 1991). For most Morrison scholars, this trajectory must be read to include the cultural and political dimensions of her work. Thus, e.g., the essayists curated by Nancy J. Peterson in *Toni Morrison: Critical and Theoretical Approaches* (Baltimore: Johns Hopkins University Press, 1997) read Morrison through deconstruction and postmodernism, but also through historicized political legacies. Morrison's work has also been read much more overtly within postcolonial discourse by, e.g., Gurleen Grewal, *Circles of Sorrow, Lines of Struggle: The Novels of Toni Morrison* (Baton Rouge: Louisiana State University Press, 1998). Her close reading of Morrison's first six novels sees them as sociopolitical works. Stelamaris Coser's *Bridging the Americas: The Literature of Paule Marshall, Toni Morrison, and Gayl Jones* (Philadelphia: Temple University Press, 1994) places Morrison's writing within the larger America, aligning her with Paule Marshall and Gayle Jones and comparing her writing with that of Gabriel García Marquéz and Carlos Fuentes. Drawing upon the

work of Houston A. Baker and Henry Louis Gates, Jr., Trudier Harris considers
how traditional oral forms such as blues and trickster narratives have influenced
Morrison. She considers Morrison's fiction up to the publication of *Beloved* in
1987, arguing for the primacy of folkloric influences, which permitted Morrison
to take up devices of oral storytelling as archival practice.

2. Morrison's M.A. thesis, written under her original name, Chloe Wofford,
was entitled "Virginia Woolf's and William Faulkner's Treatment of the Alienated" *(*Cornell University, 1955).

3. As Gates and others have pointed out, slave and ex-slave narrators wrote
under the burden of having to prove that they had indeed written their own
work, and the much-noted forewords to their accounts of their lives argued this
point. An account of one's life was not enough. An account of one's sentience
was demanded, and at all moments the narrator of a slave narrative had to perform the Cartesian paradigm, "I think." See Henry Louis Gates, Jr., *The Signifying Monkey* (New York: Oxford University Press, 1988).

4. August Strindberg, "Author's Foreword," *Six Plays of Strindberg*, trans.
Elizabeth Sprigge (New York: Avon, 1965), 64. Luigi Pirandello, *Six Characters
in Search of an Author* (New York: Signet Classics, 1998).

5. Frederick Douglass, *Narrative of the Life of Frederick Douglass, an American
Slave, Written by Himself* (New York: Dover Publications, Inc., 1995), 69.

6. Michel Foucault, "Different Spaces," in *Aesthetics, Method, and Epistemology*, ed. James F. Faubion, vol. 2 of *Essential Works of Foucault, 1954–1984* (New
York: The New Press, 1998), 49.

7. It may be that Morrison shares some of Gayatri Chakravorty Spivak's
concern, as expressed in "Can the Subaltern Speak?" that Foucault's effort to
theorize a radical liberatory politics ultimately reinstates the oppositions of
Western subject and colonized other as the basis for its emancipatory project. In
any case, Morrison's fiction expresses a desire to address the specific problematic
of the one aspiring to subjectivity, rather than the one seeking to escape the false
centeredness of a misrecognized subject position. See Spivak, "Can the Subaltern Speak?" in *Marxism and the Interpretation of Cultures*, ed. Cary Nelson and
Lawrence Grossberg (Urbana: University of Illinois Press, 1988), 271–313.

8. Roland Barthes, *The Neutral: Lecture Course at the College de France
(1977–78)*, trans. Denis Hollier (New York: Columbia University Press, 2007).

9. I am thus indebted to Nellie McKay, though I depart from her earlier
conversations with Morrison's texts. She produced some of the earliest work
on the relationship between memory and communal belonging in Morrison's
writing. See esp. Nellie Y. McKay, *Critical Essays on Toni Morrison* (New York:
G. K. Hall, 1988). McKay has also co-edited two books that have facilitated the
teaching of Morrison's work. See Nellie Y. McKay and Kathryn Earle, eds.,
Approaches to Teaching the Novels of Toni Morrison (New York: Modern Language
Association of America, 1997), and William L. Andrews and Nellie Y. McKay,

eds., *Toni Morrison's 'Beloved': A Casebook* (New York: Oxford University Press, 1999). As Morrison herself has noted, McKay's work remains notable for its early understanding of Morrison's situatedness as "an already- and always-raced writer" (*P* 4).

10. Michel Foucault, "The Thought of the Outside," in *Aesthetics, Method, and Epistemology*, ed. James F. Faubion, vol. 2 of *Essential Works of Foucault 1954–1984* (New York: The New Press, 1998), 148.

11. René Girard, *Deceit, Desire, and the Novel*, trans. Yvonne Freccero (Baltimore: Johns Hopkins University Press, 1965), 3.

12. Maurice Blanchot, "Literature and the Right to Death," in *The Gaze of Orpheus and Other Literary Essays*, trans. Lydia Davis (Barrytown, N.Y.: Station Hill Press, 1981), 27.

13. Foucault, "The Thought of the Outside," 152.

14. In the English translation of the French phrase *pouvoir savoir*, the transitive has been elided. The literal translation of *pouvoir savoir* is "to be able to know." It concerns a capacity for knowledge that is not articulated in the English "knowledge is power" or the translation of Foucault's work as *Power/Knowledge* (*Power/Knowledge: Selected Interviews and Other Writings, 1972–1977* [New York: Vintage Books, 1980).

15. On the difference between an opposition between history and fiction, and reality and unreality, see Paul Ricoeur, *Time and Narrative*, esp. vol. 3 (trans. Kathleen Blamey and David Pellauer; Chicago: University of Chicago Press, 1988).

16. See Linda Hutcheon, "Theorising the Postmodern: Towards a Poetics," in *The Post-modern Reader*, ed. Charles Jencks (London: Academy, 1991), 76–93.

17. See Terry Eagleton, "The Culture Industry: Enlightenment as Mass Deception," in *The Illusions of Postmodernism*, (Oxford: Blackwell, 1997).

18. Max Horkheimer and Theodor W. Adorno, *Dialectic of Enlightenment: Philosophical Fragments*, trans. Edmund Jephcott (Stanford, Calif.: Stanford University Press, 2002), 94–136. Adorno would continue to theorize the culture industry again and again in his later writings. The Frankfurt School's critique of mass culture echoes Nietzsche's argument that mass culture is central to modern social formations. His resistance to mass culture is argued forcefully in his praise of Wagner's work as saving art from a German culture that had been rendered mediocre by a popular system of education and the increased popularity of newspapers. See *The Birth of Tragedy* (trans. Walter Kaufmann; New York: Random House, 1967). Montaigne and Pascal had already voiced their concerns about the increasing demands of diversion and, in the eighteenth century, Goethe was deeply skeptical of the "wasting" effects of emerging mass culture, specifically newspapers. See Leo Lowenthal, *Literature, Popular Culture, and Society* (Englewood Cliffs, N.J.: Prentice-Hall, 1961), 2. Marx and Engels were much more optimistic about the free press, calling it the "eye of a people's

soul." See Karl Marx and Friedrich Engels, *Collected Works, vol. 1I* (New York: International Publishers, 1975), 142. Later, the idea of the all-seeing eye would instill a profound unease in the prospect of a "Big Brother" who is eternally vigilant, watching, invasive.

19. Horkheimer and Adorno, *Dialectic of Enlightenment*, 94.

20. Ibid., 95.

21. Ibid., 98.

22. Fredric Jameson, *Postmodernism; or, The Cultural Logic of Late Capitalism* (Durham, N.C.: Duke University Press, 1991), 17.

23. Ibid., 4–5.

24. Jameson's use of this term, *pastiche*, is itself an index of the long debate about the state of art vis-à-vis mass production. Jameson acknowledges the trajectory of the word, coming from Adorno through Thomas Mann's Doktor Faustus (Jameson, *The Prison House of Language: A Critical Account of Structuralism and Russian Formalism* [Princeton, N.J.: Princeton University Press, 1972], 16).

25. Sigmund Freud, "The 'Uncanny,'" in *Writings on Art and Literature* (Stanford, Calif.: Stanford University Press, 1997), 234–56.

26. Jameson, *Postmodernism*, 17.

27. On focalization, see Mieke Bal, *Murder and Difference: Gender, Genre, and Scholarship on Sisera's Death.* (Bloomington: Indiana University Press, 1988), esp. 86–87.

28. Freud, "The 'Uncanny,'" 204, 205.

29. Jameson, *Postmodernism*, 17.

30. Gauri Viswanathan, *Masks of Conquest: Literary Study and British Rule in India* (New York: Columbia University Press, 1989).

31. Ibid., 113.

32. Ibid., 113–14.

33. See his discussion of the inseparability of language and culture in Ngugi wa Thiong'o, *Decolonizing the Mind* (Portsmouth, N.H.: Heinemann, 1981), esp. 15–17.

34. Ibid., 15.

35. Salman Rushdie, *Imaginary Homelands* (New York: Granta, 1992).

36. Hortense Spillers acknowledges the special burden placed upon black female bodies. Not only does the origin get coded as female in the idiom of the mother tongue, but the literary response to colonialism frequently entails gestures of reclamation of the feminine. Indeed, Sharon Holland has noted that even critical readings of colonial discourse, including fictional engagements with it, have (re)"produced" women's bodies as figures upon which arguments may be staged. See Sharon Patricia Holland, *Raising the Dead: Readings of Death and (Black) Subjectivity* (Durham, N.C.: Duke University Press, 2000).

37. Derek Walcott, *Another Life* (London: Jonathan Cape, 1973), 3.

38. Bill Ashcroft, Gareth Griffiths, and Helen Tiffin, *The Empire Writes Back: Theory and Practice in Post-Colonial Literatures* (London: Routledge, 1989).

39. Ibid., 7.

40. Ibid., 38.

41. Ibid.

42. Ibid., 39.

43. Simon Gikandi, *Writing in Limbo: Modernism and Caribbean Literature* (Ithaca: Cornell University Press, 1992).

44. Ibid., 3.

45. Ibid., 9.

46. Ibid., 12.

47. Homi Bhabha, "Of Mimicry and Man: The Ambivalence of Colonial Discourse," in *The Location of Culture* (London: Routledge, 1994), 85–92.

48. Walcott dramatizes colonialism's pedagogy in chap. 11 of his book-length poem *Another Life*. On this subject of Walcott's relation to the colonial curriculum, see Yvette Christiansë, "'Monstrous Prodigy': The Apocalyptic Landscapes of Derek Walcott's Poetry," in *Mapping the Sacred: Religion, Geography and Postcolonial Literatures*, ed. Jamie S. Scott and Paul Simpson-Housley (Amsterdam: Rodopi, 2001), 199–224.

49. Walter Benjamin, "On Language as Such and on the Language of Man," in *Reflections: Essays, Aphorisms, Autobiographical Writings*, ed. Peter Demetz, trans. Edmund Jephcott (New York: Schocken Books, 1986), 314.

50. Walter Benjamin, "A Berlin Chronicle," in *One Way Street*, trans. Edmund Jephcott and Kingsley Shorter (London: Verso, 1997), p. 314.

51. Ibid.

52. Paul Ricoeur elaborates a notion of indebtedness that appears to be congruent with Morrison's poetic practice in "The World of the Text and the World of the Reader," chap. 7 of *Time and Narrative*, vol. 3; see esp. 157. Interestingly, this notion emerges as the correlate of his repudiation of the opposition between history and fiction.

53. Holland, Raising the Dead, 4. Holland's work takes up cultural anthropologist Michael Taussig's Benjaminian argument that the creation of a "space of death" is a vital psychic refuge for terrorized subjects. See Michael Taussig, *Shamanism, Colonialism, and the Wild Man* (Chicago: University of Chicago Press, 1987).

54. Saidiya Hartman, *Lose Your Mother: A Journey along the Atlantic Slave Route* (New York: Farrar, Straus and Giroux, 2007).

55. Denise Heinze, *The Dilemma of "Double-Consciousness": Toni Morrison's Novels* (Athens: University of Georgia Press, 1993); Philip Page, *Dangerous Freedom: Fusion and Fragmentation in Toni Morrison's Novels* (Jackson: University Press of Mississippi, 1995).

56. For Homi Bhabha, Morrison's fiction epitomizes the postcolonial subject's disruption of history through the creation of a "discursive time-lag" in which the present act of narrative is transformed into a "haunting memorial." Thus, for Bhabha, Morrison creates "the *unheimlich* space for the negotiation

of identity and history." See Homi Bhabha, *The Location of Culture* (New York: Routledge, 1994), 198. Bhabha's work is paralleled by that of Paul Gilroy, with notable divergence on the matter of psychoanalysis, to which Gilroy is committed. I draw upon Paul Gilroy's *Against Race: Imagining Political Culture Beyond the Color Line* (Cambridge: Harvard University Press, 2000) and Frantz Fanon's *Black Skins, White Masks* (New York: Pluto Press, 1986). By contrast, Avery Gordon's sociological reading suggests that Morrison's *Beloved* operates as a repository of memories whose shocking content overwhelms the narrative language of conventional histories. Ironically, perhaps, it is Gordon's sociological position that opens Morrison's work to more philosophical concerns. See Avery Gordon, *Ghostly Matters: Haunting and the Sociological Imagination* (Minneapolis: University of Minnesota Press, 1998).

57. Holland, *Raising the Dead*, 6.

58. In his coining of "comm(unity)," Michael Awkward has highlighted the doubled "quest" for a commonality as unity, with specific reference to black women's fiction. See Michael Awkward, *Inspiriting Influences: Tradition, Revision, and Afro-American Women's Novels* (New York: Columbia University Press, 1991), 14.

59. Page, *Dangerous Freedom*, 68.

60. Achille Mbembe argues that colonialism reduces language to commandment. See Achille Mbembe, *On the Postcolony* (Berkeley: University of California Press, 2001). In the chapter "Of Commandment," Mbembe identifies "commandment" as the forceful mode of relations between colonized and colonial rule, in which the "right" to conquer operated by reducing the right of colonized subjects. Colonial power, in the form of a right to authority, claimed for itself the language of morality, despite any contradictions with its own liberal discourses.

61. Page, *Dangerous Freedom*, 117–18.

62. Ricoeur, *Time and Narrative*, 3:157.

1. From Witnessing to Death Dealing: On Speaking of and for the Dead

1. Giorgio Agamben, *Remnants of Auschwitz: The Witness and the Archive*, trans. Daniel Heller-Roazen (New York: Zone Books, 1999).

2. Ibid., 34–35. Agamben cites Jean-François Lyotard, *The Differend: Phrases in Dispute*, trans. George Van Den Abbeele (Minneapolis: University of Minnesota Press, 1988), see esp, 33–35.

3. Agamben, *Remnants*, 34.

4. The histories of slavery, colonization, and anti-Semitism may overlap experientially and even religiously in such cases as the Ethiopian Jews or African Americas who take Judaism as their religious foundation. However, we must distinguish the experiences of the Jews in Europe from those of African

Americans. For them—drawn from vastly different backgrounds but lumped together under the category of "Africans"—the experience of history was one of forced identification on the basis of an exterior and violently imposed economy. Genealogical connection was not only discouraged but placed under active erasure, with the result that the vast majority of African Americans have no sense of anything but a vague "Africanness," which is kept alive in the designation *African American*. Jews, by contrast, share a religious orientation even though they came from vastly different geographies. In his argument that there is a certain mutual understanding of exile among Jews and African Americans, Adam Zachary Newton reminds us that Jews may trace their lineage through geographical designations in such names as *Jewish-American*, *German-Jewish*, *Russian-Jewish*, *Iranian-Jewish*, or *Argentinian-Jewish*. See, Adam Zachary Newton, *Facing Black and Jew: Literature as Public Space in Twentieth-Century America* (Cambridge: Cambridge University Press, 1999). In response to Tony Martin's preface to *The Jewish Onslaught: Dispatches From the Wellesley Battle-front* (Dover: The Majority Press, 1993), Newton responds to nomenclature and orthography by considering the graphic impact of names and naming. Thus, as Ronald Judy has, Newton considers the status of hyphenation in, for example, *African-* or *Afro-American* not only as signifying place but also as invoking, through mimicry, "a minus sign" (Newton, 8). Although I do not use the hyphen for *African American*, my own reading of the hyphen is as a bridge whose very sign is fragmentation, hence the call for such categories as African American. These names each connote "simply the latest instantiation in a long history of uprooting" (ibid.). In their plurality, each of these diasporic communities can "prove the anomaly of postexilic Jewish peoplehood, a four millennia long migration with a succession of 'landings' on multiple shores" (ibid.). These "landings" suggest "arrivals" that mark the end of purposeful journeys. Indeed, Newton goes so far as to suggest that there is a restorative promise in diaspora. If names such as *Jewish-American* and *German-Jewish* point to a long history of displacement, they also point to the concrete outcomes of forced journeys: new homes elsewhere arrived at. Thus, the very idea within diaspora holds dispersed peoples together *in* the language of a common experience. By contrast, for Newton, the name *African American* signifies place, "typography as topography, the ligature of place name compressing a continent" (ibid.). Brent Hayes Edwards reminds us that it was historian George Shepperson who formally invoked the notion of Jewish diaspora in 1965 in an attempt to include the impact of slavery within pan-Africanism's fields of interest, namely, unificatory conversations between groups of African descent, living elsewhere in the world. See Brent Hayes Edwards, "Uses of Diaspora," *Social Text* 66, 19, no. 1 (Spring 2001): 45–73; see, esp., 51–52 for his citation of George Shepperson's "The African Abroad or the African Diaspora," in *Emerging Themes of African History*, ed. T. O. Ranger (Nairobi: East African Publishing House, 1968), 152–76. See, esp. 152, as cited by Edwards. Shepperson's argument for a similarity between the "scattering" of the Jews and the enforced deportation of Africans was a precursor to the kind of argument staged by Newton.

Yet another historical difference exists between the experiences of Jews who suffered expulsion and death camps, and Africans taken into slavery to die in the Middle Passage or whose descendents have been left to feel forever that what preceded that passage has been lost in generality. Africans were desired in the so-called New and, to a lesser extent, Old Worlds because of their use value and their (enforced) capacity to produce surplus. Jews, expelled from Spain in 1492 or driven from towns across Europe during pogroms over the centuries, were expelled as undesirable and having no other use but to perform the materiality of financial transaction according to the (il)logic of anti-Semitic stereotypes. For Jews drawn into Nazism's frenzied but paradoxically rationalized attempt to eradicate racial and ethnic difference, a lumping classification similar to that experienced by Africans was at work. In his interrogation of the nature of stereotypes, Homi Bhaba points out that such generalization is its hallmark. See, Homi Bhaba, "The Other Question: Stereotype, Discrimination and the Discourse of Colonialism," in *The Location of Culture* (New York: Routledge, 1994), esp. 66–67.

For more sustained considerations of African American and Jewish American relations, see A. Stein and R. Weisbord, *Bittersweet Encounter: The Afro American and the American Jew* (Westport. Negro University Press, 1970); Paul Berman, *Blacks and Jews: Alliances and Arguments* (New York: Delacorte Press, 1994); Hasia Diner, *In the Almost Promised Land: American Jews and Blacks 1915–1935* (Westport, Conn.: Greenword Press, 1977); Michael Lerner and Cornel West, *Jews and Blacks: Let the Healing Begin* (New York: G. P. Putnam's Sons, 1995); Jack Salzman and Cornel West, *Struggles in the Promised Land: Towards a History of Black-Jewish Relations in the United States* (New York: Oxford University Press, 1997).

5. Agamben, *Remnants*, 26–31.

6. Ibid., 17.

7. Lyotard, *The Differend*, 3, cited in Agamben, *Remnants*, 35.

8. Ibid.

9. Morrison, "UTU"; in this essay, first given as a Tanner Lecture, Morrison addresses the underexamined African American presence in and contribution to the American canon and therefore to the American imaginary. The non-fictional project of this essay finds its expanded argument in *PD*.

10. Lucile P. Fultz, *Toni Morrison: Playing with Difference* (Urbana: University of Illinois Press, 2003), 16.

11. Bonnie Angelo, "The Pain of Being Black: An Interview with Toni Morrison," in *Conversations with Toni Morrison*, ed. Danille Taylor-Guthrie (Jackson: University Press of Mississippi, 1994), 261 (first published in *Time*, May 22, 1994; 120–22; see esp. 256.

12. Avery Gordon, *Ghostly Matters: Haunting and the Sociological Imagination* (Minneapolis: University of Minnesota Press, 1998), 139.

13. Bonnie Angelo, "The Pain of Being Black: An Interview with Toni Morrison," *Conversations with Toni Morrison*, ed. Danille Taylor-Guthrie (Jackson: University Press of Mississippi, 1994), 256.

14. Ibid. 257.

15. Gordon also cites Toni Morrison, "'Five Years of Terror': A Conversation with Mariam Horn," *U.S. News and World Report*, October 19, 1987, 75. See also Angelo, "The Pain of Being Black," 257. Both the Horn and the Angelo interviews are cited by Gordon.

16. One sees in Gordon's own writing the potency of haunting; her essay is interrupted by italicized repetitions, repetitions that are quotations sans quotation marks. The visual effect of the italics, the reader's double-take at the familiar lines, only freshly encountered just minutes or even seconds before and now puncturing the integrity of the "scholarly voice," foreground the effect of modernist citational practices as a practice of haunting and being haunted.

17. Susan Kessler Barnard, *Buckhead* (Charleston, S.C.: Arcadia Publishing, 2009), 62. See also Rory McVeigh, *Rise of the Klu Klux Klan: Right-Wing Movements and National Politics* (Minneapolis: University of Minnesota Press, 2009), 157.

18. Hermann J. Muller, *Out of the Night: A Biologist's View of the Future* (New York: Vanguard Press, 1935); Madison Grant, *The Passing of the Great Race; or, the Racial Basis of European History* (New York: Charles Scribner's Sons, 1936); Leslie Clarence Dunn and Theodosius Dobzhansky, *Heredity, Race, and Society* (New York: New American Library, 1946).

19. Muller, *Out of the Night*, 113.

20. Grant, *The Passing of the Great Race*, 49.

21. Ibid, 51.

22. Eugenicist philosophy was prevalent in England, America, South Africa, and elsewhere. Proponents of sometimes radically different politics agreed that eugenics was a serious matter of science, although, as we see in Muller's and Huxley's opposition to race and class prejudice, they differed in their application. For Fabians like George Bernard Shaw, eugenics could save nothing less than civilization. See George Bernard Shaw, *Sociological Papers* (London: MacMillan, 1905), 74–75. Referencing this statement and others made by both Fabians and Marxists, Diane Paul argues that: "The history of eugenics has been presented so often as though it were simply the extension of nineteenth century social Darwinism that we have nearly lost sight of the fact that important segments of the Left (as well as the women's movement) were once also enthusiastic about the potential uses of eugenics." See Diane B. Paul, *The Politics of Heredity: Essays on Eugenics, Biomedicine, and the Nature-Nurture Debate* (Albany: State University of New York Press, 1998), 14.

23. Garland E. Allen, "'Culling the Herd': Eugenics and the Conservation Movement in the United States, 1900–1940." *Journal of the History of Biology*, published online, March 13, 2012.

24. *Nuremberg Trial Proceedings*, Vol. 11, One Hundred and Ninth Day, Monday, 15 April 1946, http://www.loc.gov/rr/frd/Military_Law/pdf/NT_ Vol-XI.pdf. Grant's advice that "the most practical and hopeful method of race improvement is through the elimination of the least desirable elements in the nation" was echoed in the Nuremberg Doctors Trial, or *United States of America vs. Karl Brandt et al.* One of the doctors on trial, Gerhard Rose, claimed that he saw nothing wrong with experimenting on a few hundred concentration camp prisoners in order to improve the health of thousands of soldiers on the eastern front. See "Records of the United States Nuremberg War Crimes Trials, *United States v. Karl Brandt et al* (Case 1): November 21, 1946, to August 20, 1947," NWC, 1:72, cited in Jonathan Peter Spiro, *Defending the Master Race: Conservation, Eugenics, and the Legacy of Madison* (Lebanon, N.H.: University Press of New England, 2009), 381 and 441. Defense for another doctor, Joachim Mrugowsky, reflected the same logic that sacrifice of the weaker few benefited the stronger, especially the "Millions of soldiers" who "had to give up their lives because they were called upon to right by the state." See "Extracts from the Final Pleas for Defendant Mrugowsky," *Trials of War Criminals Before the Nuerenberg Military Tribunals*, Vol. 1 "The Medical Case," 542.

25. Harriet A. Washington, *Medical Apartheid: The Dark History of Medical Experimentation on Black Americans from Colonial Times to the Present* (New York: Doubleday, 2006).

26. Thomas Hobbes, *Leviathan, or the Matter, Forme, & Power of a Commonwealth,* ed. Richard Flathman and David Johnston (New York: W. W. Norton & Company, 1996) 28.

27. Frederick Douglass, *Narrative of the Life of Frederick Douglass: An American Slave and Incidents in the Life of a Slave Girl* (Westminster, Md.: Modern Library, 2000), 55–57.

28. William Lloyd Garrison, "Preface," in Douglass, *Narrative*, 8.

29. Douglass, *Narrative*, 18–19.

30. Ibid., 18.

31. Ibid., 55.

32. Ibid., 55–56.

33. Ibid., 56.

34. See John Greenleaf Whittier, "The Farewell of a Virginia Slave Mother to Her Daughters Sold into Southern Bondage," in *An American Anthology, 1787–1900*, ed. Edmund Clarence Stedman (Boston: Houghton Mifflin, 1900), 128–29. Whittier was a Quaker Abolitionist, whose poem "Our Countrymen in Chains" was circulated widely in broadsheets in the United States and England.

35. This is a difference between the argument that Agamben is pursuing in relation to the specific context of the Shoah and Primo Levi's witnessing of the camps. Agamben quotes Levi as resisting third-party witnessing because he is not concerned with judgment or pardon. Levi eschews the authority that Abolitionism required of Douglass. See Agamben, *Remnants*, 17.

36. Jean Fagan Yellin, "Introduction," in Harriet A. Jacobs, *Incidents in the Life of a Slave Girl: Written by Herself*, ed. Jean Fagan Yellin (Cambridge: Harvard University Press, 1987), xxxv.

37. Joycelyn K. Moody, "Ripping Away the Veil of Slavery: Literacy, Communal Love, and Self-Esteem in Three Slave Women's Narratives," *Black American Literature Forum* 24, no. 4 (Winter 1990): 633.

38. Ibid., 634.

39. As Rebekka Vaark's letter indicates, the Vaarks' farm is in a town called Milton (*M* 112). Vaark's journey passes "Fort Orange: Cape Henry; Nieuw Amsterdam; Wiltwyck," and he passes through Algonquin, Susquehanna, Chesapeake, and Lenape territories (*M* 13). Since Fort Orange is present-day Albany, Vaark's directions suggest that he has come from upstate New York.

40. Sharon Patricia Holland, *Raising the Dead: Readings of Death and (Black) Subjectivity* (Durham, N.C.: Duke University Press, 2000), 14. See, too, Orlando Patterson, *Slavery and Social Death: A Comparative Study* (Cambridge: Harvard University Press, 1982), 5.

41. Holland, *Raising the Dead*, 15.

42. Joseph Glanvill, *Some Philosophical Considerations Touching the Being of Witches: Written in a Letter to the Much Honour'd Robert Hunt Esq.* (London: James Collins, 1667).

43. Hobbes, *Leviathan*.

44. See John McWilliams's arguments about the range of economic, political, social, and spiritual strains that produced in, for example, Increase Mather and his son Cotton "a need for external force to spur covenant renewal." John McWilliams, *New England's Crisis and Cultural Memory: Literature, Politics, History, Religion, 1620–1860* (Cambridge: Cambridge University Press, 2004), 114. One such crisis emerged in the Massachusetts Bay Colony in late 1636 with accusations about unorthodox and false beliefs. In what would be known as the "Free Grace" crisis, inhabitants such as Anne Hutchinson and John Wheelwright were accused of hosting conventicles, or secret and unsanctioned religious gatherings, to propagate the charge that the Puritans were adhering to a Covenant of Works, made between Adam and God. Puritans such as John Winthrop condemned this claim as untrue and counter to the Puritan rejection of precisely the Covenant of Works, which claimed that obedience to God and good deeds were sufficient to lead to heaven. Puritans held to the belief that God's grace would be received by those who adhered to true and proper belief and the law. Hutchinson and her minister, John Cotton, believed that a Covenant of Grace was open to all, regardless of whether they adhered to the law. See David D. Hall, *The Antinomian Controversy 1636–1638: A Documentary History* (Middletown, Conn.: Wesleyan University Press, 1978), 17.

45. Increase Mather, "An Earnest Exhortation to the Inhabitants of New-England, To hearken to the voice of God in his late and present Dispensations As every they desire to escape another Judgement, seven times greater then any

thing which as yet hath been," in *So Dreadfull a Judgement: Puritan Responses to King Phillip's War, 1676–1677*, ed. Richard Slotkin and James K. Folsom (Middletown, Conn.: Wesleyan University Press, 1978), 165–206.

46. In addition to asking what it is that one hears, one also asks: What is the relationship between reading, seeing, and hearing? What is the nature of the literary images that Morrison inserts into the storytelling mode that requires a reader to see ink on paper and pass through it into the space of, not the suspension of belief, but the agreement to believe, to imagine? This is a matter of how a literary image allows us to conceptualize the question of silence as a problem of signification and not just absence. In effect, Morrison's prose is the performative redoubling of the narrative, while the narrative is itself a staging that puts the problem of silence into a scene, the mise-en-scène, somewhere between visibility and audibility, because, technically speaking, one cannot hear silence. The great problem for African American writers, or traumatized writers, is how to make others hear silence as something other than just "no one speaking." It is an ideological, political and aesthetic project. The one produces, redoubles, the other without ever being the same.

47. Morrison herself has tied these novels together: "Now what made those stories connect, I can't explain, but I do know that, in both instances, something seemed clear to me. A woman loved something other than herself so much. She had placed all of the value of her life in something outside herself." See Gloria Naylor and Toni Morrison, "A Conversation: Gloria Naylor and Toni Morrison," in *Conversations with Toni Morrison*, ed. Danille Taylor-Guthrie (Jackson: University Press of Mississippi, 1994), esp. 207–8. Speaking on the *Charlie Rose Show* on November 10, 2008, Morrison echoed this remark in referring to Florens in *A Mercy* as surrendering herself to another.

48. Ibid., 206–7.

49. Cited in ibid. 207.

2. Burnt Offerings: Law and Sacrifice

1. Even its forger cannot be fixed by any single name. He is Zechariah Morgan, freed slave. But he is also Big Daddy, Coffee, and possibly Kufi. His many names obscure him even as they announce him in his manifestation as leader, father, and liberator. He is also the only one whom God seemed to address directly and who could address God, like Moses leading his people out of bondage.

2. The Ku Klux Klan was revived in a ceremony at Stone Mountain outside of Atlanta in 1915 and reclaimed its commitment to patriotism through its idea of America and rightful citizenship. It had used economic and other forms of unrest during and after the First World War to bolster its claims that it was defending American values. Immediately after the First World War, these defenses were made in the name of morality, claiming that the threat to America came

from black men and from such "agitators for change" as suffragettes. Public performances of Klan rallies included, for example, flag ceremonies. At one flag ceremony in 1918, Klansman Wiley Doolittle's statements gave a clear indication of where the organization stood in relation to the law. He warned that those who betrayed the Klan would be "branded on the forehead and on either cheek, and the rope would be the end of traitors, in legal process of law or otherwise." Quoted in Horace C. Peterson and Gilbert C. Fite, *Opponents of War, 1917–1918* (Seattle: Greenwood Press, 1968), 223, and cited by Nancy K. MacLean, *Behind the Mask of Chivalry: The Making of the Second Ku Klux Klan* (New York: Oxford University Press, 1994), 14. MacLean also cites an Atlanta newspaper as praising Wiley Doolittle's promise of retribution for traitors, through the law or other means.

3. Ibid., 17.

4. Numan V. Bartley, *The Rise of Massive Resistance: Race and Politics in the South During the 1950s* (Baton Rouge: Louisiana State University Press, 1997), 202.

5. MacLean, *Behind the Mask of Chivalry*, 29. MacLean draws on a military intelligence reports of 1918.

6. Catherine M. Lewis and Richard J. Lewis, eds., *Jim Crow America: A Documentary History* (Fayetteville: University of Arkansas Press, 2009), xxiv.

7. The *Baltimore Afro-American* ran a story on March 7, 1931, of "the first public Communist trial held in the United States." Quoted in Lewis and Lewis, eds., *Jim Crow America*, 165–67. This volume documents the range of oppositions to Jim Crow and other forms of de facto action against African Americans.

8. Ibid., 188–93.

9. Ibid., 188, 189.

10. Jennifer E. Brooks, "Winning the Peace: Georgia Veterans and the Struggle to Define the Political Legacy of World War II," *The Journal of Southern History* 66, no. 3 (August 2000): 567, 569.

11. Ibid., 573–74.

12. Elias Canetti, *Crowds and Power* (New York: Farrar Straus Giroux, 1984), 290. Canetti's remark is the inspiration for Michael Taussig, *Defacement: Public Secrecy and the Labor of the Negative* (Stanford, Calif.: Stanford University Press, 1999), 5.

13. Don E. Fehrenbacher, *The Slave Holding Republic: An Account of the United States Government's Relations to Slavery*, ed. Ward M. McAfee (New York: Oxford University Press, 2001), 206. Fehrenbacher points out that the Continental Congress took juridical action only to secure slaves who had either fled to the British or been captured by them during the Revolutionary War. It was in response to the Abolitionist movement that slavers called for legal codification of their rights, specifically in the matter of border crossings between states. The result was the insertion of clauses about fugitive slaves into state laws and interstate agreements. Pennsylvania's 1780 law was the first to secure owners' rights (ibid., 206). While the federal 1787 Northwest Ordinance ensured that

Western territories were nonslaving, it contained a clause permitting the legal reclamation of runaway slaves who crossed into them (ibid., 207). During the Constitutional Convention of 1787, having led the way with its 1780 clause, Pennsylvania joined Connecticut's objection to a South Carolinian call to include in the Constitution a stipulation about slavers' rights. South Carolina called for runaway slaves to be subject to legal extradition, "like criminals." The reason for Pennsylvania's objection was far from altruistic. Concern centered on the financial burden this would place on states. The clause was amended to remove the burden of cost and to ensure that slaves would in fact not have any legal status before the law. This amendment effectively circumvented the possible platform that a legal hearing might have given slaves designated criminal and therefore recognized by the law. Article IV, Section Two, of the Constitution reads: "No Person held to Service or Labour in one State, under the Laws thereof, escaping into another, shall, in Consequence of any Law or Regulation therein, be discharged from such Service or Labour, but shall be delivered up on Claim of the Party to whom such Service or Labour may be due." See Constitution of the United States of America, http://www.constitution.org/constit .htm. Amendment XIII was proposed in 1866 to change this section, and it was allegedly ratified in 1868.

The clause was tested in 1791 with the kidnapping of a Pennsylvania freed slave, John Davis, by three Virginians who believed that he was a Virginian and not a Pennsylvanian slave. Davis had been manumitted, but not at his master's will. Under Pennsylvania's Gradual Emancipation Act of 1780, children born to slaves after March 1, 1780, would be free after a period of indenture, during which the master was obliged to educate them. Finkelman points out that slave owners were compensated for the cost of this education and for any financial loss caused by manumission because of the work undertaken by slaves during this stipulated period. In Davis's case, however, this compensation was not enough or not the real issue. At issue were confusion over just where the Pennsylvania/Virginia border lay and a desire by slave owners in the former's western counties to be included in the latter. Davis's owner rented him to a man in Virginia, believing that this would render the Gradual Emancipation Act void in his case. When Abolitionists returned Davis to Pennsylvania, the Virginian who had hired him sent three men to return Davis to Virginia. The three were caught and tried. See Paul Finkelman, *Slavery and the Founders: Race and Liberty in the Age of Jefferson* (Armonk, N.Y.: M. E. Sharpe Inc., 2001), 82. Finkelman points out that, while the Pennsylvania state government issued a warrant for the arrest of the three kidnappers, and while other nonslaving states also attempted to serve warrants in similar cases, politics at the national level could not afford friction over fugitives. In 1792, the Senate established a committee to consider legal ways of settling the issue of fugitives and kidnapping. George Cabot of Massachusetts chaired the committee, which included George Read of Delaware and Samuel Johnson of North Carolina. Read and Johnson were both slave owners (ibid., 93). After numerous drafts, the bill was sent to the House of Representatives on January 18. It received two readings, received a few minor changes, and was passed on February 5 with a vote of forty-eight in favor, and seven in opposition (ibid., 97). Two antislavery northerners voted for the bill on the grounds of an expedient compromise between conflicting positions on fugitive slaves. Washington signed it into law seven days later. Still, it did not satisfy slave owners, who pushed for a stronger act that would eliminate loopholes, and in 1850 Congress passed a new version.

14. In 1690, when Florens is traveling to fetch the blacksmith to save her mistress, colonial slave laws were only newly forming, and the retrieval of runaway slaves was extrajurisdictional and largely a matter for their owners.

15. Francis Newton Thorpe, *The Federal and State Constitutions, Colonial Charters, and Other Organic Laws of the States, Territories, and Colonies Now or Heretofore Forming the United States of America Compiled and Edited Under the Act of Congress of June 30, 1906* (Washington, D.C.: Government Printing Office, 1909). The full text of the article reads: "It is also agreed that the Commissioners for this Confederation hereafter at their meetings, whether ordinary or extraordinary, as they may have commission or opportunity, do endeavor to frame and establish agreements and orders in general cases of a civil nature, wherein all the Plantations are interested, for preserving of peace among themselves, for preventing as much as may be all occasion of war or differences with others, as about the free and speedy passage of justice in every Jurisdiction, to all the Confederates equally as to their own, receiving those that remove from one Plantation to another without due certificate, how all the Jurisdictions may carry it towards the Indians, that they neither grow insolent nor be injured without due satisfaction, lest war break in upon the Confederates through such miscarriages. It is also agreed that if any servant run away from his master into any other of these confederated Jurisdictions, that in such case, upon the certificate of one magistrate in the Jurisdiction out of which the said servant fled, or upon other due proof; the said servant shall be delivered, either to his master, or any other that pursues and brings such certificate or proof. And that upon the escape of any prisoner whatsoever, or fugitive for any criminal cause, whether breaking prison, or getting from the officer, or otherwise escaping, upon the certificate of two magistrates of the Jurisdiction out of which the escape is made, that he was a prisoner, or such an offender at the time of the escape, the magistrates, or some of them of that Jurisdiction where for the present the said prisoner or fugitive abideth, shall forthwith grant such a warrant as the case will bear, for the apprehending of any such person, and the delivery of him into the hands of the officer or other person who pursues him. And if there be help required, for the safe returning of any such offender, then it shall be granted to him that craves the same, he paying the charges thereof."

16. *Plessy v. Ferguson, 163 U.S. 537 (1896)*, http://supreme.justia.com/us/163/537/case.html.

17. Neil Gotanda, "A Critique of 'Our Constitution is Color-Blind,'" *Stanford Law Review* 44, no. 1 (November 1991): 54.

18. See, e.g., the conflict embedded in Justice Harlen's dissenting opinion in *Plessy v. Ferguson* when he argues that "in view of the Constitution, in the eye of the law, there is in this country no superior, dominant, ruling class of citizens. There is no caste here" (*Plessy v. Ferguson*, 559). In this, he overlooks the history in which Jefferson chose not to include African slaves or their descendents in the Constitution except to make provision for them as slaves.

19. Fehrenbacher, *The Slave Holding Republic*, 206. Pennsylvania's 1780 law was the first to secure owners' rights.

20. Michel Foucault, "Truth and Juridical Forms," in *Power*, ed. James D. Faubion, vol. 3 of *Essential Works of Foucault 1954–1984* (New York: The New Press, 2000), 4.

21. See Richard Tuck's contextualizing of Locke (particularly in conversation with Grotius, Hobbens, and Pufendorf) in *Natural Rights Theories: Their Origin and Development* (Cambridge: Cambridge University Press, 1981).

22. Locke was a founding Commissioner of the royal Board of Trade under Charles II, which met for the first time in June 1696. See Peter Laslett, "John Locke, the Great Recoinage, and the Origins of the Board of Trade: 1695–1698," *The William and Mary Quarterly*, 3rd series 14, no. 3 (JJuly 1957): 370–402. See also J. W. Gough, *John Locke's Political Philosophy* (Oxford: Oxford University Press, 1950).

23. John Locke, "First Treatise," in *Two Treatises of Government and a Letter Concerning Toleration*, ed. Ian Shapiro (New Haven, Conn.: Yale University Press, 2003).

24. Thomas Hobbes, *Leviathan, or the Matter, Forme, and Power of a Commonwealth*, ed. Richard Flathman and David Johnston (New York: W. W. Norton & Company, 1996). See chaps. 14 and 15, "Of the First and Second Naturall Lawes and of Contract" and "Of Other Lawes of Nature," 72–78 and 79–87.

25. John Locke, "Second Treatise," in *Two Treatises of Government* , sections 124, 85, 87, 123.

26. One is reminded here of Eugene Genovese's remarks about the social death experienced by slaves, a remark engaged and extended in Sharon Holland's work and also articulated by Abdul JanMohamed in his reading of Richard Wright. JanMohamed reads, through Wright, to Western political philosophy's authorization of slavery. JanMohamed traces three modes in which the black subject is death-bound: actual death, social death, and symbolic death. See Abdul R. JanMohamed, *The Death-Bound Subject: Richard Wright's Archeology of Death* (Durham, N.C.: Duke University Press, 2005).

27. Nancy V. Morrow, "The Problem of Slavery in the Polemic Literature of the American Enlightenment," *Early American Literature* 20, no. 3 (Winter 1985/1986): 237.

28. Morrison made this remark in discussion with Assia Djebar following the performance of excerpts from the opera *Margaret Garner,* for which Morrison had written the libretto, and *Daughters of Ishmael,* which Djebar had written. The event took place at Miller Theater in New York: 'Margaret Garner and the Daughter's of Ishmael," March 28, 2009, http://icls.columbia.edu/events/page/toni_morrisons_margaret_garner_and_assia_djebars_the_daughters_of_ishmael/past.

29   Michel Foucault, "The Thought of the Outside," in *Aesthetics, Method, and Epistemology,* ed. James D. Faubion, vol. 2 of *Essential Works of Foucault 1954–1984* (New York: The New Press, 1998), 147–74, esp. 157. This essay was originally published in *Critique* 229 (June 1966): 523–46. The original translation was by Brian Massumi; it was amended for the New Press edition.

30. The law makes its appearance in language when it is threatened by the transgressive talk of the younger generation, who wish to change the command to read "Be the Furrow" or some other version of the original. The older men, Harper Jury and Sargeant, resist. Jury insists that Destry, one of Luther Beauchamp's two sons, is wrong to change "Beware" to "Be." Jury stresses that "Beware means 'Look out. The power is mine. Get used to it.'" (*P* 87). Sargeant backs Jury up by trying to explain that no one can put himself in the place of God, the real law giver, as the word "Be" would attempt to do. There can be no such simultaneity. "Be" would mean "putting Him aside" and taking power for oneself. Any attempt to do is simply "Blasphemy!"

31. Michel Foucault, "Society Must Be Defended," in *Ethics: Subjectivity and Truth,* ed. Paul Rabinow, vol. 1 of *Essential Works of Foucault, 1954–1984* (New York: The New Press, 1994), 62.

32. Gloria Naylor, *Mama Day* (New York: Vintage, 1988).

33. Ibid., 5.

34. Ibid., 6.

35. Renè Girard, *Violence and the Sacred,* trans. Patrick Gregory (Baltimore: Johns Hopkins University Press, 1977); George Buchanan Gray, *Sacrifice in the Old Testament: Its Theory and Practice* (Oxford: Oxford University Press, 1925); Victor Turner, *Ritual Process: Structure and Antistructure* (Chicago: Aldine, 1969).

36. George is a similar figure in Gloria Naylor's *Mama Day,* sacrificing himself so that Cocoa can live but doing so in a private agreement with himself.

37. Derrida outlines his argument about Abraham's unspoken betrayal of his community in *The Gift of Death,* trans. David Willis (Chicago: University of Chicago Press, 1995).

38. Foucault, "Society Must Be Defended," 25.

39. Israel Knohl, *Divine Symphony: The Bible's Many Voices* (Philadelphia: Jewish Publication Society, 2003), 61.

40. Foucault, "Society Must Be Defended," 25.

41. Mieke Bal, *Death and Dissymmetry: The Politics of Coherence in the Book of Judges* (Chicago: University of Chicago Press, 1988), 9.

42. Ibid.

43. Ibid., 96, 23, 76–80, 85–86, 89–93.

44. Jean Toomer, "Blood Burning Moon," in *Cane* (New York: Liveright Publishing Company, 1975), 28–35.

45. Ibid., 31.

46. Ibid., 32, 33.

47. Ibid., 34.

48. Ibid.

49. For them, there would be none of the kind of grief that Stamp Paid and his unnamed wife suffered after their master's son took her (*B* 184).

50. Gayatri Chakravorty Spivak, "Can the Subaltern Speak?," in *Marxism and the Interpretation of Culture*, ed. Cary Nelson and Lawrence Grossberg (Urbana: University of Illinois Press, 1988), 281. See also Spivak, *The Critique of Postcolonial Reason: Toward a History of the Vanishing Present* (Cambridge: Harvard University Press, 1999), 293.

51. Walter White, *A Man Called White* (1948; Athens: University of Georgia Press, 1995), 11.

52. Walter White, "I Investigate Lynchings," *American Mercury* 16 (January 1929), 77–84. See also *The Making of African American Identity*, vol. 3, *1917–1968*, *National Humanities Center Resource Toolbox*, http://nationalhumanitiescenter.org/pds/maai3/segregation/text2/investigatelynchings.pdf.

53. Anne P. Rice, *Witnessing Lynching: American Writers Respond* (New Brunswick, N.J.: Rutgers University Press, 2003), xii.

54. Robyn Wiegman, "Anatomy of Lynching," *African American Culture and Sexuality*, special issue, *Journal of the History of Sexuality* 3, no. 3 (January 1992): 450.

55. Max Horkheimer and Theodor W. Adorno, *Dialectic of Enlightenment*, trans. Edmund Jephcott (Stanford, Calif.: Stanford University Press, 2002), 11.

*3. Time Out of Joint: The Temporal Logic of
Morrison's Modernist Apocalyptics*

1. On the forces that compelled migration, see Farah Jasmine Griffin, *"Who set you flowin'?": The African-American Migration Narrative* (New York: Oxford University Press, 1995).

2. For a sustained discussion of this phenomenon, see Charles Scruggs, *Sweet Home: Invisible Cities in the Afro-American Novel* (Baltimore: Johns Hopkins University Press, 1995).

3. Scruggs, *Sweet Home*, and Griffin, *"Who set you flowin'?"* offer readings of the trope of the north in African American literature. As stated in my Introduction, Griffin considers this trop across a range of genres.

4. Gaston Bachelard suggests that a house "constitutes a body of images that give mankind proofs or illusions of stability" (*The Poetics of Space: The Classic Look of How We Experience Intimate Places*, trans. Maria Jolas (Boston: Beacon Press, 1994), 17.

5. Ann Petry, *The Street* (Boston: Houghton Mifflin, 1946), 27.

6. Ibid., 28.

7. Ibid., 57.

8. Lorraine Hansberry, *A Raisin in the Sun* (New York: Samuel French Inc., 1988).

9. See Fredric Jameson, *Postmodernism; or, The Cultural Logic of Late Capitalism* (Durham, N.C.: Duke University Press, 1991). Jameson emphasizes the imitativeness of the postmodern aesthetic, an imitativeness that radically devalues the productive possibilities of historical thought. See esp. 17–18.

10. A helpful summary of the arguments on this issue can be found in Jonathan Arac, ed., *Postmodernism and Politics* (Minneapolis: University of Minnesota Press, 1986). See esp. Arac's "Introduction," ix–xliii.

11. See Yvette Christiansë, "Comte de Gobineau, 1814–1882," *International Encyclopedia of the Social Sciences*, 2nd ed., ed. William A. Darity (Farmington Hills, Mich: MacMillan Reference USA, 2007), 335–36. De Gobineau's work extended earlier theories of racial typologies, such as those of French naturalist Baron George de Cuvier.

12. Derek Walcott, *Bounty* (New York: Farrar, Straus, Giroux, 1997), 59.

13. See W. E. B. Du Bois, *The Philadelphia Negro: A Social Study* (New York: Schocken, 1967).

14. Jacques Derrida, *Specters of Marx: The State of the Debt, the Work of Mourning, and the New International*, trans. Peggy Kamuf (New York: Routledge, 1994).

15. T. Mark Ledbetter reads this as a restorative gesture that transforms the mark of ownership into a mark of distinction. See T. Mark Ledbetter, "An Apocalypse of Race and Gender: Body Violence and Forming Identity in Toni Morrison's *Beloved*," in *Postmodernism, Literature, and the Future of Theology*, ed. David Jasper (New York: MacMillan, 1996), 78–90. This may be so, in that she has *no option* but to accept the mark, but this would also be why the mark *cannot* be taken as restorative. The mark placed on Ma'am is a circle first and then a cross. Perhaps it is, as Ledbetter suggests but does not pursue, originally a tribal mark of identification or honor, a cipher of passage through the rites of socialization. Its location *under* her breast is intriguing, suggesting a mystery of some kind. The image of Ma'am hanging from a tree is also the moment of the mark's uselessness, since "By the time they cut her down nobody could tell whether she had a circle and a cross or not" (*B* 61). The mark, the sign of belonging to the true believers, is an unreliable cipher for communication. It is also the moment that puts the lie to the claim of the permanence of the written word, particularly on the parchment of human skin. The body is impermanent, like its memory,

which dies with it unless one makes the transition made, as has Morrison, to the nonepidermal surface of inscription upon the page.

16. Sally Keenan, "Myth, History, and Motherhood in Toni Morrison's *Beloved*," in *Recasting the World: Writing after Colonialism*, ed. Jonathan White (Baltimore: Johns Hopkins University Press, 1993), 47.

17. See Roland Barthes, *Camera Lucida*, trans. Richard Howard (New York: Hill and Wang, 1981).

18. See Walter Benjamin, "Theses on the Philosophy of History," in *Illuminations*, trans. Harry Zohn (New York: Schocken Books, 1969), 253–64. Benjamin perceives the writer of this history as a male, and as a materialist historian.

19. See ibid.

20. Walter Benjamin, "On Language as Such and on the Language of Man," in *One-Way Street*, trans. Edmund Jephcott and Kingsley Shorter (New York: Verso, 1979), 107–23.

21. Ibid., 121.

22. As Eugene Genovese points out, the paternalism of the Southern plantation owner, "like every other paternalism, had little to do with Ole Massa's ostensible benevolence, kindness, and good cheer. It grew out of the necessity to discipline and morally justify a system of exploitation." See Eugene D. Genovese, *Roll, Jordan, Roll: The World the Slaves Made* (New York: Vintage Books, 1976), 4.

23. Franz Fanon, *White Skin, Black Masks* (New York: Pluto Press, 1986).

24. The judges of the normative inhabit socially mediating and policing roles. Foucault's examples of such figures include the "teacher-judge, the doctor-judge, the educator-judge, the 'social worker'-judge," upon whom "the universal reign of the normative is based; and each individual, wherever he may find himself, subjects to it his body, his gestures, his behavior, his aptitudes, his achievements. The carceral network, in its compact or disseminated forms, with its systems of insertion, distribution, surveillance, observation, has been the greatest support, in modern society, of the normalizing power." See Michel Foucault, *Discipline and Punish: The Birth of the Prison*, trans. Alan Sheridan (New York: Vintage Books, 1995), 304.

25. This is the unity of "capacity" (*pouvoir*) and "knowing" (*savoir*) that is more fully conveyed by the French couplet *pouvoir/savoir*.

26. Mieke Bal, *Death and Dissymmetry: The Politics of Coherence in the Book of Judges* (Chicago: University of Chicago Press, 1988), 96.

27. J. Milgrom. "Sacrifice and Offerings, Old Testament," in *The Interpreter's Dictionary of the Bible*, ed. George Arthur Buttrick et al.(Nashville: Abingdon Press, 1976), 9:769.

28. See Althusser on being addressed by ideology in "Ideology and Ideological State Apparatuses: Notes Towards an Investigation," Louis Althusser, *Lenin and Philosophy and Other Essays*, trans. Ben Brewster (New York: Monthly Review Press, 1972), 127–86.

29. In the story of the runaway slave Margaret Garner, upon whom Morrison's novel is based, Avery Gordon points out that the reaction to her decision to take her child's life was so sensational that she was in fact permitted to argue on her own behalf in a Cincinnati court (*Ghostly Matters: Haunting and the Sociological Imagination* [Minneapolis: University of Minnesota Press, 1998], 157). See also Gordon's brief discussion of the backlash against the "fusions of racism, poverty, coercion, and violence" in the form of the Radical Reconstruction, but also in the Enforcement Acts of 1870 and the Ku Klux Klan Act of 1981 (ibid., 171). See also Mark Reinhardt's "Who Speaks for Margaret Garner? Slavery, Silence, and the Politics of Ventriloquism," *Critical Inquiry* 29 (Autumn 2002): 81–119.

30. Denise Heinze, *The Dilemma of "Double-Consciousness": Toni Morrison's Novels* (Athens: University of Georgia Press, 1993), 111.

31. Ibid.

32. Ibid., 23.

33. Mikhail Bakhtin, *Rabelais and His World*, trans. Hélène Iswolsky (Bloomington: Indiana University Press, 1984), 303ff.

34. Victor Turner, *The Ritual Process: Structure and Anti-Structure* (Chicago: Aldine, 1969). See also Turner, ed., *Celebration: Studies in Festivity and Ritual* (Washington, D.C.: Smithsonian Institution Press, 1982).

35. Bakhtin, *Rabelais and His World*. trans. Hélène Iswolsky. Bloomington: Indiana University Press, 1984.

36. Peter Stallybrass and Allon White, *The Politics and Poetics of Transgression* (Ithaca, N.Y.: Cornell University Press, 1986). Stallybrass and White pursue the implications of the logic of inversion with particular reference to the country fair and draw heavily on Bakhtin's notion of the Rabelaisian carnivalesque.

37. Turner, *The Ritual Process*, 95, 107, 138. See also Turner, *Celebration: Studies in Festivity and Ritual*, 168, 202.

38. This understanding of trauma as the missed encounter with the real emerges from Freud's writings on repetition compulsion and Lacan's revisiting of the story of the dream of the burning child. See Cathy Caruth's explanation and development of this notion in *Unclaimed Experience* (Baltimore: Johns Hopkins University Press, 1995).

39. Derrida, *Specters of Marx*, 10.

40. Ibid.

41. Benjamin, "Theses on the Philosophy of History," 257.

42. Benjamin in no way considers his angel of history to be dead. My reading of this possibility is provoked by a response to Rosalind C. Morris, for whom the stare is the moment in which we come closest to encountering the death of ourselves in the look of the other, and also the death of the other, whose stare severs the chain of the look. She explores this notion in the "Epilogue" to her *In the Place of Origins: Modernity and Its Mediums in Northern Thailand* (Durham, N.C.: Duke University Press, 2000).

43. Marilyn Ivy, *Discourses of the Vanishing: Modernity, Phantasm, Japan* (Chi-cago: University of Chicago Press, 1995), 22.

44. Christopher Columbus, *Libro de las profecías*, in *Raccolta di documenti e studi publicati dalla Real Commissione pel quarto centenario dalla scoperta dell'America*, ed. Cesare de Lollis (Rome: Real Commissione Colombina, 1892–94), 71.

45. In fact, the advent of the Gutenberg printing press in the 1450s contrib-uted to this privileging of texts. According to Henri-Jean Martin, millions of books, pamphlets, and tracts had been printed, distributed, and sold within fifty years of its invention. Henri-Jean Martin, *The Coming of the Book: The Impact of Printing, 1450–1800*, trans. David Gerard (London: N.L.B., 1984), 186.

46. The full sentence of this letter, dated September 13, 1501, reads: "I have said already that, for the execution of the enterprise of the Indies, neither reason nor mathematics nor map serve, plainly Isaiah's prophecy was fulfilled." Quoted in Djelal Kadir, *Columbus and the Ends of the Earth: Europe's Prophetic Rhetoric as Conquering Ideology* (Berkeley: University of California Press, 1992), 4. Kadir is referring to Columbus's *Libro de las profecías* (folio 5v). The letter to Isabella and Ferdinand appears in pt. 1, 2:82.

47. Aeneas Sylvius Piccolomini (Pius II), *Historia rerum ubique gestarum*. Quoted in Christopher Columbus, *The 'Libro de las profecías' of Christopher Co-lumbus*, trans. with commentary by Delno C. West and August Kling (Gaines-ville: University of Florida Press, 1991). All my quotes from and references to Columbus's postilles in Piccolomini are taken from West and Kling, 86–91. Writing of these postilles, West and Kling claim that: "Taken together, [they] form an exact and complete outline of the plan that was executed in 1501–2 in the compilation of the *Libro de las profecías*, or *Book of Prophecies* written by Columbus to impart his vision of the New World to Isabelle and Ferdinand of Spain. His title for the book was: *Notebook of authorities, statements, opinions and prophecies on the subject of the recovery of God's holy city and mountain of Zion, and on the discovery and evangelization of the islands of the Indies and of all other peoples and nations.*" West and Kling translated the *Book of Prophecies* from the 1892–94 edition of the *Raccolta di documenti e studi pubblicati della R. Commissione Colombi-ana*. Kay Brigham writes that the Raccolta is "Still an indispensable source" for the *Book of Prophecies*. See Kay Brigham, ed. and trans., *Christopher Columbus's Book of Prophecies: Reproduction of the Original Manuscript with English Translation*, Quintenary Edition (Fort Lauderdale: TSELF, Inc., 1991), 13. Her title for the *Raccolta* differs from that of West and Kling and reads *Raccolta di documenti e studi*, Parte 1–Volume II, ed. Cesare de Lollis (Rome; 1894).

48. Marjorie Reeves, *The Influence of Prophecy in the Later Middle Ages: A Study in Joachimism* (Oxford: Oxford University Press, 1969), 259, 430–31.

49. Ibid., 305.

50. For an account of the early slaughter of native peoples by the Spanish settlers, see Bartolome de las Casas, *A Short Account of the Destruction of the Indies*, trans. Nigel Griffin (New York: Penguin Classics, 1992).

51. Ibid., 66.

52. John Smith, "A True Relation of Such Occurences and Accidents of Noate as Hath Hapned in Virginia Since the First Planting of That Colony," In *Early American Writing*, ed. Giles Gunn (New York: Penguin Books, 1994), 99.

53. Ibid., 99.

54. Georg Simmel, "The Metropolis and Mental Life," in *The Sociology of Georg Simmel*, ed. Kurt H. Wolff. trans. H. H. Gerth and C. Wright Mills (New York: The Free Press, 1964), 409–24.

55. Karl Marx, *Grundrisse: Foundations of the Critique of Political Economy*, trans. Martin Nicolaus (New York: Penguin Books, 1973), 163.

56. See Walter Benjamin, *Charles Baudelaire: A Lyric Poet of in the Era of High Capitalism*, trans. Harry Zohn (London: Verso, 1969), also "On Some Motifs in Baudelaire," in *Illuminations*, 152–96.

4. Beginnings and Endings, Part One: Old Languages / New Bodies

1. The notion of the "standing reserve" is from Martin Heidegger. See his "The Question Concerning Technology," in *The Question Concerning Technology and Other Essays*, trans. and introd. William Lovitt (New York: Harper & Row, 1977), 3–35.

2. Sigmund Freud, *The Interpretation of Dreams*, vol. 4 of *The Standard Edition of the Complete Psychological Works of Sigmund Freud*, trans. James Strachey, Anna Freud, Alix Strachey, and Alan Tyson (London: Hogarth Press 1955), 11.

3. On the idea of the copula and magical speech, see James T. Siegel, *Naming the Witch* (Stanford, Calif.: Stanford University Press, 2006). Siegel draws on Derrida's theory of the copula and on the work of Marcel Mauss.

4. Jacques Derrida, *Limited, Inc* (Evanston, Ill.: Northwestern University Press, 1988).

5. David Aune suggests that this accusation is a broad one, covering a range of ritual practices involving food, and that Paul was not consistent in his condemnation of the consumption of meat sacrificed to idols. (The term "idol" is a problematic one, affirming a Christian position that does not countenance any competing gods—there can be no other gods, only idols). See David Aune, *Revelation*, vol. 1, *Word Biblical Commentary* (Dallas: Word Books, 1997), 191–94. Although the identity of the woman named Jezebel is hard to pinpoint, scholars including Aune, Adela Yarbro Collins, and Elisabeth Schüssler Fiorenza suggest that she belonged to one of a number of prophetic traditions with which the author of Revelation was in competition. Using documented evidence about early Christians, Collins and Aune position her in relation to the dispersed nature of the church. They conclude that both she and the author of Revelation were peregrinating prophets, although clearly Jezebel was attached to Thyatira, where a number of Gnostic sects flourished. The sect in existence after Jezebel's given dates was the Montanists, whose leading prophets were Priscilla and

Maximilla. For Schussler Fiorenza, the status of those women prophets is suggestive of a legacy that may have been left by Jezebel. See Adela Yarbro Collins, *Crisis and Catharsis: The Power of the Apocalypse* (Philadelphia: The Westminster Press, 1984); David Aune, "The Social Matrix of the Apocalypse of John," *Bible Research* 26 (1981): 16–32; Elisabeth Schüssler Fiorenza, "Apokalypsis and Propheteia: The Book of Revelation in the Context of Early Christian Prophecy," in *L'Apocalypse Johannique et l'apocalyptique dans le Nouveau Testament*, ed. J. Lambrecht (Glembloux: J. Duculot, 1980), 105–28.

6. It is not my intention to rehearse their conflict in detail. What is important for Morrison is Paul's inclusiveness as a Jew who invited non-Jews— Greeks, Romans, and all Gentiles, as well as Jews—to convert to Christianity and to resist the Mosaic law of circumcision. The arguments over this culminated in a meeting between Peter, Paul, and the other heads of the church, such as Barnabus, in Jerusalem. See Acts 9:26 ff, 11:27 ff, 15, and Galatians 1:18 ff and 2, where Paul lays out his case and account of the meeting. At stake for Paul was God's covenant with Moses (Genesis 17) and the Torah.

7. For other reasons as well, and in an analysis too detailed to engage with here, Collins concurs with Aune that, while the author of Revelation refers to himself as John, he nowhere claims to be the apostle or a disciple. She also reads the reference to the twelve apostles in Revelation 21:14 as evidence that the apostles are no longer alive. See Collins, *Crisis and Catharsis*, 26–27. See also Schüssler Fiorenza's detailed consideration of John's identity in "Apokalypsis and Propheteia."

8. The ghost in this statement is, of course, Jacques Derrida, particularly his remarks about iterability in the discourse of religion's futurity ("a discourse to come") in his essay "Faith and Knowledge: The Two Sources of 'Religion' at the Limits of Reason Alone," in Jacques Derrida, *Acts of Religion*, ed. and introd. Gil Anidjar (New York: Routledge, 2002), 83. His development of the relation between iterability, religion, and technology extends his earlier comments on the conditions of possibility for legibility. In "Signature Event Context," he points to the necessity that a (written) communication be repeatable or iterable "in the absolute absence of the addressee or the empirically determinable set of addresses." In this unbounded way, it can transmit and continue to transmit long after the addressee vanishes, thereby setting the conditions of its own possibility. See "Signature Event Context," in *Margins of Philosophy*, trans. Alan Bass (Chicago: University of Chicago Press, 1982), 315. What is iterable is the mark, the writing itself. This iterable mark opens itself to this larger, unbounded field, thus extending its sameness even as it connects with all possible alterity, difference.

9. Judith Butler, *Excitable Speech: A Politics of the Performative* (New York: Routledge, 1997).

10. Sarah Appleton Aguiar, "'Passing On' Death: Stealing Life in Toni Morrison's Paradise," *African American Review* 38, no. 3 (Autumn 2004): 517.

11. Patrick McKee, "Spacing and Placing Experience in Toni Morrison's *Sula*," *Modern Fiction Studies* 42, no. 1 (1996): 2.

12. Ferdinand de Saussure, *Course in General Linguistics*, trans. Wade Baskin (New York: McGraw-Hill, 1966).

13. Derek Walcott, "Prelude," *Collected Poems 1948–1984* (London: Faber and Faber, 1992), 3–4, lines 7–8, 4.

14. Ibid., l. 10.

15. In 1936, a contributor to *Notes and Queries* reported that he had "been hearing the phrase" for over forty years, "having first heard it in the United States in 1892" (William White, "The Nigger in the Pile," *Notes and Queries* 170 [1936], 12).

16. Madelyn Jablon, "*Tar Baby*: Philosophizing Blackness," in *Approaches to Teaching the Novels of Toni Morrison*, ed. Nellie Y. McKay and Kathryn Earle (New York: Modern Language Association, 1997), 74.

17. See Joel Chandler Harris, "The Wonderful Tar Baby Story," in *The Complete Tales of Uncle Remus* (New York: Houghton Mifflin, 2002), 6–8. The tar baby story is the second in a collection of stories told by a fictional black character, a slave named Uncle Remus who was the creation of Joel Chandler Harris. In the story, two anthropomorphic animals, Brer Fox and Brer Rabbit, try to outwit each other. Brer Rabbit is playing pranks and bossing everyone around, and Brer Fox decides to teach him a lesson. To do so, he makes a doll and covers it with tar. When Brer Fox encounters the tar baby and addresses it, he receives no response and so punches it in anger. The trap works, and he gets stuck in the tar. The more he struggles, the more he becomes entrapped. In his introduction to the stories, Harris is anxious to ensure that he has not failed to give "vivid hints of the really poetic imagination of the Negro" or to create a character who has "quaint and homely humor" and "a certain picturesque sensitiveness." See Chandler's "Introduction," xxi. For a critical response to Harris's picturesque blackness, see Robert Cochran, "Black Father: The Subversive Achievements of Joel Chandler Harris," *African American Review* 38, no. 1 (Spring 2004): 21–34. There is some contention about whether Chandler drew upon American Indian folktales about animal spirits or whether he turned to other folk traditions, including German fables, in which Reynard the Fox bears a strong resemblance to Brer Fox.

18. Linda Krumholtz, "Blackness and Art in Toni Morrison's *Tar Baby*," *Contemporary Literature* 49, no. 2 (Summer 2008): 268, 270.

19. Ibid., 263.

5. Beginnings and Endings, Part Two: The Poetics of Similitude and Disavowal at Utopia's Gates

1. "Toni Morrison Discusses *A Mercy*," with Lynn Neary, National Public Radio Book Tour, October 27, 2008; "A Conversation with Author Toni Morrison," Charlie Rose, Monday, November 10, 2008.

278 Notes to pages 189–200

2. Mary Louise Pratt, *Imperial Eyes: Travel Writing and Transculturation* (New York: Routledge, 1992), 1–11.

3. Freud discusses kettle logic in *The Interpretation of Dreams*, 4:119–20, and in *Jokes and Their Relation to the Unconscious*, vol. 13 of *The Standard Edition of the Complete Psychological Works of Sigmund Freud*, trans. James Strachey, Anna Freud, Alix Strachey, and Alan Tyson (London: Hogarth Press, 1960), 62, 206. He writes of a patient who dreamed that his neighbor had borrowed a kettle and returned it damaged with three arguments: he had not returned a damaged kettle; it was damaged when he borrowed it; and he had not borrowed it at all. For Freud the contradictions can exist at the same time in the dream and, although they attempt to mask embarrassment (that of being naked, in Freud's interpretation), they nevertheless confirm the thing they deny.

4. Jacques Lacan, *Freud's Papers on Technique, The Seminar of Jacques Lacan*: Book 1, trans. Jacques–Alain Miller and Russell Grigg (New York: W. W. Norton & Co, 1997), 129–42.

5. Susan Stewart, *On Longing: Narratives of the Miniature, the Gigantic, the Souvenir, the Collection* (Durham, N.C.: Duke University Press, 1993), 57.

6. Ibid., 61. Stewart focuses upon the miniature as the embodiment of something that is nevertheless produced by time, or our awareness of time, awareness being synonymous with interiority.

7. This accusation occurs elsewhere in Morrison's oeuvre, as in the accusation Paul D makes when he learns that Sethe had killed her own child.

8. Writing about video testimonies of Holocaust survivors, Lawrence Langer has argued that survivor shame is a more correct notion than survivor guilt because it does not diffuse or redeem the horror and suffering of the Shoah. Neither does it relieve perpetrators of culpability. See Lawrence Langer, *Versions of Survival: The Holocaust and the Human Spirit* (Albany: State University of New York Press, 1982), 36.

9. The Fifth Monarchists were one of many schismatic groups that emerged in England after the civil strife that began around the ascendancy of Charles I to the throne and culminated in strife around the rule of Charles II. Another factor in the emergence of these groups was the shift from church rule in 1641. Most were Baptists or Congregationalists, who welded biblical millennialism to antiroyalist political reform on the basis of their reading of the Book of Daniel, particularly with regard to the succession of four world orders. Fifth Monarchists opposed Charles I and supported Cromwell, believing that Cromwell would prepare the way for the return of Christ, the monarch of the fifth world order. Timothy G. Shilston argues that, despite their millennialist beliefs, the movement's leaders were far from irrational or merely violent. He argues that, with the exception of Thomas Venner, who led two uprisings in London, theirs was "a movement committed to building alliances with other sectaries and actively engaged in the political process at the highest level." See Timothy G. Shilston, "Thomas Venner: Fifth Monarchist or Maverick," *Social History* 37,

no. 1 (February 2012): 59, 57. Venner and his followers sought to bring about the thousand-year reign of Christ through rebellion. He had travelled to Salem, Massachusetts, in 1637, before moving to the West Indies to found a settlement. He returned to England in 1651. After proclaiming disappointment in Cromwell, he attempted to assassinate him and was subsequently imprisoned for two years. In 1657, after his release, he led a rebellion against the restored monarchy of Charles II. He was tried by Cromwell and sent back to prison but released over a year later. He and his followers staged a second rebellion in 1661; on its defeat, they were executed (hanged, drawn, and quartered). Shilston argues that Venner's commitment to the violent overthrow of government was "inconsistent" with the majority of Fifth Monarchists (ibid., 61). See also J. C. D. Clarke, *The Language of Liberty: Political Discourse and Social Dynamics in the Anglo-American World* (Cambridge: Cambridge University Press, 1994), 225.

10. Abbot Suger, *Abbot Suger on the Abbey Church of St. Denis and Its Art Treasures*, ed. and trans. Erwin Panofsky (Princeton: Princeton University Press, 1946).

11. Peter Thompson, "The Thief, the Householder, and the Commons: Languages of Class in Seventeenth-Century Virginia," *William and Mary Quarterly*, Third Series, 63, no. 2 (April 2006): 257.

12. Ibid.

13. Having floundered in its first two decades, the Virginia Company had learned that tobacco was the one sure source of return for investment. By 1617, ten tons of tobacco had been shipped to England from Jamestown. By 1620, tobacco exports had risen to around 100,000 pounds. See Willard Wesley Cochrane, *Development of American Agriculture: A Historical Analysis*, 2nd ed. (Minneapolis: University of Minnesota Press, 1993), 7, 14. This productivity required labor. Early efforts to draw the Native Americans into servitude failed; indentured Europeans could eventually move vertically once their indentured period was over; and this left Africans the most viable "source" of labor.

14. Gaston Bachelard, *The Poetics of Space: The Classic Look of How We Experience Intimate Places*, trans. Maria Jolas (Boston: Beacon Press, 1994), 13.

15. Ibid., 13.

16. Ibid., 17.

17. In conversation with Elisabeth Roudinesco, Derrida stresses that he was not positing any single division between humans and animals. He believes that: "there is a radical discontinuity between what one calls animals—primates in particular—and man. But this discontinuity cannot make us forget that between different animal species and types of social organizations of living beings there are other discontinuities." See Jacques Derrida and Elisabeth Roudinesco, "Violence Against Animals," in *For What Tomorrow . . . A Dialogue*, trans. Jeff Fort (Stanford, Calif.: Stanford University Press, 2004), 72–73.

18. Jacques Derrida, "Genesis and Structure of the *Essay on the Origin of Languages*," in *Of Grammatology*, trans. Gayatri Spivak (Baltimore: Johns Hopkins

University Press, 1976), 165–268. Rousseau opens his essay with the statement that "Speech distinguishes man among the animals." See Jean Jacques Rousseau, *On the Origin of Language*, in Jean-Jacques Rousseau and Johann Gottfried Herder, *On the Origin of Language: Two Essays*, trans. John H. Moran and Alexander Gode (Chicago: University of Chicago Press, 1986), 5.

19. Derrida, *Of Grammatology*, 187.

20. Ibid., 195, 196.

21. Jean-Jacques Rousseau, *Emile*, 261, quoted in ibid., 243.

Epilogue

1. Gérard Genette, *Paratexts: Thresholds of Interpretation*, trans. Jane E. Lewin (Cambridge: Cambridge University Press, 1997), 16. These peritexts consist of the cover, title page and publication details that include ISBN information.

2. Ibid., 157. Genette distinguishes between different types of epigraph, which increasingly come to replace dedications starting in the eighteenth century. The autographic epigraph is, by definition, a commentary written by the author, as opposed to the allographic epigraph "that is according to our conventions, attributed to an author who is not the author of the work" (ibid., 151). He attributes the vogue of the novelistic epigraph to the rise of the gothic novel in England. It was taken up by Sir Walter Scott, who headed each chapter with an epigraph assigned to an author (ibid., 146–47). Terminal epigraphs, which Perec names "métagraphs," come after the text; they may have the concluding effect of a moral (ibid., 149).

3. A paratext might also include reviews, advertisements, book club discussions, course syllabi, and the studies that professors and their students produce of any given text.

4. Genette, *Paratexts*, 156.

5. Valerie Smith, Introduction to *New Essays on 'Song of Solomon,'* ed. Valerie Smith (Cambridge: Cambridge University Press, 1995), 6.

6. Edward Gibbon, *The History of the Decline and Fall of the Roman Empire* (Ware, Hertfordshire: Wordsworth Editions, 1998), 582, 596. Gibbon blamed the ruin of Gaul, for example, on Rome's alliances with barbarians.

7. The term *New World* was associated with Columbus after Pedro Mártir de Angleria's history of the Spanish conquest of the Americas. See Pietro Martire d'Anghiera, *The Discovery of the New World in the Writings of Peter Martyr of Anghiera* (Rome: Istituto poligrafico e zecca della stato, Libreria dello stato, 1992), 21, 417. Elise Bartosik-Vélez argues that the *Aeneid* is "a foundational text" in the discourse of *translatio imperii*, which was also narrated as a progressive movement from Asia to the west of Europe. The notion of *translatio imperii* was absorbed by Christianity in the fourth century C.E. during Constantine's efforts to unify and codify the Church. The crowning of Charlemagne in 800 was seen

by proponents of this discourse as the ascendency of a new empire into which the Roman *imperium* had been transferred. See Elise Bartosik-Vélez, "Translatio Imperii: Virgil and Peter Martyr's Columbus," *Comparative Literature Studies* 46, no. 4 (2009): 560, 561. Bartosik-Vélez argues further that the idea of the transfer of empire, in practice a "history of appropriation," was popular during Isabella and Ferdinand's reign, with a presumption that Spain was heir to Rome's knowledge and culture after the expulsion of the Moors in 1492 (ibid., 563). This was the context in which Pedro Mártir de Angleria understood Columbus's colonization of the so-called New World.

8. Paul Saenger, *Space Between Words: The Origins of Silent Reading* (Stanford, Calif.: Stanford University Press, 2000), 9, 26 (quotation from 26). Saenger outlines the history of ancient *scriptura continua*, "possible only in the context of a writing system that had a complete set of signs for the unambiguous transcription of pronounced speech" (9). This history begins, for Saenger, with the Greek adoption of the Phoenician alphabet, which allowed the addition of "symbols for vowels." The visibility of vowels meant that, unlike in such scripts as Hebrew, "word separation was no longer necessary to eliminate an unacceptable level of ambiguity."

9. Ibid. 6.

10. Edward Tenner, *Our Own Devices: How Technology Remakes Humanity* (New York: Vintage Books, 2004), 163.

11. Jennifer DeVere Brody, *Punctuation: Art, Politics, and Play* (Durham, N.C.: Duke University Press, 2008), 64

12. Ibid., 78.

13. Denise Heinze reads Claudia's violent response to the dolls as "born of a painful childhood lesson that teaches her she can never be as beautiful or loveable as the standards of western culture dictate." See Heinze, *The Dilemma of "Double-Consciousness,"* 17. Philip Page reads the dismantling through a larger frame of psychic "splitting." He calls "the act of splitting" the dolls open an enabling one for Claudia. His reading approaches the larger issue of the reading and writing traditions into which she is inserting herself. For Page, her desire to "learn the mystery" of the dolls' voices enables the "discovery of her own voice." This discovery is understood retrospectively, in the writing of the story that Claudia has undertaken. She is, after all, looking back, and she plots the memory of dismantling the dolls within the larger frame of dismantling that she has already engaged. See Page, *Dangerous Freedom*, 38 and 51. Farah Jasmine Griffin draws the paradigmatic focus into a wider discussion about the spatialization of power, specifically, the psychic struggle in which the black subject "tries to resist efforts to dominate him or her." The space in which this struggle occurs is the space of modernity, the space of urban power, which Griffin identifies as sophisticated and whose degree of sophistication is measured by a struggle to control space and the bodies that inhabit it. Griffin sees the "invocation

of desire in popular culture forms like movies and advertisements" as one aspect of such struggle, and she identifies Wright's Bigger Thomas, Petry's Lutie, and Morrison's Pauline Breedlove as figures that succumb to this invocation. Likewise, Pecola and Hagar, from *Song of Solomon*, succumb to "the desire to meet white standards of beauty," just as Pauline does. Drawing on Houston Baker's discussion of the relation between a sense of place and a sense of personal, placed security, Griffin sees the violence of "white standards of beauty" as being part of a continuum of violence, which includes control of the (black) migrant body's "experience of time and space" through regulation. This includes the creation and, then, regulation of desire. See Griffin, "Who set you flowin'?," 102. See also Baker, *Workings of the Spirit*, 104.

14. Freud, "The 'Uncanny,'" 205.

15. Donald Spoto points out that not only was Rose the name of Williams's older sister but both his maternal and paternal grandmothers were called Rose. See Donald Spoto, *The Kindness of Strangers: The Life of Tennessee Williams* (New York: Little, Brown & Company, 1985), 173.

16. C. Lynn Munro, "The Tattooed Heart and the Serpentine Eye: Morrison's Choice of an Epigraph for *Sula*," *Black American Literature Forum* 18, no. 4 (Winter 1984): 150.

17. Ibid.

18. See, e.g., the Introduction to "The Gospel of Truth" by Harold W. Attridge and George W. MacRae, in *The Nag Hammadi Library in English*, 3rd ed., ed. James McConkey Robinson, and Richard Smith (Leiden: E. J. Brill, 1988), 38.

19. Ibid., 39.

20. Marianne Hirsch, "Knowing Their Names: Toni Morrison's *Song of Solomon*," in *New Essays on Song of Solomon*, ed. Valerie Smith (Cambridge: Cambridge University Press, 1995), 73.

21. Ibid., 73–74.

22. Richard B. Hays, "The Conversion of the Imagination: Scripture and Eschatology in 1 Corinthians," *New Testament Studies* 45 (1999): 395.

23. Martin Luther King, Jr., "Paul's Letter to American Christians," Sermon Delivered at Dexter Avenue Baptist Church, Montgomery, Alabama, November 4, 1956 (url: http://mlk-kpp01.stanford.edu/primarydocuments/Vol3/4-Nov-1956_PaulsLetter.pdf).

24. A. S. Byatt, 'Introduction,' Toni Morrison, *Beloved* (New York: Everyman's Library, 2006), ix-x.

25. The self-announcing statements of "Thunder, Perfect Mind" echo those of Eve in another Nag Hammadi text, "On the Origin of the World, II, 5 and XIII, 2." Named the principle instructor and first virgin, Eve was created by Sophia from a droplet of water ("On the Origin of the World, II, 5 and XIII, 2" 180). Eve, who was also her own midwife when she gave birth to the Lord, calls

out: "It is I who am the part of my mother; / And it is I who am the mother; / It is I who am the wife; / It is I who am the virgin; / It is I who am pregnant; / It is I who am the one that comforts the pains of travail; / It is my husband who bore me; / And it is I who am his mother, / And it is he who is my father and my lord, / It is he who is my force; / What he desired he says with reason. / I am the process of becoming. / Yet I have born a man as lord" ("On the Origin of the World, II, 5 and XIII, 2," 181). These statements reflect a grammatical similarity to those of "Thunder: Perfect Mind" and a similar definite declarative order. They also refer to self-generation. Where they differ is in their concern with the corporeality of the body in the world, albeit in a tone and content that exceed mortal corporeality. Their opacity still has some familiar, human concepts: wife, pregnancy, husband, and mother. Even the notions of one who gives birth to herself and who is mother and wife to her son is within the range of human comprehension of divine prerogatives of self-reproduction.

Hans-Gebhard Bethge reads the eschatology of "On the Origin of the World" as citational, drawing upon and demonstrating a familiarity with other texts in order to strengthen the authority of its unique, eclectic creation and redemptive narratives that draw upon different Gnostic systems. Considering the range of references, Bethge suggests a possible period and place for the text's writing, the Alexandria of the early 300s, when it was the point of convergence of intellectual and religious debates (Bethge, "On the Origin of the World [II, 5 and XIII, 2]," in *The Nag Hammadi Library in English*, 3rd ed., ed. James Mc-Conkey Robinson and Richard Smith [Leiden: E. J. Brill, 1988], 170). In its deliberate citations, "On the Origin of the World" is literary.

26. David Nirenberg, "The Politics of Love and Its Enemies," in *Religion: Beyond a Concept*, ed. Hent de Vries (New York: Fordham University Press, 2008), 492. Nirenberg does not engage traditions, religions, or economies of exchange outside of Europe and the territories with which its philosophies and religions are historically connected (e.g., the so-called Near East).

27. In *The Gift of Death*, Derrida refers to what Patočka calls "the Christian reversal" that occurs with "the Platonic incorporation of demonic mystery and orgiastic irresponsibility" which is "in turn repressed by a certain Christianity" (21).

28. Rowan Williams, "Introduction," in *Theology and the Political: The New Debate*, ed. Creston Davis, John Milbank and Slavoj Žižek (Durham: Duke University Press, 2005), 3, quoted in Nirenberg, "The Politics of Love," 492.

29. Foucault, "Of Other Spaces," 52.

30. David Wright, "Liner Notes," *HR*.

31. D. W. Griffith, *The Birth of a Nation*, ed. Robert Lang (New Brunswick, N.J.: Rutgers University Press, 1993).

32. Ibid., 45, 46.

33. Ibid.. 45.

34. Christie Anne Farnham, *The Education of the Southern Belle: Higher Education and Student Socialization in the Antebellum South* (New York: New York University Press, 1994), 148. Farnham quotes from the Autograph Book of Harriet Cook, 1852, held in the Martha F. Fannin Papers (ibid., 220).

35. Albert Wertheim, "The McCarthy Era and the American Theater," in *Insurgency in American Theatre, Theatre Journal* 34, no. 2 (May 1982): 216. Albert Maltz and the nine other writers and filmmakers who refused to answer questions before the House Un-American Activities Committee (HUAC) were popularly known as the Hollywood Ten. Their recourse to the First Amendment was ignored, and they were sentenced to prison and blacklisted. Maltz had been critical of increasing legal attempts to curtail democratic freedoms of association in the name of protecting America from Communism. Wertheim describes *The Morrison Case* as an attempt to strike back at the HUAC and McCarthyism (ibid., 216). The play's central character, Pete Morrison, is curious about many things, including Communism. He loses his job in a milieu in which fair trial is impossible, as is "the right to face one's accusers." The play was based on the actual transcript of a trial held at the Brooklyn Naval Yard (ibid., 217). Maltz had received an Oscar for his heroizing screenplay about a blinded Second World War veteran, Al Schmid, in the 1945 film *Pride of the Marines*.

36. Barthes, *Camera Lucida*, 94.

Bibliography

Abraham, Nicolas. "Notes on the Phantom: A Complement to Freud's Meta-psychology." Trans. Nicholas T. Rand. In *The Trial(s) of Psychoanalysis*, ed. Françoise Meltzer, 75–80. Chicago: University of Chicago Press, 1988.

Abraham, Nicolas, and Maria Torok. *The Shell and the Kernel: Renewals in Psychoanalysis*, Volume 1. Ed. and trans. Nicholas T. Rand. Chicago: University of Chicago Press, 1994.

Adell, Sandra. *Double-Consciousness / Double Bind: Theoretical Issues in Twentieth-Century Black Literature*. Urbana: University of Illinois Press, 1994.

Agamben, Giorgio. *The Idea of Prose*. Trans. Michael Sullivan and Sam Whitsitt. Albany: State University of New York Press, 1995.

———. *Infancy and History: The Destruction of Experience*. Trans. Liz Heron. London: Verso, 1993.

———. *Remnants of Auschwitz: The Witness and the Archive*. Trans. Daniel Heller-Roazen. New York: Zone Books, 1999.

Aguiar, Sarah Appleton. "'Passing On' Death: Stealing Life in Toni Morrison's *Paradise*." *African American Review* 38, no. 3 (Autumn 2004): 513–19.

Allen, Garland E. "'Culling the Herd': Eugenics and the Conservation Movement in the United States, 1900–1940." *Journal of the History of Biology*. Published online, March 13, 2012.

Althusser, Louis. "Ideology and Ideological State Apparatuses: Notes Towards an Investigation." In *Lenin and Philosophy and Other Essays*, trans. Ben Brewster, 127–186. New York: Monthly Review Press, 1972.

Anderson, Benedict. *Imagined Communities: Reflections on the Origin and Spread of Nationalism*. Rev. ed. London: Verso, 1991.

Andrews, William L., and Nellie Y. McKay, eds. *Toni Morrison's 'Beloved': A Casebook*. New York: Oxford University Press, 1999.

Angelo, Bonnie. "The Pain of Being Black: An Interview with Toni Morrison." In *Conversations with Toni Morrison*, ed. Danille Taylor-Guthrie, 255–61. Jackson: University Press of Mississippi, 1994.

Ashcroft, Bill, Gareth Griffiths, and Helen Tiffin, eds. *The Empire Writes Back: Theory and Practice in Post-Colonial Literatures*. London: Routledge, 1989.

285

Attridge, Harold W., and George W. MacRae. "Introduction and Translation: The Gospel of Truth." In *The Nag Hammadi in English*, 3rd ed., ed. James McConkey Robinson, and Richard Smith, 38–39. Leiden: E. J. Brill, 1988.

Aune, David. *Revelation. Word Biblical Commentary*. Dallas: Word Books, 1997.

———. "The Social Matrix of the Apocalypse of John." *Bible Research* 26 (1981): 16–32.

Awkward, Michael. *Inspiriting Influences: Tradition, Revision, and Afro-American Women's Novels*. New York: Columbia University Press, 1991.

Bachelard, Gaston. *The Poetics of Space: The Classic Look of How We Experience Intimate Places*. trans. Maria Jolas. Boston: Beacon Press, 1994.

Baker, Houston A. "Black Folklore and Black American Literature." In *Long Black Song: Essays in Black American Literature and Culture*, 18–41. Charlottesville: University of Virginia Press, 1972.

———. *Workings of the Spirit: The Poetics of Afro-American Women's Writing*. Chicago: University of Chicago Press, 1991.

Bakhtin, Mikhail. *Rabelais and His World*. Trans. Hélène Iswolsky. Bloomington: Indiana University Press, 1984.

Bakhtin, Mikhail. *Rabelais and His World*. Trans. Hélène Iswolsky. Bloomington: Indiana University Press, 1984.

Bal, Mieke. *Death and Dissymmetry: The Politics of Coherence in the Book of Judges*. Chicago: University of Chicago Press, 1988.

———. *Murder and Difference: Gender, Genre, and Scholarship on Sisera's Death*. Bloomington: Indiana University Press, 1988.

Baldwin, James. *Go Tell It on the Mountain*. London: Corgi Books, 1970.

———. *Nobody Knows My Name*. New York: Dell Publishing, 1961.

Barnard, Susan Kessler. *Buckhead*. Charleston, S.C.: Arcadia Publishing, 2009.

Barthes, Roland. *Camera Lucida*. Trans. Richard Howard. New York: Hill and Wang, 1981.

———. *The Neutral: Lecture Course at the College de France (1977–78)*, trans. Denis Hollier. New York: Columbia University Press, 2007.

Bartley, Numan V. *The Rise of Massive Resistance: Race and Politics in the South During the 1950s*. Baton Rouge: Louisiana State University Press, 1997.

Bartosik-Vélez, Elise. "Translatio Imperii: Virgil and Peter Martyr's Columbus." *Comparative Literature Studies* 46, no. 4 (2009): 559–88.

Benjamin, Walter. "A Berlin Chronicle." In *One Way Street*, trans. Edmund Jephcott and Kingsley Shorter, 293–346. London: Verso, 1979.

———. *Charles Baudelaire: A Lyric Poet in the Era of High Capitalism*. Trans. Harry Zohn. London: Verso, 1969.

———. "On Language as Such and on the Language of Man." In *Reflections: Essays, Aphorisms, Autobiographical Writings*, ed. Peter Demetz, trans. Edmund Jephcott, 214–32. New York: Schocken Books, 1986.

———. "Theses on the Philosophy of History." In *Illuminations*, trans. Harry Zohn, 253–64. New York: Schocken Books, 1969.

Benveniste, Emile. *Problems in General Linguistics.* Trans. Mary Elizabeth Meek. Coral Gables, Fla.: University of Miami Press, 1973.

Berman, Paul. *Blacks and Jews: Alliances and Arguments.* New York: Delacorte Press, 1994.

Bethge, Hans-Gebhard. "On the Origin of the World (II, 5 and XIII, 2)." In *The Nag Hammadi Library in English*, 3rd ed., ed. James McConkey Robinson and Richard Smith. Leiden: E. J. Brill, 1988.

Bhabha, Homi. "Dissemination: Time, Narrative, and the Margins of the Modern Nation." In *Nation and Narration*, 291–322. London: Routledge, 1990.

———. *The Location of Culture.* New York: Routledge, 1994.

Blanchot, Maurice. "The Essential Solitude." In *The Gaze of Orpheus and Other Literary Essays*, trans. Lydia Davis, 63–77. New York: Station Hill Press, 1981.

Blassingame, John. *The Slave Community: Plantation Life in the Ante-bellum South.* New York: Oxford University Press, 1972.

Blassingame, John, and Mae G. Henderson, eds. *Antislavery Newspapers and Periodicals.* Boston: Hall, 1984.

Braxton, Joanne M. *Black Women Writing Autobiography: A Tradition Within a Tradition.* Philadelphia: Temple University Press, 1989.

Broad, Robert L. "Giving Blood to the Scraps: Haints, History and Hosea in *Beloved.*" *African American Review* 28, no. 2 (Summer 1994): 189–96.

Brody, Jennifer DeVere. *Punctuation: Art, Politics, and Play* (Durham, N.C.: Duke University Press, 2008.

Brooks, Jennifer E. "Winning the Peace: Georgia Veterans and the Struggle to Define the Political Legacy of World War II." *The Journal of Southern History* 66, no. 3 (August 2000): 563–604.

Butler, Judith. *Excitable Speech: A Politics of the Performative.* New York: Routledge, 1997.

Byatt, A. S. "Introduction." In Toni Morrison, *Beloved*, vii–xxi. New York: Everyman's Library, 2006.

Canetti, Elias. *Crowds and Power.* New York: Farrar Straus Giroux, 1984.

Carby, Hazel. *Reconstructing Womanhood: The Emergence of the Afro-American Woman Novelist.* New York: Oxford University Press, 1987.

Caruth, Cathy. *Unclaimed Experience: Trauma, Narrative, and History.* Baltimore: Johns Hopkins University Press. 1996.

Castelli, Elizabeth. *Imitating Paul: A Discourse of Power.* Louisville, Ky.: Westminster / John Knox Press, 1991.

Certeau, Michel de. *The Writing of History.* Trans. Tom Conley. New York: Columbia University Press, 1988.

Christiansë, Yvette. "Comte de Gobineau, 1814–1882." In *International Encyclopedia of the Social Sciences*, 2nd edition, ed. William A. Darity, 335–36. Farmington Hills, Mich: MacMillan Reference USA, 2007.

―――. "'Monstrous Prodigy': The Apocalyptic Landscapes of Derek Walcott's Poetry." In *Mapping the Sacred: Religion, Geography and Postcolonial Literatures*, ed. Jamie S. Scott and Paul Simpson-Housley, 199–224. Amsterdam: Editions Rodopi, 2001.

Clarke, J. C. D. *The Language of Liberty: Political Discourse and Social Dynamics in the Anglo-American World*. Cambridge; Cambridge University Press, 1994.

Cochran, Robert. "Black Father: The Subversive Achievements of Joel Chandler Harris." *African American Review* 38, no. 1 (Spring 2004): 21–34.

Cochrane, Willard Wesley. *Development of American Agriculture: A Historical Analysis*, 2nd ed. Minneapolis: University of Minnesota Press, 1993.

Collins, Adela Yarbro. *Crisis and Catharsis: The Power of the Apocalypse*. Philadelphia: The Westminster Press, 1984.

Collins, Patricia. "Learning from the Outsider Within: The Sociological Significance of Black Feminist Thought." *Social Problems* 33 (December 1986): 514–32.

Columbus, Christopher. *Christopher Columbus's Book of Prophecies: Reproduction of the Original Manuscript with English Translation*. Quintenary Edition. Ed. and trans. Kay Brigham. Fort Lauderdale: TSELF, Inc., 1991.

―――. *Libro de las profecías*. In *Raccolta di documenti e studi publicati dalla Real Commissione pel quarto centenario dalla scoperta dell'America*. Ed. Cesare de Lollis. Rome: Real Commissione Colombina, 1892–94.

―――. *The Libro de las profecías of Christopher Columbus*. Trans. with commentary by Delno C. West and August Kling. Gainesville: University of Florida Press, 1991.

Coser, Stelamaris. *Bridging the Americas: The Literature of Paule Marshall, Toni Morrison, and Gayl Jones*. Philadelphia: Temple University Press, 1994.

Davis, Charles T., and Henry Louis Gates, Jr., eds. *The Slave's Narrative*. New York: Oxford University Press, 1985.

Davis, Thulani. *All the Renegade Ghosts Rise*. Washington, D.C.: Anemone, 1978.

De las Casas, Bartolome. *A Short Account of the Destruction of the Indies*. Trans. Nigel Griffin. New York: Penguin Classics, 1992.

Denard, Carolyn. "Blacks, Modernism, and the American South: An Interview with Toni Morrison." *Studies in the Literary Imagination* 31, no. 2 (Fall 1998): 1–16.

Dent, Gina. "Developing Africa into America: The Role of Anthropology in the Literary History of Blackness." Forthcoming Ph.D. dissertation, Columbia University.

―――. "Geopsychoanalysis: '. . . and the rest of the world.'" *American Imago* 48, no. 2 (Summer 1991): 199–231.

Derrida, Jacques. *Acts of Religion*. Ed. Gil Anidjar. New York: Routledge, 2002.

―――. "Faith and Knowledge: The Two Sources of 'Religion' at the Limits of Reason Alone." In Jacques Derrida, *Acts of Religion*, ed. and introd. Gil Anidjar, 40–101. New York: Routledge, 2002.

———. *The Gift of Death.* Trans. David Wills. Chicago: University of Chicago Press, 1995.

———. *Limited Inc.* Evanston, Ill.: Northwestern University Press, 1988.

———. *Margins of Philosophy.* Trans. Alan Bass. Chicago: University of Chicago Press, 1982.

———. "Of an Apocalyptic Tone Recently Adopted in Philosophy." Trans. John P. Leavey, Jr. *Semeia* 23 (1982): 63–97.

———. *Of Grammatology.* Trans. Gayatri Chakravorty Spivak. Baltimore: Johns Hopkins University Press, 1976.

———. *Positions.* Trans. Alan Bass. Chicago: University of Chicago Press, 1981.

———. *Specters of Marx: The State of the Debt, the Work of Mourning, and the New International.* Trans. Peggy Kamuf. New York: Routledge, 1994.

Derrida, Jacques, and Elisabeth Roudinesco. "Violence Against Animals." In *For What Tomorrow . . . A Dialogue,* trans. Jeff Fort, 62–76. Stanford, Calif.: Stanford University Press, 2004.

Development of American Agriculture: A Historical Analysis. 2nd ed. Minneapolis: University of Minnesota Press, 1993.

Diner, Hasia. *In the Almost Promised Land: American Jews and Blacks 1915–1935.* Westport, Conn.: Greenwood Press, 1977.

Donnan, Elizabeth, ed. *Documents Illustrative of the History of the Slave Trade to America.* Vols. 2 and 3. New York: Octagon, 1965. (First published 1931–32.)

Douglass, Frederick. *Narrative of the Life of Frederick Douglass, an American Slave, Written by Himself.* New York: Dover Publications, Inc., 1995.

Du Bois, W. E. B. *Black Reconstruction in America.* New York: Atheneum, 1992.

———. *Dusk of Dawn: An Essay Toward an Autobiography of a Race Concept.* New Brunswick, N.J.: Transaction, 1984.

———. *The Philadelphia Negro: A Social Study.* New York: Schocken Books, 1967.

———. *The Souls of Black Folks.* New York: Penguin Books USA Inc., 1969.

Dunbar, Paul Laurence. *The Heart of Happy Hollow.* Miami: Mnemosyne Publishing, 1969.

———. *The Sport of the Gods.* Miami: Mnemosyne Publishing, 1969.

Dunn, Leslie Clarence, and Theodosius Dobzhansky. *Heredity, Race, and Society.* New York: New American Library, 1946.

Duvall, John N. "Morrison and the Anxiety of Faulknerian Influence." In *Unflinching Gaze: Morrison and Faulkner Re-Envisioned*, ed. Carol A. Kolmerton, Stephen M. Ross, and Judith Bryant, 3–16. Jackson: University Press of Mississippi, 1997.

Eagleton, Terry. *The Illusions of Postmodernism.* Oxford: Blackwell, 1997.

Edwards, Brent Hayes. "Uses of Diaspora." *Social Text* 19, no. 1 (Spring 2001): 45–73.

Ellison, Ralph. *Invisible Man.* New York: Random House, 1972.

———. "Richard Wright's Blues." In *In Shadow and Act*, 77–94. New York: Quality Paperback Book Club, 1994.

"Extracts from the Final Pleas for Defendant Mrugowsky." In *Trials of War Criminals Before the Nuernberg Military Tribunals under Control Council Law No. 10, Nuernberg, October 1946–April 1949*, vol. 1, *The Medical Case*, 539–51. Washington, D.C.: U.S. Government Printing Office, 1949–53.

Fanon, Frantz. *Black Skin, White Masks*. New York: Pluto Press 1986.

———. *The Wretched of the Earth*. Trans. Constance Farrington. New York: Grove, 1968.

Farnham, Christie Anne. *The Education of the Southern Belle: Higher Education and Student Socialization in the Antebellum South*. New York: New York University Press, 1994.

Felman, Shoshana, and Dori Laub. *Testimony: Crises of Witnessing in Literature, Psychoanalysis, and History*. New York: Routledge, 1992.

Fenves, Peter. *Arresting Language: From Leibnitz to Benjamin*. Stanford, Calif.: Stanford University Press, 2001.

Fehrenbacher, Don E. *The Slaveholding Republic: An Account of the United States Government's Relations to Slavery*. Ed. Ward M. McAfee. New York: Oxford University Press, 2001.

Fields, Karen. "To Embrace Dead Strangers: Toni Morrison's 'Beloved.'" In *Mother Puzzles: Daughters and Mothers in Contemporary American Literature*, ed. Mickey Pearlman, 159–69. Westport, Conn.: Greenwood, 1989.

Finkelman, Paul. *Slavery and the Founders: Race and Liberty in the Age of Jefferson*. Armonk, N.Y.: E. M. Sharpe, Inc., 2001.

Foner, Eric. *Reconstruction: America's Unfinished Revolution, 1863–1877*. New York: Harper & Row, 1988.

Foster, Frances Smith. *Witnessing Slavery: The Development of Antebellum Slave Narratives*. 2nd ed. Madison: University of Wisconsin Press, 1994.

Foucault, Michel. "Different Spaces." In *Aesthetics, Method, and Epistemology*, ed. James F. Faubion, vol. 2 of *Essential Works of Foucault, 1954–1984*, 175–85. New York: The New Press, 1998.

———. *Discipline and Punish: The Birth of the Prison*. Trans. Alan Sheridan. New York: Vintage Books, 1995.

———. *Fearless Speech*. Los Angeles: Semiotext(e), 2001.

———. "Of Other Spaces." *Diacritics* 16 (Spring 1986): 22–27.

———. *The Order of Things: An Archeology of the Human Sciences*. Trans. Alan Sheridan. New York: Vintage, 1973.

———. *Power/Knowledge: Selected Interviews and Other Writings, 1972–1977*. New York: Vintage Books, 1980.

———. "Society Must Be Defended." In *Ethics: Subjectivity and Truth*, ed. Paul Rabinow, vol. 1 of *Essential Works of Foucault, 1954–1984*. New York: The New Press, 1994.

———. "The Thought of the Outside." In *Aesthetics, Method, and Epistemology*, ed. James F. Faubion, vol. 2 of *Essential Works of Foucault 1954–1984*, 147–69. New York: The New Press, 1998.

———. "Truth and Juridical Forms." In *Power*, ed. Ed. James F. Faubion, vol. 3 of *Essential Works of Foucault 1954–1984*, 1–89. New York: The New Press, 2000.

Freud, Sigmund. *Beyond the Pleasure Principle*. Vol. 18 of *The Standard Edition of the Complete Psychological Works of Sigmund Freud*. Trans. James Strachey, Anna Freud, Alix Strachey, and Alan Tyson. London, Hogarth Press, 1959.

———. *The Interpretation of Dreams*. Vol. 4 of *The Standard Edition of the Complete Psychological Works of Sigmund Freud*. Trans. James Strachey, Anna Freud, Alix Strachey, and Alan Tyson. London: Hogarth Press, 1955.

———. *Jokes and their Relation to the Unconscious*. Vol. 13 of *The Standard Edition of the Complete Psychological Works of Sigmund Freud*. Trans. James Strachey, Anna Freud, Alix Strachey, and Alan Tyson. London: Hogarth Press, 1960.

———. "The Uncanny." In Freud, *Writings on Art and Literature*, 234–56. Stanford, Calif.: Stanford University Press, 1997.

Fultz, Lucille P. *Toni Morrison: Playing with Difference*. Urbana: University of Illinois Press, 2003.

Fuss, Diana. *Identification Papers: Readings on Psychoanalysis, Sexuality, and Culture*. New York: Routledge, 1995.

Gates, Henry Louis, Jr. *The Signifying Monkey: A Theory of African-American Literary Criticism*. New York: Oxford University Press, 1988.

Gates, Henry Louis, Jr., ed. *Black Literature and Literary Theory*. New York: Routledge, 1990.

Genette, Gérard. *Paratexts: Thresholds of Interpretation*. Trans. Jane E. Lewin. Cambridge: Cambridge University Press, 1997.

Genovese, Eugene D. *Roll, Jordan, Roll: The World the Slaves Made* . New York: Vintage Books, 1976.

Gibbon, Edward. *The History of the Decline and Fall of the Roman Empire*. Ware, Hertfordshire: Wordsworth Editions, 1998.

Gikandi, Simon. *Writing in Limbo: Modernism and Caribbean Literature*. Ithaca, N.Y.: Cornell University Press, 1992.

Gilroy, Paul. *Against Race: Imagining Political Culture Beyond the Color Line*. Cambridge: Harvard University Press, 2000.

Girard, René. "Are the Gospels Mythical?" *First Things: The Journal of Religion and Public Life*, no. 62 (April 1996): 27–31.

———. *Deceit, Desire, and the Novel*. Trans. Yvonne Freccero. Baltimore: Johns Hopkins University Press, 1965.

———. *Violence and the Sacred*. Trans. Patrick Gregory. Baltimore: Johns Hopkins University Press, 1977.

Glanville, Joseph. *Some Philosophical Considerations Touching the Being of Witches, Written in a Letter to the much Honour'd Robert Hunt Esq*. London: James Collins, 1667.

Gordon, Avery. *Ghostly Matters: Haunting and the Sociological Imagination*. Minneapolis: University of Minnesota Press, 1998.

Gotanda, Neil. "A Critique of 'Our Constitution is Color-Blind.'" *Stanford Law Review* 44, no. 1 (November 1991): 1–68.

Grant, Madison. *The Passing of the Great Race; or, the Racial Basis of European History.* New York: Charles Scribner's Sons, 1936.

Gray, George Buchanan. *Sacrifice in the Old Testament: Its Theory and Practice.* Oxford: Oxford University Press, 1925.

Grewal, Gurleen. *Circles of Sorrow, Lines of Struggle: The Novels of Toni Morrison.* Baton Rouge: Louisiana State University Press, 1998.

Griffin, Farah Jasmine. *"Who set you flowin?": The African-American Migration Narrative.* New York: Oxford University Press, 1995.

Griffith, D. W. *The Birth of a Nation.* Ed. Robert Lang. New Brunswick, N.J.: Rutgers University Press, 1993.

Hall, David D. *The Antinomian Controversy 1636–1638: A Documentary History.* Middletown, Conn.: Wesleyan University Press, 1978.

Hamilton, Alexander. *Hamilton's Itinerarium: Being a narrative of a journey from Annapolis, Maryland, through Delaware, Pennsylvania, New York, New Jersey, Connecticut, Rhode Island, Massachusetts and New Hampshire from May to September, 1744.* Ed. Albert Bushnell Hart. St. Louis: W. K. Bixby, 1907.

Hansberry, Lorraine. *A Raisin in the Sun.* New York: Samuel French Inc., 1988.

Harris, Joel Chandler. "The Wonderful Tar Baby Story." In *The Complete Tales of Uncle Remus,* 6–8. New York: Houghton Mifflin, 2002.

Harris, Trudier. *Fiction and Folklore: The Novels of Toni Morrison.* Knoxville: University of Tennessee Press, 1991.

Hartman, Saidiya. *Lose Your Mother: A Journey along the Atlantic Slave Route* (New York: Farrar, Straus and Giroux, 2007

Hays, Richard B. "The Conversion of the Imagination: Scripture and Eschatology in 1 Corinthians." *New Testament Studies* 45 (1999): 391–412.

Heidegger, Martin. *The Question Concerning Technology and Other Essays.* Trans. and introd. William Lovitt. New York: Harper & Row, 1977.

Heil, John Paul. *Rhetorical Role of Scripture in 1 Corinthians.* Atlanta: Society of Biblical Literature, 2005.

Heinze, Denise. *The Dilemma of "Double-Consciousnness": Toni Morrison's Novels.* Athens: University of Georgia Press, 1993.

Hertz, Robert. *Death and the Right Hand.* Trans. R. Needham. Glencoe: Illinois Free Press, 1960.

Hirsch, Marianne. "Knowing Their Names: Toni Morrison's *Song of Solomon.*" In *New Essays on 'Song of Solomon,'* ed. Valerie Smith, 69–92. Cambridge: Cambridge University Press, 1995.

Hobbes, Thomas. *Leviathan, or the Matter, Forme, & Power of a Commonwealth.* Ed. Richard Flathman and David Johnston. New York: W. W. Norton & Company, 1996.

Holland, Sharon Patricia. *Raising the Dead: Readings of Death and (Black) Subjectivity.* Durham, N.C.: Duke University Press, 2000.

Horkheimer, Max, and Theodor W. Adorno. *Dialectic of Enlightenment: Philosophical Fragments.* Trans. Edmund Jephcott. Stanford, Calif.: Stanford University Press, 2002.

Humez, Nicholas Alexander. *On the Dot: The Speck That Changed the World.* Oxford: Oxford University Press, 2008.

Hurston, Zora Neal. *Their Eyes Were Watching God.* Urbana: University of Illinois Press, 1978.

Hutcheon, Linda. "Theorising the Postmodern: Towards a Poetics." In *The Postmodern Reader,* ed. Charles Jencks, 76–93. London: Academy, 1991.

Irigaray, Luce. *This Sex Which Is Not One.* Trans. Catherine Porter. Ithaca, N.Y.: Cornell University Press, 1985.

Ivy, Marilyn. *Discourses of the Vanishing: Modernity, Phantasm, Japan.* Chicago: University of Chicago Press, 1995.

Jablon, Madelyn. "*Tar Baby*: Philosophizing Blackness." In *Approaches to Teaching the Novels of Toni Morrison,* ed. Nellie Y. McKay and Kathryn Earle, 73–76. New York: Modern Language Association, 1997.

Jameson, Fredric. *Postmodernism; or, The Cultural Logic of Late Capitalism.* Durham, N.C.: Duke University Press, 1991.

———. *The Prison House of Language: A Critical Account of Structuralism and Russian Formalism.* Princeton, N.J.: Princeton University Press, 1972.

JanMohamed, Abdul R. *The Death-Bound Subject: Richard Wright's Archeology of Death.* Durham, N.C.: Duke University Press, 2005.

Judy, Ronald J. *(Dis)Forming the American Canon: African-Arabic Slave Narratives and the Vernacular.* Minneapolis: University of Minnesota Press, 1993.

Kadir, Djelal. *Columbus and the Ends of the Earth: Europe's Prophetic Rhetoric as Conquering Ideology.* Berkeley: University of California Press, 1992.

Keenan, Sally. "Myth, History, and Motherhood in Toni Morrison's *Beloved.*" In *Recasting the World: Writing after Colonialism,* ed. Jonathan White, 45–81. Baltimore: Johns Hopkins University Press, 1993.

King, Debra Walker. *Deep Talk: Reading African-American Literary Names.* Charlottesville: University of Virginia Press, 1998.

Kittler, Friedrich. *Discourse Networks, 1800–1900.* Trans. Michael Metteer, with Chris Cullens. Stanford, Calif.: Stanford University Press, 1990.

Knoll, Israel. *Divine Symphony: The Bible's Many Voices.* Philadelphia: The Jewish Publication Society, 2003.

Krumholtz, Linda. "Blackness and Art in Toni Morrison's *Tar Baby.*" *Contemporary Literature* 49, no. 2 (Summer 2008): 263–92.

Lacan, Jacques. "The Agency of the Letter in the Unconscious, or Reason Since Freud." In *Écrits: A Selection,* trans. Alan Sheridan, 146–78. London: Tavistock, 1977.

———. *Freud's Papers on Technique. The Seminar of Jacques Lacan: Book 1.* Trans. Jacques-Alain Miller and Russell Grigg. New York: W. W. Norton & Co, 1997.

Langer, Lawrence. *Versions of Survival: The Holocaust and the Human Spirit.* Albany: State University of New York Press, 1982.

Laslett, Peter. "John Locke, the Great Recoinage, and the Origins of the Board of Trade: 1695–1698." *The William and Mary Quarterly,* 3rd series 14, no. 3 (July 1957): 370–402.

Lehmann, Nicholas. *The Promised Land: The Great Black Migration and How It Changed America.* New York: Alfred A. Knopf, Inc., 1991.

Lemert, Charles. "The Race of Time: Du Bois and Reconstruction." *boundary 2* 27, no. 3 (2000): 215–48.

Lerner, Michael, and Cornel West. *Jews and Blacks: Let the Healing Begin.* New York: G. P. Putnam's Sons, 1995.

Levinas, Emmanuel. "Reality and Its Shadow." In *Collected Philosophical Papers,* trans. Alphonso Lingis, 1–13. Dordrecht: Martinus Nijhoff, 1987.

Lewis, Catherine M. and Richard J. *Jim Crow America: A Documentary History.* Fayetteville: University of Arkansas Press, 2009.

Locke, John. *The Fundamental Constitutions of Carolina.* London: s.n., 1670. Copy from Harvard University Library. http://gateway.proquest.com/openurl?ctx _ver=Z39.88–2003&res_id=xri:eebo&res_dat=xri:pqil:res_ver=0.2&rft _id=xri:eebo:citation:99832684.

———. *Two Treatises of Government and a Letter Concerning Toleration.* Ed. Ian Shapiro. New Haven, Conn.: Yale University Press, 2003.Lockyer, Herbert. *All the Women of the Bible.* Grand Rapids, Mich.: Zondervan, 1967.

Lowenthal, Leo. *Literature, Popular Culture, and Society.* Englewood Cliffs, N.J.: Prentice-Hall, 1961.

Lubiano, Wahneema, ed. *The House That Race Built: Original Essays by Toni Morrison, Angela Y. Davis, Cornel West, and Others on Black Americans and Politics in America Today,* New York: Vintage Press, 1998.

Lyotard, Jean-François. *The Differend: Phrases in Dispute.* Trans. Georges Van Den Abbeele. Minneapolis: University of Minnesota Press, 1988.

MacLean, Nancy K. *Behind the Mask of Chivalry: The Making of the Second Ku Klux Klan.* New York: Oxford University Press, 1994.

Martin, Henri-Jean. *The Coming of the Book: The Impact of Printing, 1450–1800.* Trans. David Gerard. London: N.L.B., 1984.

Martin, Tony, ed. *The Jewish Onslaught: Dispatches From the Wellesley Battle-front.* Dover: The Majority Press, 1993.

Marx, Karl. *Grundrisse: Foundations of the Critique of Political Economy.* Trans. Martin Nicolaus. New York: Penguin Books, 1973.

Marx, Karl, and Friedrich Engels. *Collected Works.* New York: International Publishers, 1975.

Mather, Increase. "An Earnest Exhortation to the Inhabitants of New-England, To hearken to the voice of God in his late and present Dispensations As ever they desire to escape another Judgement, seven times greater then any thing which as yet hath been." In *So Dreadfull a Judgement: Puritan Responses to King Phillip's War, 1676–1677*, ed. Richard Slotkin and James K. Folsom, 165–206. Middletown, Conn.: Wesleyan University Press, 1978.

Matus, Jill L. *Toni Morrison.* Manchester: Manchester University Press, 1998.

Mbembe, Achille. *On the Postcolony.* Berkeley: University of California Press, 2001.

McKay, Nellie Y. *Critical Essays on Toni Morrison.* New York: G. K. Hall 1988.

McKay, Nellie Y., and Kathryn Earle, eds. *Approaches to Teaching the Novels of Toni Morrison.* New York: Modern Language Association of America, 1997.

McKee, Patrick. "Spacing and Placing Experience in Toni Morrison's *Sula.*" *Modern Fiction Studies* 42, no. 1 (1996): 1–30.

McVeigh, Rory. *Rise of the Ku Klux Klan: Right-Wing Movements and National Politics.* Minneapolis: University of Minnesota Press, 2009.

McWilliams, John. *New England's Crisis and Cultural Memory: Literature, Politics, History, Religion, 1620–1860.* Cambridge: Cambridge University Press, 2004.

Micheaux, Oscar. *The Forged Note.* Lincoln, Nebr.: Western Book Supply Company, 1915.

Milgrom, J. "Sacrifice and Offerings, Old Testament." In *The Interpreter's Dictionary of the Bible.* ed. George Arthur Buttrick et al., 9: 763–71. Nashville: Abingdon Press, 1976.

Miller, J. Hilllis. *Speech Acts in Literature.* Stanford, Calif.: Stanford University Press, 2001.

Moody, Joycelyn K. "Ripping Away the Veil of Slavery: Literacy, Communal Love, and Self-Esteem in Three Slave Women's Narratives." *Black American Literature Forum* 24, no. 4 (Winter 1990): 633–48.

Morris, Rosalind. *In the Place of Origins: Modernity and Its Mediums in Northern Thailand.* Durham, N.C.: Duke University Press, 2000. Morrow, Nancy V. "The Problem of Slavery in the Polemic Literature of the American Enlightenment." *Early American Literature* 20, no. 3 (Winter 1985–86): 236–55.

Muller, Hermann J. *Out of the Night: A Biologist's View of the Future.* New York: Vanguard Press, 1935.

Munro, C. Lynn. "The Tattooed Heart and the Serpentine Eye: Morrison's Choice of an Epigraph for *Sula.*" *Black American Literature Forum* 18, no. 4 (Winter 1984): 150–54.

Nancy, Jean-Luc. *The Speculative Remark (One of Hegel's Bon Mots).* Trans. Céline Surprenant. Stanford, Calif.: Stanford University Press, 2001.

Naylor, Gloria. *Mama Day.* New York: Vintage Books, 1988.

Naylor, Gloria, and Toni Morrison. "A Conversation: Gloria Naylor and Toni Morrison." In *Conversations with Toni Morrison*, ed. Danille Taylor-Guthrie, 188–271. Jackson: University Press of Mississippi, 1994.

Newton, Adam Zachary. *Facing Black and Jew: Literature as Public Space in Twentieth-Century America.* Cambridge: Cambridge University Press, 1999.

Ngugi wa Thiong'o. *Decolonizing the Mind*. Portsmouth, N.H.: Heinemann, 1981.

Nirenberg, David. "The Politics of Love and Its Enemies." In *Religion: Beyond a Concept*, ed. Hent de Vries, 491–512. New York: Fordham University Press, 2008.

Nuremberg Trial Proceedings. Vol. 11, *One Hundred and Ninth Day, Monday, 15 April 1946*. Online at http://www.loc.gov/rr/frd/Military_Law/pdf/NT_Vol-XI.pdf.

O'Callaghan, F. B., ed. *Documents Relative to the Colonial History of the State of New York: Procured in Holland, England, and France by John Romeyn Broadhead*. 15 vols. Albany, N.Y.: Weed, Parsons, 1853–87.

Olaniyan, Tejumola. *Scars of Conquest / Masks of Resistance: The Invention of Cultural Identities in African, African-American, and Caribbean Drama*. New York: Oxford University Press, 1995.

Page, Philip. *Dangerous Freedom: Fusion and Fragmentation in Toni Morrison's Novels*. Jackson: University Press of Mississippi, 1995.

Parrott, Douglas M. "Introduction" to "The Thunder: Perfect Mind." In *The Nag Hammadi in English*, 3rd ed., ed. James McConkey Robinson and Richard Smith, 295–96. Leiden: E. J. Brill, 1988.

Patterson, Orlando. *Slavery and Social Death: A Comparative Study*. Cambridge: Harvard University Press, 1982.

Paul, Diane B. *The Politics of Heredity: Essays on Eugenics, Biomedicine, and the Nature-Nurture Debate*. Albany: State University of New York Press, 1998.

Peterson, Horace C., and Gilbert C. Fite. *Opponents of War, 1917–1918*. Seattle: Greenwood Press, 1968.

Peterson, Nancy J., ed. *Toni Morrison: Critical and Theoretical Approaches*. Baltimore: Johns Hopkins University Press, 1997.

Petry, Ann. *The Street*. Boston: Houghton Mifflin, 1946.

Pietro Martire D'Anghiera. *The Discovery of the New World in the Writings of Peter Martyr of Anghiera*. Rome: Istituto poligrafico e zecca della stato, Libreria dello stato, 1992.

Pirandello, Luigi. *Six Characters in Search of an Author*. Trans. Eric Bentley. New York: Signet Classics, 1998.

Plessy v. Ferguson. 163 U.S. 537 (1896). Online at http://supreme.justia.com/us/163/case.htm.

"Records of the United States Nuremberg War Crimes Trials, *United States v. Karl Brandt et al* (Case 1): November 21, 1946, to August 20, 1947." Records of the United States Nuernberg War Crimes Trials, National Archives, 1:72.

Reeves, Marjorie. *The Influence of Prophecy in the Later Middle Ages: A Study in Joachimism*. Oxford: Oxford University Press, 1969.

Reinhardt, Mark. "Who Speaks for Margaret Garner? Slavery, Silence, and the Politics of Ventriloquism." *Critical Inquiry* 29 (Autumn 2002): 81–119.

Ricoeur, Paul. *Time and Narrative*. Vol. 3. Trans. Kathleen Blamey and David Pellauer. Chicago: University of Chicago Press, 1988.

Robinson, James McConkey, and Richard Smith, eds. *The Nag Hammadi in English*. 3rd ed. Leiden: E. J. Brill, 1988.

Rousseau, Jean-Jacques. *On the Origin of Language*. In Jean-Jacques Rousseau and Johann Gottfried Herder, *On the Origin of Language: Two Essays*, trans. John H. Moran and Alexander Gode, 5–76. Chicago: University of Chicago Press, 1986.

Rushdie, Salman. *Imaginary Homelands*. New York: Granta, 1992.

Saenger, Paul. *Space Between Words: The Origins of Silent Reading*. Stanford, Calif.: Stanford University Press, 2000.

Salzman, Jack, and Cornel West. *Struggles in the Promised Land: Towards a History of Black-Jewish Relations in the United States*. New York: Oxford University Press, 1997.

Saussure, Ferdinand de. *Course in General Linguistics*. Trans. Wade Baskin. New York: McGraw-Hill, 1966.

Schüssler Fiorenza, Elisabeth. "Apokalypsis and Propheteia: The Book of Revelation in the Context of Early Christian Prophecy." In *L'Apocalypse Johannique et l'apocalyptique dans le Nouveau Testament*, ed. J. Lambrecht, 105–28. Glembloux: J. Duculot, 1980.

Shaw, George Bernard. *Sociological Papers*. London: MacMillan, 1905.

Shepperson, George. "The African Abroad or the African Diaspora." In *Emerging Themes of African History*, ed. T. O. Ranger, 152–76. Nairobi: East African Publishing House, 1968.

Shilston, Timothy G. "Thomas Venner: Fifth Monarchist or Maverick?" *Social History* 37, no. 1 (February 2012): 55–64.

Siegel, James T. *Naming the Witch*. Stanford, Calif.: Stanford University Press, 2006.

Simmel, Georg. "The Metropolis and Mental Life." In *The Sociology of Georg Simmel*, ed. Kurt H. Wolff, trans. H. H. Gerth and C. Wright Mills, 409–24. New York: The Free Press, 1964.

Scruggs, Charles. *Sweet Home: Invisible Cities in the Afro-American Novel*. Baltimore: Johns Hopkins University Press, 1995.

Smith, John. "A True Relation of Such Occurences and Accidents of Noate as Hath Hapned in Virginia Since the First Planting of That Colony." In *Early American Writing*, ed. Giles Gunn, 95–100. New York: Penguin Books, 1994.

Smith, Valerie, ed. *New Essays on 'Song of Solomon.'* Cambridge: Cambridge University Press, 1995.

Spiro, Jonathan Peter. *Defending the Master Race: Conservation, Eugenics, and the Legacy of Madison*. Lebanon, N.H.: University Press of New England, 2009.

Spivak, Gayatri Chakravorty. "Can the Subaltern Speak?" In *Marxism and the Interpretation of Culture*, ed. Cary Nelson and Lawrence Grossberg, 271–313.

Urbana: University of Illinois Press, 1988.————. *The Critique of Postcolonial Reason: Toward a History of the Vanishing Present.* Cambridge: Harvard University Press, 1999.

Spoto, Donald. *The Kindness of Strangers: The Life of Tennessee Williams.* New York: Little, Brown & Company, 1985.

Stallybrass, Peter, and Allon White. *The Politics and Poetics of Transgression.* Ithaca, N.Y.: Cornell University Press, 1986.

Stein, A., and R. Weisbord. *Bittersweet Encounter: The Afro American and the American Jew.* Westport, Conn.: Negro University Press, 1970.

Stewart, Susan. *On Longing: Narratives of the Miniature, the Gigantic, the Souvenir, the Collection.* Durham, N.C.: Duke University Press, 1993.

Strindberg, August. "Author's Foreword." In *Six Plays of Strindberg*, trans. Elizabeth Sprigge, 61–73. New York: Avon, 1965.

Suger, Abbot. *Abbot Suger on the Abbey Church of St. Denis and Its Art Treasures.* Ed. and trans. Erwin Panofsky. Princeton: Princeton University Press, 1946.

Taussig, Michael. *Defacement: Public Secrecy and the Labor of the Negative.* Stanford, Calif.: Stanford University Press, 1999.

————. *Shamanism, Colonialism, and the Wild Man.* Chicago: University of Chicago Press, 1987.

Tenner, Edward. *Our Own Devices: How Technology Remakes Humanity.* New York: Vintage Books, 2004.

Thompson, Peter. "The Thief, the Householder, and the Commons: Languages of Class in Seventeenth-Century Virginia." *William and Mary Quarterly*, Third Series, 63, no. 2 (April 2006): 211–20.

Thorpe, Francis Newton. ed. *The Federal and State Constitutions, Colonial Charters, and Other Organic Laws of the States, Territories, and Colonies Now or Heretofore Forming the United States of America Compiled and Edited Under the Act of Congress of June 30, 1906.* Washington, D.C.: Government Printing Office, 1909.

Toomer, Jean. *Cane.* New York: Liveright Publishing Company, 1975.

Tuck, Richard. *Natural Rights Theories: Their Origin and Development.* Cambridge: Cambridge University Press, 1981.

Turner, Victor. *The Ritual Process: Structure and Anti-Structure.* Chicago: Aldine, 1969.

Turner, Victor, ed. *Celebration: Studies in Festivity and Ritual.* Washington, D.C.: Smithsonian Institution Press, 1982.

Viswanathan, Gauri. *Masks of Conquest: Literary Study and British Rule in India.* New York: Columbia University Press, 1989.

Walcott, Derek. *Another Life.* London: Jonathan Cape, 1973.

————. *The Bounty.* New York: Farrar, Straus, Giroux, 1997.

————. *Collected Poems 1948–1984.* London: Faber and Faber, 1992.

Washington, Harriet A. *Medical Apartheid: The Dark History of Medical Experimentation on Black Americans from Colonial Times to the Present.* New York: Doubleday, 2006.

Wertheim, Albert. "The McCarthy Era and the American Theater." In *Insurgency in American Theatre, Theatre Journal* 34, no. 2 (May 1982): 211–22.

White, Walter. "I Investigate Lynchings." *American Mercury* 16 (January 1929): 77–84.

White, William. "The Nigger in the Pile." *Notes and Queries* 170 (1936): 12.

Widdowson, Peter. "The American Dream Refashioned: History, Politics and Gender in Toni Morrison's 'Paradise.'" *Journal of American Studies* 35, no. 2 (August 2001): 313–35.

Wiegman, Robyn. "Anatomy of Lynching." Special issue *African American Culture and Sexuality, Journal of the History of Sexuality* 3, no. 3 (January 1992): 445–67.

Williams, Rowan. "Introduction." In *Theology and the Political: The New Debate*, ed. Creston Davis, John Milbank, and Slavoj Žižek, 1–5. Durham, N.C.: Duke University Press, 2005.

Wright, Richard. *Eight Men*. New York: Harper Collins, 1996.

———. *Native Son*. New York: Harper and Brothers, 1940.

Yarborough, Richard. "The First-Person in Afro-American Fiction." In *Afro-American Literary Study in the 1990s*, 105–34. Chicago: University of Chicago Press, 1989.

Yaeger, Patricia. *Dirt and Desire: Reconstructing Southern Women's Writing 1930–1900*. Chicago: University of Chicago Press, 2000.

Yellin, Jean Fagan. "Introduction." In Harriet A. Jacobs, *Incidents in the Life of a Slave Girl: Written by Herself*, ed. Jean Fagan Yellin, xv–xxi. Cambridge: Harvard University Press, 1987.

Index

Abolition, 52, 53, 116, 265fn13
Abraham, 104; *see also* sacrifice
absence, 46; constitutive, 64; *see also* vanishing
Adorno, Theodor W., 11–12, 239
aesthetic, 11, 212
Africa, 97
Agamben, Giorgio, 28–29, 31, 48, 51
agency, 19–20; delusion of, 19–20; 228
alterity, 212
Althusser, Louis, 138
ambiguity, 152
ambivalent figures, 173–74
American Indians, 47, 54, 55, 204
animality, 143, 208, 215, 279fn17, Rousseau's distinctions, 208; *see also* human
apocalypse, 19–20, 56, 124, 125, 129, 133, 140, 150, 152; and slavery, 126; and signification, 136; modus operandi, 136, 153–54; theatrics, 137; sleight of hand, 149; amnesia, 153; Columbus, 153–155; hermeneutics, 153; Fifteenth Century Europe, 154–55; and similitude, 160; banality, 169; millenialist dialectic, 200; promises land 202

Bachelard, Gaston, 201, 205, 206
Bacon's Rebellion, 203–4
Bakhtin, Mikhail, 147, 178
Barthes, Roland, 5, 201, 205
Benito Cerano, 202

Benjamin, Walter, 12, 20, 150; *see also* language
Biblical narratives, 136, 147, 153, 154, 155, 167, 170, 179, 189, 232, 233; Abraham, 104; Isaiah, 154, 274fn46; Pauline references, 159, 233, 235, 238; 276fn6, 320; Revelation, 164–64, 275fn5, 166, 181; Jezebel, 164–65, 167–68, 275fn5; I Kings, 164–65; classical prophets, 166; Eve, 176–77; Song of Solomon, 232–33, 246; I Corinthians, 233; New Testament, 233; Pauline letters, 235
black masculinity, 185–86
black soldiers, 38, 80, 81, 84, 89; *See also* war
Blanchot, Maurice, 7–8
body, 63–64, 72, 129, 134, 170, 271fn15; and desire, 170–71; slave's body, 210; and inscription, 134, 137; self-inscription, 234; black migrant body, 282fn13
Brown v Board of Education, 83
Butler, Judith, 12

Capitalism, 156; and indifference, 156
carceral network, 272fn24
carnivalesque, 147–48; 273fn36
citation, 100, 124, 147, 166, 216, 217, 219, 226, 229, 230; and grief, 217; Morrison's self-citation, 240–41, 250; The Morrison Case, 284fn35

language (*continued*)
192; haunted 14, colonial curriculum, 14–18, 15; embodying culture,
16; mother tongue, 16, 256fn36; and
abrogation, 17; Roland Barthes,
5; Walter Benjamin's theory, 20;
René Girard on outside of language,
7–8; postcolonial commandment,
288fn60; performative, 76; dreams,
162, simile, 162–63; metaphor, 162;
limits, 163; contamination, 164;
women's, 177; semiological chains,
179; engendered 183–84, 185; magic,
194; tenses, 195; emotional, 199;
literary vs. analytical, 205; and hu-
man/animal 208; symbolic order,
231; testimonial language, 74; failure
of language, 74; ellipses, 241; *see also*
epigraph; simile; metaphor
law, 9–10; 68, 77, 115, 116, 126, 135, 144,
269fn30; slave laws, 82–84, 265fn13;
Fugitive Slave Laws 140, 142, 144,
266fn13, 267fn14; de jure/de facto,
78, 79–80; colonial laws, 84, 116;
Continental Congress, 265fn13; natural law, 85; natural law and slavery,
86–87; Plessy v Ferguson, 83, 84,
99, 268fn18; and haunting, 94; Dred
Scott v Sandford, 117; Brown v Board
of Education, 83; lynching, 118; juridical power 85; mother tongue, 16;
256fn36; as motto, 77–79, 91–92, 94,
115–16, 124, 176; spatial logic, 8
liberal humanism, 203
liminality, 149
literacy, 43, 139; 194
literalism, 132, 133
Laclau, Ernesto, 159
Locke, John, 84, 85, 86, 87, 198,
loss, 47, of name, 48, 69, 72
longing, 121
love, 95, 244, 245; Pauline message, 235,
238; European etiological history,
238–39
lynching, 117–18

Marx, Karl, 149, 156
masculinity, 132–33; *see also* black
masculinity
Mauss, Marcel, 143
meanings, 29; and context, 29; con-
tested, 93, 97–98
melancholia, 20, 171
memory, 33, 43, 44, 46, 49, 54, 55, 56,
64, 72, as obligation, 21, 144; as
theatre of past, 20; as distinct from
mourning, 22; *Beloved* as repository, 258fn56; and community, 24;
as injunction, 24, 25–26, 98; and
inheritance, 24, 89; and amnesia, 38;
future anteriority, 38; names, 44–45;
loss, 48; as covenant, 93; performance
of, 100; and forgetting, 200; false
memory, 201
mercantilism, 156
metaphor, 72, 92, 100, 114–15, 119,
134–35, 138, 158, 159, 162, 168, 183,
209, 217; names, 47–48; *see also* house
as
metonymy, 162, 209
millennialism, 200; 278fn9
mimesis, 106
miniature, 276fn6
miscegenation, 101, 111–12, 248, 249
misreading, 43; *see also* haunting
Modernism, 11; self-reflexivity, 16; uneasy relation of colonized, 17
modernity, 156; capitalist modernity, 106
mother, 45, 46, 56, 62, 67, 70, 128;
disappearance of, 17, 47, 49, 89, 129;
Sethe's mother, 128; resisting ideal,
175; non-biological, 169; as category
of being, 191; early socializing role,
227; in *Song of Solomon*, 234; *Beloved*,
74
mother tongue, 16, 256fn36; *see also*
language
motto, 77–79, 91–92, 94, 115–16, 124,
176; *see also* law
mystery, 76, 113, 129, 218; feminized
threat, 172

10/2/19